P9-DBS-665

The Apostolic Church in the New Testament

The Apostolic Church in the New Testament

by DAVID M. STANLEY, S.J.
Professor of New Testament Study
Regis College, Willowdale, Ontario

THE NEWMAN PRESS • 1967 • WESTMINSTER, MARYLAND

Third Printing, September, 1967

Imprimi potest:
Angus J. Macdougall, S.J.
Praepositus Provinciae Canadae Superioris Societatis Jesu
November 26, 1963

Nihil Obstat:
Thomas J. Feeney, S.T.L., J.C.D.
Censor Deputatus

Imprimatur:
✠ Ralph L. Hayes, D.D.
Episcopus Davenportensis
December 19, 1963

The *Nihil Obstat* and *Imprimatur* are official declarations that a book or pamphlet is free of doctrinal and moral error. No implication is contained therein that those who have granted the *Nihil Obstat* and *Imprimatur* agree with the opinions expressed. *Library of Congress Catalog Card Number:* 65-19453. Printed in the United States of America.

FOR

Bernard Lonergan, S. J.

ON THE OCCASION
OF HIS SIXTIETH BIRTHDAY
WITH GRATITUDE AND AFFECTION

Contents

INTRODUCTION ix

I. THE APOSTOLIC CHURCH AND HER PREACHING 1
1. Kingdom to Church 5
2. Salvation in the Primitive Preaching 38
3. The Concept of Biblical Inspiration 67

II. THE APOSTOLIC CHURCH AND HER LITURGY 91
4. "Carmenque Christo quasi deo dicere" 95
5. Liturgical Influences on the Formation of the Gospels 119
6. The New Testament Doctrine of Baptism 140

III. THE APOSTOLIC CHURCH AND THE WRITTEN GOSPEL 195
7. *Didache* As a Constitutive Element of the Written Gospel 199
8. Salvation in the Synoptic Gospels 214
9. The Gospels As Salvation History 238

IV. THE APOSTOLIC CHURCH AMONG THE GENTILES 279
10. Paul's Conversion in Acts 285
11. Paul and the Christian Concept of the Servant of God 312
12. Pauline Allusions to the Sayings of Jesus 352
13. "Become Imitators of Me": Apostolic Tradition in Paul 371

CONCLUSION 390

NOTES 395

INDEX OF SUBJECTS 463

INDEX OF NAMES 469

Introduction

THE almost universal manifestation in the mid-twentieth century of a deep-seated desire for unity on the part of the various members of a divided Christianity is a truly remarkable phenomenon which is not easily explained. Be that as it may, the modern ecumenical movement has prompted on all sides a return to the sources of the doctrine of the Church, and in particular a reassessment of the data to be found in the New Testament. "What is the Church?" is a question of paramount interest today among Catholics, no less than among Christians of the Reform. In his opening address to the second session of the Second Vatican Council, Pope Paul VI remarked: "It should not come as a surprise that, after twenty centuries in which both the Catholic Church and the other Christian bodies distinguished by the name of church have seen great geographical and historical development, there should still be need to enunciate a more precise definition of the true, profound, and complete nature of the Church which Christ founded and the apostles began to build." The Holy Father went on to point out that the Church is a mystery, "a reality imbued with the divine presence." He also observed that human thought is constantly undergoing evolution, and that consequently our conception of the Church has, through the centuries, progressed in accordance with this universal law of human thought. Since the Church is a living body, "the Body of Christ," we may speak—as indeed Pope Paul VI did

—of this development of the notion of the Church as "the self-awareness of the Church." Its evolution is governed and clarified, said Pope Paul, first and foremost "by faithful adherence to the words and thought of Christ."

There is no one who does not see that it is to the New Testament primarily that we must look, if we wish to ascertain "what the Church considers herself to be." For the New Testament is simply the written record of the testimony by the apostolic Church to Jesus Christ. Now the very personal nature of any kind of testimony quite clearly involves the self-revelation of the witness. If the concept of literary authorship appears to demand that the author put something of himself into his work, this "self-disclosure" is specially characteristic of the function of testifying. For this reason, the character and competence of the witness are, in any court of law, a matter of deepest concern. But where (as is the case with the witness of the New Testament) there is question of testimony based not only upon human experience but also upon divine faith, then "the personality" of the attestant comes sharply into play. We may rightly expect, then, to find that the apostolic Church, already in existence some twenty years before any of the New Testament literature was composed, has impressed her distinctive "personality" upon these sacred books which have been written by her members, under her direction, and marked with the seal of her approbation.

It may not be irrelevant to recall here also that this collection of apostolic and ecclesiastical writings was put together in the course of (at least) half a century, during the years that constituted the formative period of the life of the Church. During this era, under the impact of unique experiences and by specially aided theological reflection, the Church grew in the knowledge of the Lord Jesus and His work for the salvation of men. As a consequence of and in parallel with this development, the Church evolved a fuller comprehension of her own nature and her mission in this world. Precisely because the New Testament contains the record of the Church's testimony of faith and experience to Jesus Christ, we shall find that it also reflects her growth in her own consciousness of her self and her role in human history.

This means, of course, that there were certain facets of her character which were unknown or only half-consciously realized at the beginning of this formative period of the apostolic age. The early community of Jerusalem, created by the revolutionary events of the first Christian Pentecost, cannot be expected to have reached the stature of the Church as she reveals herself in the letters of St. Paul. And even within the body of Pauline writings we may find a certain evolution in the conception of the Church. Again, the picture of the Church which is discernible in the Johannine literature will be seen to possess a depth and a dimension that is not yet perceptible in the thought of St. Paul.

Such attention to and evaluation of the historical process through which the Christian revelation has been communicated to us is, together with the discerning and analysis of the many and varied literary forms found in the sacred books of the Christian Church, a notable characteristic of twentieth-century New Testament scholarship. As the late Pope Pius XII observed in his great Encyclical on "Biblical Studies and the Opportune Means of Promoting Them" (*Divino afflante Spiritu*), "if our age accumulates new problems and new difficulties, it also supplies, by God's bounty, new aids and helps to exegesis." Indeed, we venture to suggest that the study of the historical process involved in the creation of the New Testament is one of the outstanding contributions which our era can make to the understanding of the Christian revelation. Pope Pius might well have had this point in mind when, in the same Encyclical, he wrote these encouraging words: "It is therefore a mistake to maintain, as some who fail to appreciate the conditions of biblical study do maintain, that nothing remains for the Catholic exegete to add to the achievements of Christian antiquity." The Holy Father explicitly pointed out the contribution made by present-day Scripturists through the study of the kinds of literature found in the New Testament: "This study has been pursued during the past few decades with greater care and industry than formerly, and has made us better acquainted with the literary forms used in those ancient times, whether in poetical descriptions, or in the formulation of rules and laws of conduct, or in the narration of historical facts and events." Pope Pius likewise encouraged the Catholic *Neutestamentler* to continue his investigations by reminding all of the very small portion of the Bible whose meaning has been authoritatively determined by the Church. "There consequently remain many matters, and important matters, in the exposition and explanation of which the sagacity and ingenuity of Catholic interpreters can and ought to be freely exercised. . . ."

When Pope John XXIII solemnly opened the first session of Vatican II, which he had summoned for the express purpose of effecting an updating of the Church's consciousness of herself and her mission to men (*aggiornamento*), he defined the aim of this universal synod as consisting in "a doctrinal penetration and a formation of conscience in conformity with authentic doctrine, expounded through the methods of research and the literary forms of modern thought." Such an optimistic proposal by the late Holy Father, despite many misgivings on the part of certain men around him, whom he called "prophets of doom," is surely breath-taking. It is also heartening for those students of the New Testament who by profession are called upon to investigate and express the meaning of the Church as it appears on the sacred pages of our inspired books "through the methods of research and the literary forms of modern thought."

For a little more than a decade now, it has been the present writer's privilege and duty to devote himself professionally to the exposition of the New Testament in the classroom and in scientific periodicals. He considers it no little part of his good fortune to have been thus engaged during a period when the greatest interest has been taken, both by those Catholics who favor the so-called "new approach" to New Testament studies as well as by those who (to say the least) find it uncongenial, in the very questions which constitute in large measure his own stock in trade. He will always remain deeply grateful for the friendly and favorable reactions which his modest contribution to the field of New Testament studies has evoked among scholars of every Christian denomination, on both sides of the Atlantic. He is no less a debtor to those who have disagreed with his conclusions or methodology.

The present collection of essays, all of which have already appeared in print, has been put together for the express purpose of presenting a partial picture, incomplete as it is, of the Church as she witnesses to herself in the inspired writings of the New Testament. The author acknowledges with thanks the permission to reprint these studies which has been graciously given by the editors of *Theological Studies, Catholic Biblical Quarterly, Biblica,* and the *Proceedings of the Catholic Theological Society of America.* In addition he wishes to thank the publishing house of Sheed & Ward for allowing him to make use of the version of "The Conception of Our Gospels as Salvation History" which appeared in their volume *Christianity Divided: Protestant and Roman Catholic Theological Issues.* The article originally appeared in *Theological Studies.*

The idea of presenting these disparate essays in one volume did not occur to the author. He is accordingly most happy indeed to give the credit in this matter to Walter J. Burghardt, S.J., Managing Editor of *Theological Studies*, who has generously offered to select and edit the material which makes up this book. Without Fr. Burghardt's initial suggestion very probably, and certainly without his expert and invaluable help, the volume would never have seen the light of day. He cannot be held responsible for the viewpoint expressed (this remains the author's); he must be given full credit and sincere thanks for the laborious task of editing the work.

The Apostolic Church in the New Testament

I

The Apostolic Church and Her Preaching

As we have already remarked, it is by examining the several ways in which the apostolic Church gave her testimony to Jesus Christ that we may hope to discover the various facets of that "self-awareness" of the Church, of which Pope Paul spoke in his opening address to the Vatican Council. For the New Testament writers consider that to bear witness to Christ is the primary function of the Church.

To carry out this divinely-given vocation, the Church employs several characteristically human forms of activity. By means of human speech she attested from the beginning her faith in the saving significance of Jesus' death and resurrection. Thus the apostolic preaching was, if not the sole means, at least one of the principal ways in which the Church proposed to men the basic question, "What think you of Christ, whose Son is He?" (Mt 22:42). Peter attests his faith on the day of Pentecost by his proclamation, "This Jesus God has raised—a fact of which we are all witnesses" (Acts 2:32). The Church also employed the liturgy to affirm her witness to the risen Christ, thus utilizing that sacred play which is a universal human manifestation of the religious spirit. "As often as you eat this bread and drink from the cup," Paul reminds his Corinthians, "you proclaim the death of the Lord until He comes" (1 Cor 11:26). The apostolic *martyrion* was also operative in the creation of Christian literature, the inspired writings of the New Testament; and it is in the written Gospels that we can recognize above all this official attestation of the early Church. Luke states that he wrote his two-volume work on Christian origins (his Gospel and the Acts of the Apostles) in order to provide Theophilus, his aristocratic convert, with an *asphaleia*, or "guarantee" based upon the personal experience of "the original eyewitnesses," to support the Christian faith he professed after listening to the oral catechesis (Lk 1:1–4). The author of the fourth Gospel wrote his book "in order that you may grow in your belief that Jesus is the Messiah, the Son of God" (Jn 20:31). This testimony through sacred literature was directed primarily towards those who had already accepted the Christian faith. When Paul first writes to Thessalonica, he orders that his letter be read to the Christian community assembled for public worship—and this "by the authority of our Lord Jesus Christ" (1 Th 5:27). Finally, the apostolic Church gave her official witness to Christ through the dynamic force of the missionary spirit, which drove her preachers out into the Diaspora to evangelize the pagans of Hellenistic culture. Their response to the kerygma was eventually to make the Church predominantly Gentile in membership. Of all the missionaries in the first age of the Church, St. Paul became a symbol for the centrifugal movement away from the Jewish Christian milieu and for the universalist tendency which made the Church truly catholic before the close of the apostolic age.

In this first section of our study of the apostolic Church, we make a beginning by reviewing the structural development of primitive Christianity as it is presented in Acts and in the Gospel of St. Matthew. For a clear insight into the meaning of Jesus' intention to found His Church, we must consider the various stages through which the first Christians progressed as a result of the experiences which they faced during the first decades of Christianity.

The essay on the apostolic preaching describes the content and the aims of the Christian kerygma. It attempts to assess the theological significance of the primitive formulae by which the Twelve stated their faith in the divinity of Christ and their own awareness of their collective identity as the *qahal* of the new Israel. It takes cognizance also of the notable omissions in the earliest formulations of the oral Gospel—proof surely of their antiquity and their genuineness.

The third study is devoted to the difficult question of scriptural inspiration and the modern attempts to explain its nature. It has been inserted here because it provides some background for an appreciation of New Testament literature, particularly through its description of the Semitic mentality. Its relevance to our consideration of the apostolic Church is highlighted by the theory of Karl Rahner, according to whom God's initiative in inspiring the writing of the New Testament is part of the divine decree determining the existence of the apostolic Church.

1

Kingdom to Church

DURING His earthly career Jesus Christ proclaimed the coming of the kingdom of God. In the years immediately following His departure from this world the Christian Church made her appearance in history. What relation does the Church bear to the kingdom preached by Christ?

The question poses a problem which has been of paramount interest to the Christian theologian and the New Testament critic alike.[1] The present study attempts to redefine the continuity between Christ's preaching of the kingdom and the founding of the Church by tracing the lines along which, on the evidence of the New Testament, the Christianity of the apostolic age evolved, and by formulating the term of that evolution as perceived by the faith of the primitive Church. The principal sources for such an investigation are the Acts of the Apostles and the Greek Gospel of St. Matthew. Acts recounts the series of events through which the primitive community was gradually liberated from the influence of Judaism and became increasingly conscious of its missionary vocation towards pagan peoples. This experience led it to perceive that by this divinely guided growth it was realizing the notion of the kingdom announced by Christ. Moreover, it was the utilization of this experience of the Christian community in the first decades after Christ's death which had enabled Greek Matthew to express in his Gospel his very profound intuition of the kingdom's actualization in the Church.

Loisy once remarked with characteristic acerbity that the only "miracle" of Pentecost was the origin of the myth of the Church; the answer to the disciples' vain expectations of a parousiac coming of Christ in His heavenly kingdom was the disillusioning arrival of the Spirit with plans for the erection of a Church upon earth.[2] Apart from its evident cynicism, this statement has the merit of picking out one of the essential elements in the problem before us. Loisy was at least right in perceiving that the relation of kingdom to Church involved a psychological question: how did the apostolic community become aware that the kingdom of God manifested its coming through the organization of the Church?

Another important aspect of the question is the phenomenological one: By what stages did the Church finally emerge as an entity distinct from the Judaism in which she was born, and what bearing has this emergence upon the growing consciousness of the early Church that in her life the kingdom had come upon earth?

Such elements which pertain to the existential order do not readily admit of definition. But they must not, for that reason, be neglected. It is only by a study of the coming-to-be of the Church, a development of its very nature extended over a period of time, that the coming of the kingdom in the Church can be properly perceived.[3] For the coming of the kingdom, like the founding of the Church, is a *Werden*, not a *Wesen*, and their relation to one another can be grasped only through an insight into experience. To recapture the salient features of that experience in the first age of Christianity is the purpose of the following pages.

THE APOSTOLIC COMMUNITY IN JERUSALEM

The present editorial arrangement of the New Testament, by which Luke's Gospel is separated from Acts, tends to obscure the fact that they constitute a two-volume work on Christian origins. By using the closing scene of the one to form the prologue of the other, Luke underscores the unity of conception which governs the whole history. This repetition of the narrative of the Ascension extends to several of the circumstances attending it: the mention of Christ's prophecy concerning the future universal character of the apostles' mission (Lk 24:47; Acts 1:8), the nature of that mission as a *martyrion* to the resurrection (Lk 24:48; Acts 1:8), the promise of the Spirit (Lk 24:40; Acts 1:4, 5, 8), and the injunction to "remain in the city" until the reception of the Father's promise. By employing such a carefully constructed bridge Luke clearly indicates that he desires the reader to appreciate not only the continuity existing between the two great sections of his study but also the parallelism he has seen between the movement of the one and the other book. The first contains the story of Christ's work for the salvation of humanity. By laying its opening and closing scenes in the Temple, as A. M. Ramsey has remarked,[4] Luke points out the complete transformation in the conception of divine cult and of religion itself which has occurred in the course of the events he has related. I suggest that the second volume has been constructed according to a similar plan. In the opening scenes of Acts the risen Christ instructs His apostles about the nature of the kingdom of God (Acts 1:3), while its closing lines describe Paul in Rome "heralding the kingdom of God" (Acts 28:31). Consequently it is not unreasonable to suppose that Luke, with whom it is common practice to present similar sequences as a kind of diptych,[5] proposes to trace the evolution which occurred in the notion of the kingdom during the first generation of the Church's life. From the beginning of Acts he clearly enunciates this theme: the propagation of the kingdom through the apostolic testimony under the direction of the Holy Spirit.[6]

What promise for the future does Luke find in the little group which returned to Jerusalem to await "the promise of the Father"? Following an ancient source at his disposal, he points out that they numbered one hundred and twenty, sufficient in Jewish law to form a distinct community with its own sanhedrin. This sanhedrin is indicated by a repetition of the list of the Twelve with Peter at their head. They are conscious of their office, which is to witness to Christ's resurrection before the Jews and within the community.[7] With this in mind, Peter declares that a twelfth must be elected to replace the unfortunate Judas (Acts 1:21–22). The stringent conditions laid down for eligibility prove the importance of this function; and, in fact, only two of the disciples appear to qualify as candidates.

Yet the limitations of the apostles' awareness of what lies before them are only too evident in Luke's account. Their question put to the ascending Christ, "Lord, is it at this time that you will restore the kingdom to Israel?" (Acts 1:6), betrays a crassly material view of the kingdom of God, a view which may well have been operative in their election of Matthias. Why was it so necessary to have twelve witnesses rather than eleven? When, some twelve years later, James is executed, there is no move to replace him. The reason may have been that James had faithfully executed, as Judas had not, his function as witness. It is possible, however, that prior to Pentecost the apostles were concerned with filling those twelve thrones to be occupied by them (Mt 19:28) in the great eschatological judgment of Israel.[8]

Another point, to which we shall return later, deserves mention here: Peter's insistence that the candidate for apostleship should have received the baptism of John (Acts 1:22). Several of the original Twelve had been disciples of the Baptist (Jn 1:40 ff.), and Peter's remark implies that the others had also received the same type of baptism. This will prove an important factor in the constitution of Christian baptism.

Luke depicts the little community as "at one in persevering in prayer" (Acts 1:14); but it does not appear that they celebrated the "breaking of the bread," or that they attempted to win any new adherents to their way of life. They were full of expectancy, as they awaited the mysterious baptism in the Holy Spirit and the return of the Master, predicted by the angels (Acts 1:11). Their consciousness that in electing Matthias they were accomplishing what had been foretold by the prophets (Acts 1:20) proves that they somehow knew that they were assisting at the consummation of Israel's sacred history. Beyond that, they had no inkling of what was shortly to happen to them.

The Jewish feast of Pentecost brought a transformation of the community into something very different from what it had anticipated. It is likely that the disciples had conjectured that the baptism of the Spirit was to usher in the parousia of the Lord, come back to restore the sovereignty to Israel. Luke has taken pains to disclose the revolutionary character of the descent of the Holy Spirit. Tongues as of fire appeared, accompanied by a great noise as of wind; "dividing," they sat upon each of the disciples, with the result that all present fell into ecstasy and began to pray aloud in praise of God and of the wonder He had wrought (Acts 2:4).[9] Two facts emerge clearly from the account: the community was caught up in ecstasy, and they were endowed with the gift of prophecy. Recent exegesis of the passage has shown conclusively that the gift of "tongues" had no relation to preaching but was "the voice" which attracted the attention of the crowds assembled in Jerusalem for the feast of Pentecost. It was the prophetic charism,[9a] as Luke indicates, which was later exercised by Peter in his address to the multitude: "Peter then advanced with the Eleven. He raised his voice and began to prophesy to them" (Acts 2:14).[10]

The greatest change perceptible in the attitude of the disciples is their realization that the Messianic times have thus been inaugurated by the descent of the Spirit and not by the Lord's second coming. It was of this hour that Joel had spoken when he declared that Yahweh's Spirit would be poured forth, prophecy would again return to Israel, and salvation would come to all men through the Name of the Lord already identified as the risen Christ (Acts 2:16 ff.). The prophet had moreover foretold the creation of this group of God's servants, filled with the Spirit, who were the "little remnant of Israel," the Messianic community. Joseph Schmitt has rightly seen how this realization dominates the first five chapters of Acts and has insisted upon its importance as the first link between the preaching of Christ and the ecclesiology of Paul.[11] It remains to point out the limitations of this pentecostal revelation to the apostles.

The new Israel has been born in the fire of the Spirit, and Peter and the Eleven are prophets of the new Israel. But they are prophets "to the house of Israel" (Acts 2:36), to whom the Messianic promise primarily belongs (Acts 2:39); and if Peter refers at all to the call of the Gentiles "in as large a number as the Lord our God will call them" (Acts 2:39), the reference is certainly obscure.

While Luke does his best to stress the universality of this first proclamation of salvation to "men of every nation under heaven" (Acts 2:5), it must be remembered that those who heard Peter on this occasion, during one of the great national pilgrimages to Jerusalem, were all Jews of the Dispersion. Isaiah had made the Temple the focal point of reunion during the Messianic age (Is 2:2 ff.), and the Jerusalem Christians can hardly have failed to be deeply impressed by the verification of this prophecy. The Holy City must have seemed destined to be the center of the new religion on the day of Pentecost, and their experience in gaining converts during the period which followed served to heighten the impression that the expansion of Christianity was to result from a centripetal movement towards Jerusalem.[12]

Thus what is emphasized in the Lucan account of Pentecost is the function of the Jerusalem community in the formation of the Church until the Council mentioned in chapter 15: her rôle as symbol of unity in early Christianity. This is clear also from an allusion in Luke's account to the tower of Babel, mentioned in the Canticle of Moses (Dt 32:8).[13] The miracle of "tongues" is presented as a supernatural reversal of Babel's baleful influence upon the nations of the earth. In Genesis the story was made the vehicle for a religious explanation of the diversity of language upon earth with its resultant hostility between peoples. In Acts the tongues which became "divided" cause the disciples to speak one miraculous language of ecstatic prayer, which summons the men of various nations to receive, in the charismatic gifts of interpretation, a share in the outpouring of the Spirit.

Finally, Luke's narrative suggests that the coming of the Spirit was the promulgation of the Christian law: the references to fire and to the sound which marshals the crowd are reminiscent of the giving of the Mosaic law upon Sinai.[14] In his Gospel Luke refrained from giving to his "Sermon on the Plain" the interpretation which Matthew plainly put upon the "Sermon on the Mount," that of a proclamation by the new Moses of the new law. In the chapters of Acts which follow the Pentecost narrative the evidence which has been collected from earlier sources points to the disciples' preoccupation with their status as the new *qahal* of Israel (cf. esp. Acts 2:47), an attitude which is one of the results of Pentecost.[15]

It can only be explained on the supposition that they looked on the descent of the Spirit as the imparting of the Messianic law.

The first five chapters of Acts, which describe the fruits of the pentecostal experience during the first years of Jerusalem Christianity, depict an ideal, even idealized, state of affairs. There is a continued and quite remarkable increase in the number of the disciples, who enjoy popularity with their Jewish neighbors and who practice under apostolic direction heroic charity towards one another. Persecution, when it comes, is welcomed as a further proof that they constitute the Messianic community of the "last days" (Acts 4:24–31), and the wonders of Pentecost recur, endowing them with new courage and patience. A brief reference to what is almost certainly a personal reminiscence of one of the apostolic group reveals the attitude of this heroic age as one of joyfulness "for having-been-judged-worthy-to-suffer outrages for the Name" (Acts 5:41).

Three relatively long summaries with which the author punctuates his narrative serve to mark the passage of time and also to draw attention to the marvelous advance of Christianity (Acts 2:42–47; 4:32–35; 5:12–15). As has been pointed out,[16] some earlier document is the source of these résumés, but in each case their scope has been enlarged by the interpolation of an additional theme. To discover the reason for these insertions is to gain an insight into the spirit of primitive Christianity.

The first summary (Acts 2:42–47) follows the narrative of Pentecost and shows its effect upon the social-liturgical life of the disciples. It depicts them as following a course of instruction which is called "the teaching of the apostles," a presentation of the truths of the faith in the light of the exaltation of Christ and the descent of the Spirit.[17] The author of the summary insinuates that this teaching was ordinarily connected with the celebration of the Eucharist. While the Temple remained the center of public worship for these Jewish Christians, the "breaking of the bread" was the heart of their more properly Christian life. Carried out in the privacy of their homes during the course of a meal, it was characterized by joy. The disciples retained the vivid memory of how the risen Christ had come to them habitually in the course of a repast, and this sacramental coming of the Lord would remind them for a long time, as Paul testifies (1 Cor 11:26), of the much-desired second advent of the Master.[18]

The community's keen sense of the social aspects of the Eucharist is also apparent in the practice of what Luke calls the *koinōnia,* a word which may be translated by "common life" in the sense in which it is used in religious orders. A description of it has been interjected into this first summary (Acts 2:44–45): "The faithful shared everything in common; they sold their properties and their goods, and divided the proceeds amongst the community, according to the need of each one." By this interpolation its author wishes to correlate the teaching of the apostles and the Eucharist with this "communism" of the primitive Christians. Stanislas Lyonnet in a recent article has further specified this relation of the *koinōnia* to the Eucharist: the "common life" was a necessary prerequisite for participation in the "breaking of the bread."[19] The fellowship with Christ in the Eucharist demanded that disposition by which each of the first disciples refused "to call his own what appertained to him" and regarded "everything as held in common."

The second summary (Acts 4:32–35), originally devoted entirely to the social features of the community's life (Acts 4:32, 34–35), has been enlarged by an intercalated reference (v. 33) to the dynamic nature of the apostolic teaching. It is linked to the "little Pentecost" (Acts 4:31) and is thus presented as one of the tangible results of the presence of the Spirit in the community. By this procedure the author stresses the fact that the "common life" is one of the fruits of early Christian theological thought, which in its turn stems from the Holy Ghost. The *martyrion* given by the apostles "with great display of power" was accompanied not only by the miracles performed upon the sick but also by those less tangible, spiritual wonders, like the *koinōnia*, which this teaching evoked in the hearts of the disciples.

The third résumé (Acts 5:12–15), which sketches the thaumaturgical work of the apostles, is significant because of its remarkable reference to the privileged position Peter held in the esteem even of outsiders. They realize somehow that he has taken Jesus' place among the disciples, and they bring to him their sick and possessed as formerly they had to Christ (vv. 15–16; cf. Mk 6:56).

The fact that each of these summaries insists on the great favor which the community enjoyed with "the people" enables us to form some estimate of the relationship between the Jews and the Jerusalem Christians. To their fellow countrymen the little group was simply a more fervent sect of Judaism, a *hairesis*, as Paul will later term them, like the Essenes or the Pharisees (cf. Acts 24:14; 28:22; 26:5). It may also be that the Jews tended to confuse them with the movement headed by John the Baptist. The fact that the Christian community was known in Palestine as "the Way," a title probably deriving, as we shall see, from the Baptist's preaching, seems to indicate this.

What may be gathered from Luke's narrative about the Jerusalem community's conception of itself? As we have observed, the pentecostal experience revealed to the apostles the inauguration of the Messianic age and the community's identity with the new Israel. The apprehension of this truth drastically altered their entire historical perspective: the Lord, they perceived, had begun His work as Messiah and Redeemer, not by a personal reappearance in the world, but by the mission of the Spirit.[20] The old Jewish scheme of history they had already recognized as obsolete on Ascension Day; instead of one, there were to be two comings of the Christ. But now the commencement of the Messianic times without this second coming made it clear that the "last age" comprised two moments.[20a] There was a time of preparation, during which the invisible Lord by the Spirit worked through the community for the building up of a spiritual kingdom. Consequently their role in this period was to assist in aggregating Israel as a whole to the new faith. The second period was to be marked by Christ's second coming, when He would "bring the times of refreshment" and "the restoration of all things" (Acts 3:20–21). While the disciples did not know the date of this parousia, they were certain of one thing: the Lord's coming was contingent upon the conversion of Israel (Acts 3:19). In the first flush of their enthusiasm and by the phenomenal success which attended their early efforts to convert Israel, they naturally considered that the period of preparation for the Lord's advent would be a matter of comparatively little time. For as yet they were unaware of the place to be occupied by the pagan nations in the divine plan of salvation. It was to be Stephen's privilege to begin the community's education on this important point.

For the moment, they regarded themselves as the "little remnant" whose duty it was to rescue as many as possible of the "wicked and perverse generation." They called themselves "the Way." This title, I believe, they took from the Second Isaiah, whose prophecy was a favorite commonplace in their preaching: "Prepare the way of the Lord . . ." (Is 40:3 ff.).[21]

Since John the Baptist had been the first to use the passage in his call to penance (Mt 3:3), the designation of Jerusalem Christianity as "the Way" may be an indication of the close connection between it and the Baptist movement in the eyes of contemporary Judaism.

The community life of the disciples was, as we have noted, a paradisiac existence such as the prophets had foretold (Is 11:6 ff.). Full of joy, living in closest union with one another, having banished want by the sharing of their material goods, strengthened in time of persecution by the presence of the divine Spirit, they seemed to enjoy the fulness of that Messianic peace which was to mark the restoration of Israel. It is true that these Jerusalem Christians possessed a religion and a form of divine worship surpassing that of Israel; their evident belief in the divinity of Christ, their awareness of the personality of the Holy Spirit, and the "breaking of the bread" are evidence of that. Still it was the continuity between Christianity and the ancient religion which remained uppermost in their minds. The idea of receiving pagans, who had not first been converted to Judaism, was still inconceivable. The foundations of the kingdom had been laid, but the nature of the superstructure which the Lord intended to erect upon it was hidden in the future.

THE HELLENISTIC ELEMENT IN THE JERUSALEM COMMUNITY

The picture presented in the opening chapters of Acts is an idyll. Such a state of things was not to last. Indeed, it could not last, if the primitive community was to discover its full destiny and to develop that independence of Judaism which the complete universal coming of the kingdom of God demanded. It was the vocation of a group of Greek-speaking

Jews amongst the Jerusalem disciples, whom we may call the Hellenistic element, to dispel the idyllic atmosphere of the first years, which, however beautiful, tended to confine the new religion without the ambit of Judaism. These men, who were to commit Christianity to a course of action which would ultimately result in the admission of Gentiles within her ranks, make their appearance in Luke's story, characteristically enough, with the first signs of real dissension within the Jerusalem community (Acts 6:1).

However, the impact of this group of Hellenist Christians has already been felt in Acts' earlier chapters. The so-called Hellenistic character of some of the most ancient sources used by Luke has long been a puzzle to the critics. It is now explained by the presence of these men in the Jerusalem community from its inception. Among their more important contributions to early Christian theological thought were the elaboration of a rudimentary apologetics based on the Greek Bible, the working-out of the theology of the Name (*Kyrios*), one of the clearest proofs of the primitive faith in Christ's divinity, and the speculation upon the servant role of the suffering and glorified Christ.[22] It may also be that the presence of anti-Jewish feeling in the examples of the Jerusalem kerygma found in Acts should be credited to them. At any rate, by their creation of a series of scriptural arguments for the truth of Christianity, which were intended for use among Greek-speaking peoples, and their reflections upon Christology, the Hellenists were already forging weapons that could be used in the great missionary enterprises of the future Church.

The greatest figure in the group was undoubtedly that of Stephen, a man "full of grace and of power," endowed with many of the charismatic gifts displayed by the apostolic college (Acts 6:8) and possessing the clairvoyance and fearlessness of the ancient prophets. A Jew, he was versed in the Scriptures; a Hellenist, he was without any of the narrow chauvinism which tended to cramp the Christian spirit of many of the "Hebrews." If the long discourse attributed to him in Acts be characteristic of his doctrine, Stephen liked to dwell upon the infallible triumph of the divine plan over every obstacle that human malice could devise to thwart its execution. At the heart of such a conception of sacred history lies a profound intuition of the central truth of the apostolic preaching: Christ's death at the hands of the Jews and His resurrection by the power of God the Father. This insight resulted in the first Christian interpretation of the Old Testament; and the histories of Abraham, Joseph, Moses, and the prophets revealed to Stephen the relatively ephemeral nature of Judaism, as well as the basic incompatibility between the practice of Christianity and Judaism. In the context of Acts, Stephen's *plaidoyer* is addressed to his Jewish judges, and as such it insists upon Israel's characteristic sin, the clinging to what is of passing value in code and cult as if it were definitive. Actually, however, the martyr's interpretation of Old Testament history contained a warning to his fellow Christians, pointing out the anomaly of their position vis-à-vis Mosaic customs and the danger attendant upon the clinging to such practices.

But it was through his death that Stephen was destined to fix this lesson firmly in the mind of the primitive Church. Luke's account of the first martyrdom, drawn from an earlier source, proves that the disciples had been impressed by its close resemblance to the Master's passion. By dying on the charge of teaching that "Jesus will destroy this Place and change the traditions which Moses bequeathed to us" (Acts 6:14), Stephen reminds his brethren that Jesus had been condemned by official Judaism for declaring Himself "greater than the Temple" (Mt 12:6; 26:59) and setting Himself above the law of Moses (Jn 19:7).[23]

If the community of Jerusalem was slow to realize the inexorable logic of Stephen's teaching, the leaders of the Jews were not; and the persecution which broke out as a result of Stephen's death put an end forever to the ideal conditions in which hitherto the Christians had lived. Except for the absence of their exalted Lord, they had seemed almost to dwell in heaven, possessing the best of the two worlds of Israel and Christianity. Stephen's message brought the community down to earth, reminding them that it was in this world that they must struggle, even to death, to establish the kingdom, before they might hope to enjoy its glories in another world. In the divine call of Abraham, of Joseph, of Moses, with its peremptory demand to sever all attachment to people or country, Stephen had perceived types of the Christian vocation. But before this little seed which he implanted in the minds of the Jerusalem community could germinate into the missionary spirit of Antioch, a further divine intervention was required.

THE COMMUNITY'S GENTILE MISSION REVEALED TO PETER

Pentecost had revealed to the apostolic community the spiritual nature of the kingdom. Stephen had hinted at a further stage of development in suggesting a broader and more universalist outlook. It was Peter's experiences at Joppa and Caesarea which were destined to add a new dimension to the plan of Christian expansion.

The episode connected with the baptism of Cornelius the pagan is clearly of great importance in Luke's eyes. Like the conversion of Paul, it is recounted three times, and with each retelling fresh light is thrown upon its meaning. Logically, if not chronologically,[24] it takes precedence over a similar phenomenon at Antioch. The initiative in admitting pagans directly into the Christian communion belongs, as of right, to the head of the Jerusalem community. Luke is at pains to point out that this unprecedented event is clearly willed by God. Before answering the call of Cornelius, Peter is supernaturally informed that a creative act of God Himself has abolished the impurity formerly attaching to non-Jews: "What God has purified, call not impure" (Acts 10:15). And this principle is seen to operate effectually in Peter's subsequent attitude towards social intercourse with the Gentiles (Acts 10:28; 11:3, 9, 18; 15:9).

In obedience to the vision, Peter accepts the hospitality of Cornelius, preaches the gospel to his household; and, when the Spirit descends upon the group as upon the first Pentecost, he orders that they be baptized.

This admission of Gentiles who had not come to the Christian faith by way of Judaism was a remarkable step towards the realization of the universal character of the kingdom. The disciples who had followed Jesus in Galilee were aware that somehow the Gentiles were to be called to a share in the Messianic blessings as the prophets had foretold. Still it seems, from the explanations Peter is forced to give upon his return to Jerusalem, that they had not conceived it possible that pagans should be admitted *ex aequo* with the chosen people. Despite Luke's characteristic remark that the community "glorified God" (Acts 11:18), it appears, from the difficulties that arose at Antioch, that for some time they regarded Cornelius' conversion as an exception to the general rule. What is significant, however, is that the issue, in Peter's mind, is settled once for all; when he appears at the assembly in Jerusalem some years later, he will merely reassert the principle revealed to him that day by the sea in Joppa.

A curious remark of Peter's in his account of the Cornelius episode to the brethren of Jerusalem deserves to be noted for the light it sheds upon the process by which the apostles had come to recognize the institution of the sacrament of baptism. ". . . The Holy Spirit descended upon them, just as upon us at the beginning. And I recalled the Lord's remark: 'John,' He said, 'baptized with water, but you will be baptized in the Holy Spirit' " (Acts 11:15 ff.). His recollection of this logion of the Lord is given by Peter as his reason for allowing Cornelius and his family to be baptized. What led Peter to such a conclusion? Why not consider these pagans who had received the Spirit, just as the apostles themselves had, members of the Church? It would seem that those who received the Holy Ghost on Pentecost were considered to constitute the Messianic community without any reception of baptism. Moreover, in the very words of Christ which Peter recalls, the Johannine baptism with water is opposed to the baptism with the Spirit. Yet Peter had said at Caesarea: "Surely no one can prevent the water from baptizing those who have received the Holy Spirit even as we did?" (Acts 10:47).

What led the apostles to practice a sacrament, defined in the fourth Gospel as a rebirth of "water and the Spirit" (Jn 3:5)? As we have already remarked, the reception of John's baptism had been a condition for candidature to the apostleship. Peter, Andrew, John, Philip, and Nathanael seem to have been disciples of the Baptist; and since the disciples of Christ had also practiced this rite (Jn 4:2), the rest of the Twelve as well as the other disciples gathered in the upper room had also received it. With the reception of the baptism in the Spirit, the apostles were given a profounder insight into the antithesis: John with water, Christ with the Spirit. They had received the waters of Johannine baptism, and now Christ had baptized them in the Spirit. It was a "validation," a "sacramentalization," of the Johannine baptism. Water and the Spirit were henceforth to form a new reality, the Christian sacrament of baptism.[25]

THE "NEW CREATION" OF ANTIOCH

With the sure instinct of the true historian, Luke connects the foundation of Antiochian Christianity with the death of Stephen (Acts 8:4; 11:19). Stephen's influence is felt not only in the fact that the founders of Antioch were Hellenists, but also in their departure from the ordinary rule of preaching only to the Jews (Acts 11:20). Their evangelization of the pagans met with unprecedented success, and the result was a community predominantly pagan in origin. Furthermore, three factors in the formation of the Antiochian Church resulted in a strikingly new formula of Christianity.

Joseph Barnabas, a Levite of Cypriot origin (Acts 4:36), who enjoyed the confidence of the heads of the Jerusalem community, was sent to supervise the new foundation at Antioch. As leader of the new church, he displays the qualities which had earned him the sobriquet "Barnabas,"[26] by encouraging the novel experiment at Antioch whereby Jewish and Gentile Christian lived in Christian fellowship, and by promoting a marked growth in the congregation. Barnabas possessed, moreover, a rare gift for judging men; and the man he picked as his lieutenant was Saul of Tarsus, whom he had already sponsored in Jerusalem when Saul had been an object of fear and suspicion to the other Christians. Barnabas knew that Saul had retired to his own city of Tarsus because of his failure at evangelization in Jerusalem. There he sought him out and succeeded in getting Saul's co-operation. Barnabas' realization that Saul's talents could best be used in a mixed community like that of Antioch was a stroke of genius, from which both Saul and the Antiochian Christians were to profit.

Saul had returned to Tarsus with only the memory of a vision in which Christ had informed him that his vocation was to preach the gospel to the pagan world (Acts 22:17–21).

Perhaps also he still remembered Stephen's conception of a Christianity conscious of its freedom from the Mosaic law and the Temple cult. In any case, it was at Antioch that Stephen's principle was being put into practice for the first time; and the year Saul spent there under Barnabas' direction prepared him for his future mission to the pagans. The example given him in the art of governing a congregation composed of some Jewish and many pagan Christians would serve him later in founding churches like Philippi, Thessalonica, and Corinth. The development of a completely Christian liturgy, centered in the Eucharist, would provide Saul with a form of cult that could be easily transplanted to new foundations. His period of training came to an end the day the Holy Spirit manifested His will regarding himself and Barnabas. The great missionary era of the Church was begun.

Luke points out that the completely distinctive character of Christianity was realized for the first time not at Jerusalem but at Antioch (Acts 11:26). There the group of disciples appeared as a "new creation" by contrast with both paganism and Judaism. This was due to the absence of the Temple's influence in their Christian life, together with the fact that the majority of the disciples were converts from paganism. The Jerusalem community had been, in fact, no less Christian, but it remained to some extent under the shadow of the Temple. At Antioch it was easier to forget the ancient discrimination between Jew and Gentile, where there was no "wall of separation" to divide Jewish Christians from the rest, as when the Jerusalem community assisted at the public liturgy of Israel. Until certain Christian pharisees invaded Antioch (Acts 15:11), there were no such distinctions.

Owing to the distance from the Temple, the Eucharistic celebration became the center of the community's cultic life in a way it had never been in Jerusalem. It is significant that we find the word "liturgy" applied to the "breaking of the bread" first at Antioch (Acts 13:2). In Jerusalem, "liturgy" continued to signify the gorgeous ceremonial of Judaism.

The most important feature of the new spirit manifested by Christian Antioch was her answer to the divine call to the missions among the Gentiles. In Jerusalem the community tended to await the coming of the pagans to the center of the new religion, the Temple. It is Antioch which first obeys the command of Christ to carry His gospel "to the end of the earth." Her Hellenist founders had not forgotten Stephen's teaching that the Almighty had been a wanderer Himself during the greatest period of Israel's religious life, the march through the desert, that He "does not dwell in structures built by human hands" (Acts 7:48). They were aware that the Eucharistic liturgy, which was the center of their Christian life, could be carried out wherever the preachers of the gospel were to be found. It was scarcely an accident that the Spirit should summon the first missionaries of Antioch while they were engaged in the Eucharistic cult.

This divine revelation of the fully universal nature of the kingdom of God was to be brought home to the apostolic Church through the missionary experiences of Paul. His travels throughout Asia Minor and Europe illustrate, in Luke's story, the witnessing "to the end of the earth" which the risen Christ had mysteriously pointed out as an element in the coming of the kingdom. Moreover, as events were to prove, Paul was destined to enlarge considerably the early Christian view of the history of salvation.

The Jerusalem community had held firmly to two principles which she knew to be divinely revealed: the gospel must first be preached to Israel (Acts 2:39; 3:26; 5:31), and the parousia of the Lord was delayed only until Israel as a collectivity had accepted Christianity (Acts 3:19–20). Paul made the first of these his guide in preaching the gospel; wherever he went, he first announced the kingdom to the Jews of the Dispersion. Yet everywhere, as Luke testifies, he met their almost unanimous opposition to Christianity. In many places the only obstacle to their killing him out of hatred for his message was the power of imperial Rome (Acts 17:5 ff.; 18:12 ff.; 21:31 ff.; 23:12; 25:2 ff.).[27] By contrast Paul was very successful in his attempts to convert the pagans. According to Acts, Paul's most sustained effort to convince the Jews of the truth of Christianity was at Ephesus, where he devoted three months to the task (Acts 19:8); it seems that he did not succeed in making a single convert among his own race. Now it is interesting to note that it was around this point in his career, in the opinion of many commentators,[28] that Paul seems to have undergone a change of opinion with regard to the proximity of the Parousia. At any rate, by the time he wrote to the Roman Church from Corinth, about the year 56, he had clearly formulated a theology of history according to which, by her rejection of the gospel, Israel had yielded her place in the kingdom to the pagan nations and would only accept Jesus as the Christ "when the full number of the Gentiles has come in" (Rom 11:25–26). Whether Paul had been granted a special revelation on this point, we do not know. It is, however, not improbable that this conclusion was simply the result of his missionary experiences during the height of his career as an apostle. Once he had arrived at this conclusion, he must have seen the conversion of Israel as a hope indefinitely deferred, and with it the second coming of the Lord. For the earlier belief, stated by Peter, was not found to be incorrect: the Parousia was still contingent upon the collective entry of the Jews into the kingdom. Paul's discovery was that this conversion itself was, in its turn, contingent upon that of the Gentiles. In the early days of Palestinian Christianity Israel's acceptance of the faith would, it had seemed, be almost spontaneous, a matter of no time at all; and the Lord's coming had in consequence appeared near at hand. It took the greater part of Paul's missionary activity to change that outlook. By the time Matthew's Gospel, as we possess it in Greek, came to be written, the divine plan for the propagation of the gospel was known throughout the Christian Church. This realization of the delay in Christ's second coming was, I believe, an important factor in turning Paul's attention to the mysterious phenomenon of the Church herself and in promoting, perhaps chiefly through his instrumentality, the conviction in apostolic Christianity that the coming of the kingdom was to be identified with the organization of the Church.

THE END OF JERUSALEM'S IMPORTANCE IN APOSTOLIC CHRISTIANITY

In the early years Jerusalem had seemed destined, with the Temple, to be the center of Christianity. But Acts reveals a gradual movement away from the capital of Judaism. The Hellenistic element is driven out by persecution. Peter, more and more occupied with his pastoral visits to new foundations, finally goes off "to another place" (Acts 12:17). About the same time the apostles themselves appear to have sought new fields of evangelization. Paul, frustrated in his apostolate in Jerusalem, lives a year at Antioch and then begins a series of expeditions which lead him eventually to Rome.

Jerusalem had but one more function to perform in the history of the early Church: to promulgate the definitive charter of Gentile liberties. This she did in the Council of Jerusalem, in the presence of Peter, Paul, and others, if not all, of the apostles. Luke makes it clear that this formal acknowledgment of the fully revealed divine plan for the coming of the kingdom emanates not from Peter but from the Jerusalem community, in the person of James, her bishop. Peter, for whom the question was settled long ago at Caesarea, is simply present as "the legate of Christ."[29] It was fitting that Jerusalem, the mother church and primitive guardian of orthodoxy, should publicly accept the declared will of God before disappearing, as she would soon after, with the advance of Titus' armies, into history. Her chief glory was ever to have submitted to that divine will, no matter what it cost her. Her original conception of the kingdom of God had been very different from the reality as it evolved under the impact of events. Once the tide turned in the direction of the Gentiles, Jerusalem's task was ended, and the focal point of Christianity was henceforth to be located elsewhere.

In Acts Luke sketches the gradual revelation to the early Church of what Christ had meant in His postresurrection discourses by "the kingdom of God." It is consonant with our author's purpose that, after its recurrence in this place (Acts 1:3), he makes no reference to the phrase during the part of his narrative which deals with the Jerusalem period, but only when he comes to Paul's missionary activity.

The phrase is first mentioned upon Paul's return to Lystra from Derbe; he and his companions "encouraged the spirits of the disciples, urging them to persevere in the faith, 'for,' they said, 'it is by many trials that we are to enter the kingdom of God'" (Acts 14:22). It is clear from the context that by perseverance in "the faith" Paul means continued loyalty to the Church which he has organized among the disciples (v. 23 speaks of his establishing a hierarchical body), the only means of entry into the kingdom. In Ephesus, as has been pointed out, Paul spent three months, as Luke remarks, "trying to persuade them [the Jews] about the kingdom of God. But . . . some hardened their hearts and refused to be convinced, vilifying the Way before the assembly . . ." (Acts 19:8). This passage shows that to reject the Way is to reject the kingdom of God. In his farewell discourse to the "seniors" of the Ephesian Church, Paul describes his part in organizing the Church among them as a "heralding of the kingdom" (Acts 20:25). The preaching of the kingdom, rejected by the Jews, has resulted at Ephesus in the founding of a Gentile Church.

These three passages depict in miniature the connection between the kingdom of God and the Church which Luke has revealed to his reader by recounting the missionary experiences of Paul. The Church is the way to the kingdom; to reject the Church is to refuse God's kingdom; the coming of that kingdom upon earth was effected by the apostolic organization of the Church among the Gentiles. In Christ's earthly life, as Luke has shown in his first volume, the preaching of the kingdom was greeted with incredulity on the part of His fellow countrymen. When it ripened into hatred for His message, this incredulity compassed His death. But it was by the death of Christ and His resurrection that the coming of the kingdom into this world was definitively inaugurated. In Paul's lifetime the preaching of the kingdom met with this same Jewish incredulity and hatred. Through this apostolic experience Paul came gradually to comprehend the successive stages in the divine plan for the establishment of the kingdom. From all eternity God had decreed that Israel's exclusion from the kingdom through lack of faith should lead to the call of the Gentiles, whose conversion in turn would provoke that of the Jews. Such a scheme of things was necessary in order that Christianity should be liberated from the thrall of Judaism, and by withdrawing herself from the shadow of the Temple should actualize the potentiality for true universalism which was an essential quality of the kingdom of God.

All of this Luke implies when at the very end of Acts he describes Paul's activity in Rome as a "heralding the kingdom of God" (Acts 28:31). A few days after his arrival in that city Paul had, in the Jewish assembly, "borne testimony to the kingdom of God" (Acts 28:23), trying to persuade them by scriptural arguments about the Messianic character of Christ. When he meets with this last refusal, he states that "God's salvation has been sent to the Gentiles" (Acts 28:28). Acts closes with the preaching of the kingdom to the Gentiles, thus reminding the reader that the divine revelation concerning the coming of the kingdom, with which the book began, has reached its term.

KINGDOM AND CHURCH IN THE GOSPEL OF MATTHEW

A brief review of the first Gospel will clarify the relation between the coming of the kingdom and the founding of the apostolic Church. It will also, in addition to providing a confirmation for Luke's interpretation of the experience of the apostolic Church, throw considerable light upon the purpose of Matthew, who writes at the close of the developments we have been describing.

Like any other Gospel, that of Matthew narrates the story of Jesus' public life culminating in His passion, death, and resurrection. What is peculiar to Matthew's Gospel, however, is a very clearly marked progression in the dramatic movement centering in Jesus' preaching of the kingdom of heaven. This proclamation of the kingdom arouses greater and greater opposition during the Galilean ministry, which reaches its peak in Jesus' refusal to give any sign "except the sign of the prophet Jonah" (Mt 12:38–42), and His terrible warning "to this wicked generation" that the state of having positively rejected the kingdom will be worse than their first state of ignorance regarding it (12:43–45). In the sequel Jesus devotes Himself to the instruction of His faithful disciples; apart from certain controversial episodes, He leaves the Jews to themselves. Meantime the Jewish opposition turns to hatred, draws down upon itself the angry fulminations of the sevenfold woe in chapter 23, and achieves its purpose in the passion and death of Jesus.

During this latter part of his Gospel Matthew dwells with increasing insistence upon another theme: to replace the Jews who have rejected the kingdom, the divine plan calls for the admission of the Gentiles. This motif appears in a series of parables, most of which are found only in this Gospel: the parable of the Eleventh Hour (20:1–16), of the Two Sons (21:28–32), of the Vineyard (21:33–56),[30] of the Wedding Feast (22:1–14).[31]

Matthew had made use of another device to highlight this presentation of the drama of Jesus' preaching of the kingdom: five lengthy discourses, artificially constructed from the logia of Christ scattered throughout the traditions of the public life, which form a kind of midrash on the narrative sections which precede and delineate various aspects of the kingdom of heaven.[32] The Sermon on the Mount (5:1—7:29) prepares for the coming of the kingdom and promulgates its new code. The missionary discourse (10:5–42) contains Jesus' plan for the promotion of the kingdom among the Jews of Palestine. The discourse in parables (13:3–52) portrays the mysterious nature of the kingdom and explains, in effect, why it is rejected by the Jews, and why during the rest of the story Jesus will content Himself with instructing only His faithful followers. The fourth sermon (18:1–35) is an instruction to the disciples on the mutual duties of the members of the kingdom. The final discourse (24:3—25:46) contains Christ's prediction of the end of the world of Israel, the ruin of the Temple, which is presented as the externalization of the coming of the kingdom in His death and resurrection.

A re-examination of these discourses in the light of Form Criticism reveals another source upon which Matthew had drawn: the experience of the apostolic Church. The recognition of this element in the Matthean picture of the kingdom of heaven gives a completely new insight into the purpose of the Evangelist. By adding this new dimension to his picture of the kingdom as preached by Christ, Matthew has set in parallel the experience of the apostolic age and that of Jesus' earthly life. This experience of the primitive Church during the thirty years which followed the Master's death has verified what He stated about the coming of the kingdom. Thus within the description of the coming of the kingdom we are enabled to discern the figure of the nascent Church.

The Sermon on the Mount teaches the proper dispositions for the receiving of the kingdom when it comes, and presents what we might call the "prehistory" of the kingdom. The Beatitudes which form its exordium recall the two great classes of Israel who were types of the subjects of the kingdom: the *'anawim* and the prophets.[33] Christ insists upon the exact observance of the law of Moses, as He did throughout His earthly career (5:17–20). By this means alone the will of God will be perfectly accomplished, and this is the *conditio sine qua non* for the coming of the kingdom, as the Our Father (6:9–13) shows. Yet the passage which immediately follows the exhortation to observe the old law promulgates, by a series of six antitheses, the new law of the kingdom. It is a code of perfection, but a code which concerns those who live in this world. It outlaws hatred, impurity of mind, divorce, perjury, vengeance; it insists on love of enemies (5:21–48). Like the command to leave to God all care of material needs (6:25), which Acts testifies was carried out in the apostolic *koinōnia,* this new legislation is the charter of the primitive Church. Yet, in this first discourse, which occurs in Matthew's Gospel before the constitution of the apostolic college (10: 1–5), the picture of the future Church is only discreetly hinted at. The disciples are to be the prophets of the kingdom (5:12), a theme which Matthew introduces immediately after the Beatitudes; he will refer to it again in three subsequent discourses.[34] For the present, until "heaven and earth pass away" (5:18) as a result of Christ's death and resurrection,[35] the kingdom is still in the future.

With the missionary discourse there appears a curious blending of the experiences of the little band of apostles, sent to preach the coming of the kingdom, with that of the apostolic age. The instruction of the newly-chosen Twelve concerns at first only their immediate mission in Galilee (10:5–16). They are forbidden to evangelize pagans or even Samaritans; their message, like that of John the Baptist and Jesus Himself, concerns something still in the future: "The kingdom of heaven is near at hand." Abruptly, without warning, the whole setting is shifted (vv. 17–42); the apostles are dragged before "governors and kings" to present the *martyrion* (v. 18) to Christ's resurrection described in Acts. Thus there is no longer any question of announcing the coming of the kingdom: it is now proclaimed as having come through Jesus' death and exaltation. The "coming of the Son of Man," the divine visitation identified with the destruction of Jerusalem, will find the apostles still engaged in this missionary activity.[36]

This deliberate foreshortening of historical perspective reveals a deep insight on the part of the Evangelist. He has perceived that the kerygma of the apostolic Church is a continuation of Jesus' preaching of the kingdom, although he is aware that the kerygma is centered upon the historical act of man's redemption by which the kingdom is come upon earth, and is aimed at attracting new members to the community. In short, Matthew has seen that the organization of the Church is an integral part of the coming of the kingdom.

By the time the instruction in parables is reached in the first Gospel, Jesus' preaching has been rejected by the majority of the Jews; in consequence the rejection of Israel comes very much to the fore. Matthew cites Is 6:9–10 at greater length than Mark. He includes two parables, not found elsewhere, which bear upon Jewish incredulity: that of the Hidden Treasure and the Pearl of rare value, which insist that entry to the kingdom entails the sacrifice of everything, even of the law of Moses. Matthew still has Israel in mind when at the end of the sermon he recalls a personal experience of his own, the riches of the "scribe become a disciple of the kingdom," possessing the old as well as the new (v. 52).

Two other properly Matthean parables describe the kingdom existing in this world as found in the apostolic Church at the date of writing. It contains the wicked as well as the good, "all sorts of things" (13:47), the just with the "promoters of scandals and iniquity" (v. 41). Included in this sermon is the parable of the Sower with the explanation of it that was current in the primitive Church. Here we find allusions to the presence within the kingdom-become-Church of the lukewarm who have been seduced by riches (v. 22) and of the halfhearted who apostatize in time of persecution (v. 21).

The point of departure for the fourth discourse is the disciples' question concerning "the greatest in the kingdom of heaven" (18:1 ff.). The narrative section preceding this exhortation on the mutual duties of members of the kingdom has recounted the promise of the primacy to Peter (16:18–19) and the incident of the Temple tax (17:24–27), which proves Peter's privileged position among the Twelve. The lessons which Christ gives are for the community which Peter will shepherd: the dangers of scandal, solicitude for the "lost sheep" (Jesus has already described His own mission in these terms, 17:24–27), fraternal correction (here the word *ekklēsia,* mentioned in the promise of the primacy, again occurs), the spirit of forgiveness (illustrated by a Matthean parable, the two debtors, 18:23–35, which probably concerns relations between Gentile and Jewish Christians). There is an imperceptible transition in this sermon from the real child, present at the beginning, to the humble and simple members of the future Church.

The last discourse, which foretells the end of the world of the Old Testament, dramatically depicts the definitive coming of the Church in the divine visitation of the glorified Christ which terminates the existence of the Temple. Throughout the greater part of the apostolic age, the Christian community still clung to the traditions and cultic practices of Judaism. In this apocalyptic event Matthew sees the vindication of the universality of the new religion. The "*sēmeion* of the Son of Man" (24:30) displayed triumphantly above the devastation of Jerusalem is that *sēmeion* which Isaiah foresaw raised up by the Lord for the Gentiles, and for those lost of Israel and the dispersed of Judah (Is 11:12): the kingdom come as the Church.

Three parables, which seem to reflect the organization of the Church at the time this Gospel was written, are inserted towards the end of the eschatological discourse. All three concern the eschatology of individuals, and thus provide a valuable insight into the Church's realization of the indefinite period of time during which she must exercise her mission before the parousia of her Lord. The parable of the Steward (24:45–51) concerns the particular judgment of the apostles and the other administrators of the kingdom upon earth; that of the Ten Virgins, who appear as spouses of Christ (25:1–13), suggests that there are already groups of specially consecrated contemplatives, of which Tabitha and the widows of Joppa may well be an earlier example (Acts 9:36 ff.); the parable of the Talents (Mt. 25:14–30) depicts the particular judgment of those who form the body of the faithful. By the time this Gospel was composed, therefore, the death of individual Christians before the Parousia was an accepted fact. The doctrine which we saw stated by Paul concerning the unlimited delay of the Lord's second coming is now common to the whole Church.

This eschatological discourse upon the ruin of the Temple performs a double function in the framework of the first Gospel. It serves to introduce the climax of the kerygma, the Passion and Resurrection narratives; as such, it explains the cosmic effects of the redemption depicted as a passing of the old heavens and the old earth in the creation of the new world. But it sets a term as well to the experience of the apostolic Church which Matthew has also depicted in these five sermons—the experience of the coming of the kingdom in the Church as a result of the preaching of the Gospel. Matthew composed his Gospel at a period when the whole evolution of primitive Christianity described by Luke in Acts has resulted in a Church, in which pagans have replaced the Jews who have rejected the good news of salvation. The center of religious interest has already shifted from Jerusalem to distant Rome, whither Peter and Paul have migrated. As a result, the mystery of the establishment of the kingdom of heaven upon earth has been clarified for the apostolic Church; the entry of the pagans into the kingdom has taken precedence over that of Israel, and with it the unlimited duration of the life span of the Church has been recognized.

The purpose of the twofold theme, or rather of a single

theme developed on two different historical levels, now becomes clear to us. Matthew has attempted in one volume what Luke has accomplished in two books: to show the coming of the kingdom of heaven as realized in the organization of the apostolic Church. He uses the literary scheme of presenting the preaching of Jesus in five great sermons primarily to expose the meaning of the passion and resurrection of Christ: Jesus' proclamation of the coming of the kingdom fulfils Old Testament prophecy in a way so unexpected by the Jews that they reject Him, and so yield place to the Gentiles. A secondary purpose appears, however, in the references made in these same sermons to the apostolic preaching of the gospel: the heralding of the kingdom of God as come definitely upon earth through the principal act of Christ's redemptive work is the principal means of organizing the Church. The apostolic community has perceived, Matthew tells us in effect, that the rebuff met by Jesus in His attempts to convince Israel of the truth of His message is paralleled by the failure of the nascent Church to win over the majority of the Jews to Christianity. In the case of Christ Himself this attitude of Judaism led ultimately to His death; in the case of the apostolic community it led to the establishment of the Church as it existed when Matthew's Greek Gospel was written.

The date of the founding of the Church is a matter of much debate among theologians. Christ is considered by some to have founded it upon the cross; by others, when He rose as the glorified Head of the Mystical Body on the first Easter; by a third group, when He sent the Holy Spirit at Pentecost. Luke's account of Christian origins in Acts indicates a solution to the problem along quite different lines: the coming of the kingdom which coincided with the founding of the Church was an evolutionary process extended over a period of time. Greek Matthew, who constructed his Gospel to underscore this same truth, has carefully marked the beginning and the end of the continuous movement which is the founding of the Church, by means of the first and the last of five great discourses. The *terminus a quo* is the Sermon on the Mount, by which Jesus inaugurates His preaching of the kingdom; the *terminus ad quem* is the destruction of the Temple, the divine manifestation of the coming of the glorified Son of Man in His kingdom-become-Church.

2

Salvation in the Primitive Preaching

THE purpose of the present essay is to determine as exactly as the sources at our command will permit the manner in which the apostolic community of Jerusalem arrived at a Christian doctrine of salvation, and to evaluate their initial formulation of it. This level of theological development may be best described as that of the primitive preaching. Chronologically and geographically, its lines of demarcation remain tantalizingly vague.[1] The Palestinian kerygma continued to be employed in its original form by Paul, for example, long after he had embarked upon the evangelization of the Greek mainland and even after he had elaborated the grandiose soteriological themes which characterize his later letters.[2] Fortunately, however, the vagueness which frustrates any attempt to situate our period historically affects only the terminal point. Its origins, which are of paramount importance for the comprehension of the maturer phases of New Testament thought, can be narrowed down to the moment when the fundamental truth of the Christian revelation first flashed upon the minds of the apostles, namely, that Yahweh's long-promised salvation had become reality in Jesus Christ. It is, moreover, possible to discern with a fair degree of accuracy the lineaments of this somewhat rudimentary stage of Christian soteriology with its theological insights and modalities of expression which, however imperfect or lacunary, set the pattern that would be followed by the great Pauline and Johannine syntheses.

The true value of these early doctrinal affirmations, however, lies much deeper than their function as a point of departure for subsequent, richer theological reflection. They have, in the first place, a claim on our interest and reverence inasmuch as they pertain to the inspired literature of the New Testament. A more basic reason derives from the fact that Christianity is in essence a historical religion, possessing revelation that is essentially involved with time, and not merely a collection of theological propositions. Accordingly, the very development of doctrine within the books of the New Testament is inspired and meaningful in itself. The Christian reality to which the various sacred writers attest is always greater than any formulation of it, however admirable or technically accurate. If we are to grasp the *res christiana* as God intended we should grasp it, we cannot afford to neglect the temporal, the contingent, as well as the organic nature of the New Testament revelation. To select only what appears to be the most perfect form in which the various dogmas are set forth, while rejecting the cruder, more fragmentary, less apt enunciations of them, is to ignore the historical character of Christian revelation.[3]

In order that we may evaluate the achievements and the deficiencies of the most primitive conception of salvation known to have existed in Christianity, three major influences in its creation must be taken into consideration: the Old Testament doctrine of salvation, Jesus' formation of the first disciples through His public ministry, death, and resurrection, and (the most significant factor of all) the pentecostal experience of the apostolic community.

PRINCIPAL OLD TESTAMENT SOTERIOLOGICAL THOUGHT-PATTERNS

It will be well to begin by reminding ourselves that the problem of formulating a Christian soteriology was basically a Jewish problem. The first Christians were almost exclusively of Jewish origin and consequently conceived the new revelation of which they were the depositaries in a characteristically Semitic fashion, one quite distinct from the way in which a group of Greeks might have envisaged it. They were, in addition, acquainted with the notions of salvation so prominent in the sacred books of Judaism. It was inevitable, therefore, that the primitive preaching should be conditioned by the soteriological thought-patterns of the Old Testament.

It was only in the postexilic period of Israel's history that salvation acquired those spiritual, transcendent, and individual (as opposed to collective) qualities which in the Christian dispensation came to be associated with the term. In earlier ages the Israelite thought of salvation merely as a deliverance from present, national, terrestrial calamities. Security and happiness in this life were the essence of salvation. The root *'ys* from which the various Hebrew terms for it are derived means "to be broad, spacious." Positively, the notion involves an exercise of strength which gains victory; negatively, it connotes liberation from danger, misfortune, hostile powers—above all, from death and Sheol. J. Pedersen has pointed out how different it is from the Hellenistic idea of *sōtēria,* which denotes deliverance from the miseries and limitations of man's present material existence.[4] To Israel, salvation primarily implied security and prosperity in this life, bestowed by the protective strength of Yahweh, sole source of protection (Jg 7:2). It compassed the whole of man's nature and his contemporary existence. The Greek conception of "saving our souls," so familiar to modern theological thought, would have been quite unintelligible to the ancient Israelite. When finally the Old Testament writers became aware of some kind of salvation after death, they did so thanks to the revelation of a bodily resurrection, not through the alien idea of the soul's immortality. Despite fundamental differences, it is one of the most notable characteristics of New Testament soteriology that throughout the course of its development it appears to have remained within the Hebraic frame of reference in this regard.[5]

The event which gave rise to the Old Testament conception of salvation was Israel's redemption out of Egyptian bondage, from which Yahweh had rescued her in order to form for Himself a people of His own acquiring.[6] The fact that Israel had received her status as God's own people by this momentous liberation accounts for the national and collective overtones which clung for so long a time to the Old Testament salvation idea. It was only after the Exile, when Israel's national aspirations were recognized as doomed to failure, that salvation was related to the individual and became more spiritual.[7] The great prophets of the Exile, Jeremiah (Jer 31:29–31) and Ezekiel (Ez 18:1–32; 34:2–20), adopt the individualist viewpoint. In the book of Isaiah, there is attention to the universal (Is 2:2–4) and eschatological (Is 25:8; 45:8; 51:6; 61:10) character of Yahweh's salvation. Deutero-Isaiah particularly universalizes and spiritualizes the notion of "the land" (Is 43:3 ff.; cf. also Is 60:21; Ps 69:34–37; 3:8; 47:4 ff.).

The wisdom literature of Israel revives in a striking way the interest in individual salvation (Jb 5:15; 22:29; 26:2; Prv 2:7; 20:22). Still, in these authors the question of individual retribution finds no solution which reaches beyond the grave.[8] The book of Wisdom provides an answer by adopting the Greek notion of the immortality of the soul (Wis 5:15).

Such a doctrine, however, was a deviation from the customary thought-patterns of ancient Israel and it offered little help to the early Christian thinkers.[9] It is instructive to observe how rarely, if ever, the idea of an immediate reward after death seems to have occurred to the writers of the New Testament.[10] In the Old Testament the problem of divine retribution was solved satisfactorily only when, towards the end of her history, Israel accepted the belief in the future resurrection of the body. While it is possible to recognize gropings after this doctrine in earlier texts (Is 26:19; Ps 49:15; Jb 19:25), the first clear enunciation of it is found in Dn 12:2–3. By the time the author of 2 Maccabees wrote his *histoire édifiante* of the last Jewish struggle against Hellenistic impiety, there are at least certain groups of thinkers in Judaism who take the belief for granted (2 Mac 12:43–45; cf. 14:46) and who have abandoned the old traditional notion of Sheol (2 Mac 15:12–16).

It was also only very gradually that Israel focused her Messianic hopes upon the coming of an individual Christ. The divine promises prior to the Exile are obscure on this point, although they do assert that Yahweh's salvation is to be brought to Israel through some human intermediary, "the seed of woman" (Gn 3:15), "the seed of Abraham" (Gn 12:1–3; 17:4–8), "the ruler" of the tribe of Judah (Gn 49:10), the covenanted people under Moses (Dt 28:1 ff.), "the offspring of David" (2 S 7:12–16; 1 Chr 17:13; cf. Ps 89:27–38). The collapse of the Davidic dynasty during the Exile did not entirely snuff out this hope (Jer 23:1–8; Ez 21:27; 34:23). Moreover, the composition of the Servant Songs towards the end of the Babylonian captivity inaugurated a new trend in Israelitic Messianism. They set forth a soteriology in which Yahweh's Servant is designated as the divine organ of salvation. He is the new lawgiver (Is 42:1–4), and also the lamb immolated as a sin offering by suffering and death (Is 53:3–12) to expiate the "sins of the many." His exaltation will provide new grounds for hope not only to Israel but also to the pagan nations. The possibility of identifying the Servant with the Davidic king of earlier prophecy is implicit in the fact that both are depicted as the bearers of Yahweh's definitive salvation. Old Testament Messianism reaches its climax in the book of Daniel, where the future kingdom of the saints is symbolically represented by an apocalyptic figure, the "Son of Man," at once human and superhuman.[11] With this conception Israelite soteriology reaches a stage beyond which it cannot develop before receiving the New Testament revelation of the incarnate Word.

It remains to refer very briefly to three notions connected with Old Testament salvation doctrine which stem from Israel's experience of the covenants Yahweh made with the patriarchs and, on Sinai, with His people: the kingdom of God, the Day of Yahweh, and the idea of the remnant. In the earliest Israelitic traditions (Ex 15:18; Jg 8:23; 1 S 8:7) Yahweh was acknowledged as ruler of His people, indeed as king of the whole earth (Ex 19:6). In a later age the hope of Israel's restoration found support in the belief that God's dominion over His people was unending (Is 33:22; Zeph 3:15). Faith in the effective and final establishment of Yahweh's sovereignty epitomizes the protogospel of Deutero-Isaiah (Is 52:7). Already in the postexilic prophets this eschatological intervention may be seen to include the termination of the present world, postulating the creation of "the new heavens and the new earth" (Is 65:17 ff.; 66:22; Za 14:6–9). The transcendent nature of the divine dominion over the universe is emphasized by Dn 12:1 ff., while Israel's delivery is pictured as taking place in heaven rather than upon earth.[12] Like the theme of the kingdom of God, that of the Day of

Yahweh depicts this final divine intervention in human history, Yahweh's judgment. A minatory note, however, is distinctive of the latter conception: it is a day of darkness (Amos 5:18), of anger (Zeph 2:2), of vengeance (Is 34:8; 53:4), when God will judge Israel's foes and save His people. Yet the infidelity of many among the chosen people raised the question of the reconciliation of Yahweh's justice with His undoubted faithfulness to His promises. A means of resolving this tension was found in the doctrine of the remnant, which runs like a thread throughout the Old Testament prophetic books.[13] The pre-exilic prophets (Amos, Mi, Is) consider the Palestinian survivors of the depredations of the Assyrians Salmanasar, Sargon, and Sennacherib as the remnant, while the prophets of the Babylonian captivity (Jer, Zeph, Ez) think of the exiled Jews as constituting this favored group who become the bearers of the new salvation. After the Exile, the remnant is identified with that section of the people who returned to rebuild the Temple (Za 13:8 f.; Esd 9:8). We shall have occasion later to remark on the importance of this theme in the ecclesiological thought of the primitive Christian community, which Paul was to develop in his epistles (Gal 6:16; Rom 9:27–29).

JESUS' LIFE AND TEACHING PREPARE NEW TESTAMENT SALVATION DOCTRINE

When we turn to the New Testament to discover the earliest Christian conception of salvation, our principal sources are undoubtedly the records embodied in Acts of the preaching emanating from Jerusalem during the period consequent upon the first Pentecost.[14] Its dominant characteristic may be described as pre-eminently pentecostal, since it was the miracle of Pentecost which, as we shall attempt to demonstrate, revolutionized the faith and thinking of the disciples. Yet it was Christ's preparation of His disciples for this pentecostal revelation, by instruction and by permitting them to share in the significant events of His earthly career up to the moment of His ascension, which enabled them to profit by this supreme experience and which, together with the Old Testament, assisted them in formulating the good news of the kerygma. Accordingly, it is necessary to consider these formative influences before attempting an examination of the apostolic preaching.

When Christ inaugurated His public ministry, He entered a world which felt acutely the need for salvation. On the evidence of the New Testament itself, there were already a number who "looked for the consolation of Israel" (Lk 2:25; cf. Jer 17:6; Is 40:1) or "who were expecting the redemption of Jerusalem" (Lk 2:38). Recently the documents of the "Damascus" covenanters of Qumrân have introduced us to another group of pious Jews among whom the hope of an imminent coming of the Lord's anointed had been kept bright. To prepare for this long-awaited event, they had seceded from the degraded cult and compromised priesthood of Judaism by a retreat into the desert of Judah, where they exercised their vigilance by a strict observance of the law. Their sectarian writings witness to the need of the help Christ came to bring. It appears most strikingly in their constant fluctuation between two extremes of sentiment, a feeling of utter sinfulness on the one hand, and a deep confidence in the merciful forgiveness of Yahweh on the other.[15] Confronted with this dilemma, they strove to make themselves worthy of the eschatological salvation which the Messiah would effect, by fidelity to the teaching of the "Master of Justice" and a practice of the law which included the proper interior dispositions of mind and will. John the Baptist's preaching is remarkably close to the doctrine of Qumrân in theme and spirit,[16] although he does not seem to have insisted so strongly on the observance of the law. John stressed the need of *metanoia* as the requisite disposition for the reception of the kingdom of God, which he declared to be near at hand. The purpose of the baptism he administered was principally to reveal the identity of the Messiah, the bearer of the definitive salvation through the Spirit (Jn 1:33–34). "I have come baptizing with water in order that He might be made known in Israel" (Jn 1:31). The only quality of the imminent Messianic salvation which the Baptist's preaching disclosed was its necessary relation to the Spirit of Yahweh.

In His public life Jesus announced the coming of the kingdom of God. If, on a superficial view, His message seems to have been identical with John's (Mt 3:2; 4:17), still the Gospel accounts make it plain that Jesus' very presence had already in some sense effected salvation.[17] Jesus could assure His Pharisee interrogators that "the kingdom of God is in your midst" (Lk 17:21). While He refused the title of king (Jn 6:13; 18:33), still He did identify Himself as "the Son of Man," thereby asserting a relation between His person and the Old Testament figure symbolizing the Messianic kingdom (Dn 7:13, 18). Moreover, at His triumphal entry into Jerusalem, Jesus not only accepted the royal acclamations of the crowd by which they unwittingly connected this coming with the Messianic salvation, but, it would seem, He deliberately planned the whole demonstration for the instruction of the disciples.[18]

It was mainly through the medium of the parable that Jesus attempted to give the people at large some elementary notions about the supernatural salvation connected with the kingdom. From the parable collections preserved by the first two Evangelists, two features of this salvation clearly emerge. On the one hand, it is essentially eschatological in character, and thus to be achieved fully only through Yahweh's final judgment.[19] Yet on the other, there already exists, or at least will exist in the proximate future, a form of salvation homogeneous with that future, all-embracing, eschatological salvation.[20] Like a hidden treasure (Mt 13:44) or an inestimable pearl (Mt 13:45–46), salvation may be found in this world, provided a man be ready to sacrifice "everything with joy" for its acquisition.

With the failure of the Jewish people generally to respond to His preaching, Jesus devotes His attention to a little band of disciples. Under His divine pedagogy, their minds are gradually enlightened until their loyal devotion to Him as rabbi and prophet finds its supreme expression in the Petrine avowal in the neighborhood of Caesarea Philippi: "You are the Christ" (Mt 16:16; Mk 8:29; Lk 9:20). This statement marks the peak of Jesus' self-revelation during His public life. Before the disciples can grasp the mystery of His divinity, they must pass through the dark night of His passion and death, experience those momentous meetings with the risen Lord, and receive the Holy Spirit in their baptism with the pentecostal fire. The Johannine discourse after the Last Supper underscores the necessity for such a long and arduous approach to the supreme Messianic secret.[21] As long as Jesus remained with them, the disciples' loyalty to Him rested upon too human grounds. Before they could attain the knowledge of His divinity, this natural "faith" in Jesus as the Christ must suffer a total eclipse through the terrible events which culminated in Calvary.[22]

Jesus' appearances to the disciples after His resurrection were devoted to rebuilding their loyalty and devotion to Himself into something immeasurably greater than it had ever been during His earthly life (Lk 24:46). The expressions employed by the Evangelists in referring to their new faith in the risen

Jesus as the Messiah prove how much more solid and supernatural this paschal belief was than anything they had formerly known.[23] At the same time they assert that a new dimension must still be added to this faith before the disciples can witness effectively to the risen Lord (Lk 24:48–49).

A less obvious but far more important purpose which lay behind these postresurrection appearances may be discerned in their peculiar character. Jesus appeared to the disciples suddenly, without warning. His departure is, oddly enough, never mentioned by the Evangelists except once (Lk 24:31), where the strange expression "He became invisible" is employed. The disciples were struck with terror, thinking they saw a ghost (Lk 24:37), or at best were filled with a strange uneasiness: they "knew it was the Lord," yet they "dared not ask 'Who are you?' " (Jn 21:12). The lesson Jesus was thus endeavoring to teach them was one which is central to the Christian doctrine of salvation, the notion of presence.[24] It was a lesson which would be mastered only after the descent of the Holy Spirit.

Jesus' final departure from the disciples at His ascension into heaven also constituted an important step in the revelation of salvation. Acts' account of it appears to suggest that, even at the close of the forty days' intercourse between the risen Christ and His disciples, they had not acquired a clear insight into the supernatural nature of the kingdom of God. They still looked for "the restoration of the sovereignty to Israel" (Acts 1:6) and cherished the dream of an earthly theocracy. Jesus' definitive departure from this world shattered their hopes of a terrestrial kingdom in much the same way as His death had shattered their hopes of an earthly Messiah. The Ascension also made a drastic change in what might be called the disciples' theology of history. On leaving them, it seems clear that Christ had let them know that this occasion was the termination of postresurrection appearances.[25] After His disappearance the angelic message of Jesus' second coming in glory provided the disciples with a new hope and radically altered the old scheme of sacred history which until now they had taken for granted. As Jews, they had been led to expect but a single coming of the Christ,[26] in which history would find its culmination as well as its climax. Now they became aware that God's plan included two comings of His Christ. The new data solved certain problems which had arisen in their minds. The time of Israel's restoration remained hidden in the mysterious counsels of "the Father" (Acts 1:7). The universal judgment of the awful "Day of Yahweh" was deferred. The risen Jesus had told them He was to be "the judge of living and dead appointed by God" (Acts 10:43). This judgment, they deduced, was somehow connected with His glorious parousia.

At the same time, these new insights created fresh problems. How much time was to elapse before the Lord's return? What was the meaning of the period interjected into the divine plan of salvation between His ascension and His second coming?[27] Prior to Pentecost, the disciples possessed only a few clues to the mystery. Jesus had left them with the command to carry the good news of the gospel "to the end of the earth" (Acts 1:8), to initiate into discipleship not merely their fellow countrymen but "all races" by baptism and teaching (Mt 28:18). All this, together with His promise to remain continually, though invisibly, present in their midst "until the end of the world," seemed to suggest that human history was destined to continue for an indefinite period. And if, as was only natural, their intense devotion to the Master prompted them to hope for His speedy return, they were quite aware that nothing He had ever said gave any basis for such an expectation (1 Th 5:1–2).

One point He had made clear. They were to remain in Jerusalem until their reception of the promised Spirit of truth (Lk 24:49), who, as Jesus had told them in explaining the necessity of His departure, was to "lead them along the way to the full truth" (Jn 16:13). The sending of this Holy Spirit, as they would realize only at Pentecost, involved Jesus' exaltation to the Father's right hand.

Accordingly, it is now evident why Pentecost is rightly considered the *terminus a quo* of the disciples' comprehension of the meaning of Christian salvation.[28] To evaluate properly the effects of the pentecostal revelation, it is now necessary to consider the content of the apostolic kerygma.

THE PRIMITIVE PREACHING

In order to take proper cognizance of the remarkable theological insights as well as of the inevitable[29] inadequacies in their expression, we propose to discuss the primitive preaching in terms of the motive which prompted the leaders of the Jerusalem community to launch upon their work of evangelization. A study of the sermons summarily reproduced in Acts shows a threefold conviction to have been operative in the minds of the disciples: a profound sense of the consummation of sacred history, a vivid recollection of Christ's injunction to give testimony to Himself, and a pressing desire to invite their own race first and foremost to adopt the proper dispositions for attaining the kingdom of God.

The Consummation of Israel's Religious History

From the day of Pentecost itself the apostolic community appears to have adopted towards history an attitude which differed radically from any they had hitherto displayed. They proclaim that an event of primary importance to Israel has taken place: the culmination of her sacred history. The "last days" foretold by "all the prophets from Samuel onwards" (Acts 2:17; 3:24) have become a contemporary reality. The preachers display an acute awareness of witnessing to, indeed of participating in, the consummation of the Messianic hopes of the Old Testament.[30] Their conviction rests principally upon three supernatural facts: the permanent bestowal of Yahweh's Spirit, their own transformation by that divine Gift into the nucleus of the new *qahal* of Israel, and (as cause of these two *Heilstaten*) Jesus' exaltation as "Son of God in power" (Rom 1:4).[31]

Perhaps the most surprising feature of the disciples' newfound attitude is their assurance that the Messianic era has been ushered in, not by the glorious parousia of the risen Lord, but by the spectacular, charismatic descent of the Holy Spirit. It is noteworthy that the Messianic blessings which the apostles imparted from Pentecost onwards are spiritual blessings: the remission of sins and the gift of the Spirit. Moreover, they now asserted that by this gift of the Spirit Yahweh had fulfilled "the promise" (Acts 2:39) made to Abraham (Acts 3:25) and to Moses (Acts 7:17 ff.), renewed to David (Acts 13:23), and recalled incessantly by the prophets (Acts 10:43). The complete novelty of this belief reveals the revolutionary nature of Pentecost. Not only was the disciples' view of Israel's restored theocracy lifted to an infinitely higher plane; in addition, they recognized that the inauguration of the new theocracy was due to a mysterious Presence in their midst, which was neither that of the Lord Jesus, enthroned in heaven until "the time of the restoration of all things" (Acts 3:21), nor that of "the Father," who by exalting His Son had fulfilled His Old Testament promises in this gift of the Spirit (Acts 2:33).

The disciples had already learned the divine nature of the Spirit from the Old Testament. Did they recognize His new presence as that of a divine Person? It would seem that certain qualities of their experience of the Spirit could not but remind them of Jesus' promise to send "another advocate" (Jn 14:16), who should assist them in bearing witness to their Lord (Jn 15:26). If in the beginning the Spirit made His coming felt as a mysterious divine force through various sensible manifestations,[32] still it is clear that the apostles quickly learned to distinguish such external phenomena from His abiding, invisible activity in the hearts of the faithful, whose intimate and delicate character unmistakably postulated the presence of a divine Person.[33]

One of the *récits* in the earlier section of Acts seems particularly to suggest the apostles' awareness of the personality of the Holy Spirit.[34] Peter declares before the Jerusalem Sanhedrin that the Spirit together with the apostles attests the Father's glorification of Jesus. "This [Jesus] God has exalted to His right hand as Prince and Saviour to grant repentance to Israel as well as remission of sins. Now we are witnesses of these facts, as well as the Holy Spirit, whom God has given those who are obedient to Him" (Acts 5:31–32). In this incident it is the significance of testimony as the autonomous act of a responsible being which is to the fore. The context of the courtroom would alone suffice to show this. But the nature of the apostolic testimony itself postulates in addition the existence of a person-to-person relationship. This is shown here by Peter's avowed personal *engagement* to the Father through obedience (Acts 5:29) as well as by his implied self-commitment to the risen Jesus by his discipleship. When, therefore, Peter equates the relationship of the Spirit as witness to the salvific acts of the Father, or to the status of His Son, with these personal relationships of his own, he is equivalently affirming his awareness of the Spirit's divine personality.[35]

A second aspect of the disciples' belief in the consummation of Israel's history, as we have noted, is the conviction that under the domination of the Spirit they form the new Messianic community.[36] It was through their "baptism by a Holy Spirit" (Acts 1:5)—an experience which, they are well aware, could never be repeated in quite the same manner in the case of those who would later join their ranks[37]—that they have become the remnant foretold by Old Testament prophecy,[38] enjoying a privileged group-existence, set apart from the "wicked and perverse generation" (Acts 2:40) of their former coreligionists who refuse to accept the gospel. They constitute the *qahal* of "the saved," whose increment, through the administration of Christian baptism (Acts 2:41), is the work of the risen Lord (Acts 2:46). This consciousness of their vocation as the congregation of the new Israel of "the last times" led them very early to seek in "the Scriptures" the inspiration and guidance in the government of the *ekklēsia* which would provide directives for its future destiny.

In a recent study of the first five chapters of Acts, Joseph Schmitt has demonstrated how clearly their sources reflect the influence of Deuteronomy, "the law of the ideal Israel in eschatological times."[39] His conclusions regarding the formative value of the Deuteronomic code in the case of this primitive ecclesiology are borne out by a study of other passages in the apostolic kerygma and the Synoptic Gospels where there is question of the constitution and function of the Church.[40] We wish to mention one of the passages cited by Dr. Schmitt, which combines two Old Testament texts that appear to have been commonplaces in the early preaching, so as to provide us with what is possibly one of the most primitive New Testament definitions of salvation.

The first quotation is Moses' prediction concerning "the

prophet like me" (Dt 18:15–18). "Now Moses has declared that 'the Lord our God *will raise up* a prophet from your brethren like me. You will obey him in whatever he will say to you. Any man who will not heed that prophet will be exterminated from the people'" (Acts 3:22–23). On Peter's view, Moses was referring to "these days," the period following the descent of the Holy Spirit. He then seeks to establish the identity of the prophet Moses had described by a reference to the divine promise given Abraham: "Through the instrumentality of your seed, all the tribes of the earth *shall be blessed*" (Gn 12:3; 22:18; Acts 3:25). Peter's conclusion provides a sketch of the risen Christ's role as Saviour which is evidently composed with the help of his two Old Testament citations. "By *raising* His Servant, God has sent Him to you first of all *to bless* you, by turning each of you from your iniquity" (Acts 3:26).[41] This precious text provides one of the most primitive expressions of the concept of Christian salvation preserved in tradition. Jesus' resurrection is clearly indicated as a major factor. What is perhaps not so immediately evident is precisely how Peter understands the mission of the risen Lord to confer the Messianic blessings upon His people. He cannot refer to the appearances of Jesus to the disciples after the Resurrection.[42] Nor is it possible that he is thinking of the Parousia, already mentioned in this discourse.[43] The inclusion of the promise to Abraham provides the best clue. We have already seen that in the apostolic preaching it was considered to have been fulfilled by the gift of the Holy Spirit. Accordingly, it becomes clear that in this early conception of Christian salvation the mission of the glorified Jesus to bless the Jewish people was carried out through the presence of the Spirit in the apostolic community. Aware of the distinction between the Son and the Holy Spirit, the apostles nonetheless conceived their activity in the present age as one and the same.

In the same way at a later date Paul would assert without any apologies that "the Lord is the Spirit" (2 Cor 3:17).

At times the message of salvation was formulated solely in function of Jesus' exaltation. "God has exalted Him to His right hand as Prince and Saviour, to grant repentance to Israel, as well as remission of sins" (Acts 5:31). The interest of texts like this one[44] is that they formulate the doctrine of salvation solely in terms of Jesus' glorification, and thus attest the belief of the apostolic community in another dogma essential to our study, the divinity of Christ. Like the more succinct credal formula found in the Pauline epistles, "Jesus is *Kyrios*" (1 Cor 12:3; Rom 10:9), this series of texts affirms the contemporary character of the universal sovereignty of Christ oriented towards His role as Saviour. For the expression of this article of faith, the primitive Church employed Ps 110:1: "The Lord said to my Lord, 'Sit upon my right hand until I make your enemies [serve as] your footstool.'"[45] The prominence of the *sessio ad dexteram Patris* in the Palestinian kerygma is due to its having been the foundation of the apostolic belief in Jesus' divinity. Peter's pentecostal discourse traces the psychological process by which this realization dawned upon the first disciples. First, there was the pre-pentecostal belief in "Jesus the Nazarene, a man accredited to you by Yahweh through acts of power, miracles, and signs." Then, as a result of the gift of the Spirit, they learned that "having been exalted to God's right hand and having received from the Father the promise of the Holy Spirit, He has poured out what you both see and hear." As a result, we have the creation of the new faith: "Therefore let all the house of Israel know for certain that God has made Him *Kyrios* and Messiah, this Jesus whom you have crucified" (Acts 2:22–36). Peter begins by calling Him "a man" and concludes by acknowledging His reception of the divine Name, *Kyrios*.

To an age like ours, habituated to more refined, or at any rate more Greek, formulations of the hypostatic union which are a legacy from the Council of Chalcedon, such unsophisticated modes of expression may well seem theologically naïve, if not scandalous. Yet their very clumsiness or lack of theological refinement bears witness to their authenticity.

Two variations on this theme must be mentioned here. Transposed in eschatological terms, this assertion of Jesus' divinity appears as His appointment "by Yahweh as judge of living and dead" (Acts 10:42). Paul's address at Athens preserves this article of faith in a very early form. "For He has set a day on which He intends to judge the world in justice through the intermediary of a man whom He has marked out; and He has offered proof of this to all by raising Him from the dead" (Acts 17:31).

The second motif is the theology of "the Name," which provides what is perhaps the clearest evidence that from the beginning the Jerusalem community acknowledged the ascended Christ as God. Its close connection with the theme of the contemporary reign of the glorified Jesus may best be seen in three strophes of a hymn which is of Palestinian provenance,[46] cited by Paul:

> For this, God has exalted him beyond all limit
> and has graciously bestowed on him the Name
> surpassing every other name,
>
> in order that, at Jesus' Name,
> all should prostrate themselves: inhabitants of heaven,
> of earth, of the infernal regions,
>
> and every tongue take up the cry
> "Jesus is *Kyrios!*"
> to the glory of God the Father. (Phil 2:9–11)

In this canticle, which resumes the soteriological message of the Jerusalem Church, the exaltation of Jesus is concretely expressed as the conferring of "the Name," *Kyrios*. The significance of this act of the Father is underscored in terms of the resultant universal adoration accorded Christ by every rational creature.[47]

From the day of Pentecost itself, this theology of the Name holds a position of first-rate importance in the apostolic doctrine of salvation. Peter connects it with the entry into history of "the last times," the *raison d'être* of his citation of Joel appearing in the last line quoted: "and it will come to pass that every man who invokes the Name of the Lord [i.e., Christ] will be saved" (Acts 2:21). In the succeeding episodes recorded by Luke, the references to "the Name" recur like a litany. Faith in the power of this Name on the part both of Peter (Acts 3:6) and of the man lame from birth (Acts 3:16) has resulted in the miracle of his healing (Acts 4:10). In this Name alone is salvation to be acquired (Acts 4:12). It is the source of all "healing and signs and wonders" by which the gospel is to be propagated (Acts 4:29–30). By its invocation the original pentecostal phenomena recur to strengthen and encourage the community beset by persecution (Acts 4:31). "To be accounted worthy to be dishonored for the Name" evokes the profoundest joy in the hearts of the disciples (Acts 5:41). Finally, this profession of faith in the power of Jesus' new Name is so characteristic of the rite of initiation into the Messianic community that it is commonly referred to as "baptism in the Name of Jesus" (Acts 2:38; 8:16; 10:48; 19:5; 22:16; 1 Cor 1:13 ff.).

It is to be noted that this theology of the Name replaces, in the ancient sources at Luke's disposal, the expression "the kingdom of God" retained by the Synoptic narratives. Its value may be seen in the fact that it reflects the manner in which the disciples received the divine revelation of the establishment of that kingdom. In other words, the definitive coming of the divine sovereignty was, for the primitive Church, concretized and epitomized in one unique moment of the history of salvation, the conferring of the divine Name *Kyrios* upon Jesus at His exaltation to God's right hand.

The Apostolic Testimony

Our discussion of the first aspect of the soteriological conception found in the primitive preaching centered around two metahistorical facts, the new presence of the Spirit and the celestial exaltation of the risen Lord.[48] While in the present section we shall have to deal with certain events which are primarily of the historical order and which, as such, necessarily occupy a place in the kerygma, yet it must be remembered that it is their *heilsgeschichtlich* quality which gives them their principal importance in the message of salvation. Moreover, it is this same aspect of the kerygma which determines its nature as testimony rather than as proof. Proof is in place (and is sufficient) where there is question of truth in the merely intellectual order. When, however, that order is transcended to compass a truth like that of the Incarnation, then proof is inadequate[49] and testimony must be invoked.[50] The Bible is almost exclusively concerned with testimony. Even where there is question of the existence of God, the sacred authors, while providing abundant testimony to the existence of the one true God of Israel, are nowhere concerned to prove His existence.[51] Consequently, with regard to Christ's resurrection, one would look in vain to the apostolic preachers for any proof of the fact. On the other hand, they are constantly asserting that it is their business to attest to its reality. The transcendent superiority of testimony over proof may be gauged by the fact that, while proof compels the assent of reason only, testimony demands an *engagement* of the whole man, mind, heart, and, above all, will. For this reason, the term "proof" has never formed part of the biblical vocabulary of salvation, while testimony is a key word in the soteriologies of both Testaments.[52] It is by testimony, the kerygma, not by proof, as Paul reminds us, "that God has been pleased to save those who have faith" (1 Cor 1:21).[53]

Which, then, were the events which formed the object of the *testimonium apostolicum*? They fall under three main heads: the resurrection of Christ, His death, and the ministry of His public life. Of these three, His resurrection receives the greatest emphasis, since belief in it was basic for the disciples' realization of Jesus' role as Messiah, Saviour, Son of God. This paschal faith was an utterly new creation and marked an absolute beginning. Although it was almost immediately supported by the testimony drawn from "the Scriptures," still, as John is at pains to point out, the belief in Jesus' resurrection was prior to any understanding of the Old Testament prophecies regarding it (Jn 20:8). It was rather the disciples' awareness that Jesus had been raised from the dead by the Father which led them to read the Old Testament with the eyes of their newly-acquired Easter faith. The same is true regarding their anticipation of "the last times."[54] The Messianic hope, which in any case had been extinguished by Jesus' passion and death, did not impel the first Christians to "postulate" His resurrection. As we have already seen, it was not this event but the descent of the Spirit which revealed the advent of the Messianic era.

Thus Jesus' resurrection dominates the kerygma by its very nature. In addition, it was upon command of the risen Christ that the apostles undertook their *martyrion*, the office of witnessing in which they were assisted by the Spirit, the gift of the risen Lord in return for their obedience of faith (Acts 5:32).[55]

Together with Jesus' resurrection, the message of salvation contains a reference to His death. While it is habitually announced as the work of the Jews and pagans,[56] its salvific value is not neglected. That death, though perpetrated by evil men, formed an integral part of God's design (Acts 2:23; 3:18): it was "for our sins" and "according to the Scriptures" (Acts 8:32–35; 1 Cor 15:3). In addition, the primitive community learned very early, doubtless from Hellenists like Stephen, to recognize as types of Jesus in His rejection and persecution by His own people certain Old Testament figures: Joseph (Acts 7:9), Moses (Acts 7:25–29, 35, 39), the prophets (Acts 7:52), the Suffering Servant of Yahweh (Acts 8:32–33). Finally, the repeated insistence upon Jesus' exemption from the common law of corruption reveals how clearly the apostles had understood the divinely triumphant nature of His death (Acts 2:25–31; 10:40; 13:34–37).

Essential to an appreciation of the salvific nature of Jesus' death was the apostolic faith in His divinity. That faith, as we have seen, owed its origins to the pentecostal revelation that Jesus had been exalted to the Father's right hand. Once they were in possession of this truth, the apostles quickly learned to employ it in evaluating the earlier stages of Jesus' career. If He were revealed as divine in His exaltation, He had been already divine in His death and even in His earthly life.[57] Thus we are able to trace genetically the development of the kerygma. With Christ's resurrection and exaltation as point of departure, the doctrine of salvation reached out to embrace first His death, then His public ministry as part of the divine plan. At a somewhat later date it may perhaps have included the significant features of Jesus' infancy and childhood, although this obviously biographical interest is one sign of the difference between the preached and the written Gospel.

The recognition of the divinity of Christ poses a delicate problem. What prevented the disciples, upon their realization of this dogma, from asserting that there was more than one God? A negative answer, which we must not overlook, may be found in the uncompromising monotheism which the apostles had inherited from Judaism and which undoubtedly made such an admission psychologically impossible. Yet the pentecostal revelation had altered several of their Old Testament beliefs so radically that the force of this argument is considerably diminished. A more convincing reason is to be sought, I believe, in the manner in which the truth of Jesus' divinity was revealed to the disciples. This modality is discernible in the formulae which were first employed to express the revelation. Perhaps the most frequent is that constructed on the pattern of Ps 110:1: "God has exalted Him to His right hand as Prince and Saviour . . ." (Acts 5:31; cf. also 2:33; 1 Pt 3:22; Rom 8:34; Ap 5:1). The same idea was expressed by the assertion that Jesus' reception of the divine Name *Kyrios* was the crowning act of His glorification (Acts 4:12b; Phil 2:9–11). Thus we find the early Christian community acknowledging Jesus' divinity as *a sharing with the Father* of the divine prerogatives of universal dominion and judgment as well as of the divine Name.[58] At a later theological period this truth will be expressed as the *unitas naturae divinae.*

If we recall the existentialist character of Semitic thought, habitual with these Palestinian Christians, we can see in their insistence upon the close harmony between the salvific acts of Christ and the Father a further affirmation of this same truth. The exalted Jesus is proclaimed as one with the Father in sending the Holy Spirit (Acts 2:33). In the case of Jesus' death and resurrection, this unity of operation is so emphasized that He appears as a merely passive instrument in the hands of Yahweh. God uses the Jews and Romans as tools to put Jesus to death. Then He raises Jesus and exalts Him to a participation in His own divine power. Our appreciation of the primitive awareness of this unity of action is deepened if we recall that, as a matter of fact, early Christian thought had also perceived that Jesus had actively participated in the work of salvation. The popular Servant theology,[59] which portrayed His self-oblation in union with the Father's will, shows this as regards His death. The equally ancient article of faith, "Jesus rose from the dead" (Acts 10:41; 17:3; 1 Th 4:14), in which the act of rising is attributed to Christ, indicates it for His resurrection. The predominance of those formulae which give pre-eminence to the Father's initiative does reveal, however, the way in which the apostolic community normally represented to itself the perfect unity of operation of the Father and the Son, the counterpart in Hebraic thought-patterns of our unity in nature.

Around the two main events proclaimed in the primitive preaching, Jesus' death and exaltation, a cluster of logia and miracle stories culled from the oral traditions of Jesus' public ministry quickly gathered (Acts 2:22; 10:37–39). The miracles were considered a necessary object of the apostolic testimony inasmuch as they were proof of Jesus' Messianic anointing by Yahweh (Acts 10:38; 4:27; Lk 4:18). At a later stage of theological reflection they were considered as the first step in the earthly establishment of the kingdom of God, since they marked the beginning of the overthrow of the satanic dominion over man (Mt 8:29; 10:1; Lk 10:18).

Invitation to Repentance, Faith, and Reception of Christian Baptism and the Holy Spirit

The apostolic attestation to God's "good news of peace through Jesus Christ" (Acts 10:36) issued in the call to *metanoia*, repentance for sin and a change of heart vis-à-vis the divinely-designated Saviour of Israel, Jesus of Nazareth (Acts 2:38; 3:25–26; 5:31; 11:18; 13:38; 17:30). This involved an act of faith in Jesus' divinity and in the presence of the Holy Spirit as the fulfilment of God's Old Testament promises of salvation (Acts 2:36; 4:10–12; 13:39–40; 17:31). To seal and publicize this profession of Christian faith, as well as to enter the community of the saved, the reception of baptism was necessary (Acts 2:38; 8:36, 38; 10:47). The final sign of full acceptance by the Christian community of the neophyte was the imparting of the Holy Spirit by the apostles (Acts 2:38; 8:15–17; 9:17; 19:5–6).

Such was the concept of salvation which the Jerusalem Church expressed in her kerygma. Salvation had been definitively acquired for the human race by Jesus of Nazareth through His mortal life, death, and resurrection. It had been revealed to mankind only in His exaltation, which was itself manifested through the descent of the Holy Spirit, whose presence, in turn, had made of the disciples the Messianic congregation of the new Israel. The Old Testament promises of salvation had been fulfilled in the unexpected disclosure of Jesus' divinity and the divine personality of the Holy Spirit. The kingdom of God had become a heavenly reality by the conferring upon Jesus of the divine Name *Kyrios*; it had been inaugurated upon earth by the new presence in the community of the Spirit, who thus bestowed on the disciples their vocation as the remnant. Moreover, the hope of the parousiac return of the Lord Jesus, who by the exercise of the eschatological judgment would consummate the consolidation of His kingdom, made the apostles aware that "the last times" consisted of two moments: one of preparation for Christ's second coming, the other "the times of refreshment," "the period of the universal restoration" (Acts 3:20–21), connected with the Lord's return.[60] Simultaneous with that event would occur "the resurrection of the just and the unjust" (Acts 24:15) together with the glorious transformation of the faithful still alive (1 Th 4:17; 1 Cor 15:51). In that hour the eschatological salvation described by Jesus' parables would be achieved.

THE LIMITATIONS OF THE PRIMITIVE SOTERIOLOGY

It remains to point out the omissions and imperfections in this earliest conception of Christian salvation. In the first place, there is scarcely any mention made of the pre-existence of Christ.[61] As a result, no place is found for the Incarnation in this primitive soteriological scheme. It would seem that we are dealing with a period when the consequences of Christ's divinity had not been pushed back beyond His public ministry. For a more developed theology which will embrace the salvific meaning of the Word's becoming man, we must await the writing of the fourth Gospel.[62]

While the assertion of certain critics that the death of Jesus is not regarded as salvific in the primitive preaching is demonstrably unfounded,[63] still it must be admitted that its salvific values were not fully exploited. This was due, in part at least, to the polemic and apologetic preoccupations of the early years, which resulted in the obscuring of the Father's part in "handing over" His Son to death. The Palestinian kerygma highlighted the part played by the Jews in the *traditio* of Jesus to the pagans. It will be only in the Pauline theology, once anti-Jewish propaganda is left aside, that the "handing over" is explicitly and consistently attributed either to the Father (Rom 8:32; 4:25) or to Jesus Himself (Gal 2:20; Eph 5:2, 25). When this point is finally clarified, and not beforehand, it will be possible to elaborate the positive aspects of

Christ's salvific death as a death to self, to the law, to sin and death.[64]

The beneficiaries of salvation at this early stage are considered almost exclusively as the Jewish people. The Jerusalem community does not seem to have received, as yet, a clear intuition of the mission to the pagans.[65] There is no hint of any operation of that centrifugal force which was shortly to characterize Christianity, the going forth to preach to the Gentiles.[66]

The sacramental theology of this period, so far as it is revealed in the sources we possess, remains in a very elementary stage of development. The effects of baptism, regarded as the necessary rite of initiation into the community, are thought of under the negative aspect of the remission of sins. The bestowal of the Holy Spirit is associated exclusively with the imposition of the hands of the apostles (Acts 8:14–16). The first affirmation of the immediate connection between the Spirit and baptism occurs in the fourth Gospel (Jn 3:5). The Eucharist is not mentioned anywhere in the kerygma—possibly a hint of the attitude which would later evolve into the *disciplina arcani*. One of the Acts' summaries, deriving from a more ancient source, associates it with "the teaching of the apostles" (Acts 2:42),[67] not with the preaching. While it is difficult to say whether the sacrificial aspects of the Eucharist were adverted to before Paul (1 Cor 10:14–21), that sacrament was, in the earliest tradition, associated with the Last Supper (1 Cor 11:23 ff.), with the repasts taken with the risen Christ (Acts 2:46),[68] and with the Parousia (1 Cor 11:26).

Finally, there is no evidence of any reflection upon the teleology of salvation. Nowhere in the primitive preaching is there any mention of God's love, which appears so prominently in the Pauline and Johannine soteriologies (Gal 2:20;

Rom 5:8; 8:32; 1 Jn 4:10; Jn 3:16). At most, there is implicit reference to what Paul will call "the justice of God," His fidelity to His Old Testament promises of salvation (Acts 2:33, 39; 7:17; 13:23, 32; 23:21).

3

The Concept of Biblical Inspiration

THE purpose of this essay is twofold: to review and assess the significant contributions made to the problem of biblical inspiration in contemporary research, and to suggest some areas in which work might profitably be done in the future.

SIGNIFICANT CONTRIBUTIONS IN CONTEMPORARY RESEARCH

I believe that many new insights have been provided in our time by the studies of Pierre Benoit,[1] Joseph Coppens,[2] Karl Rahner,[3] and Bernhard Brinkmann;[4] and I shall attempt to present their work in summary form. As regards further possible theological speculation, I wish to amplify a suggestion made recently by my colleague, R. A. F. MacKenzie: "Since the theory of instrumental causality has been so usefully developed, and has done so much to clarify—up to a point—the divine-human collaboration in this mysterious and wonderful work, what is needed next is fuller investigation of the efficient and final causalities, which went to produce an *OT* or *NT* book."[5] Since the days of Franzelin and Lagrange,[6] treatises on inspiration have tended to emphasize the human aspects of the Bible and the activity of the sacred authors. It is perhaps more opportune nowadays to turn our attention to God's function as efficient-exemplary cause of the Bible and ask ourselves just why inspiration was necessary in the divine plan of God's self-revelation to men.

Christianity's traditional attitude toward its sacred books, both those received as a legacy from Israel and those produced by its own apostolic writers, has always been reverently maintained by the Catholic Church as part of the deposit of faith. It is the belief that these sacred books were written under a peculiar divine influence, so that God is rightly regarded as their Author, and in consequence the Christian Bible is a normative record of those truths which God has deigned in His mercy to reveal to us.

All this, of course, is axiomatic in Catholic theology, and such a statement has the air of a truism. Yet, such a simple-seeming statement involves not a few difficult problems. Indeed, before we can discuss these questions fruitfully, it will help to determine more accurately three notions which this statement contains: (1) What view should be taken of the Bible itself, considered as a whole? (2) What does the word "author" signify, particularly when applied to the divine source of this written revelation? (3) What is meant by truth from the biblical viewpoint?

The Nature of the Bible

What, then, is the nature of the Bible? What approach will best reveal to us the meaning of our sacred literature? There are, broadly speaking, two attitudes which have been taken, historically, to the Scriptures: the critical method, which enjoyed such a vogue in the nineteenth and early-twentieth centuries, and that which Dom Célestin Charlier has called the psychological method,[7] which might also be termed the theological method.

The critical method, practiced by rationalist liberals like

Wellhausen, Gunkel, and Loisy, was essentially an intellectual approach in the narrow sense. Its inventors were engrossed in comparing the Bible with other forms of literature and often enough were intoxicated with the heady discovery that the Scriptures were very human documents. These men belonged to an age obsessed with the search for scientific objectivity, with the making of factual inventories, with the recovery and criticism of documentary sources; and they were imbued with a crusading iconoclasm bent on destroying the old-fashioned view held by so many earnest Christians that the Bible had somehow dropped ready-made from its celestial home, a kind of divine oracle without any necessary relation to time, human culture, or history.

While it would be unjust to slight the contributions made by these scholars to biblical science, it must be admitted that they were children of an age notorious as a low point in religious thought, both philosophically and theologically.[8] It was an age blissfully unaware of the profound differences separating the culture and genius of the Semitic peoples from the thought-forms and civilization of the Greek-formed West.[9] It suffered most of all from the fact that, in its anxiety to acquire what it considered a detached, purely scientific view of the essentially religious, personal Semitic viewpoint, it had unconsciously adopted the basically irreligious *Weltanschauung* of ancient Greece.[10]

The pernicious effects of this rationalist approach to the Bible are well known: a disdainful neglect of the divine origin of the Scriptures and an ever-increasing skepticism and infidelity toward the Judeo-Christian revelation based on the denial of its historical character. In such circumstances it is not surprising that biblical inspiration should become confused with that "inspiration" exhibited by the world's great literary artists who had created the classics, while inerrancy, conceived in the image and likeness of nineteenth-century liberalism, was categorically denied to the Bible.

In the face of such a destructive onslaught, the Catholic theologian bent every effort to devise an apologetic that could save the eternal values of the ancient Christian faith. Not ill-equipped, in many instances, with the scientific methods and erudition of his opponents, the Catholic scholar endeavored to turn these very weapons against their unbelieving inventors.[11] This meant, inevitably, that the Catholic critic was forced to meet his adversary on the adversary's ground, and it need surprise no one that today many of his arguments appear as outmoded as the opinions he was trying to refute. He tended to accept the excessively idealistic view of historical and scientific truth, the quite modern concept of authorship, and, more generally, the almost exclusively intellectual approach to the Bible characteristic of his own Greek education. I mention all this merely because it forms part of the picture of the Catholic attitude to the study of biblical inspiration prior to Pius XII's *Divino afflante Spiritu*, and not in any spirit of criticism which would be disrespectful to the affirmations of the Church found in encyclicals like *Providentissimus Deus*.[12]

What is the theological or psychological approach to the Scriptures, the newer and more comprehensive view of the Bible's meaning? It is a method that was born partly of a generally felt dissatisfaction with the old, purely literary Higher Criticism, partly of a growing desire to recover the religious values which Christian tradition had always found in the Bible, and partly of the widening of scientific horizons by fresh discoveries in archeology, ethnology, and psychology. Scholars began to realize the necessity of attending not merely to the literary context, immediate or remote, of the inspired books, but also to the historical, cultural, racial milieus in which the Bible had been produced. They became conscious of the singular nature of Semitic thought-patterns, dominated by an existentialist interest in living reality.[13] Where the Greek mind was haunted by the problem of the one and the many, Semitic dialectic was fascinated by the spiritual mystery of the unity of all things. It found in the symbol, rather than in the abstract concept, a natural vehicle of expression.[14] The religion of the Hebrews had begun, not with a metaphysical deduction of God's existence, but with a vital, supernatural experience of the living God veiled in awful mystery upon cloud-wrapped Sinai.

This new awareness of the character of the Semitic religious genius produced in modern biblical scholarship the realization that "none of the human factors which have influenced the birth, formation, and final shape of the sacred Book can be withdrawn from the productive and formative activity of the Holy Spirit."[15] These words of Dom Charlier suggest that for a comprehensive understanding of divine inspiration we must consider the effects of this charism not only upon the written or oral sources, the various redactors and glossators of the sacred books, but upon the entire ambient culture in which God's activity had worked for generations as an energizing leaven. As Charlier remarks, "Inspiration is, then, infinitely more than the communication by God of a kind of mechanical influx which subordinates to it the literary activity of certain free instruments; it is the productive, all-embracing penetration, by the Holy Spirit's vivifying action, of the whole history and life of the people of God."[16]

Permit me to cite but one consequence of this new attitude which has a bearing upon the doctrine of biblical inspiration: the recently renewed interest in the spiritual sense of the Scriptures as understood and exploited by the Fathers of the

Church and by the modern creation of biblical theology.[17] This viewpoint is important for a proper study of the Bible's inspiration, because it rests ultimately upon what we might call an "incarnational" conception of our sacred literature. Scripture is not the mere projection of divine ideas upon human events or human formulations, providing God's word with some sort of figurative connection with time and space. The divine scriptural word is, like the incarnation of the personal divine Word, a profoundly real entry of God into human existence. "Just as the substantial Word of God became in every way like man, sin excepted, so the words of God (His revelation) expressed in human language became completely like human language, error apart. That is what St. John Chrysostom meant by his magnificent praise of the divine condescension found, as he repeatedly affirms, in the sacred books."[18] This familiar doctrine of Pius XII is a faithful echo of the patristic teaching regarding scriptural inspiration. We shall refer to it again in a moment in discussing our next point, the concept of author as applied to the Bible.

The Concept of Author in Biblical Inspiration

One of the most elusive ideas in the treatise on biblical inspiration is the notion of author, as applied both to God and to the sacred writer. Clearly, of course, it is an analogous concept, since there is question of the collaboration of God and man.

To characterize the inspired writers, the modern doctrinal affirmations of the Church have applied the very precise modern concept of literary authorship to them.[19] The idea of authorship entertained by the ancient world comes much closer, as R. A. F. MacKenzie has stated, to the notion of patron; witness the Jewish custom of placing under the egis of

Moses, David, and Solomon, the law, the Psalter, and the wisdom literature.[20] Today we have perhaps a better grasp of the complexity of the process by which many of our sacred books were composed and so can solve more satisfactorily than was possible fifty years ago the questions created by modern criticism's denial to certain Old and New Testament figures of immediate literary authorship of books traditionally regarded as their work.[21]

As regards the divine authorship, we must re-examine the meaning of the Church's age-old assertion that "God is Author of Sacred Scripture." The expression, it appears,[22] was first employed in the doctrinal battle waged by the fourth- and fifth-century African Church against Manichean dualism. Just as the existence of the two "authors" of the universe was denied by the councils of the period, so the one God was acknowledged as unique "author" of the new and old covenants.[23] *Auctor* in these decrees is probably employed in its primary meaning, "producer, originator." This seems clear from the Second Council of Lyons' use of *archēgos* in the Greek text, in which it simply reproduces the earlier formula.[24] While Augustin Bea has sought to show that the term "author" had the literary sense in these ancient documents,[25] it is difficult to see that his argument is really conclusive. Karl Rahner has pointed out the danger of too facilely equating *auctor* with literary author.[26]

Moreover, there is need of careful investigation into the precise sense in which, in many patristic writings, Scripture is said to be divinely inspired. It may well be that these texts merely affirm prophetic inspiration, which does not necessarily provide a basis for God's literary authorship. In any event, we have to examine the grounds for attributing such literary authorship to God. As applied to human writers, the notion involves certain stylistic individualities which bear a close relation to a man's character, temperament, and background—qualities which cannot be applied to the divine Author of Holy Writ. Accordingly, it is very much a question whether the insistence of theologians since Franzelin's day that God is literary Author of the Bible is an explanation of the dogma of inspiration, or whether this is simply a matter which was not defined.[27]

Again, there is a very real problem connected with the assertion of the double authorship, human and divine, of Scripture. God's literary authorship in no way impairs that of the inspired writer, who cannot be reduced to the status of a secretary. In fact, God's authorship does not merely tolerate the co-operation of men; it demands it. Yet the attribution of literary authorship to God must somehow put Him in the same category as the human author. Any vague comparison seeking to describe God's activity as a kind of concursus, in which the divine causality remains transcendental, provides no basis for the kind of predication of which we are speaking. We must be able to show precisely how God and man can be truly called authors of any biblical book. Nor, as Rahner remarks, can we sufficiently explain the individual literary qualities of each hagiographer by simply stating that God permits him to work "in a free and personal manner."[28]

How, then, describe the divine literary authorship of the Bible? How can we justify the attribution to God of authorship of books written by men? Can it be done without prejudice to the real, yet subordinate, authorship of the sacred writers?

We might attempt an answer to these questions by beginning with the notion that the Scriptures are the record of God's personal dealings with men. God's purpose in entering human history is twofold: to save men and to reveal Himself to them. This purpose was accomplished by God's giving of

His Son as redeemer of men and revealer of the Father. The written record of this *Heilsgeschichte*, the Bible, is God's self-revelation.[29] However, it is obvious that God cannot reveal Himself to men except in human language—which is only to say that God cannot reveal Himself except in terms of man's reaction through faith to His self-revelation. In other words, God's will to have the Bible written as He intended necessarily involves the hagiographer's personal reaction, personal testimony, to God's manifestation of Himself.[30]

Indeed, since any author always puts something of himself into his book, I think it is safe to say that the notion of self-revelation provides the basis for the analogous concept of authorship we are seeking. Since the Bible as salvation history is *primarily* God's self-revelation, God must be regarded as principal Author of Scripture. At the same time, and of necessity, the Bible, written by men, is an epiphany of those men's response of loving obedience and faith to God's message. It is also a self-revelation on the hagiographer's part, in which he records his personal reply in the dialogue between God and man which is *Heilsgeschichte*. For the human author is not a mere secretary; nor can he be, if God's aim is to be achieved. In consequence, the hagiographer must contribute something of his own: not merely his individual way of expressing the divine word (his literary genre), but also his own faith's response to God's message. The Bible is accordingly, *at one and the same time*, God's self-revelation and that of the inspired writer. While these two are to be distinguished, they must not be divided up materially, as if, for instance, Jesus' words in the Gospels are the divine element and the Evangelist's remarks the human. The entire narrative is necessarily a divine-human word.[31] Failure to appreciate this incarnational character of Scripture has sometimes led to a wrong emphasis upon the *ipsissima verba Christi* as employed in theological proofs. Of course, the text contains Christ's words, but it reproduces those words as already interpreted, to a greater or lesser degree, by the Evangelist. He is author no less of these logia than of the rest of his Gospel. Still, these (and all the other words of Scripture) are, in the first place, God's words also, even those containing the writer's own reflections, because they constitute, in their entirety, God's chosen way of revealing Himself to men. This remains true even of those scriptural books like the Epistle to the Romans, where, it might appear, we have merely Paul's reaction to God's self-revelation. The Apostle's stated aim corrects such an impression. He writes to expose "the good news" as "God's dynamic force effecting salvation" (Rom 1:16).

Here it might help to employ the analogy provided by *Divino afflante*, to which we have already referred. God is *personally* present in history through the incarnation of the Son, who assumed a human nature without diminishing its human spontaneity or other human perfections. On the contrary, these were immeasurably enhanced by the hypostatic union. Moreover, the only way God could enter humanity personally was by assuming a human nature without becoming a human person. Similarly, God could only be Author of Scripture through the exercise of a uniquely divine prerogative, the employment of men as real authors, not secretaries. God cannot reveal Himself, as He has willed to do, without causing the sacred writer to reveal himself, giving his individual response and expression to this divine-human work which is the Bible.

The Semitic Conception of Truth

We must now recall briefly the difference which separates the Semitic concept of truth from the Greek. Greek philosophy considers truth as the perfect conformity of the mind to reality, found properly in the speculative judgment.[32] Yet it was not through minds formed by Hellenistic culture (a rare exception might be made for the book of Wisdom and possibly Hebrews) but through the Semitic mentality that God gave us His revelation. Hence, if we wish to understand the charism of inspiration and God's purpose in bestowing it, we must appreciate Israel's attitude to truth.[33]

To the Semite, truth is essentially something which is lived. It is a matter not of speculation but of experience—and, in its deepest sense, experience of God. Knowing is basically a personal encounter. Adam "knew his wife" by having intercourse with her—one of the most personal and intimate experiences possible for a human being. Adam knew God by encountering Him personally. In the fourth Gospel, we are urged to "live the Truth," because it pertains to the existential order of Christian living. Conversely, faith belongs to the order of doing: in fact, it is the only thing Christ commands us "do," if we wish "to perform the works of God" (Jn 6:28–29).

It was to communicate their love of Truth (to the Semitic mind, loving and knowing are correlatives) that the inspired writers undertook their task. Their primary purpose was not the propagation of truths, the composition of a body of doctrines, but the attraction and conversion of men by exhortation, consolation, reprimand, and encouragement, so that they might "live the Truth." The Bible contains truth (one need hardly add) in our Western, intellectual sense. But the value of the Scriptures, on the view of its Semitic authors, far surpassed any merely negative quality of inerrancy. It was the dialogue between God and man: a written dialogue, containing divine testimony to the living God, which sought primarily to involve men personally by eliciting their proper response in this dialogue, the wholehearted self-commitment of man in his total being through faith, an engagement "person to person" with the God who acts to reveal Himself.

RECENT CONTRIBUTIONS TO INSPIRATION THEOLOGY

The Work of Pierre Benoit

The theological thought of Pierre Benoit on scriptural inspiration is conditioned by Thomistic principles and may be characterized by its emphasis upon Scholastic method rather than upon the historical context in which the Bible was produced.[34]

He begins with a discussion of the instrumentality of the sacred writer, a subject to which he has made a significant contribution. He situates this instrumentality between the instrumental activity such as that of the waters of baptism, which would exclude real authorship, and that instrumental activity proper to the soul under the influence of God's natural concursus. The sacred writer is an instrument because he does not act on his own initiative, nor does he receive complete knowledge of the supernatural message he expresses.[35] Yet his individuality is not suppressed: he is moved to compose his book "in a free and personal manner."[36]

There are three main points in Benoit's presentation of the nature of inspiration: (1) his distinction between prophetic and scriptural inspiration, (2) the varying effects of the charism upon the speculative and practical judgment of the human author, and (3) the consequently analogous nature of scriptural inspiration.

Following St. Thomas' treatment of prophecy, we must distinguish between revelation, in which God gives both the means of representation (sensations, phantasms, ideas) and also the "light" to make a true judgment, and scriptural inspiration, where only the "light" is God-given, the inspired writer employing his own ideas and phantasms. However, to avoid the difficulties of Franzelin's system,[37] we must again distinguish between the divine effect on the speculative and that on the practical judgment. The illumination of the speculative judgment which provides divine certitude is prophetic inspiration. On the other hand, scriptural inspiration which affects the practical judgment is primarily an impulse of the will. It directs the practical reason of the writer to carry out his purpose of writing a book. Normally, both practical and speculative intellects are inspired in varying degrees, according as there is question of teaching truth. This is the first illustration of the analogous nature of the concept of inspiration. It permits Benoit to assert that, while the whole Bible is inspired in every part, there can be question of the "negative privilege" of inerrancy only when there is some teaching.[38]

The analogous nature of the concept of inspiration may be further illustrated by the way it extends proportionally to all the faculties which come into play in composing a book, as well as to the entire contents of Scripture, to all the authors and redactors who produced any given book, and to all the real senses of Scripture.[39]

Biblical inerrancy is not the final cause of inspiration, nor its sole consequence, since God did not have the Bible written merely to teach doctrine but for the spiritual guidance of its readers. How explain the so-called "errors" in the Bible? In the past, failure to distinguish inspiration clearly from revelation led to unsatisfactory solutions like the restriction of inspiration to matters of faith and morals, an exaggerated appeal to "implicit citations," or to the theory of "historical appearances." To define the limits of biblical inerrancy, formal instead of material criteria must be used. These come down to three questions: what attitude does the author adopt toward his subject?

What degree of affirmation does he employ in speaking of it? How far does he demand acceptance of his views?

Only at the end of his study does Benoit refer to the study of *genera litteraria* as a solution for the problem of inerrancy. Quite frankly, one might wish he had begun with this method, adopted officially by the magisterium, which enables us to maintain the absolutely fundamental principle that the Bible contains no error. Pedagogically speaking, it has always seemed to me that this point of departure produces upon the inquirer a much healthier psychological effect.

The Contribution of Joseph Coppens

In reviewing Benoit's exposition in *Initiation biblique*, Joseph Coppens, the celebrated Louvain scholar, criticized several points, of which three have relevance here: (1) the Bible can contain false "affirmations," provided they are not "taught";[40] (2) the "teaching" of the sacred writers is restricted to "objectively religious and supernatural truths" and to natural and profane truths which the author considers "in their religious and supernatural significance"; (3) the only kind of error excluded by inspiration is that which would compromise the objectively religious and supernatural truths of its teaching.[41]

In a subsequent article Coppens takes issue with the three principles which we pointed out earlier as fundamental to Benoit's view of inspiration: the theory of the twofold inspiration of the Bible (i.e., the distinction between scriptural and prophetic inspiration), the distinction between judgments as speculative and practical, and the rejection of material criteria in ascertaining the author's meaning.[42] He questions whether Benoit's subdividing of inspiration into purely scriptural and prophetic is really useful or founded in reality. He prefers to restrict prophetic inspiration to passages where there is also question of some revelation.[43] As regards Benoit's categories of judgment, he finds the terms "speculative" and "practical" vague and inadequate: it is not evident that practical judgments never include a speculative aspect. Terminologically, Coppens would prefer to call them judgments of *apprêt* and *arrêt*: the first connotes an approximative, provisory judgment; the second, a definitive affirmation which the writer intends to teach, engaging his (and God's) authority and demanding the reader's assent.[44] Finally, while Coppens admits that material criteria alone are insufficient for judging the author's mind, he insists they are necessary because they include "the classical means of evaluating the doctrinal signification of a scripture text."[45]

The Thought of Karl Rahner

With the brilliant essay of Karl Rahner, a new element is introduced into the recent discussion of the nature of biblical inspiration: the historical process in which the divine influence actually operated.[46]

Rahner's thesis may be expressed as follows. The formal, predefining act of the divine Will by which God founded the Church of the apostolic age (the *Urkirche*) includes the inspiring of Scripture as one of the constitutive elements of the process by which the Church was divinely instituted. The Scriptures were not merely occasioned by the foundation of the *Urkirche*, nor were they a result of it. God's authorship of Scripture through inspiration was an essential moment in the production of the *Urkirche* and derives its peculiar character from the divine founding of the Church. Thus, scriptural inspiration is "simply God's authorship of the Church insofar as this has a relation to Scripture as a constitutive element of the *Urkirche* itself."[47]

How does Rahner conceive God's founding of the Church? By a will-act which is absolute and which is eschatological. It is absolute because included in the decree of the incarnation, prior to any decision of human liberty. It is eschatological because, in contrast with the election of Israel, it constituted the definitive *Heilsveranstaltung* in Christ and the Church, i.e., the definitive presence of divine grace in the world as the eschatological event of God's mercy, the consummation of history.[48]

What does Rahner mean by the *Urkirche* and how does he understand its function in the history of salvation? It might be called the Church-*in-fieri* during the apostolic age, which was directed by God in such a manner as to determine the character of the Church as an institution historically perceptible and destined to be indefectible. Involved in this work of foundation was not merely Christ but also the group of disciples He had gathered during His public life, who later enjoyed the absolutely unique experience of Pentecost. God's relationship to this *Urkirche* was a very special one: only through this first generation does He have a relation to succeeding generations of Christians. For revelation closed with the death of the last apostle, and Peter and the apostolic college possessed, in addition to the office handed on to their successors, an untransferable function in the Church.[49]

But the founding of the Church took the form of an evolutionary process extended in time.[50] There were events in her coming-to-be which were not destined to specify the Church's complete status, i.e., Temple worship and certain Judaizing practices. Hence the eschatological character of the Church endowed her with a clear self-consciousness of her own divinely intended nature and gave her the power to prune away any pseudo-Christian phenomena attending her emergence from the matrix of Judaism.

How does Rahner justify his view that the writing of Scripture under divine inspiration formed a constitutive element of the Church's founding? Granted that by His divine direction of the historical process through which the *Urkirche* evolved into the Church, God decreed to found the Church, then the *Urkirche* had necessarily to contain certain essential elements (the "deposit of faith," the primacy, apostolic succession, the sacraments). Now the formation of (at least) the New Testament belongs to these constitutive elements, because the Scriptures are the Church's book. Only she can recognize their inspired character or interpret them definitively. If the Scriptures are the word of God, they are just as fundamentally the Church's self-expression of her faith.[51] Like the apostolic preaching, the writing of the New Testament formed part of the initial phase of the Church's existence which was to remain normative throughout her subsequent history. It was because the *Urkirche* was aware of the necessity of preserving a record of her faith, her traditions, her very development, that she confided these things to writing.[52]

This remarkable theological synthesis provides Rahner with a satisfactory explanation of the divine-human authorship of Scripture. God is Author of Scripture because He willed its composition as an essential part of the *Heilsgeschichte* through which He revealed Himself by means of a supernatural historical *Heilsgemeinde*, which thus objectifies itself in the Book. God is principal Author, since this historical process exhibits within our world effects wrought by God alone. However, since God willed that the Church record in writing her awareness of her true nature and mission, the apostolic writers who evince this Christian faith are also real, though subordinate, authors. Moreover, just as the divine activity which presided over the developments by which He formed the *Urkirche* into the Church necessarily came to a conclusion once the Church was fully constituted, so too the history of God's authorship of Scripture *eo ipso* reached a conclusion as one of the events of this *Heilsgeschichte*.[53]

Rahner is also able to explain how the Church recognized the inspired character of Scripture.[54] The Church's long hesitation about the canonicity of certain New Testament books makes it historically improbable that any revelation of the New (or Old) Testament canon was expressly given through any of the apostles. So does the fact that the *Epistle of Barnabas* and Hermas' *Shepherd* were once regarded as canonical. We must, says Rahner, distinguish an implicit revelation of a book's inspiration and canonicity (which necessarily occurred before the death of the last apostle) and the expressly conscious, reflexive advertence to these qualities. He shows how the implicit awareness of the inspired character of his writings was present to the sacred author himself. Insofar as the New Testament authors were aware that they formed part of the concrete life of the Church-*in-fieri* expressing herself through Scripture (a knowledge which is supernatural), these writers can be said to have been conscious of their inspiration without perhaps reflecting upon it.

This magnificent contribution by one of the most original thinkers in the contemporary Church constitutes a landmark in the study of biblical inspiration. I have found only one difficulty with it: no room appears to have been left for the possibility of the composition of an inspired book after the death of the last apostle. Since Rahner demands a revelation to the Church of the New Testament canon, a revelation that would of necessity have been given before the death of the apostles, it is hard to see, in his theory, how the Catholic critic could avoid an aprioristic rejection of certain fairly cogent arguments for dating 2 Peter in the second century. We shall find a rather convincing solution to this problem in a significant article of Bernhard Brinkmann.[55]

Further Contributions by Bernhard Brinkmann

The German theologian Bernhard Brinkmann, of the Jesuit faculty of St. Georgen in Frankfurt, asks two pertinent questions: (1) How did the Church recognize the inspired character of the books of Scripture? (2) Why does the canon of Scripture contain only a certain number of books when, as Rahner for instance admits, there were other inspired writings?

He answers the first question by giving the common theological opinion that, since inspiration is a supernatural event, it can only be known through revelation. He holds, however, that this fact is revealed by way of conclusion, not explicitly.[56] He rejects, moreover, a view (held also by Rahner) that some kind of revelation is necessary for the inclusion of inspired books in the scriptural canon.[57]

Brinkmann's reasons for his views are based on the silence of the First Vatican Council regarding the criterion of inspiration, and on the belief found in both Jewish and Christian tradition that the deciding factor is the prophetic origin of the sacred books. The New Testament books were believed to contain the Christian rule of faith by the early Church because they had originated with the apostles, who, like the Old Testament writers, were prophets, instruments of God.[58] Accordingly, everything the apostles wrote, like everything they preached, was considered part of the *regula fidei*. The selection of certain of these inspired writings to form the canon of Scripture was left to the Church's choice, a choice which is positive but not exclusive.

One important consequence of this view is Brinkmann's assertion that a book could be written by some associate or successor of an apostle in the second century and be accepted as canonical, provided it faithfully recorded apostolic revelation.[59]

Brinkmann's most important contribution, in my opinion, is his thesis that the canon of Scripture is the result of the Church's infallible choice. He rightly refuses to postulate a special revelation, of which there is no trace anywhere and which is excluded by the history of the canon.[60]

AREAS OF FURTHER THEOLOGICAL INVESTIGATION

Since theology has made such advances in the understanding of biblical inspiration, we may well ask whether there is room for further development. I should like to indicate some questions which still invite exploitation.

In the first place, as I remarked in the beginning, the theologian might profitably reinvestigate the final cause of scriptural inspiration. Why did God inspire the sacred writers? Why is inspiration necessary to produce a book God willed to author through the medium of men? This question can be answered satisfactorily only by adopting a more religious view of the Bible than that taken by the old liberal critics. Let me illustrate from the history of Gospel criticism.

To defend the historical credibility of the Gospels, Catholic apologetics devised a system which rightly denounced the suggestion that the accounts written by the Evangelists were the mere product of the faith (or imagination) of the first disciples. There was, however, a tendency to deny that any theological interpretation had been put upon the facts narrated and to maintain that the logia attributed to Jesus were the *ipsissima verba Christi*.[61] In short, a valiant effort was made to make the Gospel stories conform to the canons of the nineteenth century's conception of history.

Today considerable work has been done upon the notion of religious history. It is now realized that there is such a thing as metahistory, which does not suffer the yardstick of secular history to be applied to it. We admit more readily that there is religious interpretation (and necessarily so) in the sacred history of Jesus' life and death, and that it is insufficient to treat His resurrection like any other historical fact.[62]

This more profound view of scriptural historical narration can provide a valuable clue to the purpose of the Bible's inspiration. If it were merely a question of profane history, the accuracy of the authors' statements could be checked by any valid historical method. If, however, the sacred writers are endeavoring to describe the irruption of the divine into human history through the incarnation of God's Son, we find a new necessity for inspiration: to ensure the validity of that theological interpretation essential to the type of religious history contained in the Bible. This question of the relation of inspiration to symbolic history would reward the attention of the theologian.

We also need a theological investigation of God's total purpose in inspiring the sacred books. We have seen that this divine aim is not only doctrinal. Scripture is addressed to the whole man in his concrete existence, not merely to man's intellect. It was written "that you may persevere in your belief that Jesus is the Messiah, God's Son, and that through your belief you may have life in His name" (Jn 20:31). It provides food for the Christian life in a way in which the infallible pronouncements of the magisterium do not. The Bible is the "testimony of living experience, which tends to stir emotions and will, as well as enlightening the mind," whereas the Church's authoritative declarations are "intended to appeal only to the intellect. . . . Naturally the same Authority guarantees the affirmations of theology (those which are *de fide*), but it does not *make* them; and the text that is adduced in support of the affirmation is functioning only on the rational, logical level, while its affective, imperative values are in this context necessarily disregarded."[63]

The task of defining the total purpose of Scripture and of scriptural inspiration is not easy. It involves a careful and complete elaboration of biblical theology—which has yet to be done. Still, it represents an ideal toward which the theologian and the biblical scholar can work.

Meantime, there are other, smaller issues to be settled. Rahner's splendid theory of the inspiration of the New Testament needs careful working out so that it can be applied to the Old.[64] I believe, too, that it would be profitable to follow up Rahner's lead by investigating the mediatorial role of the Church in the inspiration of Scripture. Could we not learn more about the function of the inspired writers as men of the Church?

The theologian might re-examine the discriminating attitude of the Church in the period when she was forming the scriptural canon, as Brinkmann has suggested. She was not concerned with selecting writings that were simply error-free, but with apostolically authentic doctrine.[65]

Finally, I suggest that two analogies with the practice of the Church in regard to the conferring of the sacraments and to preaching might well deepen our understanding of biblical inspiration. To confer any sacrament validly, the minister must intend to do what the Church wishes him to do. Might not this principle illustrate the way in which God influenced the New Testament writers? They intended to do what the Church wished, i.e., to compose a written record of the apostolic preaching and teaching. Is not such an intention implicit in Paul's letter to the Churches of Corinth and Galatia, and in Luke's prologue?[66]

The second analogy derives from the Church's traditional attitude toward the necessity of a kind of "apostolic succession" in the valid, efficacious preaching of the word of God. To the bishop, as successor of the apostles, belongs the office of preaching. He shares this function with others by communicating faculties to them for that purpose. To preach without faculties is analogous to hearing confessions without faculties. This lofty conception of the preacher's role, postulating an unbroken chain that preserves communion with the apostles for the promulgation of the spoken word, provides a counterpart to the way in which biblical inspiration assures the Church of the apostolic authority of the written word of the New Testament.

II

The Apostolic Church and Her Liturgy

A STUDY of the manner in which the apostolic Church celebrated public worship provides a deep insight into her "self-awareness," that consciousness of her mission to men and of her belief in Jesus Christ. It is noteworthy, I believe, that Yahweh's intention in forming Israel as His own People is represented by the author of Exodus as liturgical in scope. "Thus says Yahweh, the God of Israel: 'Let my people go, that they may hold a feast for me in the desert' " (Ex 5:1).

Moreover, it is to be remembered that there is a certain parallel between the conventions governing liturgy and the literary forms through which the sacred writers expressed the salvation history both of the Old Testament and the New. While cultus must be the sincere expression of real religion by means of external rites, performed by duly appointed ministers of the religious community, still by the very fact that it is "service of the people," i.e., a social activity, the cultus is governed by forms or patterns which limit individual expressions of piety. On the other hand, by the fact that these religious actions are the official gestures of the People of God, in the Old Testament as in the New, they reveal much about the basic beliefs of the community, which are incarnate, so to speak, in these external rites. Thus the sacramental quality of the liturgy of the apostolic Church will disclose many significant features of the Church herself.

The first essay deals with a number of hymns cited in the New Testament which express a remarkably advanced Christology and bear witness to the early Christian awareness of the interpersonal relationship between the community and the Holy Spirit. At this very early stage in the development of the Church, contrary to what some have thought, there was little use made in public worship of the Psalter (note, however, the prayer of the Jerusalem congregation, Acts 4:24–30, which shows how the Church could express her faith in the Messiahship and divinity of her Master through the Psalms). It appears that both in the baptismal and in the Eucharistic liturgies the hymn was the most common expression of worship. Various credal formulae, also quoted in the New Testament, were likewise employed to proclaim the common faith of the gathered community.

Our second study reviews the influence exerted by early Christian cultus upon the composition of the four Gospels. It has been recognized for some time that Israel's public worship exerted a profound influence upon certain parts of the Old Testament. The liturgical recital of God's "judgments" (*mishpatim*), or mighty deeds in favor of His People, has left its mark not only upon many of the Psalms, but also upon certain narratives (cf. Gn 1; Ex 19:14–20; Jos 24:2–28). Remnants of creeds are also found not infrequently in Israelite literature (cf. Dt 26:5–9; Jos 24:2–13). In the New Testament also, as most scholars agree, the narratives of the Passion probably originated as separate compositions intended to provide readings for public worship. It would appear that Paul wrote some, at least, of his letters for the same purpose (cf. 1 Th 5:27; Col 4:16). The first two Gospels contain very ancient liturgical accounts of Jesus' institution of the Eucharist (Mt 26;

26–29; Mk 14:22–25), and the Gospel of Matthew closes with a citation from a baptismal formula (Mt 28:19). The supreme importance of the Eucharistic liturgy for the primitive Church can be demonstrated from the way in which it has left its mark upon other New Testament narratives, preserved undoubtedly as illustrations of the meaning and efficacy of this sacrament (cf. the twofold reporting of the feeding of the crowds in the wilderness in Mt and Mk, or Luke's account of Paul's shipwreck in Acts 27:33–36). In the same manner, the earliest baptismal liturgies have impressed themselves on several New Testament narratives. Finally, the ancient liturgical practices of Israel are occasionally reflected in some New Testament narratives.

The third study in this section is devoted to the understanding of baptism, the rite of Christian initiation, in the early Church. It is an attempt to present the biblical theology of this sacrament. The many comparisons and figures employed by the New Testament writers to describe baptism and its significance for the Christian life reveal their concern to portray it as one of the efficacious means whereby the believer is made to participate in the significant episodes of Christian salvation history. These inspired authors teach that it is only by sharing or experiencing personally those redemptive acts whereby man's salvation became a reality in Jesus Christ that we are to be saved. They were also fully aware that the great saving events of the whole *Heilsgeschichte* (Old Testament as well as New) imparted the significance as well as the efficacy to the Christian sacraments.

assemblies of the disciples was attributable to the Eucharistic liturgy. "Breaking the Bread at home, they partook of the Food with transports of joy and utter simplicity of mind, while they sang God's praises" (2:46–47). The last words of this citation appear to indicate that this joy, inspired by the presence of the risen Master, was normally expressed in song.[1]

It is the captivity epistles, however, that give us the most specific and circumstantial accounts of the primitive Christian use of hymns in public worship. Two particularly deserve to be cited, since they provide an insight into the function of hymn singing in early Christianity. In Col 3:16 we read: "May the word of Christ dwell within you, rich in wisdom, as you instruct yourselves by means of songs, hymns, inspired canticles, and sing gratefully with all your heart to God." While it is improbable that Paul intends to distinguish three categories of sacred songs, the purpose of this public or liturgical singing is made clear. By means of hymns the Christian community *instructs* herself and at the same time offers cultic prayer to God. Thus there is question here of what Heinrich Schlier has called "Kultlieder der Gemeinde."[2] As Schlier points out, these hymns were in every sense of the word "community hymns": they originated within the community, and their authorship, by way of contrast with the later Gnostic hymns, remained anonymous; they remained the property of the community and were, in the course of time, continually reworded or readapted to the community's varying liturgical needs;[3] most important of all, they are the voice of the community, the *alter Christus*, and hence Paul refers to this liturgical hymnody as the *logos tou Christou*, "Christ's word." Paul has emphasized the oneness of the community in the last half of the preceding verse, which serves as introduction to this statement: "you have also been called in one Body to (the peace of Christ); hence express your gratitude" (Col

3:15b). The voice of the Body is the *logos tou Christou*, which is thus to be distinguished from the kerygma (*logos tou Kyriou*, or *logos tou Theou*), as also from the *didachē*,[4] exemplified in the written Gospels and in the New Testament letters. Kerygma is the "word of the Lord" proclaimed by the missionaries of the apostolic age to the non-Christian world with a view to its conversion. The "teaching" is that deeper, theological interpretation of the events announced by the kerygma, made by the authoritative teachers of the Church for the believing Christian, either as an individual or as a member of the community. The *logos tou Christou* is addressed by the community, assembled for its liturgical functions, to itself, the Body of Christ, for the purpose of mutual or reciprocal instruction and edification. The effect of this communal "voice of Christ," singing gratefully to God with undivided heart and mind, is the fuller realization of its complete oneness with the Head and of its members with one another.[5]

The second passage occurs in Eph 5:18–20: "Stop getting drunk on wine, which only leads to licentiousness. Seek instead to be filled with the Spirit, by reciting songs, hymns, inspired canticles, by singing to the Lord and chanting His praises with all your heart, giving thanks always for everything in the person of our Lord Jesus Christ to God the Father." As is evident, the text is parallel to that from Colossians which we have been discussing. However, there are two variations in the present passage which throw further light on the nature of these early hymns. The Colossians text spoke of the hymns as sung "to God"; here there is question of "singing to the Lord and chanting His praises." The term *Kyrios* here, as normally in Paul's writings, is a title of the risen Christ and denotes His divinity. In point of fact, there is no real difference between the hymns sung to God and those addressed to Christ. This is not only because He, like the Father, is a divine Person. Since the whole movement of the redemption accomplished by Christ originates with the Father, a song to Christ as Redeemer is a hymn in praise of the Father.[6]

The explicit mention of the Holy Spirit in this text is also of considerable importance, since it clarifies the meaning of *pneumatikos* used to describe the songs in both texts. The liturgical use of hymns by the Christian community is "inspired," not merely because they have a religious and theological character, but also because, as "Christ's word," they entail the charismatic activity of the Spirit of Christ. On Paul's view, it is through the liturgical recitation of such hymns that the community becomes "filled with the Spirit," to whose activity, as stated earlier in this letter (Eph 4:4), the unity of the "one Body" is due.

It is instructive to observe that both our texts speak of the reciprocal or mutual edification of the community as one of the primary functions of this liturgical chant: *didaskontes kai nouthetountes heautous,* and *lalountes heautois.* How fundamental, in early Christian worship, this function of the hymn was deemed by the Christians themselves, is attested by a pagan source, from which the title of this present essay is drawn: the now famous letter written by the younger Pliny to his master, Emperor Trajan.[7]

In the year 112, Caius Plinius Caecilius reported to Trajan on his efforts at stamping out Christianity in Bithynia. The document refers, somewhat obscurely, to two distinct liturgical functions in which the second-century Christians were accustomed to participate.

They [the Christians] insisted, however, that their whole crime or error came to this: they had the custom of meeting on a certain fixed day, before daybreak, to sing a hymn, alternating among themselves, to Christ as God; and to bind themselves solemnly by an oath, not with any criminal intent, but to avoid all fraud, theft, adultery, unfaithfulness to their promises, or denial of "the deposit"[8] if summoned to do so. After dispatching this business, it was their habit to disband, reassembling once more to take food, which is, however, of an ordinary and innocent kind. . . .

There has been considerable debate among scholars as to the precise nature of these two religious services, held on "a certain fixed day" (undoubtedly Sunday). It appears probable, however, that the first was a baptismal liturgy, held in the early morning hours, while the second is undoubtedly "the Lord's Supper," celebrated in the late afternoon or evening.[9] It is Pliny's description of the baptismal rite which interests us at the moment, despite its brevity and possible omissions. The reference to the taking of an oath (*seque sacramento . . . obstringere*) has been identified as the recitation of the Decalogue, or the abjuration of a catalogue of sins such as appears occasionally in the New Testament.[10] The mention of a liturgical hymn sung on this occasion by the whole community appears to be remarkably accurate, in the light of the Pauline passages we have been studying: *carmenque Christo quasi deo dicere secum invicem*. The final phrase, which might seem to suggest the choral recitation of the Psalter,[11] undoubtedly is an attempt to express the liturgical practice, referred to by Paul, of community hymn singing, or the *logos tou Christou*. These hymns, as Pliny asserts, were principally concerned with the divinity of Christ.

We should like to study briefly, in the pages that follow, some of these very ancient Christian hymns, preserved in various parts of the New Testament. Since there is no shortage of citations of such hymns on the part of the inspired authors, we shall confine our attention to the following passages: Phil 2:5–11; Ap 5:9–10, 12, 13; 15:3–4; Eph 5:12; 1 Tim 3:16; Col 1:13–20; 1 Pt 1:3–5; Jn 1:1–18.[12]

PRIMITIVE EXPRESSION OF THE DOGMA OF CHRIST'S DIVINITY

Before we discuss the Christological conceptions reflected in these examples of early hymnology, it will be helpful to recall how gradual was the process through which the disciples were made aware of their Master's divinity. Moreover, it will also be useful to sketch out the general lines along which they attempted to express, by means of biblical symbols, their first insights into this central dogma of their new Christian faith.

On the testimony of all four Evangelists, the message of John the Baptist constitutes the beginning of the revelation of the mystery of Jesus to the first disciples. The essence of John's preaching is contained in the proclamation that "the kingdom of heaven is at hand" (Mt 3:2) and that "a mightier one than I is following me" (Mk 1:7). This mysterious person is to be the arbiter of God's eschatological judgment and the dispenser of a baptism "with a Holy Spirit and fire" (Mt 3:11). While there was a tradition, preserved for us in the fourth Gospel, that John had introduced some of his followers to Jesus (Jn 1:35 ff.), who subsequently became His disciples, still it would appear fairly certain that they did not immediately recognize in their new Master the Messianic figure announced by the Baptist. That they considered Him a rabbi greater than John may be inferred from the fact that they left John to attach themselves to Jesus. The fourth Gospel suggests that they were drawn to Him by some winning quality in His personality (Jn 1:38–39). The Synoptic accounts of the call of the first apostles simply record the fact of their vocation and omit any indication of the psychological reactions of these men to their new rabbi.

As they followed Him, listening to His doctrine and witnessing His miracles, they came to regard Him as a prophet, and one greater than the prophets of the Old Testament. At one privileged moment of the public life, which the Gospel tradition has linked with Caesarea Philippi, Peter, and through his lips the whole apostolic group, expresses the truth, divinely revealed, that Jesus is the Messiah.

Yet, despite this precious grace accorded to them, the disciples' idea of Jesus' Messianic function remained mixed with contemporary Jewish imaginings and dreams of a temporal, earthly "restoration" of Israel's hegemony among the nations. Hence their faith in Jesus as the Christ had necessarily to undergo a complete eclipse as a result of the terrible events of His sufferings and death.[13] It was only from the instructions given by the risen Lord in His postresurrection appearances that the disciples began to gain a proper notion of the spiritual nature of Jesus' Messianic mission and of the function of His passion as revealed by "the Scriptures" (Lk 24:44–46). The *terminus ad quem* of this new paschal faith is, of course, the miracle of Pentecost and the gift of the Holy Spirit, who leads them "into the whole truth" (Jn 16:13).[14] Jesus' sending of the Spirit reveals to them His own enthronement at God's right hand; and this uniquely divine prerogative discloses to them His identity as only-begotten Son of the Father, who had assumed a human nature to establish God's dominion upon earth. He is to return again to earth at the end of time, and by a glorious second coming complete the work of subjecting the universe to His divine sovereignty.[15]

Once the apostolic community was in possession of these divinely revealed truths, a certain amount of reflection was needed to reveal their full significance[16] and to discover ways of expressing in human language the mystery of Christ's divinity. In the first place, the revelation of the divine Sonship of the exalted Lord Jesus imparted a completely new significance to His earthly career and His death. Revealed as Son of God in His glorified state, He had been Son of God during His mortal life and had pre-existed as Son of God before His incarnation.

Is it still possible to recapture some of the thought-processes by which these conclusions were reached? It would seem that we have some indications in the choice of themes used by the apostolic age to express these truths. The New Testament reveals three principal patterns followed by the most ancient Christian symbolism expressive of the dogma of Christ's divinity: Jesus' enthronement at the right hand of God; the suffering and glorified Servant of Yahweh; and the theme of the Son of Man and second-Adam motif. Each set of symbols, which can be traced back ultimately to the Old Testament, was used by Jesus during His earthly teaching.

The enthronement idea as found in the apostolic preaching was based upon Ps 110:1 (cf. Acts 2:33–35). Under a slightly different form, it appears as the notion that Jesus has been "constituted Son of God in power" (Rom 1:4), a borrowing from Ps 2:7 (cf. Acts 13:33). Christ Himself, in preaching the coming of the *basileia tou Theou,* had hinted that it had, in His own person, become a contemporary reality (Lk 17:21); and He had prophesied to the Sanhedrin, on the eve of His death, His imminent elevation to God's right hand (Mk 14:62).

The Servant theology, which originated in the Palestinian Christian communities and enjoyed great popularity among the preachers and writers of the apostolic age, was founded upon the Deutero-Isaian Servant Songs, especially the passage found in Is 52:13—53:12. There can be little doubt that Jesus had referred to Himself as the Suffering Servant in logia like that found in Mk 10:45.[17] While the theme was widely used by the theologians whose inspired writings constitute so much of the New Testament Christology, it was almost never employed by St. Paul to describe Christ and His redemptive work. In the Pauline letters, the Servant theme is developed into a theology of the apostolate, the Deutero-Isaian texts being almost invariably applied to Paul himself.[18] In the Johannine literature the Servant motif is merged with that of the paschal lamb, to present Christ as "the Lamb of God, who carries the world's sin" (Jn 1:29). The sacrifice of the paschal lamb, an annual commemoration of Israel's deliverance from Egypt, provides the redemption symbol so prominent in New Testament writings. In John's account of the Passion, Jesus appears as the new Paschal Lamb. Since, however, the passover sacrifice was not one of expiation or atonement, the Johannine writings combine this paschal symbolism with that of the Servant, where the notion of vicarious satisfaction is so dominant. Such a synthesis is almost suggested by the Deutero-Isaiah, who describes the Servant as "a sheep led to the slaughter" and "a lamb that is dumb before its shearers" (Is 53:7). This composite picture of the "Lamb of God" is considered by the author of the Apocalypse as particularly apt to express the divinity of Christ, as will be seen presently.

Finally, the title by which Jesus habitually designated Himself during His public life, "Son of Man," an apocalyptic figure appearing in Dn 7:13–18, provided the starting point for a series of symbols developed by the pen of St. Paul: the theme of the last or second or new Adam.[19]

It is these three symbols that we shall find employed in the Christological hymns cited throughout the New Testament. Occasionally these themes will be combined in order to bring out more strikingly the faith of the primitive Church in the divinity of Christ and in the salvific efficacy of His mission among men. An illustration of such combination in prose is provided by the first chapter of the fourth Gospel, where the Evangelist presents the disciples' testimony to Jesus by means of seven titles: Lamb of God (Jn 1:29), rabbi (Jn 1:38), Messiah (Jn 1:41), the prophet foretold by Moses (Jn 1:45), Son of God and King of Israel (Jn 1:49),[20] and Son of Man (Jn 1:51).

HYMN TO CHRIST AS SUFFERING AND GLORIFIED SERVANT

In one of his most simple and most personal letters, that to the Philippian Church, Paul cites part of a hymn, undoubtedly familiar to his addressees from its use in the liturgy (Phil 2:5–11). The song, which celebrates Christ's work as Redeemer, is inspired by the fourth Servant Song (Is 52:13—53:12). Since the hymn, which is probably of Palestinian origin,[21] may be presumed to antedate this early Pauline letter,[22] it is particularly valuable as an early monument to the highly developed Christology of Palestinian Christianity.

> Who, while He kept His character as God,
> did not consider His divine equality
> something to be proudly paraded.
>
> No, He despoiled Himself
> by taking on the Servant's character,
> becoming similar to mortal men.
>
> And looking outwardly like any other man,
> He carried self-abasement, through obedience,
> right up to death, yes, death by the cross.

Therefore did God in turn immeasurably exalt Him,
and graciously bestow on Him the Name,
outweighing every other name;

that everyone, at Jesus' Name,
should bow adoring: those in heaven,
on earth, in the infernal regions,

and every tongue take up the cry,
"Jesus is Lord,"
thus glorifying God His Father.

The conception is a simple one, almost naive in some respects; yet it is profoundly theological. When He might have claimed the divine honors, which were always His by right as pre-existent Son of God, still He freely chose, for the carrying out of His redemptive mission, the lowly way of humiliation and suffering. The carefully-worked-out contrast in the first and second strophes between the Son's "character as God," which He retains always, and "the Servant's character," which He adopts at His incarnation, is proof of the accuracy of thought and clarity of expression attained by the Palestinian Church quite early in the apostolic times. Yet the archaic character of this Christology is also manifest in the view that the "becoming similar to mortal men" is rather part of the humiliation of "taking on the Servant's character," than an ennobling or divinization of human nature. This latter viewpoint, so characteristic of a more Hellenized Christology, makes its appearance in Christian literature only with the fourth Gospel.

As L. Cerfaux has ably demonstrated,[23] the movement of the third and fourth strophes is patterned upon the Deutero-Isaian picture of the suffering and glorified Servant of Yahweh, whose most characteristic quality had been his obedience to the divine will,[24] which he had crowned with the sacrifice of his own life (Is 53:12).

To reward the fidelity of his Servant, Yahweh had exalted him in the sight of kings and nations (Is 52:13–15), prolonged his life, and given him the spoils of the mighty (Is 53: 10–12). The reality of this prophecy's fulfilment in Jesus' exaltation surpasses all human thought or imagination. It is expressed here as the bestowal of "the Name outweighing every other name." This new Name is the divine title *Kyrios*, which in the Greek Bible was constantly used for the sacred tetragram Yahweh. When we recall that a name, for the Hebrews, was not equivocal as in Western thought, but expressed the nature of the person to whom it was attached, this gift of God's own Name to Jesus signifies the revelation of His divinity through His glorification.[25] The assertion that the Name was accorded to Jesus *as a grace* by the Father has caused surprise among commentators.[26] Yet such a theologically naive expression is not only valuable as proof of the archaic character of the hymn's Christology, but also as a reflection of the wonder and amazement which the revelation of Jesus' divinity caused in the minds of the first disciples.[27]

Just what the conferring of the divine Name upon Jesus signified in the milieu in which the hymn was composed may be gathered from the imaginative description of the cosmic liturgy in which all creatures inhabiting the Hebraic three-storied universe join to adore the God-man and to offer the doxology *Jēsous Kyrios*, a simple and archaic form of the Christian credo[28] and a touchstone of orthodoxy.[29] This acclamation is equivalently an act of praise of God the Father, author of Christ's salvific work and revealer of His Son's divinity.

HYMNS TO CHRIST AS DIVINE LAMB

In the Apocalypse the risen Christ is constantly represented through the symbolism of the lamb slain for man's redemption (Ap 5:6; 7:14; 12:11) and now enthroned in glory (5:6; 7:17; 22:1) upon the mountain of Sion (14:1). He is, as Lamb of God, the heavenly Temple (21:22) and the lamp which constitutes the heavenly city's sun (21:23). Throughout this book of Johannine revelations, there recurs a series of hymn citations in honor of God's exalted Lamb which are expressive of Christ's divinity. Three sections of one of these songs are to be found in the seer's description of the celestial liturgy (5:9–10, 12, 13).

You have the right to take the Book
and to open its seals,
for you were sacrificed
and have redeemed for God
with your blood
men of every tribe and tongue
and folk and race;
and you have made them for our God
a kingdom of priests.
And they will rule the earth.

It is the right of the sacrificed Lamb
to receive power and riches
and wisdom and strength and honor
and glory and praise.

To Him who sits upon the throne,
and to the Lamb,
praise and honor
and glory and power
for endless ages. Amen.

These acclamations, of a pronounced liturgical character,[30] give us some insight into the beginnings of the Christian liturgy. They are called "a new song" (Ap 5:9), which designates them as specifically Christian,[31] and which reminds us also of "the new Name" (2:17; 3:12) given to the risen Christ at His exaltation.[32] The Lamb symbol, which we tend to connect with the paschal lamb, more probably reminded the early Christians of the Deutero-Isaian Servant.[33] The taking of "the Book," the plan of divine Providence for mankind, symbolizes Christ's universal dominion over human history and is, consequently, a reference to His divinity. This truth is also brought out by the parallelism between this hymn to Christ and that in praise of the Father as Creator found in the preceding chapter (4:11). The acclamations to the divine Lamb in the second and third strophes are reminiscent of the vision of the Son of Man in Dn 7:14. The conceptions of the death of Christ as sacrificial and of the Christian people's sacerdotal vocation make it not improbable that these hymns were used, in the communities within the Johannine sphere of influence, during the celebration of the Eucharist.

There is a citation from a hymn which the author calls "the canticle of Moses, the servant of God, and the canticle of the Lamb" (Ap 15:3). This song, which is inspired by the canticle in Ex 15:1–18, is a composition in honor of the risen Christ as Lamb of God. The titles applied here to Christ, as well as several of the expressions in this brief strophe, are taken from the Old Testament, where they have reference to Yahweh.[34]

Great and wonderful your works,
O Lord God, Ruler of creation:
faithful and true your ways,
O King of Nations.
Who, Lord, will not revere
and glorify your Name?

For you alone are holy:
For all nations will draw near
and bow down before you:
For your saving judgments are shown forth.

CHRIST'S DIVINITY AND THE ENTHRONEMENT THEME

The most ancient examples of the apostolic preaching frequently make use of the enthronement theme in teaching the divine Sonship of Jesus Christ. This motif is found in several of the early credal formulae cited by New Testament authors where Jesus is described as "seated at God's right hand" (Ps 110:1), or with everything "subjected beneath His feet" (Ps 8:6), or as having received the new divine Name *Kyrios*.[35] This enthronement theme, which provided such a popular vehicle for the expression of Christ's divinity (cf. Rom 1:4), was employed in two ways: to describe Christ's eschatological function as "Judge of the living and dead" (Acts 10:42), or to portray Christ's actual role as Saviour, exercised by His intercession in heaven (Rom 8:34; Heb 7:25) or His intervention in this world through the Spirit (Acts 3:26).

This second view of the operation of the enthroned Christ in the sacrament of baptism is illustrated by two fragments of a hymn, taken from an early baptismal liturgy, which in the opinion of modern commentators belong together: Eph 5:14 and 1 Tim 3:16.

Wake up, you sleeper,
and arise from death,
and Christ will light you up . . . (Eph 5:14)
who was revealed through His humanity,
was justified by the Spirit,
was beheld by angels,
was proclaimed amongst nations,

was believed in throughout the world,
was taken up in glory. (1 Tim 3:16)

The first section of the hymn describes the action of the glorified Christ in terms of an awakening from the sleep of "death," that state of separation from the "God of the living" which is our heritage from the first Adam (Rom 5:12) and which can include both the sinful state resulting from personal sins in this life and eschatological death (eternal damnation) in the next. More positively, the work of the exalted Christ in the sacrament of baptism is an "illumination," a new creative act, analogous to the divine creation of light at the beginning.[36]

The attribution of such a uniquely divine operation to Christ is followed by a rather elaborate presentation of the enthronement motif consisting of three pairs of verses arranged antithetically. This triple structure appears to have been modeled upon the three steps involved in the coronation of an ancient Oriental king, which we know to have been in use in Egypt and Mesopotamia.[37] That ceremonial consisted of (1) the *elevation* of the monarch to the divine dignity, (2) his *presentation* to the gods of the national pantheon, (3) his *enthronement*, or accesssion to supreme power in the state.

The author of Hebrews employs this same manner of presenting the revelation of Christ's divinity, but uses, instead of a hymn form, a series of Old Testament citations which aptly illustrate the three steps by which Jesus is glorified. He is proclaimed Son of God by the Father Himself (Heb 1:5; Ps 2:7). He is presented by the Father to the angels for their adoration and submission (Heb 1:6–7; Ps 96:7). Finally, He accedes to divine supremacy at the Father's right hand (Heb 1:8–13; Ps 110:1).

In our hymn, Jesus' "elevation" is described in terms of His death and resurrection. Through the mediation of His sacred humanity, "justified" or glorified at His resurrection,[38] Jesus has been revealed as Son of God.[39] In the second pair of lines, we have Christ's "presentation" to the angels and to the world. This seems to refer to two events connected with Pentecost: the completion of Christ's glorification, which enabled Him to send the Spirit (Jn 7:39; Acts 2:33), and His proclamation through the apostolic preaching to "the nations" assembled in Jerusalem for that feast (Acts 2:5). Finally, the last two verses describe Christ's "enthronement" or "accession to divine power," which, as we saw, was one primitive way of denoting the revelation of His divinity. The hymn describes this revelation in terms of the universal acceptance of the Christian faith by pagans as well as by Jews, and then in terms of Christ's *sessio ad dexteram Patris*.[40]

The eschatological values present in this enthronement theme (Christ's constitution as universal Judge at the end of time) were, as Acts shows, frequently exploited by the apostolic kerygma. Peter is represented as foretelling the coming of "the times of refreshment from the presence of Yahweh," when "He will send Jesus, the Messiah destined for you. It is He whom heaven must keep until the period of the universal restoration, of which God spoke long ago through the lips of His holy prophets" (Acts 3:20–21). It is this doctrine which has inspired the theological viewpoint displayed by the baptismal hymn quoted in 1 Pt 1:3–5.

> Blessed be God, Father of our Lord Jesus Christ,
> who for His boundless mercy regenerated us
> in view of a living hope
> through Jesus Christ's resurrection from death:
> in view of an inheritance
> incorruptible, unsullied, never fading,
> preserved in heaven:[41]
> ready to be revealed in the final hour.

In this hymn the idea of the Christian life as a rebirth effected by the Father is exposed in wholly eschatological terms: "a living hope," "an inheritance preserved in heaven," "a salvation to be revealed" through the final judgment. M. E. Boismard has shown that the passage in Tit 3:4–7 is, from several points of view, parallel to our hymn, and he appears to be right in regarding Tit 3:4–7 as inspired by the themes utilized by the hymn. However, they differ fundamentally in this: Tit 3:4–7 accentuates the present effects of baptism and regards Christian salvation in terms of the actual possession of the "renovation of the Holy Spirit" (3:5) and of justification (3:7).

The hymn in 1 Pt 1:3–5, on the contrary, seems to be orientated along the lines of the words attributed to Peter in Acts 3:20–21. The "living hope" or "inheritance" is *in concreto* the exalted Christ Himself, who after His "resurrection from death" is "preserved in heaven," "ready to be revealed in the final hour" (or, as in Acts 3:21, "He whom heaven must keep until the period of the universal restoration"). The "living hope," or "inheritance," or "salvation" will only pass into the grasp of the Christian fully at the eschatological judgment, when he is finally united with the risen Lord by his own glorious resurrection.

HYMN TO CHRIST AS SECOND ADAM

The opening section of Paul's letter to the Colossians contains a substantial quotation from a hymn in praise of the God-man's intervention in the creation and the redemption. In the opinion of some commentators, the song was originally pre-Christian, then recast in honor of Christ for use in the early liturgy of baptism.[42] What is perhaps more easily demonstrable is the presence of the Adam motif in this hymn, revealed in the use of terms like "image" and "first-born," as also in the development of the creation theme and that of the Body of Christ.

Who snatched us from the tyranny of darkness,
set us instead beneath His own dear Son's dominion,
in whom we possess our ransom,
the remission of our sins.

Who is the image of the unseen God,
first-born before all creatures;
for in Him all things have been created,
things of heaven, things of earth,
things seen as well as things unseen,
Thrones and Dominions,
Principalities and Powers.

All things have been created by Him, for Him:
yes, He personally exists before all else.
All things in Him keep their coherence:
yes, He personally exists as Head of the Body, His Church.

Who is Beginning,
first-born from among the dead,
so that He might in every order take precedence;
for in Him God was pleased to lodge His whole creation,
and through Him reconcile all things to Him,
things of earth and things of heaven,
achieving peace by means of His blood, shed on the cross.

We have included vv. 13–14, which refer to the Father (the original hymn was probably trinitarian in inspiration), because they introduce us to the principal theme, that of the "first-born," used in describing the functions of the incarnate Son. The phrase "the Son of His love," a Hebraism meaning "His dear Son," may be equated with the term *prōtotokos.*

Moreover, these lines show in two ways that the hymn which follows is a composition in honor of the God-man, the Son qua incarnate.[43] First, by "the dominion of the Son" is meant the Church on earth, the Body of Christ as incarnate Son. Second, "our ransom, the remission of our sins" is conceived here, as habitually with Paul, *in concreto*, as it exists in the glorified humanity of Christ, the first *homo redemptus*.

The two main functions of the incarnate Son which the hymn commemorates are His part in the creation of the world and His redemptive work of reconciling "all things." As L. Cerfaux has pointed out, the poem does not focus attention upon the various moments in Christ's career, but rather upon the effects, in the religious sphere, of His intervention in the two great orders of creation and redemption.[44]

In the order of creation, He appears as "first-born before all creatures." As only-begotten Son, He is "first-born" with reference to the Father's eternal act of generation. His humanity, however, permits Him to be ranked first among all creatures, since they have been created "in Him, by Him, for Him." As incarnate Son, He constitutes the perfection of creation, produced "for Him"; He forms the center of creation's unity and harmony, its meaning and reality, all created "in Him." Indeed, considering that His mediation in this order is total, everything has been created "by Him."[45] Finally, as incarnate Son, He is "Image of the unseen God," a phrase which suggests His existential relationship with the Father, and His relationship as revealer with other creatures. The phrase also suggests the comparison with Adam (Gn 1:26), created to God's image and likeness, and first-born, in one sense, of all humanity.

However, it is in the order of the redemption that the primacy of the incarnate Son as second Adam is most evident. Here the whole universe may be compared with a body which is perfectly unified by its principle of coherence, the incarnate Son, who is Head of that Body known as the Church. As Redeemer, He is termed simply "Beginning": His atoning death begins man's peace with God, just as His resurrection begins man's own future resurrection. Again Christ's mediation is total: the universal reconciliation is "through Him" and "to Him," for the whole created universe is "in Him" as His complement.[46]

HYMN TO THE INCARNATE WORD

In the prologue to the fourth Gospel (Jn 1:1–18) we have another hymn in honor of the incarnate Son, which probably existed in some form or other before that Gospel was composed.[47] The theme is that of the triple coming of the Word in creation, in the Mosaic covenant, and in the new covenant effected by the Incarnation. The history of Christ's earthly career is not recounted, except in broadest outline: His war with "the darkness" is mentioned, and its eventual success is suggested. The fact that it is the Son of God who became incarnate is of great importance: it explains the possibility of man's divine adoptive filiation, as well as the revelation of the unseen God to man.

As has been pointed out,[48] the movement of the poem is cyclic: heaven to earth to heaven. This may be a conscious attempt by the author to reproduce the movement of the Christian salvation history as it was conceived in the school of John. The work of salvation in Jesus Christ was accomplished by a twofold movement: the coming into the world of the Word become man, and His passing from the world to the Father.[49]

From the beginning, the Word already was;
the Word was at home with God.

In fact, the Word was God.
He it is who from the beginning was at home with God.
All through Him came into being:
apart from Him, there existed nothing.
The life of what was made was found in Him:
yes, the Light of men is Life.
And that Light keeps shining in the darkness;
for the darkness has never put it out.
The real Light that illumines every man
was making His appearance in the world.
He was already present in the world
(the world was made by Him);
still, the world did not recognize Him.
He came to His own land;
yet His own folk would not have Him.
But as for those who did accept Him—
He gave them power to become God's children:
He whom never flesh and blood,
but only God had fathered.
Thus the Word became a mortal man:
He pitched His tent among us.

And we have beheld His glory,
glory from His Father as only Son,
the essence of God's mercy and fidelity.
Yes, of His abundance we have all received our share,
grace instead of grace:
(the law was a gift through Moses:
this mercy, this fidelity came into being through Jesus Christ).
God no man has ever seen;
His only Son, who shares the secrets of His Father's heart,
has personally acted as interpreter.

The doctrine of the divinity of Christ is presupposed throughout the hymn. Jesus Christ is identified with the Logos who has assumed man's nature and with the "only Son" of God.

The divine nature of the Logos is categorically asserted in the opening lines of the poem, while the distinction of Persons between the Father and the Logos is also aptly expressed.

The most striking development on the divinity of the incarnate Word is attained, however, by the use of the Old Testament symbol of the Mosaic covenant, and particularly of the great scene (Ex 33:18—34:10) depicting Moses' meeting with Yahweh. Details in this episode which appear to have influenced the composition of our hymn are Moses' request to be shown God's "glory" (Ex 33:18), and the description of God, heard by Moses during the theophany, as characterized by mercy and fidelity (Ex 34:6). The final stanza of the present poem exhibits these themes. To "have beheld His glory" is to have recognized Christ's divinity through some sensible manifestation (in this case, the sacred humanity), which in the Old Testament was called the *kābōd* or "glory" of God. The hymn describes this "glory" in terms of the divine *hesed* and *emeth*, the "mercy and fidelity" characteristic of Yahweh's saving activities in the Old Testament on behalf of His covenanted people, and now incarnate in Jesus Christ. Because He is divine, Christ can impart a share in these qualities to men, who thus receive "the power to become God's children." Because He is divine and "only Son" of the Father, He can perform His role as revealer of the "God no man has ever seen."

CONCLUSION

From this brief résumé of some of the New Testament hymns dealing with the theme of Christ's divinity, their double value as testimony of primitive Christian faith will, we hope, have become evident. In the first place, these lyrical compositions almost certainly date, for the most part, from a period preceding the writing of our Gospels, or even of Paul's epistles. They must, therefore, have been composed prior to 50 A.D. Thus they constitute an important part of the most ancient testimony to the Church's belief in the divinity of Christ. In the second place, they provide a most valuable insight into the development undergone by this basic Christian dogma, both by disclosing how the apostolic age advanced towards a more perfect expression of her belief, and by providing some indications of the psychological processes through which, under divine grace, the first Christians arrived at a realization of this mystery.

5

Liturgical Influences on the Formation of the Gospels

THE title of this essay may sound somewhat strange. The part played by Scripture (and particularly the Gospels) in fashioning the Church's liturgy is patent to all. What influence, however, can liturgy have had upon the formation of the Gospels? Accordingly, it may not be inopportune to make a beginning by stating just what we mean by those liturgical influences which concurred in the creation of our four canonical Gospels.

One of the lasting and legitimate gains made by New Testament criticism during the past twenty or thirty years has been the investigation and segregation of the various interests which governed the production of the Gospels. We have learned much about the nature and purpose of these books by examining the motives which guided the Evangelists in the selection and arrangement of their materials. Among these formative factors, the apostolic preaching, or kerygma, is the most obvious and most influential.[1] Papias tells us that Mark wrote down the Gospel as Peter preached it, while Irenaeus states that Luke made a book of Paul's preaching.[2] It is clear enough that the first three Gospels bear the unmistakable traces of the oral style. It has also been shown that certain apologetic interests prompted the inclusion of episodes in which Jesus defended His work, His ideals, or His disciples from His opponents' criticism. The edification, encouragement, or doctrinal instruction of the Christian community also contributed to the shaping of the Gospels. Indeed, these books were written primarily for the deepening and enlightenment of the faith of those who had already come to believe in Christ and His work of redemption. "These things have been written," said the fourth Evangelist, "that you may persevere in your belief that Jesus is the Messiah, the Son of God" (Jn 20:31).[3]

In the present study I should like to suggest that there was another influence, the liturgy, which also contributed to the writing of the Gospels. Such a liturgical influence must not be taken to mean what many Form Critics call the "divine cult" of Christ, which on their view deformed or radically altered the picture of the "historical Jesus."[4] By liturgical influence I mean the effects which public worship exerted upon the writings of the Evangelists. Liturgy is here understood to include the public worship of ancient Israel as well as that of the primitive Christian community. The Christian liturgy comprised the Eucharistic sacrifice, the administration of the sacraments, the celebration of feasts, as well as what is known nowadays as "liturgy of the Word."

We shall find four types of liturgical influence which have left their marks on the Gospels: (1) the practice of liturgical recital, (2) the incorporation of early Christian liturgical formulae, (3) the effect of Christian cultic observances and symbolism upon the writing-up of certain episodes, and finally (4) the reflection of the liturgical cycle of feasts, either Jewish or Christian.

Before we discuss these various liturgical influences, however, we must attempt some description of the liturgical life of the apostolic Christian community.

The Acts of the Apostles provides us with several summary

sketches of the life of the earliest Christian community in Jerusalem (Acts 2:42–47; 4:32–35; 5:12–16). The first of these concerns our investigation directly, since it enumerates the principal causes of the marvelous solidarity exhibited by the first Christians. "They were assiduously devoted to the teaching of the apostles and to the common life, to the breaking of the Bread and to prayers. . . . All the Christians lived a community life and possessed everything in common. They sold their property and their possessions, and shared the proceeds with everyone, according to the need each had. Day by day, frequenting the Temple in a body as well as breaking the Bread at home, they took food with boundless joy and an unworldly attitude, praising God and enjoying popularity with the whole [Jewish] people" (Acts 2:42–47). In this passage the apostolic Christian life is resumed under four heads: instruction in the teaching of the apostles, a communal existence by sharing material possessions, the "breaking of the Bread" or celebration of the Eucharist, and the recitation of prayers.

Some years ago Stanislas Lyonnet pointed out what a close connection, on the view of the author of this summary, existed between the "breaking of the Bread" and this primitive Christian "common life." "For the author of Acts, the 'breaking of the Bread' is not a by-product, or sort of liturgical rite which one might carry out for oneself: it is much rather the powerfully influential rite in which the community character, informing the whole of the Christian life, is expressed and affirmed."[5] That is to say, the Eucharistic liturgy provided the motivation and supernatural dynamism which effectively realized this remarkable experiment in the practice of Christian social justice. The Christian community prepared itself for the worthy reception of the Eucharist by sharing all earthly goods in common. And conversely, the communal partaking of the Eucharist, in which the risen Lord distributed

His grace among His disciples, gave them the supernatural force to live as a community, "possessing everything in common." Thus the Eucharistic liturgy, as Lyonnet has correctly seen, was the principal element in forming the community character of the primitive Christian Church.

I should like to develop this insight still further, and suggest that the "teaching of the apostles" was also effectively inspired by the "breaking of the Bread." From the manner in which he has constructed his sentence, it would appear that Luke saw a close relationship between the apostolic teaching and the community of goods, the one describing the doctrinal, the other the social, phase of early Christian life. "They were assiduously devoted to the teaching of the apostles and to the common life, to the breaking of the Bread and to prayers." If the Eucharist provided the inspiration and the dynamic for the "common life," it was surely not without its effect on the form taken by the "teaching of the apostles" within the community. One might expect that the liturgical influence upon Christian living had its parallel in the liturgical influence upon Christian teaching.

For, it is to be noted, the phrase "teaching of the apostles" does not refer to the kerygma or preaching by which outsiders were converted to Christianity. It was rather a deeper, more theological instruction in the Christian faith already accepted at baptism. As I have pointed out elsewhere,[6] this apostolic teaching was directed to the Christian community, providing a fuller formation in doctrine. In the first years, it was given orally by the apostles at community gatherings where the Eucharist was celebrated. Eventually this teaching was written down on various occasions by the New Testament writers, and it appears, for example, in the four Gospels.

Acts provides us with some evidence that this oral instruction of the community was traditionally associated with the

Eucharistic sacrifice, as may be seen from the incident at Troas when Paul revisited that well-established church (Acts 20:7–12). When the Christians assembled on a Sunday to "break Bread," Paul discoursed to them at some length upon Christian doctrine. In his Assisi conference, Augustin Bea drew attention to the novelty of this Christian practice, which united sacrifice with the reading and explanation of the Bible.[7] Even in Israel the sacred liturgy of the Temple was separated from the religious instruction of the people which was given in the synagogue. From its origins apostolic Christianity, on the other hand, in imitation, as Bea remarks, of Christ's own example at the Last Supper,[8] made doctrinal teaching a part of her liturgy. A striking example of this new attitude is found in Paul's remark that the liturgical re-presentation of the Last Supper is a *proclamation* of "the death of the Lord" (1 Cor 11:26). The term "proclaim" used in this text by the Apostle is constantly employed elsewhere in the New Testament for the preaching of the gospel. Is it possible to discover why St. Paul would use this word to describe the Christian Eucharistic sacrifice?

THE LITURGY AND THE WORD

While we know very little about the early liturgical setting in which the "breaking of the Bread" was celebrated, there are indications of at least two forms which the "liturgy of the Word" assumed from the earliest days. The first we may call the Passion recital; the second was the use of hymns.

The accounts of the Passion presented by the four Evangelists have certain common characteristics which set them apart from the rest of the Gospel narratives. The exponents of Form Criticism,[9] who insist so much upon the episodic, piecemeal character of our Gospels, have always been struck by the continuous, detailed nature as well as the structural similarity of the Passion narratives. The peculiar nature of the Passion stories may perhaps be best illustrated from the fourth Gospel, where the differences in vocabulary and literary flavor which distinguish the first seventeen chapters from the account of the Passion in chapters 18 and 19 can be readily observed. John's manner of recounting both Jesus' miracles and His discourses stands in marked contrast with similar accounts in the Synoptics. Yet the Johannine Passion differs so little in vocabulary and style from the Matthean, Marcan, or Lucan versions of it that it might be thought to have been composed by one of these other writers.

The most probable explanation of this phenomenon, which can be verified by a rapid reading of the four Passions, is that in relating the story of Jesus' sufferings and death these sacred writers had of necessity to guide themselves by some previous written account or accounts, which were already popular in the Christian communities. This is the only plausible explanation for the remarkable way in which John curtailed his great originality of thought and expression when he came to the Passion section of his Gospel.

Why did the story of the events, beginning with the Last Supper and culminating in Jesus' death and burial, assume a definite, written form so early in the apostolic age? The best answer, I believe, is to be found in the creation of a Christian liturgy. This time-honored association of the recital of the Passion with the sacramental re-presentation of "the death of the Lord" explains why Paul can refer to the Eucharistic liturgy as a "proclamation." Moreover, the manner in which the Passion is narrated by each of the Evangelists may be taken as the first illustration of liturgical influence upon the writing of the Gospels.

Further confirmation of this liturgical use of the Passion in early Christian communities may be derived from the prominence given it in such hymns as we may, with a fair degree of certainty, recover from the text of the New Testament. In a recent study of some of these hymns, I drew attention to their value as evidence for the very early and very precise formulation of the dogma of Christ's divinity.[10] It is also interesting to observe how all of them, in one way or another, contain references to Jesus' sufferings and glorification. These hymns, probably written for liturgical use in the administration of baptism or the Eucharist, may, together with the pre-Gospel Passion accounts already referred to, be rightly considered an initial step in the process which ended in the composition of the Gospels. Their very liturgical character will lead us to expect that a similar liturgical influence may be discovered in the work of our Evangelists. It is now time to illustrate this influence with further examples.

INCORPORATION OF CHRISTIAN LITURGICAL FORMULAE

The first illustration I should like to propose is the incorporation by the sacred writers of liturgical texts into their narratives. The most obvious instance of this occurs at the conclusion of the first Gospel, where the risen Christ gives His disciples their apostolic mandate.

> "Complete authority has been conferred on me
> in heaven as upon earth:
> therefore, go and make disciples
> of all the nations,
> by baptizing them
> 'in the Name of the Father,
> and of the Son,
> and of the Holy Spirit'. . . ." Mt 28:18–19)

Into this text, as many modern Catholic commentators admit,[11] the Evangelist has incorporated the baptismal formula already in common use in the Church of his day. The clearly liturgical character of the carefully constructed phrase with its highly developed Trinitarian orientation makes it very probable that the inspired writer has made Christ's command to baptize more explicit by introducing the words familiarly used in administering the sacrament. To assume that our Lord Himself would have made such a precise allusion to the Trinity antecedent to the pentecostal revelation is to shut one's eyes to the historical process by which Christian dogma was gradually imparted to the apostolic Church.

A similar example may be found in the Marcan account of the institution of the Eucharist (Mk 14:22–24). Modern non-Catholic critics have tended to deny the historical character of these verses because they contain no reference to the Passover supper. Moreover, it is claimed, the stereotyped, lapidary quality of these lines is not at all like the vivid, detailed description so characteristic of Mark, which can be found in the verses immediately preceding which form the introduction to this scene (vv. 12–21). It is sufficient, I think, to read these laconic lines to appreciate the force of these critics' contention that they have been interpolated into the text from elsewhere. "Now during the meal, He took some bread, blessed it, and broke it; He gave it to them and said, 'Take it. This is my body.' Then He took a cup, gave thanks, and gave it to them, and they all took a drink from it. And He said to them, 'This is my blood, covenant blood, to be shed for the rest of men.' "

Pierre Benoit has suggested a much better explanation of this abrupt change of style.[12] He admits an interpolation, but an interpolation due to Mark himself. When Mark comes to the description of Jesus' words and actions at the Last Supper in instituting the Eucharist, the Evangelist simply borrows the liturgical formula used in the Roman Church (tradition tells us Mark wrote his Gospel for Roman Christians) and inserts it into his text. Naturally, any reference to the Passover rite in such a liturgical recital would be omitted as unnecessary. Moreover, Benoit is also able to explain Mark's omission of Jesus' command of reiteration, which is retained by Luke and Paul, "Do this as a memorial of me" (Lk 22:19; 1 Cor 11: 24–25). As Benoit remarks, this is a rubric; and a rubric is not recited: it is simply put into execution.[13]

Mention may be made here of an interesting theory advanced by Oscar Cullmann, regarding the Marcan text recording the incident of Jesus' blessing the little children (Mk 10: 13–14).[14] Cullmann cites several texts in Acts containing traces of a primitive baptismal formula where the word "hinder" recurs (Acts 8:36; 10:47; 11:17). We shall cite only the first of these, in which the Ethiopian vizier remarks to Philip: "Here is water. What is to hinder my being baptized?" (Acts 8:36). When Jesus wishes to bless the children, He says to the disciples: "Allow the little children to come to me. Stop hindering them." Cullmann, while admitting that the story has nothing directly to do with baptism, suggests that it was preserved in the Gospel "to recall to the remembrance of Christians of that time an occurrence by which they might be led to a solution of the problem of infant baptism."[15]

LITURGICAL INFLUENCES ON GOSPEL NARRATIVES

We must now review a group of episodes which either owe their selection to liturgical interests or display some liturgical influence in the manner in which they are narrated.

In Mk 7:31–37 the cure of a deaf man whose speech was impaired presents a certain ritual character. In healing him, Jesus inserts His fingers into the man's ears, puts some of His own saliva on the man's tongue, and employs the word

"Ephphatha."[16] In Mk 8:22–26 we have an unusual miracle: the gradual cure of a blind man. Jesus again puts some of His own saliva on the man's eyes, lays hands on him, inquiring whether he can see anything. The man can see, but very imperfectly. Once more Jesus lays His hands on him, and the man's sight is completely restored. Mk 6:13 contains a detail about the mission of the Twelve which is not recorded by the other Evangelists: "and they anointed many sick people with oil and cured them." This aspect of the apostles' thaumaturgical activity was undoubtedly preserved on account of its symbolic significance for the sacrament of extreme unction.

In Lk 4:25–27 there is reference to two Old Testament miracle stories in which it is possible to see some sacramental typology.[17] The first is taken from the Elijah-cycle: the prophet's miraculous multiplication of the oil and meal for the widow in Sarepta (1 K 17:1–16). This miracle of the food which was constantly renewed might be considered a type of the Eucharist. The second story concerns Elisha's cure of the leper Naaman (2 K 5:1–15). The sevenfold washing in the River Jordan justifies the exploitation by the Fathers of the Church of its baptismal typology.[18]

It is, of course, in the fourth Gospel that we find the sacramental symbolism of the various miracles performed by Jesus developed most effectively. Oscar Cullmann remarks that one of John's principal aims is to show that the risen Christ, who is present always in the Church and in the sacraments, is the same Jesus of the public life.[19] The thesis is illustrated primarily with respect to the sacraments of the Eucharist and baptism. Thus the symbolism the Evangelist finds in the miracle of Cana (Jn 2:1–11) is at once baptismal (the water is changed into wine in jars used for Jewish purification rites) and Eucharistic (wine is a common biblical symbol of blood). The cure of the paralytic at the pool of Bethesda (Jn 5:1–9) with its simultaneous cure of disease and of sin, in which Christ replaces the healing angel, is baptismal in meaning. So also is the restoring of his sight to the blind man (Jn 9:1–39) whom Jesus commands to wash in a pool which, according to John, bears Christ's name (Siloe being interpreted as "Sent," that is, a synonym for the Messiah). Jesus' multiplication of the loaves (Jn 6:1–13), to which we shall have to return presently, is obviously Eucharistic. The same may perhaps be said of the cleansing of the Temple (Jn 2:12–22) and of Jesus' washing of the disciples' feet (Jn 13:1–20).[20] The incident of the piercing of Jesus' side, in which miraculous blood and water poured forth, contains an allusion to both the Eucharist and baptism, as the Fathers have pointed out.[21]

Bruce Vawter attempted, a few years ago, to carry somewhat further the investigation of Johannine sacramental symbolism.[22] He saw in the anointing at Bethany a reference to extreme unction, while Mary (constantly a symbol of the Church for John) by her presence at Cana's wedding "forecasts the sacramental nature of Christian marriage, once the glorification of Jesus is accomplished."[23] There are several Gospel narratives which, I believe, contain certain peculiar characteristics that can only be explained properly by the influence of the Christian liturgy. One of the best examples of this is John's version of the multiplication of the loaves (Jn 6:1–13). For the Evangelist, this episode is a type of the Eucharistic repast of the Church. He accordingly presents Jesus as the Messiah who gathers His followers about His own table and anticipates, by satisfying their desire for food, the Messianic banquet of the kingdom of God. John's story is strikingly different in several details from those found in Matthew, Mark, or Luke, as a brief comparison will show.

In the fourth Gospel the crowds come to Jesus, not to seek cures (as Mt 14:14 implies) or to be taught (as Mk 6:34

states), but rather to be fed. This can be seen from the first remark Jesus makes on catching sight of them: "Where shall we buy some loaves of bread, in order that these men may have a meal?" (Jn 6:5). John's allusion to the feast of the Pasch (Jn 6:4), constantly interpreted in the New Testament as a type of the Eucharist, also underscores the meaning of this incident. This meal in the wilderness of Trans-Jordan is thus related to the Passover supper, commemorating Israel's redemption from Egypt. It is, however, John's manner of describing Jesus' actions in performing the miracle which reveals his Eucharistic interpretation of the event. The Evangelist employs the same expression used in the Lucan narrative of the institution of the Eucharist (Lk 22:19): "And taking bread, after giving thanks, He broke and gave it to them saying, 'This is my body, to be given on your behalf.'" In the Johannine account of the multiplication of loaves we read: "Jesus then took the bread and, after giving thanks, He gave it round to them. . . ." In contrast with Matthew or Mark, John pictures Jesus Himself as feeding the crowd, "after giving thanks" over the bread, a Eucharistic term, and not merely "blessing" it, as in Matthew and Mark. Only in John do we find Jesus' command (which has reference only to the bread, not the fish), "Collect the pieces which are left over, lest any of them be wasted." The sequel to the episode is also peculiarly Johannine: "Now the people, seeing the sign He had performed, began to say, 'This man is really the Prophet who is to come into the world.'" Popular Jewish tradition had long associated the restoration of the manna provided by Moses with the works of the Messiah. And the manna is for John (Jn 6:31–33, 49–50) a symbol of the Eucharist.

Further instances of the influence of the Eucharistic liturgy upon the form taken by evangelical narratives may be seen in Luke's writing. We wish here to refer to a story found in Acts just before Paul and his companions suffer shipwreck (Acts 27:33–37), because it throws light upon the meaning of an episode in Luke's Gospel. "Until day began to dawn, Paul kept urging everyone to take food. 'For a fortnight now,' he said, 'you have been constantly on the watch, fasting the whole time and eating nothing. So I beg of you to take some food, because this is necessary for your safety. Not one of you will lose so much as a hair of his head.' Saying this and taking bread, he gave thanks to God before everyone, and breaking the bread he began to eat. Everyone took heart and they, in turn, took food. We were, in all, two hundred and seventy-six on board."

While there can be no question here of Paul's consecrating the bread (which all the sailors shared with him), still, on the other hand, there is little doubt but that Luke has told the story in such a way that it might serve to illustrate the effects of the Eucharist. Paul's remark, "This food is necessary for your safety" (the same Greek word means both safety and salvation), is most probably intended to remind the reader that it is the Eucharist which is the food of salvation. Paul's actions are, moreover, described according to the Eucharistic sequence: he took bread, gave thanks, broke it, and ate. Luke thus treats this episode in the way he and the other New Testament writers make use of Old Testament stories: for its typological value.

This story taken from Acts enables us to understand the incident of Jesus' breaking bread with the two disciples at Emmaus. "And it happened, after He took His place at table with them, that He took bread, blessed it, and having broken it, gave it to them. They, for their part, had their eyes opened, and they recognized Him" (Lk 24:30–31). Later, on returning to Jerusalem, these two favored disciples announce to the rest "how He became known to them through the breaking of the bread" (Lk 24:35). Here again there is no question of the celebration of the Eucharist by the risen Christ. Luke has told the story for its Eucharistic significance and has allowed Eucharistic terminology to influence his manner of describing the event, so that later Christians may learn that it is "through the breaking of the bread" that they will learn, by faith, to recognize Christ.

The Lucan account of the Last Supper (Lk 22:14–20) is a splendid instance of liturgical influence upon Gospel narrative. In fact, it might be called a piece of liturgical artistry. Luke presents, not a historical account of the institution of the Eucharist, but rather what one might almost call an "impressionist" picture-sequence, portraying the liturgical meaning of the Eucharistic sacrifice.[24] He does this by means of two carefully-worked-out tableaux which parallel each other very exactly. The first is a stylized version of the ancient Israelite ritual, the Passover supper, of which Luke has retained only the two elements that typify the Eucharist: the paschal lamb and the final ritual cup of wine. The second scene is a dramatic portrayal of the sacrifice of the new Israel, the Eucharistic liturgy.

Moreover, in order to show how the old Jewish liturgy recalling the exodus from Egypt is fulfilled in the new Christian sacrifice, the Evangelist manages to convey the impression that it is the same cup of wine, used by Jesus in celebrating the Pasch, which He later consecrates, thus constituting it the ratification of the new covenant between God and the Christian people.

This deeply theological and highly artistic literary conception has caused modern non-Catholic critics a good deal of difficulty. They tend to regard the twofold mention of the cup as the result of a textual interpolation. Their attempts to amend the text, by eliminating the consecration of the wine, is unacceptable to Catholics. In point of fact, this objection to what is termed the "longer form" of our text springs from a basic misunderstanding of what Luke is trying to express, viz., the meaning of the Eucharist as the Christian Pasch. He wishes to show that the Eucharist is the liturgical re-presentation of the supreme act of redemption performed by Jesus Christ which provides the basis of the new alliance. If we reread Luke's text with this in mind, the beauty of this liturgical lesson can scarcely be missed.

"And when the hour had arrived, He took His place at table surrounded by the apostles. Then He told them: 'I have been longing eagerly to eat this paschal lamb with you before my passion. I assure you, I shall not any longer eat it until it finds its fulfilment in God's kingdom.' Taking a cup, after giving thanks, He said: 'Take this and share it with one another. I assure you, I shall not drink the product of the vine from now on until God's kingdom becomes a reality.' "

Thus far the reader is given a neatly tailored account of the Passover ritual. It is to be noted that, after each of the significant items is mentioned (the paschal lamb and the cup of wine), Luke reports the words of Jesus which predict that this time-honored liturgy will reach its culmination in the Christian Eucharist. By the phrase "God's kingdom," which is to become a reality through Jesus' passion, Luke understands the Church.

In the second part of his diptych the Evangelist portrays the institution of the Eucharist. "And taking bread, He broke it, after giving thanks, and gave it to them, saying: 'This is my body, to be given on your behalf. Do this as a memorial of me.' Similarly, the cup also, at the end of supper, saying: 'This cup is the new covenant sealed with my blood, to be shed on your behalf.' "

One small detail in this second picture is of some importance: Luke's use of the definite article before the word "cup." In his account of the Passover rite, Luke had described Jesus as "taking *a* cup," while here he pictures him as taking "*the* cup," that same cup, to consecrate it. This significant literary device is the *trait d'union* uniting the two scenes into a harmonious unity. It explains the profound connection between the Israelite and the Christian liturgies. In fact, it might also be regarded as Luke's commentary upon a remark of his master, St. Paul: "Christ, *our* paschal lamb, has been sacrificed" (1 Cor 5:7).

ISRAELITE LITURGICAL INFLUENCES ON THE GOSPELS

We have finally to inquire whether the liturgical observances of Israel have left any traces upon our Gospels. Given the origins of Christianity, it would be surprising if these books did not in some way reflect the sacrificial and festal practices of the old religion.

The accounts of Jesus' Transfiguration, which are given by the first three Evangelists, contain, I believe, some references to the feast of Booths or Tabernacles. Peter, who sees in this dazzling apparition the inauguration of the Messianic times, to which the feast of Tabernacles looked forward, automatically remarks: "Let us put up three booths: one for you, and one for Moses, and one for Elijah" (Mk 9:5; Mt 17:4; Lk 9:33). A feature of the feast of Tabernacles was the erection of little bowers of branches under which every Israelite must live during seven days (Lv 23:42–43). These booths, recalling the Hebrews' forty years in the desert, also symbolized the mansions of the just in the Messianic kingdom.[25] Another principal event during the feast was the nightly illumination of the Temple, recalling the "blazing pillar" (Wis 18:3) that accompanied Israel during her nocturnal flight from

Egypt (Ex 13:21). All three accounts of the Transfiguration agree in making light its predominant characteristic and employ various metaphors to describe the brilliance of Jesus' countenance and the brightness of His clothing. In addition, the Matthean and Lucan narratives describe the cloud which overshadowed the disciples as "a *bright* cloud." And when we consider that Luke implies—by his remark, "Peter and his companions had been overcome by sleep" (Lk 9:32)—that the event took place at night, we have a further connection with the fiery cloud of the Exodus and the nightly illumination of Tabernacles. The Messianic expectations which this feast aroused in late Judaism are reflected in the presence of Elijah at the Transfiguration, since he was believed to return as precursor of the Christ (cf. Mal 3:1–3; 4:5–6; Sir 48:10). The appearance of Moses recalls the feast of the "Joy of the Law" celebrated at the close of the seven-day festival of Tabernacles. It marked the termination of the liturgical reading of the five books of Moses. Thus the Evangelists' accounts of the Transfiguration seem to indicate that, in their eyes and that of the apostolic Church, this mystery was the fulfilment of the liturgical symbolism of the greatest of all Israelite feasts, that of Tabernacles.

Jean Daniélou has remarked upon the relation between the narratives of Jesus' triumphal entry into Jerusalem and the feast of Tabernacles.[26] The palm branches carried by Jesus' disciples, the chanting of the hosanna (Ps 118 formed part of the music sung at the feast of Tabernacles), and the procession, all suggest the liturgy of this feast.[27] Daniélou concludes that "the entry with the palms appears as the realization of the true feast of Tabernacles at the end of days."[28] Whether or not one would admit Daniélou's further contention, viz., that Jesus' Messianic entry into Jerusalem occurred, not immediately before the last Pasch of His mortal life, but at the end of the month of September, when Tabernacles was observed, it seems clear that the Gospel accounts of this mystery of Jesus' public life display some influence of the liturgy of that Jewish feast.

Again, it is interesting to note how the beginning and the close of Luke's Gospel are dominated by liturgical themes. In the opening scene, Zachary is engaged in performing the age-old rite of the evening incense-offering. Indeed, as René Laurentin has pointed out in his new fascinating study of this Infancy Gospel, the perspective of these first two chapters of Luke is determined by three motifs which are basically liturgical: Jerusalem, the Temple, and Israelite cult.[29] At the end of his Gospel, the Evangelist suggests how, thanks to the events which have intervened since the opening section of his book, the whole concept of divine cult has been revolutionized. He pictures the apostles, after Christ's ascension from Mount Olivet, as returning to worship the Father in the Temple. "But they in turn [the apostles], after having adored Him [Jesus Christ], returned to Jerusalem with great joy. And they were constantly in the Temple glorifying God [the Father]" (Lk 24:52–53). Here we have Luke's conception of the new religion expressed in liturgical terms: the apostles adore the God of Israel, whom they now know as the Father, after adoring His Son, Jesus Christ.

Finally, it remains to consider, by means of a few instances, how much the narratives and even the whole structure of the fourth Gospel owe to the liturgy of Israel. The first example we might mention is John's representation of Jesus as the new Paschal Lamb, at the moment of His condemnation by Pilate. "Now Pilate, after hearing these words, had Jesus brought out and took his seat on the bench in the place called Lithostrotos, or Gabbatha in Hebrew. It was the day for the preparation of the paschal lamb. The time was around noon" (Jn 19:

13–14). This reference by John to the hour when Pilate imposed the death sentence has long constituted a difficulty, since it appears to contradict Mark's statement that "it was about nine in the morning when they crucified Him" (Mk 15:25). The solution, it seems, is to understand John's remark as a theological rather than a chronological one. At noon on the day of preparation, the priests in the Temple began the slaughter of the lambs to be used at the Passover supper (which, according to the official, lunar calendar of Jerusalem, was celebrated the evening of Jesus' death). The Evangelist merely wishes to point out Christ's role as the new Pasch, by stating that He was condemned to death at the hour of the "preparation" of the paschal lambs.

The most pervading influence of Jewish liturgy to be seen in the fourth Gospel, however, is the way John appears to have articulated the whole structure of his Gospel by means of the Israelite feast-cycle. The most satisfactory analysis of John's plan, it seems to me, is that worked out by Donatien Mollat.[30] He shows how the Evangelist has grouped the various events and discourses he records around three Passover feasts (Jn 1:19—3:21; 6:1–71; 11:55—19:42), a Sabbath (Jn 5:1–47), a feast of Tabernacles (Jn 7:1—10:21), and a feast of the Dedication of the Temple (Jn 10:22—11:54). Two sections of the Gospel are intentionally left unrelated to the Jewish calendar: the interlude in Samaria (Jn 3:22—4:54), because Jesus is sojourning in the land of schism; and the events of Christ's risen life (Jn 20:1—21:23), when John discards the Israelite liturgical cycle for the new, Christian "first day of the week" (Jn 20:1).

We may conclude this study of the liturgical influences operative in the formation of our Gospels by recalling a thesis Karl Rahner has stated in his brilliant essay on inspiration, as it concerns the New Testament.[31] For Rahner, the Gospels, like the other New Testament books, are the literary expression of the Church's profound and infallible consciousness of her God-given function and her divinely directed life. The inspired writers were somehow aware that, in writing their Gospels, they were recording for Christian posterity this awareness of the apostolic Church as regards her mission and her character. Because they shared this common early Christian consciousness, the Evangelists possessed a norm for selecting those incidents from the life of Christ or those utterances of His which displayed the nature of the institution He founded.

If Rahner's theory is valid, then we can expect the Gospels to exhibit the various facets of the Church's life. They will, in the first place, express her teaching role, which will include the development of that body of doctrine left her by her Founder, as well as the unerring interpretation of the meaning of Jesus' words and actions. They will reflect, secondly, the Church's defense of her beliefs and of the Christian way of life. They will, finally, reflect the liturgical life of the Church, her public worship of the Triune God.

Thus, as we have undertaken to suggest in this chapter, the Evangelists will record those words and actions of Christ which form the basis of the Church's liturgical practices. They will employ the data provided them by tradition to imbue their Christian readers with a sense of liturgical worship, by underscoring the symbolism of the sacraments. They will occasionally incorporate key texts from the liturgy of their age in order to show how it took its origin from the words and will of Christ, or to point up the analogy between the Church's liturgical actions and the more significant words and gestures of Jesus during His earthly life.

To become a Christian in the full sense of that word, it is necessary to relive by personal experience all the great events of the divinely-inspired salvation history. The Church has been entrusted with the two great means by which the individual Christian can realize this: the Scriptures and the liturgy. Since, as we have tried to show, these two have operated in conjunction from the earliest age of Christianity, it is only to be expected that the nascent liturgy of the Church should have left some impression on the inspired records of New Testament salvation which are our four Gospels.

6

The New Testament Doctrine of Baptism

ACCORDING to Paul, there are two sources upon which the apostolic Church drew in its attempts to express the various aspects of the Christian mystery: the experience of the first disciples, and the events of Israel's sacred history as they found them recorded in "the Scriptures." In the concluding doxology of his letter to Rome, Paul expresses his conviction that God will strengthen and deepen the Christian faith in that community "through my gospel and the kerygma of Jesus Christ—the revelation of a mystery, wrapt in silence throughout countless ages, but now disclosed—and through the prophetic Scriptures" (Rom 16:25–26). The experience of Jesus' first disciples must be characterized by the events which formed its climax. It was predominantly paschal and pentecostal, an experience of the risen Christ and of the Holy Spirit. Yet it also included the happenings of Jesus' public life and even the career of John the Baptist. As for the insights into the meaning of Christianity which the inspired writers of the New Testament drew from the Old, they are the fruit of a profound and acute consciousness of the harmony existing between the two phases of the divine plan of salvation, the old and the new dispensations.[1] This awareness leads Paul to formulate the hermeneutical principle which is the foundation of any Christian reading of the Old Testament: "these things occurred as examples of ourselves" (1 Cor 10:6); "whatever was written in the past has been written for our instruction" (Rom 15:4).

These two factors, which presided over the development of Christian theology as it makes its appearance in the New Testament, merit closer inspection.

THE CHRISTIAN CONCEPTION OF SALVATION

As I have pointed out elsewhere,[2] the real novelty of the Christian notion of salvation lies in the primitive Church's realization of her possession of the Holy Spirit, whose presence had formed her into the new Israel and had revealed to her the divinity of the exalted Lord Jesus. Accordingly, it is to the pentecostal experience of the first disciples that the explicitation of their specifically Christian beliefs must be ascribed. Rudolf Bultmann has recently been insisting upon the character of Christianity as an event,[3] and it is thanks to him, as L. Malevez remarks,[4] that the modern theologian has been led to ask himself the question "how, on the one hand, Christ, who has appeared historically and visibly before us, and, on the other, the Spirit, who operates invisibly, succeed in forming a single Word." This integration of the activity of the risen Christ with the operation of the Holy Spirit, which constitutes the unique character of the Christian encounter with God, springs historically and theologically from the events of the day of Pentecost—a point of which, perhaps, Bultmann has not taken sufficient cognizance.

Thus it is this transforming presence of the Spirit, at once the gift of the glorified Christ through the mediation of His risen humanity (Jn 7:39) and the witness to Christ's *sessio ad dexteram Patris* (Acts 2:33), which distinguishes Christianity, a radically eschatological religion, from the Judaism contemporary with Christian origins, characterized by a forward-looking Messianism and a scrupulous devotion to the Mosaic code. Where the Jew looked to Yahweh for salvation through the sole intermediary of the law, the apostolic Christian, aware that he already possessed salvation in part through the risen Christ's gift of the Spirit, hoped to obtain salvation's fulness through the one Mediator, his Lord Jesus, exalted at God's right hand. To appreciate how wide was the gulf which separated the Messianic and legalistic outlook of the best circles of contemporary Judaism from apostolic Christianity, we have only to recall the contrast that exists between the exegesis of certain Old Testament texts elaborated by the sectaries of Qumrân and the understanding of those same texts which is evidenced by New Testament writers.

One passage is Is 40:3 ff., which holds such a prominent place in the Gospel traditions concerning John the Baptist's preaching. In the Qumrân community rule, it is explained in function of the Torah:[5] it is the assiduous study and scrupulous observance of the Mosaic law which will prepare the convenanters for the coming of the Messiah. According to our Evangelists,[6] the Baptist employed this text not to inculcate the practice of the law but rather to insist upon *metanoia,* a radical change in men's religious attitudes, finding expression in the social virtues of justice and charity, as the necessary preparation for the advent of the Christ. It is as heir of Israel's prophetic traditions, not of her legalism, that the New Testament portrays John the Baptist.[7]

A second passage, Jer 2:13,[8] is explained in the sectarian writings as follows: "The well is the law, and they who digged it are the penitents of Israel who went forth out of the land of Judah and sojourned in the land of Damascus" (CDC 8, 6). The writer of the fourth Gospel, on the other hand, in what is almost surely a reference to this same text, indicates

Christ as the well: "If any man thirsts, he must come to me and drink—that is, he who has faith in me. According to the scriptural saying, 'from His heart shall flow floods of living water'" (Jn 7:38).[9]

The immediate cause of this divergence of the Christian from the Jewish point of view was Pentecost, which transfigured the Messianic expectations of the apostolic Church into a firm faith in the presence of their risen Lord among them through the Holy Spirit. Thanks to it, they are made aware of Jesus' divinity, of the Spirit's personality, of the inauguration of "the last times" in its first phase, which would extend until the eagerly awaited day of Christ's parousia. Moreover, they began, in the light of the Spirit, to reassess the theological significance[10] of the events of Jesus' earthly life and the work of the Baptist. This deeper penetration into the meaning of the events which formed the Christian kerygma of salvation would attain its full perfection in the fourth Gospel, but it can be seen already operative in the Synoptic literature.[11] That this whole development is the result of the apostles' encounter with the Spirit is attested by the last of the Evangelists: "the advocate, the Holy Spirit, whom the Father will send in place of myself, will teach you everything and will recall to you all I have myself spoken to you" (Jn 14:26).

THE CHRISTIAN VIEW OF ISRAEL'S SACRED HISTORY

How early the Christian community began to seek, in the great events of Old Testament salvation history, clues for the interpretation of the *res christiana,* is difficult to say. The first extensive use of the method, which Jesus had Himself undoubtedly employed in His public teaching and which the author of Hebrews will ultimately erect into a system of Christian hermeneutics, is credited in the New Testament to

Stephen (Acts 7:2–53). It is very probable that it was further developed in the Hellenist-founded Church at Antioch (cf. Acts 13:16–41), which became the heir of Stephen's viewpoint and which was mainly responsible for the formation of Saul as future apostle of the Gentiles. The basis of this method of Old Testament interpretation is the insight that there exists a fundamentally identical pattern in God's dialogue with His people in the old dispensation and in the new which supplanted it. This conviction is expressed in Hebrews' remark that, while the old law was ephemeral and relative, and "brought nothing to fulfilment," still it served God's providential purpose as "introduction to a brighter hope" (Heb 7:19). Because they were aware that the Old Testament history bore a transcendental relation to the Christ-event,[12] the preachers and inspired writers of the apostolic age made use of that history to express their experience of the Christian mystery in all its aspects.[13]

A concise formulation of this principle may be seen in St. Thomas' discussion of the *sensus spiritualis*. "The course of history is so ordered that such a meaning may be taken from it. This prerogative of so ordering history belongs solely to Him who through His providence governs history, God alone. Just as a man, in order to signify something, may employ words or imaginary comparisons, so God, for the expression of some things, employs the course of history, which is subject to His providence."[14] On the view of the New Testament authors, this sense of Israel's sacred history is revealed in "the Scriptures." Moreover, it is this interpretation of the events of this ancient salvation history, *as it is recorded upon the sacred page*,[15] which unveils their true meaning. The characteristically modern question, "What 'really' happened in the crossing of the Red Sea, the capture of Jericho, the restoration after the Exile, etc.?", is alien to the mind of these writers.

To their way of looking at the sacred past, what *really* happened is what God has deigned to announce to them in the Book. It is crucial for any appreciation of this long-forgotten viewpoint to recognize how justified the New Testament authors were in employing that religious-historical perspective which springs from a deep consciousness of the consistency of God's salvific action throughout the course of Hebrew and Christian history. Thanks to this insight, the prophets and inspired scribes of the New Testament were enabled to discern the full signification of Christ's redemptive activity.

FRAME OF REFERENCE OF NEW TESTAMENT SACRAMENTAL THEOLOGY

In view of what we have thus far said, it will not be surprising to discover that the New Testament writers constantly employed as frame of reference for their explanation of the meaning and efficacy of Christian sacramental symbolism a threefold division of the history of salvation. This division is related to the coming of Jesus Christ, which gives to the story of God's dealings with men its essential significance. It comprises (1) the period before Christ, (2) Christ's earthly and mortal life, (3) Christ's glorified and heavenly existence, which extends to include the life of His Body, the Church on earth. As we hope to demonstrate by a study of the New Testament doctrine of baptism, it was on this triple level that the inspired authors primarily sought to discover the meaning of the Christian sacraments, those "signs of the end"[16] which effectively reproduce, for subsequent generations of believers, the pentecostal experiences of the first disciples.[17] Moreover, the "natural" symbolism of the sacramental elements, washing (water), food (bread, wine), healing or strengthening (oil), which strikes our modern mentality as so important,[18] does not appear to have constituted for the apostolic age the prima-facie signification of the sacramental signs. If they employed such symbolism, as they occasionally did, it was simply because they had found it already designated by the events of their sacred history. At any rate, we venture to assert that this natural symbolism of the sacramental system never carried the same weight with the New Testament thinkers as did the other, to us less obvious, symbolism.[19]

One of the best examples of New Testament sacramental theology, in which these three levels of sacred history are employed, is found in the Johannine discourse on the Bread of Life (Jn 6:26–65), which teaches the efficacious symbolism of the Eucharist. The reader's attention is concentrated upon the importance of symbolism almost from the beginning of the sermon. "Then what sign (*sēmeion*) do you perform, that we may see and find faith in you?" (v. 30). A reference to a Psalm, commemorative of the miracles of the Exodus and the wandering in the desert, gives Jesus the occasion to point out the true relation between the manna, "the bread from heaven" (Ps 78:24–25), and the Eucharistic bread, "the truly divine bread from heaven" (Jn 6:31–32). Next, the meaning of the Eucharist is sought in the life-giving Incarnation of the Son of God (vv. 33–35), in Jesus' public ministry (vv. 38–40),[20] in a reference to the words of institution and to Jesus' redemptive death: "It is my flesh, given for the life of the world" (v. 51).[21] In the sequel, the Eucharistic symbolism is shown to derive also from Christ's exaltation and His gift of the Spirit (vv. 61–63).[22] As is evident from a literary analysis,[23] the key word in this dialogue-discourse, "bread," is used in four different senses to designate the bread of the miracle of multiplication, the manna, the Word Incarnate, and the Eucharist. What must be noted, however, is that these four meanings are closely interrelated. Each of the first three adds a new depth to the Eucharistic symbolism attaching to the fourth sense, the body of the exalted Christ, who bestows, in this sacrament, the Holy Spirit upon those who have faith in Him.

SYMBOLISM AND SACRAMENTAL EFFICACY

There are two important consequences which flow from this New Testament view of the symbolism of the Christian sacraments. It provides, in the first place, a vehicle for the expression of the efficacy of the sacraments in the order of grace. Secondly, it enables the inspired writers to distinguish sharply this sacramental efficacy from magic.

Because of their sensitivity to the divine orientation of Israel's history towards the central events of salvation, the New Testament writers were well aware that behind the Old Testament figures of the Christian sacraments lay the dynamic will of God with its creative power. Moreover, familiarity with the Old Testament had taught them the efficacious value of the signs which Yahweh had granted to His people: the rainbow, circumcision, the sprinkled blood ratifying the covenant given through Moses.[24] This creation of effective symbolism was for them but another instance of a divine activity: the imposition of names, upon things at the creation of the world, upon persons in the course of Old Testament history. On the biblical view, such God-given names were not equivocal (as in Greek philosophy) but expressed the reality of the things or persons to which they had been attached.[25] Thus, in regard to the sacramental symbols, whose meaning had been divinely determined by means of their types occurring throughout sacred history from the creation to the apostolic age, the New Testament authors found means to express their efficacy by relating them to the revealed salvation history. The efficacious symbolism of the Eucharist, for example, as the divine "bread from heaven" "giving life to the world" comes not only from the words of institution but also from the feeding of God's people with manna, from Jesus' multiplication of the loaves during His public ministry, and, above all, from the glorification of His sacred humanity endowing it with the power of communicating the Spirit, author of the divine life of grace.

This linking of sacraments to sacred history also enabled the New Testament writer to remove any misapprehension that there was something magical about the operation of these signs. The Johannine discourse on the Eucharist warns the Christian emphatically against such a false view, by means of references to each of the three levels of sacred history from which the sacrament derives its effective symbolism. The first caveat is connected with the miracle of multiplication. "I can assure you that you are looking for me, not because you have seen signs, but because you ate some of the loaves and had your fill" (Jn 6:26). Instead of recognizing the sign of some deeper mystery in the miraculous bread, the Jews have eyes only for bread in the "sign," or miracle. Faith on the part of the recipient is necessary for full sacramental efficacy. The second warning, like that of Paul to the Corinthians (1 Cor 10:5), recalls an incident of Old Testament history. "Your fathers ate manna in the desert, but they are dead" (v. 49). God's favor is not bestowed through the sacrament without man's co-operation. The final warning occurs through Jesus' remark stressing the relation between His glorified humanity and the Spirit in this sacrament. "The Spirit it is who bestows life: the flesh counts for nothing" (v. 63). This statement refutes any crassly materialistic view of the consumption of Christ's body in the Eucharist, and indirectly stresses also the need of the proper dispositions in those who receive it.

Given the attitude of the New Testament authors toward sacramental symbolism, we shall endeavor to present a synthesis of their teaching on the nature of baptism and its effects by relating it to the three levels of sacred history which we have already discussed. We shall begin by recalling the great episodes in the Old Testament which contributed to the meaning of the sacrament. Then we shall discuss the events of Jesus' earthly life which the Evangelists narrate in order to explain the origins of baptism. Finally, we shall review the effects of Christ's exaltation and His sending of the Spirit, upon the symbolism of this rite of initiation into His Body, the Church.

The method will be found to possess the advantage of removing certain false questions from a discussion of the origins of baptism. The imposition upon exegesis and theology, at the close of the Middle Ages, of a methodological viewpoint (the product of the enthusiasm of the discoverers of canonical law) which we may call "juridical," has long exercised a preponderance as unwarranted as it is deleterious.[26] Thus, with reference to baptism, there is much effort spent in attempting to determine the precise moment at which Christ instituted it. Such legalism can, at times, lead to some rather bizarre "theological" conclusions: for example, insistence upon the reception of Christian baptism by the apostles some time before the first Holy Thursday, to safeguard the validity of their reception of orders and the Eucharist.[27]

In contrast with such methods, the one here adopted after the example of the New Testament writers themselves has the merit of directing attention to the precise meaning of the sacramental sign which is baptism, and so revealing to us its purpose and its effects.

BAPTISMAL SYMBOLISM DRAWN FROM OLD TESTAMENT HISTORY

In the course of a striking description of the genesis of Christian thought as "essentially a transformation of images," effected by the death of Christ ("the decisive act of transformation") and the presence of the Spirit in the apostolic Church, Austin Farrer very aptly observes that "since the process is of the rebirth of images, it is to the matrix of images, the Old Testament, that the Spirit continually leads; for here are images awaiting rebirth; all this is Christ, could we but see how and why; the Spirit will teach us."[28]

When we turn to a consideration of the Old Testament images exploited by the New Testament writers in their endeavor to describe the baptismal mystery, we find that in their works they lay under tribute almost all the great *gesta Dei* in Israel's salvation history: the creation, the Deluge, the promise to Abraham with its sign, circumcision, the exodus from Egypt, the wandering in the desert, the covenant established through Moses, together with the poignant presentation of it in the prophetic writings as Yahweh's espousals with His people, and (perhaps) even Israel's crossing of the Jordan under Joshua.

The Creation

Because of the fact that the accounts of creation stand at the head of the biblical revelation in the beginning of Genesis, we have long been accustomed to open our catechetical instructions by the question "Who made the world?", and to give to that problem a place of primacy which it never actually enjoyed in Israel's religious experiences of her God.[29] Moreover, the logical structure of Scholastic theology has assigned to the treatise on creation a place which has led us to regard that divine activity as cosmological rather than soteriological.[30] Accordingly, it comes as something of a surprise to find a theologian like Paul describing Christ's redemptive work as a "new creation" (2 Cor 5:17). At best, we think it an arresting metaphor expressive of the novelty of the Christian order.

However, the Old Testament view was that the covenant was primary in God's self-revelation to Israel. The point of departure of Old Testament religion was, historically speaking, summed up in the dictum "You shall be my people, and I will be your God" (Jer 31:33; Ex 19:5). God carried on His part of the dialogue with Israel through a long succession of saving acts performed in their favor. As a result, the Old Testament places quite a different emphasis upon the doctrine of creation. Secondary in Old Testament revelation, both historically and theologically, to the covenant idea, the doctrine of creation was incorporated relatively late into the Hebrews' sacred accounts of their own origins, where it functioned as a kind of prologue to the story of that people's relations with their covenant-God.[31] And so it happened that creation was set forth in that literature as the beginning of the mighty wonders Yahweh had wrought for Israel. Because they were accustomed to consider cosmic origins as the beginning of the salvation history, the later Old Testament writers found it quite natural to express the eschatological salvation of "the last times," the climax of Yahweh's interventions on behalf of His chosen people, as a second and more marvelous creation. The view of Deutero-Isaiah is that Yahweh will work Israel's definitive salvation *as creator* (Is 43:18–19; 48:6 ff.; cf. also 65:17 ff.), for the reason that God's creation of the universe is thought of as pertaining to the same theological category as His covenant (Is 51:15–16; cf. also 66:22). This conception of the saving event is, I believe, the basis of the biblical view that the *eschaton* must correspond to the beginning, that eschatology, in other words, is determined by protology or ktisiology.

What is true of Old Testament literature holds good also for that of the New, in which the creation theme is pressed into the service of soteriology.[32] In fact, it may be asserted that the concept of "the new creation," together with its counterpart, the idea of regeneration or birth anew, forms the most apt expression of the salvation revealed in Jesus.[33] Paul portrays the Christian who has, through faith and baptism, found a share in Christ's redemption, as "a new creature" or "a new creation" (Gal 6:15; 2 Cor 5:17), while the notion of rebirth is found applied to various aspects of Christian salvation in a series of New Testament writings (Mt 19:28; Jn 3:3 ff.; Eph 2:4–6; 1 Jn *passim*; 1 Pt 1:3, 23; 2:2). Paul is thinking of baptism in terms of creation when he states: "We are indeed His work, having been once created in Christ Jesus in view of good works, which God prepared beforehand for us to practice" (Eph 2:10). The thought of baptism is also perhaps implicit in James' remark: "Of set purpose, He engendered us through the message of truth, in order that we might be a kind of first fruits among His creatures" (Jas 1:18). The very original Pauline conception of Christ as the last Adam, the new Adam, the second Adam, which he first hit upon in a period of controversy (1 Cor 15:22, 45) and then made the focal point in his soteriology (Rom 5:12 ff.), was at a later period recast to express the mystery par excellence, the new Christian unity of Jew and Gentile in the Body of Christ (Eph 2:15; 4:12–13, 24). The inauguration of this "new Man" in the lives of individual Christians is the unrepeatable rite[34] of baptism. "Do not play one another false, seeing that you once stripped off the old man with his practices and put on the new man, newly formed in the image of his creator . . ." (Col 3:9–10).[35]

Of all the divine activities in the beginning, it was the creation of light which the author of the first creation-account in Genesis appears to have found most impressive and mysterious (Gn 1:3). It strikes the modern reader as strange that the priestly writer should have described light's creation before that of sun or moon. Apart from the motives dictated by a practical apologetic interest,[36] it would seem that light, in the author's estimation, held a paramount position among God's irrational creatures. It was considered of no less importance by the author of the fourth Gospel, who saw that the life emanating from the Word "was the light of men" (Jn 1:4). And he can think of no better way to describe the Word Himself than as "the true light which illuminates every man" (Jn 1:9). Accordingly, this biblical emphasis upon the creation of light provided an apt vehicle for the presentation of New Testament baptismal doctrine.

The whole episode of the healing of the man blind from birth (Jn 9:1–41) forms a kind of baptismal catechesis, in which Christ, the author of the sacrament, figures as "light of the world" (Jn 9:5). In what is primarily a reference to his own conversion by the Damascus road, Paul includes the baptismal experience of his readers and recalls the biblical account of the creation of light. "The God who had said, 'Light, shine out of darkness,' is He who has shone into our hearts to produce the illumination of the knowledge of God's glory reflected upon the countenance of Christ" (Cor 4:6). He urges the Colossians to persevere "in thanking the Father, who entitled you to share the lot of the saints in the light, who once rescued us from the dominion of darkness and transferred us into the realm of His dear Son, in whom we possess the redemption, the remission of sins" (Col 1:12–14). After reminding the Gentile Ephesians that "once you were sheer darkness, but now light in the Lord," the Apostle urges them to "conduct yourselves as children of light" and to avoid "the sterile works of darkness," "since everything that comes to light is light" (Eph 5:8–13). This last obscure remark seems to contain a promise of victory for all believers through their rejection of pagan immorality, and thus forms an introduction to what is probably a fragment of a baptismal liturgy:

> Awake, you slumberer,
> and rise from the dead!
> Then Christ will illuminate you. (Eph 5:14)

A clear reference to baptism as an illumination occurs in the famous Hebrews' passage on "impossible repentance." "It is in fact impossible to renew again, by bringing to repentance, those who have once been illuminated, who have tasted the heavenly gift, who have received a share of the Holy Spirit, who have savored the glorious word of God and the dynamism of the world to come, and yet have fallen . . ." (Heb 6:4–6).

Finally, in connection with the use of the creation theme to expound baptismal doctrine, we must mention the paradise motif, which New Testament writers do not neglect. The very brief Marcan description of Christ sojourning in the desert among wild beasts after His baptism by John is couched in terms of the new Adam in the new paradise.[37] In the Apocalypse, baptism is called "the river of life" (possibly also "the tree of life") by the adaptation of a text from Ezekiel,[38] which in turn draws on the descriptions of the terrestrial paradise in Gn 2–3.[39]

Noah: the Deluge and the Ark

The Petrine letters make use of the symbolism of the Deluge in exposing their teaching on baptism. The first instance occurs in a discussion of the cosmic effects of Christ's death and resurrection: "God's patience, in the days of Noah, waited eagerly while the ark was being made ready, in which a few people, eight persons to be exact, were saved by the water, which now saves you also—I mean its antitype, baptism" (1 Pt 3:20–21). Such a conception of the Deluge as a saving act of Yahweh may be traced back to the book of Genesis itself. There, in fact, we may distinguish, skilfully interwoven in the account of the flood, two quite different emphases.[40] The Yahwist writer, more concerned with man's sinfulness, takes a pessimistic view of this destructive flood; the priestly writer, on the other hand, who loves to dwell on the divine activity, stresses it as a divine act of salvation, issuing in the Noachic covenant which God plans to establish (Gn 6:18; 9:11, 16) with the man He has delivered from the midst of the wicked. There is, however, also one remark of the Yahwist which provides a probable source for the later theological developments on the Deluge: "Yahweh did away with all being existing on the surface of the earth, from man to beasts, reptiles and birds. They were blotted off the earth, so that Noah alone was left, and those who were with him in the ark" (Gn 7:23).

In late Judaism there was a tendency to consider the Deluge in its more positive and salutary aspects, and to connect it with the remnant doctrine, as we see from Ben Sira's "Praise of the Fathers":

> Noah was found perfectly just,
> in the time of wrath he was the offshoot.

> Thanks to him a remnant was left upon earth
> when the Deluge occurred. (Sir 44:17)

A remarkable passage in Deutero-Isaiah compares the return from the Exile with the Deluge: both are saving judgments of Yahweh executed in favor of His people.

> "For a little moment did I forsake you:
> but with great pity will I bring you back to me.
> In an outburst of wrath I hid my face
> for a moment from you:
> but with eternal kindness will I take pity on you,"
> says the Lord, your redeemer.
> "Because like the days of Noah is this to me.
> As I swore that the waters of Noah
> should no more pass over the earth,
> so have I sworn to be angry no more with you,
> nor to rebuke you." (Is 54:7–9)

Israel's restoration thus appears as a "new deluge," a mighty act of salvation. It is this line of thought which culminates in the Petrine theology of baptism.[41] Jesus' own reference to the Deluge in His description of His own divine visitation in triumph upon the ruins of the Temple (Mt 24:37–41)[42] undoubtedly was a formative factor in such a development.

The second Petrine passage does not make such a clearly baptismal use of the Deluge story, although it does appear to regard the Flood as a means of Noah's salvation: "He did not spare the ancient world, but preserved eight persons among whom was Noah, a preacher of holiness, by inflicting the Deluge upon the godless world" (2 Pt 2:5).[43]

Abraham: the Promise, Circumcision

As the "father of us all" (Rom 4:16), Abraham commanded the attention of the inspired writers of the New Testament as he did those of the Old. "No one has been found equal to him in glory," says Ben Sira (Sir 44:19b). Paul, who likes to dwell upon Abraham's faith, describes its object as God the Creator, who "raises the dead and summons nothingness to existence" (Rom 4:17), thereby making it equivalent to the Christian's faith in Christ's death and resurrection (Rom 4:23–25). Hebrews mentions this same aspect of Abraham's faith, and remarks that his recovery of his son Isaac, the result of his belief that "God is powerful enough even to raise the dead," was "a parable," or type—either of the general resurrection or of Christ's (Heb 11:17–19). However, the author of Hebrews devotes most of his praise of Abraham's faith to its connection with the divine promise (Heb 11:8–18), mentioned repeatedly in the book of Genesis (Gn 13:15–17; 15:5; 17:5–8; 18:18).

In Paul's earliest sketch of a baptismal theology (Gal 3:26—4:7), the sacrament figures as the means whereby the Gentiles, who cannot be considered Abraham's *sperma,* or heirs by blood of the divine promise made to him (cf. Gal 3:16), can lay claim to his inheritance. A parallel argument is worked out in Rom 4:9–12 in terms of faith and justification, the complementary elements in New Testament baptismal doctrine. As Paul Démann has pointed out,[44] the question of descendance from Abraham became an acute problem in predominantly Gentile Christian communities, whose members, unlike the Jewish Christians, had no racial ties with the greatest of the patriarchs; what basis of hope had they of sharing the blessings God had promised to Abraham? In answering that question, Paul shows how important was Abraham's promise in the biblical doctrine of salvation, and how it enters into the signification of baptism. He lays the groundwork for his argument by providing his reader with a typically rabbinical piece of exegesis on the use of *sperma* in the singular. "Now it was to Abraham that the promises were addressed, and to his descendant. Scripture does not say 'and to his descendants,' as if there were question of more than one. It points only to one,' 'and to your descendant,' that is, to Christ" (Gal 3:16). The argument, which involves baptism, is stated somewhat later in the same chapter. "You are all God's sons by faith in Christ Jesus. You have all indeed, because baptized in Christ, put on Christ. There is no room for 'Jew' or 'Greek,' no room for 'slave' or 'free,' no room for 'male' or 'female': all of you constitute but one Man in Christ Jesus. And if you are Christ's, you are Abraham's descendant, heirs according to the promise" (Gal 3:26–29). The "putting on Christ," an effect of baptism, is clearly intended by Paul as equivalent to "constituting one Man in Christ Jesus."[45] In other words, we are dealing here with an instance of the doctrine habitually taught by Paul: the identification of the Christian with Christ (1 Cor 6:17; 2 Cor 5:14; Gal 2:20). It is essential to his line of argumentation here. This adoptive Abrahamitic filiation of the Gentiles becomes in turn a type of the divine adoption which it was Christ's mission to bestow through the gift of the Holy Spirit (Gal 4:4–6). Thus one might say that, on Paul's view, Abraham's significance in baptismal theology is a profound one: he forms, with Christ, a link in the supernatural chain uniting the Christian to the Father as an adoptive son. Hence there is no break in the history of salvation as it is unfolded in sacred history.[46] God's part in the dialogue between Himself and men is a consistent one, and Abraham is not without his influence upon the meaning of baptism.

The Pauline description of baptism as a "circumcision of the soul in the Spirit" (Rom 2:29), or "a circumcision not operated by human hand, the circumcision of Christ" (Col 2:11), further reveals the importance of Abraham for our study. It is indeed, as Charles Masson remarks, "a singular way of speaking to Christians."[47] Yet, in the ensemble of Pauline teaching, it is natural enough. In Rom 4:9–12, Paul has proven that Abraham's circumcision was a sign (*sēmeion*) and a seal (*sphragis*) of his justification by faith. In calling baptism a spiritual circumcision, Paul is affirming that it is the sign and seal of Christian faith, relating all believers to their father Abraham (Rom 4:16). The *sphragis* motif, at least as found in Pauline letters, is most probably connected with the theme of Abraham and his circumcision (cf. the use of *sphragizein* in the context of "the promises" in 2 Cor 1:22; Eph 1:13; also Eph 4:30).

Moses: the Exodus, the Wandering, the Covenant

Of all the saving judgments of Yahweh recorded in the Old Testament, it is the deliverance of Israel from Egyptian bondage which provides the New Testament writers with the basic analogue for Christ's redemptive work. When they employ the terms *lytron, apolytrōsis, agorazein,* and *peripoiēsis* in attempting to expose the meaning of Christian salvation, they are thinking primarily of the Exodus, by which Yahweh purchases for Himself a people "of His own acquiring" by assuming the onerous task of freeing them from Pharaoh's power and leading them through the desert to the Promised Land. Given the first-rate importance of these episodes in Israel's salvation history for New Testament soteriology, it is natural that they should bulk large in the formation of baptismal symbolism.

The figure of Moses is glorified in the New Testament, and his importance as a type of Christ is dwelt on repeatedly. Stephen depicts him as dispenser of salvation to his people, though rejected by them (Acts 7:25), and gives him a title nowhere predicated of him in the Old Testament, that of "savior" (Acts 7:35). Hebrews praises Moses' faith, through which he "esteemed the opprobrium of the Christ as riches superior to the treasures of Egypt" (Heb 11:26).

For Paul, it is the passage through the Red Sea and the protection afforded the Hebrew people by the cloud which gives a deep insight into the meaning of baptism. "I would not have you forget, brothers, that our fathers—all of them—dwelt under the protection of the cloud. All of them passed safely through the sea. And all of them in the cloud and in the sea were baptized into union with Moses" (1 Cor 10:1–2). The tradition Paul follows regarding the cloud, which varies from that of Exodus (cf. Ex 13:21; 14:19–20), is preserved in Ps 104:39.[48] Nor does he think too closely, in describing the Hebrews' baptism in the sea, of the detail recorded in Ex 14:22, where the crossing is made dry-shod. Jacques Guillet describes Paul's almost ruthless manner of dealing with Old Testament typology. When he assigns a typical value to extrinsic analogies which the modern mind finds difficult to accept, Paul does so in virtue of his fundamental insight. Israel, by leaving Egypt at Moses' word to follow Yahweh in the desert, took a step which, religiously speaking, is comparable to the Christian renunciation of the world and adherence to Christ through baptism.[49]

The author of Hebrews makes use of Israel's march through the desert to present his conception of the Christian life here below.[50] In such an original comparison, baptism figures as the Christian point of departure on this pilgrimage: it is "the initial assurance." "We have become confederates with Christ, provided we preserve, firm until the end, the initial assurance" (Heb 3:14).[51] Later in his letter the writer describes this Christian people "wandering in the desert" as forming a sacred procession to the heavenly temple, in which baptism once more figures as the initial step. "Let us approach with an upright mind, in fulness of faith, our minds cleansed from an evil conscience and our bodies washed with pure water" (Heb 10:22). In such a liturgical context the reference to baptism as pure or holy water recalls the ritual ablutions prescribed by the Mosaic code (cf. Nm 5:17) and the purifying water promised to Israel in her regeneration during the Messianic age (Ez 36:25). The verb *brantizein*, here translated as "cleanse," properly means "sprinkle," and its use here, especially in such proximity to Heb 9:20, evokes the sprinkling of the people by Moses with the blood of the covenant (Ex 24:8). The sacramental power of the water of baptism in purifying the soul is stressed in the present text.[52]

Since mention of Moses recalls the covenant made by God with the Hebrews, we must mention an Old Testament image of that covenant which is employed by Paul in describing baptism: the figure of espousals. In exhorting husbands to love their wives, Paul remarks that "Christ loved the Church and handed Himself over for her, that He might sanctify her by cleansing her with the bath of water, accompanied by the word, in order to bring the Church to Himself in all beauty, without flaw or wrinkle or anything of the kind, but to be consecrated and faultless" (Eph 5:25–27). The same figure occurs in two other Pauline passages, in which the baptismal theme is at least implicit. "I experience a divine jealousy with regard to you, since I betrothed you to a single spouse: I presented you, as a pure virgin, to Christ" (2 Cor 11:2). In Romans, Paul depicts the Christian community's liberation from the law in terms of a marriage dissolved by death. "And so, brothers, you likewise have been put to death so far as the law is concerned by the Body of Christ, in order to belong to another, to Him who was raised from the dead, that we might produce fruit for God" (Rom 7:1–6).

It was by means of this same image that Hosea had expressed the love of Yahweh for His people, affianced to Him by the covenant. "That is why I shall lead her, by my seductions, into the desert, and shall speak to her heart. . . . And she shall respond there as in the days of her youth, as the day she came up from the land of Egypt. . . . I shall make for them a covenant. . . . And I will betroth you to myself forever" (Hos 2:14 ff.). This most expressive figure keeps reappearing in subsequent prophetic writing (Jer 2:1—3:22; Is 51:4–8; 61:10). There is one passage in Ezekiel's magnificent allegory, based on this theme, which may have influenced Paul's writing of the passage in Ephesians cited above: ". . . and I swore an oath to you and entered into a covenant with you. . . . So you became mine. Then I bathed you with water and washed your blood from you, and I anointed you with oil" (Ez 16:8–9). The successive exploiting of the marriage symbol to express the meaning and vicissitudes of Yahweh's covenant with Israel reaches its climax in the Pauline letters, where it signifies Christ's union with the Church effected by the sacramental bath of baptism.

Here we might also mention the symbolism of anointing, which appears both in Paul and in John. "It is God who gives us as well as you our firm adherence to Christ. It is He who anointed us and also put His seal on us and gives us His guarantee by the Spirit in our souls" (2 Cor 1:21–22). "You have been anointed by the Holy One" (1 Jn 2:20). "You still retain in yourselves the anointing you received from Him, and you do not need to have anyone teach you" (1 Jn 2:27). The ritual of anointing was prescribed in the covenant given on Sinai for priests (Ex 29:7) and for the sacred furniture of the tent of testimony (Ex 30:25 ff.). At a later period the kings (1 S 10:1; 16:13) and sometimes the prophets (1 K 19:16) were anointed to signify their reception of Yahweh's Spirit for their office. This custom influenced the Johannine and Pauline descriptions of baptism as a *chrisma,* imparting the permanent possession of the Spirit (cf. also Is 61:1).

Joshua and the River Jordan

The great Old Testament miracle of the crossing of the Jordan by the chosen people to take possession of "the land" under Joshua is described in the same grand epic style as was the crossing of the Red Sea (Jos 1:11—4:18). In the New Testament it is remarkable that the writers, apart from one or two passing references (Acts 7:45; cf. also Heb 4:8), do not appear to have made any use of it. However, it may not be out of place here to mention an episode in the fourth Gospel (Jn 10:40–42) which may contain a reminiscence of Joshua's crossing of the Jordan. The passage forms the prelude to what Louis Bouyer calls "the center of the Gospel," the resurrection of Lazarus, which, if it does not contain any direct reference to baptism, is certainly baptismal in its general spirit.[53]

Rather abruptly, the Evangelist places Jesus in Perea on the other side of the Jordan. As Sir Edwyn Hoskyns observes,[54] the author is not concerned to give any details of the Perean ministry (cf. Mt 19:1 ff.; Mk 10:1 ff.), but to draw attention to the significance of the locality by this topographical note. He takes cognizance of the fact that this was "where John had baptized" (v. 40), and that many, as a result of John's preaching, had found faith in Jesus "there" (v. 42). It is while Jesus is beyond the Jordan that word is brought to Him of Lazarus' illness in Bethany. Upon receiving it, Jesus "remained two days in the place where He was" (Jn 11:6), and finally sets out with a promise to His disciples that they will see an act of God's glory (11:4, 15). Upon His arrival in Bethany He finds Lazarus dead four days. Such attention to the time element recalls a feature of the narrative of the crossing of the Jordan (Jos 1:11; 3:1–5). As Jesus promised His followers that they should experience God's power, so Joshua informs the Hebrews that "tomorrow the Lord is going to perform wonders among you" (Jos 3:5). Admittedly, the connection between this Old Testament story and the passage in the fourth Gospel is a tenuous one,[55] yet such typology would explain some of the obscure features of the narrative which follows in John, and would account for the baptismal use of both Joshua's crossing the Jordan and the resurrection of Lazarus in the patristic catecheses.[56]

Conclusions

After this rapid review of those saving judgments of Yahweh in the course of Old Testament history which, in the estimation of New Testament writers, have concurred in creating the symbolism and efficacy of baptism, we may now summarize the results of our investigation thus far.

Just as God created the world by His dynamic word, so through the rite of baptism this same creative activity is employed to produce in the neophyte a comparable renovation which makes of him "a new creature." Moreover, it is part of God's plan of salvation that the creation of the universe should affect the symbolism of this sacrament, which is a new exercise of the divine creative dynamism. More particularly, baptism's signification has been determined by God's creation of light and by the fact that the Word-made-flesh enters the world as "the true light, illuminating every man," to impart that life which is "the light of men." Jesus' own baptism by John, after which Christ retires to the desert as the new Adam with dominion over the wild beasts, enjoying familiarity with the angels, gives Christian baptism the power

sign, so also they were aware that the events of Jesus' public life were directed, in part at least, to that same divine purpose. Accordingly, we must now devote some space to an investigation of the meaning of John the Baptist's role in the New Testament story, to the teaching and miracles of Jesus which in the Synoptic Gospels are recorded for their relation to baptism, and to the sacramentalism of the fourth Gospel, which contains such a profound rethinking of the theology of baptism.

The important place which baptism will be found to occupy in the Gospels is primarily due to the essential function of that sacrament in the life of the Church. Thus, it is no accident, for instance, that the schema of the apostolic kerygma included the work of John the Baptist as "the beginning of the good news of Jesus Christ" (Mk 1:1).[57] This interest in baptism is no doubt also due to the fact that, in the Judaism contemporary with the New Testament, ablutions of various kinds were widely practiced (Mk 7:4; Lk 11:38). The author of Hebrews includes "teaching about baptisms" (Heb 6:2), or the discrimination between various baptismal rites, among the rudiments of Christian instruction. The recent recovery of certain sectarian documents belonging to the Jewish community of Qumrân reveals great insistence upon frequent lustrations. While these "baptisms" have practically no significance for an understanding of the Christian sacrament, one interesting point in rabbinical theology regarding proselyte baptism deserves mention. It appears that the reception of a Gentile convert into Judaism consisted of a threefold rite: circumcision, baptism, and a sacrifice. Thanks to circumcision and baptism, the non-Jew "entered the covenant" and became a full-fledged Israelite. Still, a burnt offering had to be made by him before he could be admitted to any sacrificial meal. It seems that this ritual rose from Jewish consciousness of the necessity, for a Gentile proselyte, of repeating the triple experience of the *qahal* of Israel which prepared the people for the Sinaitic covenant. They were circumcised "a second time" (an inference from Jos 5:2–3); they were baptized in the desert (Ex 19:10); and they shared the covenant sacrifice (Ex 24:3–8).[58] This awareness of the need of repeating, in the life of the individual, the collective experience of Israel of God's saving judgments, we have already seen displayed by the New Testament writers who revert to Old Testament events to express the mystery of Christian baptism.

John the Baptist and "the Restoration of All Things"

The inclusion of John in the New Testament message of salvation must be credited neither to his personality nor to his teaching, about which so little is said, but to his divinely directed function, that of baptizing.[59] In the Gospels Jesus points out the necessity and divine origin of this baptism (Lk 7:29–30) and appears to regard John's mission as comparable to His own (Mt 21:23–27). He also describes John's role in the history of New Testament salvation as somehow related to "the restoration of all things" (Mt 17:11; Mk 9:12). It is to be observed, however, that while Jesus states that "Elijah has already come" and identifies him as John (Mt 17:12–13), He never actually says that John brought about "the restoration of all things." In order to grasp the precise meaning of this mysterious phrase, we must first recall John's mission as the Gospels present it, and investigate the nature of Johannine baptism.

John is clearly represented by the Synoptics as an Old Testament prophet. Like his predecessor, he is a "herald" of the future kingdom. He is Isaiah "crying in the desert" (Mt. 3:3) proclaiming "the word of God" which "came to him" as it had come to the Old Testament prophets (Lk 3:2). He is Elijah, by his garb (Mt 3:4; 2 K 1:8), by the angelic pronouncement that he will be "endowed with the spirit and power of Elijah" (Lk 1:17), and by Jesus' declaration that he is "the Elijah who is destined to come" (Mt 11:14). He is even "something more than a prophet" (Mt 11:9), because he is the messenger immediately preceding the Christ (Mal 3:1). According to the fourth Gospel, John's prophetic function is specifically "to give testimony" (Jn 1:7, 31).

John's baptism also pertains to the prophetic order. It was the visible sign of *metanoia,* the change of heart necessary for re-establishing good relations between Israel and Yahweh which the coming kingdom demanded. It involved an act of faith and hope in Yahweh's Anointed One. As Paul explains at Ephesus, "John practiced a baptism of repentance, telling the people they should make an act of faith in Him who was to come after him" (Acts 19:4). This *metanoia* was expressed by the public confession of sins (Mt 3:6; Mk 1:5) and immersion in the River Jordan. John himself described the rite as a lustration "with water, aimed at a change of heart" (Mt 3:11), or "a baptism in token of a change of heart, which looked to the forgiveness of sins" (Mk 1:4). It was a symbol of the right dispositions for the coming kingdom; it was not a rite of initiation into that kingdom. It prepared men to receive the preaching of Jesus and to await a baptism of an entirely different order (Mt 3:11).

This doctrine of the two baptisms, one provisory, the other definitive, Messianic, eschatological, is very important in New Testament baptismal theology. It has, however, long been a question with the New Testament critics whether such a conception really went back to the Baptist or was an invention of early Christian apologetic interests. There has been a tendency to regard the phrase "in the Holy Spirit" (Mk 1:8; Mt 3:11; Lk 3:16) as put into John's mouth at a later period to prove the superiority of Christian baptism over Johannine. Joseph Schmitt has shown by a careful study of texts appearing in the Dead Sea literature that there is a good possibility that these Synoptic logia, ascribed to John, are authentic.[60] It is interesting to note also that the Old Testament notion of fire as symbol of the divine judgment, which appears in John's description of Christ's baptism (Mt. 3:11; Lk 3:16), finds an echo in the *Manual of Discipline*, where there is also question of an eschatological purification.[61]

The value of John's description of Christian baptism lies in its stress upon the essentially eschatological nature of the sacrament. Old Testament prophecy characterizes the Messianic age as an era when Yahweh will pour out His Spirit in abundance upon men (Jl 3:1–5), and also as the terrible "Day of Yahweh" (Amos 7:4; Is 30:27–30; Mal 3:2), when God is to pass a judgment whose searching, relentless character is symbolized by fire. John's originality consists in his insight into the nature of Christian baptism as specified by these prophetic descriptions of the Messianic times. This relation of baptism to the *eschaton* holds an important place in the New Testament conception of it. On Pentecost Peter would make it clear to his hearers that the "baptism with the Spirit" received by the apostolic group had inaugurated the days of the Messiah and was a sign of the imminence of the eschatological judgment (Acts 2:16–17). He was to point out, moreover, that the newly established means to "save yourselves from this perverse age" and to enter the new Israel of the "last days" was baptism "in the name of Jesus Christ" (Acts 2:37–41). While the later experience of the apostolic Church would greatly clarify this eschatological aspect of baptism, still the credit for first describing it as a "sign of the end" rests with John.

According to the fourth Gospel, the Baptist also presents

another facet of Christian baptism: its close relation to Christ's death. The Evangelist describes John as contrasting his baptism with the person, rather than the baptism, of Christ. "He who sent me to baptize with water had said to me, 'He upon whom you see the Spirit descend and rest, is He who baptizes with a Holy Spirit.' And I have seen, and I have continued to testify that He is the Son of God" (Jn 1:33–34). This same Gospel records a Johannine saying which prophesies Jesus' future sacrificial death: "Here is the Lamb of God, He who is taking away the world's sin" (Jn 1:29, 36). The context in which this is uttered makes it clear that a connection is intended between the baptism "with a Holy Spirit" brought by Jesus and His death for the sin of the world. Baptism's efficacy stems from this future liberation by the Lamb of God.

We must now attempt to answer the question we raised earlier, as to the part played by John in "the restoration of all things." The theme was, in late Judaism, connected with the return of Elijah:

> Remember, I am sending you Elijah the Tishbite
> before the dawning of the great and manifest day of the Lord,
> who will re-establish (*apokatastesei*) the right attitude of father to son,
> the right attitude of a man to his neighbor. (LXX: Mal 3:22–23)

Ben Sira repeats this doctrine, employing the same phraseology, in his praise of the prophet Elijah:

> Who, it is written, is to come with reproofs at the appointed time,
> to quiet anger before it becomes wrath,
> to correct (*epistrepsai*) the attitude of father to son
> and to establish (*katastesai*) the tribes of Jacob. (Sir 48:10)

In the New Testament this same Elijah motif is recalled in the angel's announcement to Zachary of John's birth: "And he shall be His forerunner, inheriting the spirit and power of Elijah, to correct (*epistrepsai*) the attitude of fathers to sons and the rebellious by the wisdom of holy men, to prepare for the Lord a readied people" (Lk 1:17).

While it is clear from this last citation that Elijah's work of "restoring all things" falls upon John, the New Testament also ascribes the same function to Christ Himself. On Ascension Day the disciples evidently expect the risen Lord to perform this office: "Lord, are you at this time restoring (*apokathistaneis*) the sovereignty to Israel?" (Acts 1:6). In reply, while remarking that the revelation of this chosen time has been reserved by the Father's providence to Himself, Christ promises His own the gift of the Holy Spirit, who thus appears involved in this restoration. After Pentecost Peter is aware that the *apokatastasis pantōn* is to be the ultimate task of the parousiac Christ, "whom heaven must hold until the era of the restoration of all things" (Acts 3:21). Paul, in turn, connects it with the redemptive activity of the "second Adam," by whom "the rest of men will be restored (*katastathēsontai*) to holiness" (Rom 5:19). To the Ephesians he speaks of God's eternal plan of salvation, "which He decreed to put into effect in Him, as the economy of the fulness of time: to gather (*anakephalaiōsasthai*) all creation, in heaven as well as upon earth, under one head, Christ" (Eph 1:9–10).

Hence, on the one hand, it appears that the change of heart preached by John, with the external rite of baptism which symbolized it, begins "the restoration of all things" by preparing men to receive the kingdom with the proper dispositions. On the other hand, the establishment of the kingdom or sovereignty of Christ over all creation is effected by His death and resurrection, while His return in triumph at the end of the period during which His kingdom is advanced in His Church is to carry salvation to its perfection. Accordingly, "the restoration of all things" is a continuous process, initiated by John's baptism but carried on by the Church in obedience to the office imposed by the Master in virtue of the universal power conferred on Him by His death and resurrection:

> Therefore, go and make disciples
> of all the nations,
> by baptizing them . . .
> and by teaching them
> to carry out everything
> that I have enjoined upon you. (Mt 28:19–20)

A deeper insight into the continuity between John's baptism and the Christian sacrament will be gained by the experience of the apostolic Church during her first years, which will lead her to a fuller understanding of the antithesis "John with water—Christ with the Spirit." The discussion of this doctrinal development must be left for the next section of this study.

At the time of the Council of Trent there was a great deal of debate about a proposition which stated that "Christ's baptism did not nullify John's baptism, but merely added the promise to it." It is instructive to note that while the wording of the proposition is open to criticism in certain respects, the Tridentine Fathers did not condemn it, but were content to anathematize the assertion that John's baptism had the same force as Christ's.[62] In point of fact, the New Testament would appear to make some sort of connection between the two baptisms, as will be seen from a study of the accounts of Jesus' baptism by John in the Jordan.

Jesus' Baptism by John

This important episode, narrated with some detail by each of the Synoptics (Mt 3:13–17; Mk 1:9–11; Lk 3:21–22) and referred to by the fourth Gospel (Jn 1:32–33), enables us to clarify the relations seen by the New Testament writers between John's baptism and the Christian sacrament. That this narrative, so full of paradox, should have found a place at all in the Gospels is proof of its essential value to Christian dogma. The author of Christian baptism accepts John's inferior baptism. Moreover, the theophany on this occasion of the Spirit who descends "like a dove" does not seem, from the accounts of the first two Evangelists, to have been witnessed by any bystanders; and, presumably, the same holds true for the heavenly voice. The fourth Gospel adds that John also beheld the vision (Jn 1:32). What, then, is the purpose of this divine manifestation? While it was included in the apostolic preaching as Jesus' Messianic anointing (Acts 10:38), it is for its significance to Christian belief that it is recounted in the written Gospels. According to the fourth Gospel, the episode shows the continuity between Johannine and Christian baptism. "That He might be made known in Israel—that is why I came baptizing with water" (Jn 1:31). The verses immediately following make it clear that it was precisely Jesus' manifestation as author of the sacrament of baptism of which John spoke. This scene, in which all the elements that are to constitute that sacrament are disclosed—the Spirit, the water, the presence of the triune Godhead—is the epiphany of baptism.[63]

Baptismal Symbolism in Jesus' Public Ministry

From the accounts of the public life in the Synoptics we can gather no more than obscure hints of the significance of Jesus' miracles and teaching for New Testament baptismal doctrine. Mark has preserved the account of two miracles in his Gospel which may contain some general sacramental teaching. The first, the cure of a deaf man whose speech was impaired (Mk 7:31–37), is of an unusually ritualistic nature, and its influence from earliest times upon the baptismal usages of Milan and Rome can be seen in the use of saliva and the word *ephphatha*.[64] The second miracle is the gradual healing of a blind man (Mk 8:22–26), narrated immediately after the disciples have displayed their lack of comprehension of the miracles of the multiplication of loaves (Mk 8:14–21). That the man recovers his sight only progressively in two stages seems intended to teach the disciples the deeper meaning and sacramental efficacy of Jesus' symbolic actions. However, it will be only in the fourth Gospel that the healing of blindness will be narrated because of its baptismal significance.

As regards Jesus' teaching in the first three Gospels, it is possible that the mysterious ejection of the man who came improperly clad to the wedding feast in the Matthean parable (Mt 22:11–14) indicates the necessity of baptism for entry into the Church.[65] There are also two logia of Jesus in which His future redemptive death is described as a "baptism" (Mk 10:38; Lk 12:50). They remind the reader of the essential relation of baptism to Jesus' death for men.[66]

While the only evident theological interpretation of Jesus' miracles by the Synoptics is that they constitute the initial attack upon Satan's hold on the world of men through deformity, disease, or death,[67] in the fourth Gospel several of the miraculous "signs" performed by Christ are interpreted as symbolic of baptism. At Cana the transformation of water used for "the purification of the Jews" into wine, which symbolizes the new dispensation of the Spirit,[68] is called a manifestation of Jesus' "glory" (Jn 2:1–11). This first sign given by Jesus to His disciples to evoke their faith in Him prepares the way for the doctrine of new birth in the dialogue with Nicodemus, for the self-effacement of the Baptist before

Jesus, and for the substitution of "living water" for that from Jacob's well[69]—all of which are important for the theology of baptism.

The theme of the conversation between Jesus and Nicodemus is the mysterious rebirth effected by the Christian sacrament, and the author surrounds the scene with an air of mystery.[70] Nicodemus, a Pharisee, learned, upright, full of the earthy realism of Hebrew wisdom, learns the absolute necessity of baptism, described in characteristically Johannine *double-entendre* as a birth "anew," or "from above" (Jn 3:3, 5). A proof of how closely, in the early preaching, baptism was related to the kingdom theme is shown by the fact that it is only here, in the entire fourth Gospel, that the phrase "the kingdom of God" occurs. This rebirth is effected by "water and Spirit." In this statement of Jesus, the most precise definition of baptism in the New Testament, we see how the material symbol realizes what it signifies, the communication of the Holy Spirit, of whom, in this Gospel, water is constantly presented as a symbol. The necessity of baptism arises from the hiatus existing between the natural (*sarx* for John connotes human nature in all its creaturely weakness) and the supernatural (Jn 3:6–7), whose mystery is described by a common biblical metaphor, the wind (Qoh 11:5; Sir 16:20–21). The efficacy of the sacrament is traced back to the harmony between the material sign and the heavenly reality, to which Jesus Himself testifies (vv. 10–13). This harmony will be established through Jesus' redemptive death and exaltation, of which Moses' bronze serpent, "a symbol of salvation" (Wis 16:6), is the sign, and which in turn is a divine saving judgment or proof of the Father's love (vv. 14–19).

The fourth Gospel also mentions the practice, by Jesus' disciples during the public ministry, of a baptismal rite, which was doubtless akin to John's baptism, possibly a sign of attachment to Jesus as a disciple. This much is certain: it was not the Christian sacrament.[71] For one thing, John, who is represented here as still practicing his baptism (Jn 3:23), would have ceased his mission, whose purpose would have thus been achieved. Moreover, as Père Lagrange remarks, the reason why the Evangelist goes to such lengths to correct (Jn 4:2) a possible false impression (Jn 3:22) that Jesus Himself performed this rite is precisely to avoid giving this baptism the character of the Christian sacrament.[72]

These allusions to the Baptist and his baptism form the background against which the meeting of Jesus and the Samaritan woman at Jacob's well is introduced by the Evangelist. John's last proclamation in this Gospel that Christ, as "God's ambassador, announces God's message, since He bestows the Spirit without stint" (Jn 3:34), and Jesus' desire to avoid the publicity which His ministry has caused by eclipsing that of John, as well as His decision to retire to Galilee through Samaria, are so many elements which form the prologue to the discourse on the "living water." This promise of "living water" which quenches the soul's desire for God and which becomes in the believer "a fountain of water welling up into eternal life" (Jn 4:13–14) is closely related to Christian baptism. In a later chapter the Evangelist himself informs us that this "living water" is the Holy Spirit (Jn 7:39). Jesus' description of the future worship of God "in Spirit and in truth" (Jn 4:23), far from promulgating a religion "of the heart" free from all external ceremonial, is complementary to the earlier sacramental teaching regarding the necessity of spiritual rebirth given to Nicodemus.[73]

The next scene in which a baptismal interest comes to the fore[74] is the cure of the man blind from birth who washes in the pool of Siloe (Jn 9:1–41).[75] As Jesus pronounces the words "I am the light of the world," He "anoints" the blind eyes with mud and commands the man to go to a pool, the name of which is interpreted by the Evangelist as "the One sent," that is, the Christ (the word actually means "conduit"). By the use of this symbolic etymology the writer shows that he has seen, in this command to wash in the pool which bears Christ's name, a symbol of baptism; and the reader is *ipso facto* given an insight into Jesus' reference to Himself as "light of the world." Christ's concluding remarks in this episode also draw attention to its baptismal signification: "I am come into this world for a judgment: that the sightless may see, and those who see may become blind" (Jn 9:39). The Johannine "judgment," which we have already seen mentioned in the Nicodemus *récit*, is the equivalent of the Pauline notion of redemption.[76] It is through baptism that the neophyte participates in this divine saving judgment of Christ.

A puzzling feature of the fourth Gospel's account of the Last Supper is, of course, the omission of the institution of the Eucharist; and the same might be said of the absence of any single scene which could be construed as the historical moment when baptism was instituted. C. K. Barrett has recently suggested a reason for this procedure which may well be correct. "The truth (in John's view) seems to be that they hang not upon one particular moment or command, but upon the whole fact of Christ in His life, death, and exaltation, and that they convey nothing less than this whole fact."[77]

There is, however, in the Johannine account of Christ's washing of the disciples' feet (Jn 13:1–15), a logion of Jesus which surely refers to baptism, and may also contain a veiled allusion to the Eucharist. The presence of such sacramental overtones would explain the evident importance of the incident in John's eyes, revealed by its solemn introduction (vv. 1–3) and by Jesus' concluding remark: "I have given you an example (*hypodeigma*),[78] in order that you may perform the same service as I have performed for you" (v. 15). The logion which touches on baptism is Jesus' observation that "the man who has taken a bath has no need of washing, but is entirely cleansed" (v. 10). This bath which needs no repetition is baptism, which can be received but once.[79] The *pedilavium* which is contrasted with it and which is declared to be a *sine qua non* of "having a part" with Christ (v. 8) is probably a symbol of the Eucharist.[80] John has thus juxtaposed the two principal Christian sacraments in order to point out their relation to each other.[81]

Conclusions

The incidents of Jesus' public ministry which come into the written Gospels from the apostolic preaching have played their part in determining the New Testament theological developments on baptism. John's principal office, "the restoration of all things," which he performed by his baptism of repentance, gave Christianity its orientation as a "baptist" movement.[82] John's prophetic role is centered in his prediction of the future baptism with the Holy Spirit, whose eschatological nature he was the first to point out. He also drew attention to baptism's essential connection with Jesus' atoning death. In fact, John's providential mission and his part in the universal restoration is precisely to reveal to Israel the author of the Christian sacrament.[83] Thus it is in baptizing Jesus that John's activity reaches its consummation; and the theophany which occurs on that occasion is a divine revelation of the nature of baptism. The scene discloses the manner in which Christ will elevate the Johannine symbol into an efficacious sign of the grace which, when once glorified, He will bestow by means of the Holy Spirit.

The baptismal significance of Jesus' public ministry, hinted at by the Synoptics, is highlighted in the fourth Gospel. Cana reveals the sacrament as the new wine of the Messianic banquet, whose purifying powers surpass any of the "purifications of the Jews." The conversation with Nicodemus depicts baptism as a new birth or birth from above, effected by the water of baptism, an effective symbol of the presence of the Spirit. The Samaritan interlude insists upon this symbolic value by describing baptism as "living water" and Christianity as a religion "in spirit and in truth," or one whose sacramental practices are efficacious in the supernatural order. The cure of the blind man at the pool of Siloe shows how baptism produces the illumination of faith in a soul properly disposed to "the light of this world." The episode repeats an idea already present in the Nicodemus discourse: baptism is the sacramental symbol of that divine judgment which Jesus has entered the world to bring about. Jesus' remark to Peter during the *pedilavium* underscores the absolute necessity of baptism, yet its all-sufficient power to renovate the Christian. Finally, the omission of any words which suggest Jesus' institution of this sacrament at one specific moment, like the similar omission of the institution of the Eucharist, may be construed as an *argumentum confirmans* for the method we are employing in our investigation of New Testament baptismal doctrine. It is to the Christ-event in its totality, summing up in itself the whole New and Old Testament revelation of Him, that baptism and the other Christian sacraments owe their existence, their symbolism, and their efficacy.

BAPTISMAL SYMBOLISM AND CHRIST'S EXALTATION

In this final section we shall consider the effects upon baptismal symbolism of Christ's exaltation and of those experiences of the Body of Christ, His Church, which are revealed to us in the New Testament as the fruits of His *sessio ad dexteram Patris*. Under Christ's exaltation we include not only His resurrection, ascension, and the sending of the pentecostal Spirit, but also, following the conception found in the fourth Gospel, His salvific death on the cross. The experiences of the primitive Christian community which gave them, in the first years, a more profound insight into the meaning of the sacrament which they began to confer on Pentecost, are likewise of paramount interest. Thus we shall be led to inquire into the signification they ascribed to baptism and its relation to the "imposition of hands," the sense of the obscure formula "baptism in Jesus' Name," the developments which caused a fuller understanding of the antithesis "John with water—Christ with the Spirit," and to review the earliest traces of primitive baptismal ritual found scattered through the New Testament.

Jesus' Death and Resurrection

A salient feature of the Johannine view of the redemptive death of Christ is its character as the initial phase of Jesus' glorification.[84] John habitually thinks of Christ's salvific work as a "passing from this world to the Father" (Jn 13:1, 3), in which the first step is His being "lifted up from the earth" upon the cross. This theological viewpoint enables John to present Jesus' death as a foretaste of Pentecost and to show how it is related to the two sacraments of baptism and the Eucharist. Accordingly, the episode of the piercing of Jesus' side with a lance is particularly significant in John's writings. The victory of the Christian faith rests ultimately upon Him "who came through water and blood and Spirit, Jesus Christ; not in water only, but in water and blood. And the Spirit is the one who attests this, since the Spirit is truth. The witnesses are three: the Spirit and the water and the blood. And these three are one" (1 Jn 5:6–8). The passage is a reminiscence of the eyewitness account of the scene on Calvary (Jn 19:35), written to deepen the faith of the Christian reader: "One of the soldiers pierced His side with a lance, and immediately blood and water issued forth" (Jn 19:34). There can be no doubt, given John's solemn attestation to the truth of this event and his reference to it in the first Johannine letter, that the Evangelist attaches supreme importance to this symbolism. The whole sacramental orientation of the fourth Gospel, whose purpose is to show how, in baptism and the Eucharist, Jesus brings eternal life to the world, permits us to see in the water a symbol of baptism, in the blood a symbol of the Eucharist, the two sacraments which are primary "witnesses" to Christ's work of redemption. There is a third essential witness, the Spirit. Here we recall the singular expression used to describe Jesus' death: "and having bowed His head He handed over the Spirit" (Jn 19:30). This departure from the normal and idiomatic Greek expressions found in the Synoptics[85] must be intentional on John's part. The Evangelist has seen in Jesus' last breath the first outpouring of the Spirit. This detail adds further meaning to the blood and water issuing from Christ's side. It is by baptism and the Eucharist that the Spirit is principally communicated.

In Pauline theology the death and resurrection of Christ form one act by which the Father effects man's salvation: "He was handed over for our sins and raised for our justification" (Rom 4:25). According to Paul, this double act of the redemption transcends time and terminates also in the Christian's dying and rising with Christ by means of baptism. Paul uses the baptismal rite of immersion to express this conception in a paragraph of Romans: "You are surely aware that we, who were baptized into Christ Jesus, were baptized into His death. We were then buried together with Him by this baptism into His death that, just as Christ was raised from the dead by the glory of the Father, so we also may live by a new kind of life. For if we have grown together with Him into the likeness of His death, so also shall we grow with Him into the likeness of His resurrection" (Rom 6:3–5).

The expression of Paul's thought in the last sentence is complicated by the mixing of two metaphors: we have "grown into Christ," and we have been "fashioned after the pattern of His death and resurrection."[86] Paul probably did this deliberately to underscore the reality of what occurs in baptism.[87] Since we are dealing here with a transitional stage in Paul's thought, we do not find any explicit statement of the relation of the sacramental effects of baptism to Christ's resurrection. This aspect will be made clear in a subsequent stage of Pauline baptismal theology: "Buried together with Him in baptism, you have also been raised together with Him by it through faith in the power of God who raised Him from the dead. Yes, you who were dead because of your sins and physically uncircumcised, He has raised together with Him" (Col 2:12–13). Of Paul's insight into the nature of baptism there can be no doubt: its symbolism has been made efficaciously sacramental by the twin events of Christ's death and resurrection.

Christ's Ascension into Heaven

Once Paul successfully integrated the resurrection into his baptismal theology, he was able to incorporate also Christ's ascension and His enthronement at God's right hand: "But God is so rich in mercy that through the great love He had for us, even though we were dead because of our sins, He brought us back to life together with Christ (it is by His loving favor you have been saved), and raised us together with Him and made us sit down in heaven in union with Christ Jesus" (Eph 2:4–6). The ascension of which Paul is speaking is that "theological ascension," as Pierre Benoit terms it,[88] the completion of Jesus' exaltation, His constitution as "Son of God in power through resurrection of the dead" (Rom 1:4). In virtue of this phase of the mystery of Christ the symbolism of baptism is further enhanced. The stark realism of the idea that the Christian has already been admitted to heavenly glory through baptismal union with the glorified Christ stresses Paul's realization of the Christian's present possession of the Messianic blessings and his definitive triumph over the forces of evil. This latter element is probably also present in the mysterious reference in Petrine literature to Christ's *descensus ad inferos* to "make a proclamation to the spirits in prison" (1 Pt 3:19).

An important effect of Christ's ascension upon New Testament baptismal doctrine is, without any doubt, the creation of the first disciples' faith in His divinity, as Peter's first speech in Acts makes clear. "Now having been exalted to God's right hand and having received the promise of the Holy Spirit from the Father, He has poured out this which you yourselves both see and hear. . . . Therefore, let the whole house of Israel know for a certainty that God has made Him Lord and Christ —this Jesus whom you, for your part, have crucified" (Acts 2:33–36). But since the revelation of Christ's enthronement as God's Son belongs properly to Pentecost, it is to that mystery that we must now direct our attention.

Pentecost and the Practice of Christian Baptism

The risen Jesus had, in virtue of His exaltation and universal dominion acquired through it, commanded His disciples to administer Christian baptism (Mt 28:18–20). He had likewise announced an event which was intended to prepare them for that ministry and for which they were to wait: "the promise of my Father," an investiture with "power from on high" (Lk 24:49), a baptism "with a Holy Spirit" (Acts 1:5). In expectation of its reception, the apostles elect Matthias to succeed the apostate Judas. While they thus seem to have been aware that the Messianic era would be opened by this mysterious "baptism," they doubtless thought of it as the return of Christ in His parousia. It is important for the connection between Johannine and Christian baptism that they felt it necessary to choose a man who had been with Jesus Christ during the whole of His public ministry, "beginning from the baptism of John" (Acts 1:22). Whether this ambiguous phrase means (as it probably does) that the candidate must have received John's baptism, or whether it means that he had to have been present at John's baptism of Jesus, Johannine baptism was in some way involved in the prerequisites for apostleship. In the light of the fact that the only baptism received by the apostles was "baptism with a Holy Spirit" in the fires of Pentecost, this previous connection with Johannine baptism is highly significant for an understanding of Christian baptism.

The pentecostal descent of the Holy Spirit produced a revolution: it created the Christian faith in the hearts of the disciples. They were made aware of Christ's divinity, of the personality of the Holy Spirit, of the inauguration of "the last times" by the Spirit's presence in their midst. Most important for our present study, they became conscious that they now formed, under the hegemony of the Spirit, the *qahal* of the new Israel.[89] This creation of what had been merely a group of Jesus' loyal adherents into the Church of the New Testament was the immediate result of their "baptism with a Holy Spirit."

Since this unique experience, which could never be repeated in the lives of any other men, had constituted these disciples as the Church, they had no need of receiving the Christian sacrament of baptism. Yet this same consciousness of the unique character of their own experience led them, according to the evidence of the New Testament (Acts 2:41), to impart Christian baptism to those who wished to be added "to the number of the saved" (Acts 2:47). In fact, we may say that the apostles looked upon the reception of this sacrament as reproducing, *so far as that was possible,* their own pentecostal experience.

This view appears in Pauline baptismal theology as a theologoumenon. He declares to the Thessalonians that "God chose you from the beginning to be saved through consecration by the Spirit" (2 Th 2:13). His plea for unity at Philippi is based on "whatever participation there is in the Spirit" (Phil 2:1). To prevent the Galatians from succumbing to the temptation to accept circumcision, he asks: "Did you begin with the Spirit only to end now with the flesh?" (Gal 3:3). In enumerating for the Corinthians those sinners who "will not have any share in God's kingdom," he observes: "Some of you used to be like that. But you have been washed, you have been consecrated, you have been justified, by the power of our Lord Jesus Christ and through the Spirit of our God" (1 Cor 6:11). This last text implicitly shows how baptism, through its efficacious power to transmit the Spirit, is the sole rite of initiation into God's kingdom. Later in this same epistle Paul expresses this idea in more characteristic terms: "We have all—Jews or Greeks, slaves or free men—been baptized by one Spirit to form one Body, and we have all drunk of the one Spirit" (1 Cor 12:13).

Such theological development is the fruit of the earlier experiences of the primitive apostolic community, an important example of which is Peter's evangelization of Cornelius and his household at Caesarea. Before Peter had time to finish his catechetical instructions or to baptize this group, "the Holy Spirit fell upon all those listening to the gospel" (Acts 10:44), and they were caught up in ecstasy. Luke describes the phenomenon with the terms he had used for that of Pentecost. Peter himself, in giving an account of the happenings to the Jerusalem community somewhat later, is aware also of the similarity between the two situations: "The Holy Spirit fell upon them exactly as upon us in the beginning" (Acts 11:15).

Yet Peter's decision to have these Gentiles baptized seems to belie his words (Acts 10:48). He had, in fact, recognized an essential difference between this experience of Cornelius and his family, and that of the disciples on Pentecost. While the pentecostal event had transformed the apostolic assembly into the *ekklēsia*, the "new Israel," this later descent of the Spirit was simply proof to Peter that God willed to have these pagans admitted to the already existing Church by means of baptism.

An incident recounted much later in Acts also draws attention to this essential difference between the baptismal experience of the first disciples and those who subsequently joined the Church. Paul met a group of John's disciples living at Ephesus who had received Johannine baptism and who, after receiving baptism "in the Lord Jesus' Name," experienced, at the descent of the Holy Spirit, the same kind of ecstasy as that of the apostles on Pentecost (Acts 19:1–7). But the entry of these Johannites into the Church is evidently very different from the formation of the apostles into the Church. Both groups had received John's baptism; both had received the descending Spirit with charismatic effects. The difference between them lies in the necessary reception of

Christian baptism by the Ephesian converts. Accordingly, we are now in a position to point out the dangerous inadequacy of the statement debated at Trent, that "Christ's baptism did not nullify John's baptism, but merely added the promise to it." While it is possible to apply this to the experience of the apostles, it is entirely misleading to predicate it of any other who joined the Church after it had been founded upon these first disciples.

Thus, from the earliest practices of the primitive community, baptism appears as the initiation rite into the "new Israel," the unique means of being saved from "this perverse age" (Acts 2:40). Like Johannine baptism, the Christian sacrament was necessarily to be received with *metanoia.* But in contrast to John's rite, baptism really effected the remission of sins (Acts 2:38). Still, it would seem that in these early days a distinction was made (which certainly had disappeared by the time Jn 3:5 was written) between the effect of baptism and that of the imposition of hands. The one was regarded as the means of admission to the Church and it remitted sin; the other imparted the Spirit. This view is illustrated by Philip's apostolate in Samaria (Acts 8:5–17). The deacon Philip baptized those Samaritans who professed faith in the gospel; but a visit from Peter and John was necessary that they might lay their hands on them to communicate the gift of the Holy Spirit.[90] Yet even in these early years some awareness of the communication of the Spirit by baptism appears indicated in Acts. At Caesarea, after the Gentiles' reception of the Spirit, Peter says: "Surely no one *can hinder the water,* so that these men may be baptized?" (Acts 10:47). It is difficult to explain this astonishing personification of the baptismal water except in terms of Peter's awareness that the water was the efficacious symbol of the living Spirit.

"John with Water—Christ with the Holy Spirit"

Another remark of Peter's in connection with the Cornelius episode makes it necessary to return to a consideration of the relations between Johannine and Christian baptism. Here it is a question of the evolution in the apostolic understanding of the antithesis "John with water—Christ with the Holy Spirit." In his account of the Caesarean miracle of tongues to the Jerusalem community, Peter describes how "the Holy Spirit descended upon them, just as upon us at the beginning. And I recalled the Lord's remark: 'John,' He said, 'baptized with water, but you will be baptized in the Holy Spirit'" (Acts 11:15–16). Peter's apologia for admitting these pagan converts to Christian baptism is based upon his recollection of this logion of Christ. To discover the logic in this train of thought, we must realize the fuller sense which Peter has seen in this antithesis.

In the Gospel record where the saying occurs, it is put in the mouth of the Baptist (Mt 3:11; Mk 1:8; Lk 3:16; Jn 1:31–33) to point out the contrast between John's purely symbolic baptism and the efficacy of the future Christian sacrament. Peter had, as a disciple of John (Jn 1:40–41), received his baptism. At Pentecost he had undergone the "baptism with a Holy Spirit," whose effect, he was well aware, had been to create the Church out of himself and his fellow disciples. As a result, Peter saw a deeper meaning in this antithesis, which he had learned both from John and Jesus. Christian baptism owed something to John as well as to Christ. The ritual ablution with "flowing" water[91] was a legacy from Jesus' precursor; the efficacy of its newly created symbolism came from the risen Christ and His gift of the Spirit. John with water and Christ with the Spirit had each contributed (though on vastly different levels) to the sacrament.[92] The antithesis was henceforth to be understood as the definition of baptism (Jn 3:5). Cornelius' reception of the Spirit reminded Peter of his own pentecostal experience, which had shed such light on the meaning of this antithesis and had been the signal to practice Christian baptism, and he had Cornelius baptized.

Baptism "in Jesus' Name"

The meaning of the phrase, baptism "in Jesus' Name," has long been debated by New Testament scholars. St. Thomas appears to have thought that in the early years of the primitive Church baptism was so administered "by a special revelation of Christ" or a "dispensation," either to increase devotion to the holy Name or because, as Ambrose observes, the Name implies the whole Trinity.[93] The difficulty which St. Thomas and other Catholic theologians have experienced in explaining this disconcerting baptismal rite, unfortunately so well attested by the New Testament, arises from the supposition that they must explain how baptism could have another "form" (in the Scholastic sense) than the Trinitarian formula pronounced by the minister of the sacrament.[94] However, the New Testament evidence shows, I believe, that such an assumption is unwarranted.

Peter tells those who have come to the faith on Pentecost: "Repent, and let each of you have himself baptized in Jesus Christ's Name for the remission of his sins, and you will receive the gift of the Holy Spirit" (Acts 2:37–38). The Samaritans converted by Philip's preaching were "baptized in the Lord Jesus' Name" (Acts 8:16), as also were the Johannites of Ephesus by Paul (Acts 19:5). Ananias' remark to the blinded Saul after his conversion gives us a clue to the meaning of this descriptive formula: "Arise, be baptized, and be washed from your sins by invoking His Name" (Acts 22:16).

This text shows that the invocation of Jesus' Name at baptism was made not by the minister of the sacrament but by the neophyte. A remark of Paul to the Corinthian community, whose unity was menaced by a certain partisan spirit, gives another hint: "But was it Paul who was crucified for you? Or were you baptized in Paul's name?" (1 Cor 1:13). The invocation of Jesus' Name by the candidate for baptism was a declaration of his willingness to become a follower of Christ, a desire springing from his belief in the redemptive value of Jesus' death and leading him to seek entry into the unity of the Church. Baptism, for Paul, is the sacrament of the unity of the Body of Christ (1 Cor 12:13; Eph 4:4–6).

We must now ask what was meant specifically in the early Church by the phrase "Jesus' Name." As the citation of an early hymn in the letter to the Philippians shows (Phil 2:9–11), it denoted not the holy Name "Jesus," but the new Name *Kyrios*, conferred on the exalted Christ at His enthronement at God's right hand (cf. also Heb 1:4–5). The acclamation *Jēsous Kyrios* was a popular credal formula, expressing faith in the divinity of Christ;[95] and the great devotion which is manifested in Acts towards this Name is a sign of the central position of this dogma from the beginning of the Church (Acts 2:21; 3:6; 4:12, 29–30, 31; 5:41).

Thus it becomes clear that baptism was referred to as "in Jesus' Name" because its reception was accompanied by the neophyte's act of faith in the principal mystery of Christianity. At the same time, it must not be forgotten that this revelation of Jesus' divinity, expressed as the Father's bestowal of the divine Name *Kyrios* on His Son, was given simultaneously, on Pentecost, with the revelation of the Spirit's personality. Accordingly, in confessing that "Jesus is *Kyrios*" (Phil 2:11; 1 Cor 8:6; 12:3; Rom 10:9; 2 Cor 4:5), the Christian implicitly acknowledged the Father as source of Jesus' glory and the Spirit as gift of his glorified Master.

By the time that Greek Matthew was written in the last decades of the first century, the Trinitarian formula, pronounced (it would seem) by the minister of baptism, had come to be regarded, at least in the community where that Gospel originated, as an essential part of the baptismal rite. It is for this reason that the Evangelist places these highly important words in the mouth of the risen Christ (Mt 28:19). It is probable that in the early days, when it was almost entirely a question of admitting adults to the community, the religious meaning of baptism was regarded as sufficiently well designated by the candidate's profession of faith in the lordship of Christ.[96] With the introduction of infant baptism, however, the need of having this designation made by someone else (obviously the minister himself) resulted in a gradual change of custom.[97] With time also, the Trinitarian formula, which had been implicit in the early baptismal profession, was made explicit. This point of development had been reached well before the writing of the Greek edition of the first Gospel.

In this connection a word must be said about a Pauline text which is commonly supposed to refer to the "matter and form" of baptism: "Christ loved the Church and handed Himself over on her behalf, that He might consecrate her by purifying her in the bath of water accompanied by a word" (Eph 5:26–27). Are there any grounds for assuming that *en hrēmati* designates the "form" of the sacrament? The word *hrēma* is employed by Paul elsewhere in what is almost certainly a credal formula (probably used in the baptismal ceremony) to denote the profession of faith *"Jēsous Kyrios."* "But what does it [Scripture] say? 'The word (*to hrēma*) is close to you, on your lips and in your mind!' It refers to the word of faith (*to hrēma tēs pisteōs*) which we preach, namely, that if you confess with your lips 'Jesus is *Kyrios*' and you believe with your mind that God has raised Him from the dead, you will be saved" (Rom 10:8–9). In Hebrews the same term appears in a description of the neophyte at his baptism as "having tasted God's fair word (*kalon Theou hrēma*)" (Heb 6:5). Both texts show that *hrēma* is the ordinary expression for the baptismal profession of faith; and this is probably what the Ephesians text refers to also.

Conclusions

Jesus' glorification—if by that term we understand the mysteries of His death, resurrection, ascension, enthronement as *Kyrios*, and the consequent sending of the Spirit to create His kingdom, the Church—played a dominant role in shaping the symbolism of baptism. Indeed, as a passage in Acts (which, in the opinion of critics, comes from a primitive source) indicates, the apostolic community firmly believed that her risen Master's promise of continual presence in her midst as Emmanuel (Mt 28:20; cf. also Mt 1:23) was fulfilled in a dynamic way in the baptismal liturgy. This ancient text, referring to this liturgical presence of Christ, is found in a summary of one of Peter's early discourses: "By raising His Servant, *God has sent Him to you* first of all, *to bless you,* by turning each of you from your sins" (Acts 3:26). As has been shown elsewhere,[98] this presence of Christ is realized through the operations of the Holy Spirit in baptism. A similar notion is found in Paul's writing, where he speaks of the baptismal experience of a Jewish convert to Christianity: "Yet to this day, whenever Moses is read, a veil hangs before their minds. 'But when anyone turns to the Lord, the veil is snatched away.' The Lord is the Spirit; and where the Lord's Spirit is present, there is freedom. And all of us, while with unveiled face we reflect, as in a mirror, the glory of the Lord, are being transformed into the same image with ever-increasing glory, as [one would expect] by the Lord who is the Spirit" (2 Cor 3:15–18).[99] This same theological conception we have already seen operative in the fourth Gospel, whose author desires to show, for the benefit of "those who have not seen" the Jesus of the public life but "have believed" the apostolic testimony, how the exalted Christ, who lives on in the Church, particularly through the sacraments of baptism and the Eucharist, is the same Jesus who lived among men, died, and rose from the dead.[100]

As a consequence of this truth that the risen Lord through His Spirit dwells in His Church and in the individual Christian, the experiences of the apostolic Church, reported in the New Testament, became formative factors in the development of baptismal symbolism. At Pentecost the apostles became aware that Christian baptism was the means of communicating the Spirit they themselves had received. If at first they did not express this doctrine with complete clarity, it is found enunciated in the Pauline and Johannine theologies. While they saw from the beginning the superiority of the Christian sacrament in comparison with John's rite, they gradually recognized the providential part John had played in the history of baptism. The signification of this sacrament as unique means of admission into the Body of the exalted Christ demanded on the part of the recipient a profession of faith in the divinity of the Lord Jesus. This led to its being commonly designated as "baptism in Jesus' Name." Before the close of the apostolic age, however, the practice of having the minister pronounce the liturgical formula "In the Name of the Father, and of the Son, and of the Holy Spirit" became universally adopted.

III

The Apostolic Church and the Written Gospel

ONE of the principal ways in which the apostolic Church bore witness to her risen Lord—a continuing testimony that would be available to future generations—was through the composition of the four Gospels. To appreciate the purpose and the character of these sacred books, we should recall in the first place that the word *euangelion* in the New Testament denotes the apostolic preaching. Thus the writings of Matthew, Mark, Luke, and John all bear in varying degrees the unmistakable traces of the spoken word. It is also to be remembered that in the New Testament the terms *kērygma* and *euangelion* are predicated primarily and properly of the preaching of the apostles, and only in a secondary, derivative sense are they applied to Jesus' own preaching. Jesus is the source of this testimony of the apostolic Church—it was inaugurated only by His divine injunction. He is, moreover, the principal object of this Good News—it is the apostles' attestation to Him and to His redemptive mission. Jesus Christ, however, was not the immediate author of the kerygma, which, as the personal and public or official *martyrion* of the Twelve to His resurrection, was created by Peter and the other members of the apostolic college.

This origin of the apostolic preaching serves as a reminder that the Gospels have human beings as their authors—men who wrote under the special influence and aid of the Holy

Spirit. They are, in consequence, the words of Matthew, Mark, and their fellow Evangelists, witnessing to Jesus' life and teaching. This fact should help us to maintain the proper perspective in evaluating what are usually referred to as the *ipsissima verba Jesu.* It should always have been evident, of course, that with the exception of some half-dozen Aramaic words, we possess our Lord's sayings only in Greek translation (which by its very nature contains interpretation, adaptation, reformulation). What we have in our Gospels—and herein lies their superlative value as the Church's official guide to the Christian way of life—are not Jesus' words *in themselves,* but Jesus' words as attested and understood and explained for us by the official witness of four privileged members of the apostolic church. It is the words of the Evangelists which are inspired: it is they who authored the Gospels which the Church proposes as the norm of Christian belief. These books were composed under the direction of the Church and sealed with her unerring approval. They contain beyond any shadow of doubt the divine revelation given us through Jesus Christ, but they contain that revelation embodied in the Church's witness of Christian faith.

We ought not to be surprised, therefore, if these authors appear to display a certain freedom in recording the sayings of Jesus—a freedom similar to that which they employ towards "the Scriptures," citations of the Old Testament in their works. They were evidently not concerned to provide a mere word-for-word rendition of what Jesus said. A glance at the diverging ways in which the Evangelists have exploited Jesus' logia will convince anyone of the truth of this assertion: e.g., the saying about the lampstand (Mk 4:21; Mt 5:14–15; Lk 11:33), or that concerning the future revelation of what is now hidden (Mk 4:22; Mt 10:26–27; Lk 8:17; 12:2–3).

The same applies to their manner of recording various episodes in Jesus' earthly life: the authors' main concern is the *propter nos et propter nostram salutem,* the Christian understanding of these actions of the Master. Divine Providence could easily have forestalled the invention of the tape recorder, if verbal transcription had been essential to the Church.

This Christian understanding of the revelation brought by Jesus was imparted to the apostles, as John likes to remind his reader (Jn 2:19; 12:16), only with and as a result of Jesus' exaltation. The hermeneutical principle which the Evangelists employed in expounding the sacred significance of the *dicta et facta Jesu* was the Lord's death and glorification. It is these twin events which lay at the heart of the apostolic kerygma with its imperative summons to Christian belief (*metanoia*). It is these same two events which control in varying degrees the inclusion and exposition of certain data regarding Jesus' public ministry. Consequently, each saying, each episode in the Gospels is to be assessed in function of its relation to the central event witnessed to by the apostolic Church. And it is also by means of this hermeneutical principle that we should attempt to solve the vexed question of the historical quality of the Infancy narratives.

The first essay in this section exposes the character of the New Testament writings, in contrast with the oral preaching, as *didachē.* The "teaching of the apostles" within the community of faith has impressed itself on the letters of Paul as well as on the writings of the four Evangelists. It is essentially a theological exploration of the Christian mystery, the work of *fides quaerens intellectum.* The Gospels were written by believers for believers. They may, indeed they must in the interests of Christian apologetics, be read at times merely as human documents worthy of credence because of the first-rate evidence they offer, which is based upon personal, competent experience. They can, however, only be fully appreciated when seen through the eyes of Christian faith.

The second study seeks to analyze the conception of salvation presented in the Synoptic Gospels. While these writers have certain common points of view, which in fact they share with the fourth Evangelist, yet each has his own personal approach to Christ, each exposes his own individual notion of Christian salvation. It does no service to Christianity, nor does it aid our comprehension of any particular author's insight into Christ, to neglect the tensions which persist between the various New Testament writers' conceptions of the Christian religion. It is actually the mark of heresy (a Greek term which means "picking and choosing") to select but one or other viewpoint exclusively, or even to emphasize one author's characteristic teaching to the neglect of the others.

The last essay seeks to describe the New Testament concept of sacred history by discussing the nature of the four canonical Gospels as salvation history. How does religious history, as recorded in the Bible, differ from secular, scientific history? Through what forms of literature did the Evangelists seek to present the Christian history of salvation? How is our understanding of salvation history enlightened by a study of what Pius XII has called "the distinctive genius of the sacred writers"? The modern answers given these questions form part of the so-called "new approach" to the Scriptures. Its chief quality, from which have flowed its best achievements, consists in the clear insight into the nature of revelation as historical process.

7

Didachē As a Constitutive Element of the Written Gospel

THE ancient ritual prescribed for episcopal consecration in the *Pontificale Romanum* refers repeatedly to preaching and teaching as among the principal duties of the bishop.[1] Thus the liturgy, with its unfailing sense of Christian tradition, reminds the new prelate that, as successor of the apostles, he inherits these two functions which the New Testament depicts them as exercising in spreading the gospel.

Some years ago C. H. Dodd made an important contribution to New Testament studies by pointing out how carefully the inspired writers distinguish between preaching and teaching. Preaching he defined as "the public proclamation of Christianity to the non-Christian world," while teaching included "ethical instruction," "apologetic, that is, the reasoned commendation of Christianity to persons interested but not yet convinced," and finally "the exposition of theological doctrine."[2] Since, however, these definitions do not appear to include adequately all the examples of teaching or of preaching given in the New Testament, or even to distinguish with sufficient precision the one notion from the other, it will be necessary to clarify these conceptions before we can discuss the influence of the apostolic teaching upon the literary genre we call a Gospel.[3]

PREACHING IN THE NEW TESTAMENT

The two words most commonly translated by the English verb "to preach" in the Greek New Testament are *kēryssein* and *euangelizesthai*.[4] As has been pointed out,[5] these terms represent a much more dynamic activity than their counterparts in any of our modern languages. *Kēryssein* connotes fundamentally the proclamation by the *kēryx*, or herald, of a message, not his own, made in the name of another, upon whom its authority depends. *Euangelizesthai* signifies properly the act of bearing good news, the *euangelion*. In the Septuagint both words are used to describe the activity of the Old Testament prophets: Jonah's message of salvation to the Gentiles is kerygma;[6] Second Isaiah employs the verb *euangelizesthai* for the proclaiming of God's future act of universal redemption.[7]

In the New Testament, John the Baptist appears as the preacher par excellence. The burden of his kerygma is the proximity of the kingdom, the establishment of divine sovereignty in this world: "The kingdom of God is at hand" (Mt 3:2; Mk 1:4; Lk 16:16; Jn 1:19 ff.; 1:29; 1:35 f.). To prepare for the advent of this kingdom, John announces the need of a profound change in man's religious attitude (*metanoia*) and the reception of baptism as symbol of this interior renovation. The Gospels define John's function in the new economy almost entirely in terms of *kēryssein*. Luke is the only Evangelist who speaks of him as a teacher. John taught his disciples to pray (Lk 11:1), and once at least he is addressed by an interlocutor as rabbi or teacher (Lk 3:12).[8] It is true that frequent reference is made by all the Evangelists to the fact that John gathered disciples about him;[9] but they also appear to suggest that this was only a passing phase. John did not intend to found a "school," but instructed his disciples to look for the Christ and to become His disciples (Jn 1:35 ff.; Mt 11:2 ff.). On the other hand, John's role as preacher is underscored by the constantly recurring theme of Elijah redivivus: he is to fulfil his vocation *en pneumati kai dynamei Ēliou* (Lk 1:17); he enters upon his public life dressed in the garb of Elijah (Mt 3:4); in him Elijah has returned (Mk 9:13); he is the last of the Old Testament prophets (Mt 11:13). Like the prophets, John announces a message that is not his own but the Word of the Lord which "comes upon" Him (Lk 3:2); and the message concerns an event which lies in the future. Nothing that John can do can usher in the coming kingdom: it is only the creative power of the Word he bears that can make the kingdom a reality.

If the Evangelists present preaching as the most characteristic feature of John's work, they seem to consider it less so in the case of Jesus. In the beginning of His public ministry, it is true, Jesus is frequently described as preaching by the Synoptics, and His message appears to be the same as that of the Baptist: The kingdom of God is at hand; repent, and believe the gospel (Mk 1:14; Mt 4:17, 23; Lk 4:44). Moreover, when the Twelve are sent on their first missionary journey, Jesus commands them to preach this same message. Once this episode is concluded, however, Jesus is pictured as devoting Himself almost exclusively to the occupation which appears in the Gospels as most characteristic of Him—teaching.[10] Thus the Evangelists would seem to insinuate that the role of herald of the divine Word, inasmuch as it implies a distinction between the Divinity and the bearer of the announcement, does not properly become Jesus Christ.

At any rate, the inspired writers are conscious of a distinction in the meaning of the term "preaching" as applied to John and to Jesus. The kingdom proclaimed by Christ is not entirely in the future: Jesus' very presence among men marks

ing is the conversion of Jews and pagans to the Gospel. The response to it is described as the "hearing of faith" (Gal 3:2; Rom 10:17). The kerygma centers in the redemptive death and exaltation of Christ as the inauguration of the Messianic times; and to this essential proclamation there is prefixed a survey of Jesus' public ministry, introduced by the work of John the Baptist.[17] Finally, it includes a summons to *metanoia*, now concretized in the act of faith in Jesus' divinity and Messiahship, and to aggregration in the visible community by the acceptance of Christian baptism.

This is preaching, or kerygma, in its most proper sense, as we see it employed as a technical term by Paul.[18] As will be evident from what we have said, the term is only analogous when applied to John's preaching or to that of Jesus. Before the central act of the redemption had taken place, it was a question of announcing the *coming* kingdom, or, at most, its inceptive foundation through Jesus' miracles. The apostolic preaching, on the other hand, announces the kingdom as *having come* through Christ's death and resurrection and the descent of the Holy Spirit. It is these historic facts which have transformed the kerygma into a "divine power leading to salvation" (Rom 1:16).

Modern Gospel criticism has devoted a good deal of attention to this apostolic preaching and has rightly seen it as a major factor in the determination of their literary genre. The Gospels retain many vestiges of the oral catechesis. They do not attempt to present a chronological account of the life of Christ and are in no proper sense biographical. Like the kerygma, they propose the various phases of Christ's salvific work.

While this kerygmatic character of the Gospels has been stressed, and with good reason, there is evidence also that the evangelical *genre littéraire* owes much to another influence, that of the Apostolic "teaching." It may be recalled at this point that the Evangelists did not write primarily for a non-Christian public, but rather to give their Christian readers a deeper insight into the events heralded by the apostolic preaching. Luke makes this clear in his dedicatory exordium: his declared purpose is "to write an ordered account for you, most noble Theophilus, in order that you may perceive the authentic character of the oral instructions you received."[19] Luke sets out to arrange his material in such a way as to provide Theophilus, already a believer, with a profounder grasp of the truths of Christianity. The intention of the author of the fourth Gospel might seem, at first sight, to be different: "These things have been written in order that you may believe that Jesus is the Christ, the Son of God, and that through faith you may attain life in His Name" (Jn 20:31). However, as Père Mollat points out,[20] the Evangelist is addressing Christians, whose faith he wishes to deepen. "Eternal life" for St. John means the full experiential knowledge of the Father and the Son (Jn 17:3), which presupposes the "teaching" which he endeavors to impart in his Gospel.

To demonstrate adequately the influence of the apostolic *didachē* upon the form of our written Gospels, it will be necessary to isolate the element of *didachē* in the New Testament and to attempt a definition of it. Accordingly, we wish to consider the teaching of Jesus Himself and then that of the apostolic Church.

JESUS AS TEACHER

The Gospels mention the fact of Jesus' teaching more frequently than they do that of His preaching;[21] and, what is much more significant, they multiply examples of this teaching.[22]

Matthew applied the verb *didaskein* to the "sermon" on the Mount (Mt 5:2 ff.), and while he does not expressly use the term in connection with the four great discourses which follow it, he clearly regards them also as *didachē*.[23] What is the function of these speeches, which Matthew has constructed out of various logia of Jesus found in tradition, in the plan of the first Gospel? They constitute, in the first place, a commentary on the object of Jesus' kerygma, the coming of the kingdom of heaven: its code of perfection, its essentially missionary character, its mystery, its social aspects, its complete universality in contrast with the Judaism it is to replace. Moreover, each discourse sets forth an interpretation of the events of Jesus' public life immediately preceding it.[24] Thus it is clear that Matthew's Gospel does not depend, for its form, merely upon the kerygma as we see it proclaimed in the Acts of the Apostles. The teaching of Jesus has also influenced its structural framework. The Matthean discourses do not serve merely to punctuate the narrative sections; they give an insight into their meaning and assist in highlighting the movement of the whole story. Without them, the first Gospel would indeed be kerygma. It would not be a written Gospel.

Of the four, Mark's Gospel is nearest in form to the apostolic preaching. Tradition tells us that Mark simply recorded what Peter preached as well as he could remember it. Inasmuch as the second Gospel has any plan at all, it appears to be that of the Petrine catechesis. It is instructive to observe that Mark devotes little space to Jesus' teaching. Yet even his Gospel cannot be defined as pure kerygma. The various elements have been arranged in such a way as to bring out the meaning of the events proclaimed—specifically, the meaning of the mystery of Jesus.[25] Moreover, Mark does not fail to refer to the teaching of the Master. Indeed, as Père Lagrange has keenly observed, Mark has his own theory concerning the nature of Jesus' public teaching.[26] For him, the parable becomes the symbol of the merciful way the Lord taught the crowds in Galilee—a pedagogy well suited to their capacity to understand (Mk 4:33) and calculated to pique the supernatural curiosity of the man of good will, who would thus be led to seek further clarification. Jesus' instruction of the disciples is of a higher nature: "in private He explained everything to His disciples" (Mk 4:34). One instance of this second kind of teaching is, for Mark, the prediction of Christ's passion and resurrection, in connection with which the word *didaskein* is used (Mk 8:31; 9:31). This example is particularly helpful for perceiving the distinction between teaching and preaching in the Gospels. The subject matter is the same as that of the kerygma. Still, it is *didachē*, on Mark's view, because it is addressed only to the disciples who had already found faith in Jesus (cf. Mk 8:29) and also because it reveals the Christological sense of the Old Testament prophecies concerning the sufferings and glorification of the Messiah.[27]

Indeed, *didachē* bears an essential relation to the understanding of "the Scriptures."[28] This aspect is set in relief by Luke's first example of Jesus' teaching, the scene in the Nazareth synagogue (Lk 4:15 ff.). We have already referred to this episode to show how the miracles Christ mentioned are in themselves kerygma. Their use here to point up the meaning of the prophet's words is *didachē*: *telos gar Nomou Christos* (Rom 10:4). The pericope illustrates clearly the relation of teaching to preaching in the New Testament. The insight into the Christian sense of the Old Testament which Jesus imparted is what impressed His hearers and the Evangelists with the "newness" of His teaching and distinguished it from the instruction of their scribes and Pharisees (Mk 1:28; Lk 4:36; Mt 7:29). This clarification of "the Scriptures" and of certain events in Israel's history during the march through the desert is exemplified also by the discourse on the bread of life in the fourth Gospel (Jn 6:59), which John regards as teaching. Moreover, it also brings out the function of *didachē* as an explanation of the meaning of Christ's own actions: the miracle of the multiplication of loaves is seen as a type of the future Eucharist.[29]

These instances of Jesus' teaching enable us to grasp its salient features and to distinguish it from preaching. The kerygma proclaims the coming of the kingdom; *didachē* explains the nature of the kingdom and reveals it as the perfect fulfilment of the Old Testament. The kerygma announces the definitive divine intervention in human history which is to be realized in Christ's death and resurrection; the teaching of Jesus' public life is a pedagogical preparation of His disciples, calculated to make them understand the salvific meaning of these events when they occur.

In this connection one final observation is in order. The Evangelists insist repeatedly that during His earthly life Jesus' teaching was never very well understood by the disciples. Each Evangelist has his own view of this lack of comprehension, but each dwells on it.[30] It is, moreover, noteworthy that there is but one occasion mentioned in the Gospels upon which the Apostles are said to have "taught"—and that without any injunction from the Master! Mark observes that upon their return from the first missionary voyage they "announced to Him all that they had done and had taught" (Mk 6:30). The Evangelist has already told his reader that Jesus' purpose in gathering the Twelve about Him was "that He might send them to *preach* and to have power to exorcise the demons" (Mk 3:15); and he describes the apostles' work on this first mission as preaching, casting out devils, healing the sick (Mk 6:13). From Matthew we know that Jesus had sent His disciples to preach the near approach of the kingdom (Mt 10:7).

The fact that Mark says the disciples taught on this occasion does not, I believe, warrant the inference that, at least in his eyes, teaching and preaching are synonymous.[31] It is more likely that the Twelve carefully reported to the Master on their attempts at teaching because He had not commanded it, and they wished to expose their doctrine for His approval. Since there is no other record in the Gospels of any further teaching on the part of the apostles, it is likely that this first essay in *didachē* was not very successful. Nor was it the wish of Jesus—and for the reason already mentioned: the apostles did not sufficiently understand His teaching during His earthly life.

As a matter of fact, the command to teach is given the apostles only after His resurrection by the exalted Christ. In virtue of His endowment with full and universal power as a result of His glorification,[32] Christ sends His followers "to make disciples of all the nations by baptizing them . . . and by teaching them to observe whatever I have enjoined upon you . . ." (Mt 28:19 f.). From Luke we know that Christ's teaching of His own went on during the postresurrection period: it was mainly an opening of their minds to understand "the Scriptures" (Lk 24:45).[33] They themselves were not, however, to attempt to teach until "endowed with power from on high" (Lk 24:49). The reason for this injunction is made clear at the beginning of Acts (1:6): until the coming of the Holy Spirit, the apostles had never quite succeeded in grasping the essentially spiritual nature of the kingdom. During Christ's public life they were only capable of preaching its coming, not of teaching its meaning and character. Like the Old Testament prophets, they could proclaim the future coming of the kingdom with only a very imperfect understanding of it. Pentecost was to bring them the power to teach Christianity by initiating them into the mysteries hitherto concealed from them.

With the descent of the Holy Ghost, they were to realize that the inauguration of the kingdom of God was due to the Spirit's coming and not to the return of Christ in glory to set up a terrestrial dominion.

THE HOLY SPIRIT AS SOURCE OF THE APOSTOLIC TEACHING

In the fourth Gospel Jesus recalls the prediction that in the Messianic age God Himself would instruct His people: "It is written in the prophets, 'they will all be taught by God' " (Jn 6:45; Is 54:13; Jer 31:33). He points out to the Jews that the only way to come to Him, to become His disciple, to understand His teaching, is through the teaching of the Father (Jn 6:44 f.). The Father's teaching has guided Him during His earthly mission (Jn 8:28); in consequence, His teaching is not His own but that of the Father "who sent me" (Jn 7:16). When, in the course of His last conversation with His disciples after the Last Supper, they have demonstrated more clearly than ever before their lack of understanding, He promises them that "the Paraclete, the Holy Spirit, whom the Father will send in my Name, will teach you everything and recall to you all that I have spoken to you" (Jn 14:25). The Holy Spirit will thus, by reminding them of Jesus' instructions during His mortal career, provide the basis for their *didachē*. But the Spirit "of Truth" is not to act merely as a mnemonic aid: "He will introduce you to the truth in its entirety" (Jn 16:13). He is to open their minds to the deeper perception of the meaning of Jesus' teaching.

THE TEACHING OF THE APOSTLES

The insight given by the pentecostal Spirit into the lifework of Christ and into the *raison d'être* of Israel's sacred books is thus presented by the New Testament as the chief element in the creation of the apostolic teaching. The kerygma proclaimed the accomplishment of the Old Testament in Christ's work for man's salvation. The apostolic *didachē* may, therefore, be defined as the induction into the *sensus plenior* of the kerygma.

Oddly enough, though Luke refers to the "teaching" of the Apostles as a technical term in Acts, he gives the reader only one example of it: Paul's discourse to the seniors of the church of Ephesus (Acts 20:18–35). This instruction to the pastors of the Christian flock is based upon a logion of Christ's not recorded elsewhere: "It is more blessed to give than to receive" (v. 35). An autobiographical sketch of Paul's own apostolic activities provides a first commentary on this saying of the Lord's (vv. 18–24): his reliance on Christ, his complete frankness in both preaching and teaching (*anangeilai kai didaxai*, v. 20), his readiness to give his own life in order to carry out the commission he has received from the Lord. The second section (vv. 25–35) is an application of Jesus' words to their own pastoral office: they have been constituted "overseers" of the Church by the Holy Spirit with full jurisdiction; they must guard the purity of doctrine against heretics; they must look to the Lord, who is the chief builder of the Church, for their "inheritance," without seeking worldly advantages. Dom Jacques Dupont has commented upon the many parallels between this discourse and the pastoral letters of Paul, where frequent examples of this same type of teaching are to be found.[34]

Indeed, the Pauline epistles furnish one of the best examples of the apostolic teaching to be found in the New Testament. Written to those who have already been converted by the kerygyma, they contain abundant instances of a profounder explanation of the truths of the faith and their practical application to the Christian life.[35] That Paul regarded his letters as a form of *didachē* may be seen from a remark he makes to the Thessalonians: "Steadfastly preserve the traditions which you have been taught either orally or through one of our letters" (2 Th 2:15). Paul always carefully preserves the distinction between preaching and teaching. His own knowledge of Christianity, he tells the Galatians, was derived directly from Christ. "Neither did I receive it [the gospel] from any human being, nor was I taught except through a revelation of Jesus Christ" (Gal 1:12).[36] Eph 4:20–21 provides a similar example: "But you did not thus learn Christ, if at least you have heard Him preached and taught in a manner consonant with the truth which is in Jesus." Once the Apostle has established a church by his preaching, the activity which engages him is *didaskein*. "For this reason I sent Timothy to you . . . who will relate to you my journeys in Christ, how everywhere in every church I teach" (1 Cor 4:17).

This teaching is concerned with a deeper instruction in the Christian way of life that results in the living of the dogmas grasped in a profound manner. "Go on living your life in Christ, [who is] the Lord, just as you have received Him: being rooted in and built on Him and made firm in the faith as you were taught . . ." (Col 2:6).[37] Both this text and the one from Ephesians just cited insist upon the identity of the exalted Christ with the Jesus of the public life, and show in consequence Paul's awareness that the authority of his *didachē* derives from the "truth which is in Jesus," the Jesus who worked and taught in Galilee.

At the same time, the teaching of the apostolic Church does not consist merely in a reiteration of the *ipsissima verba Christi*. Aware that the Holy Spirit had revealed to them the infallible meaning of the Master's instructions, the apostolic teachers do not hesitate to *develop* His teaching: to apply it to the concrete situations in which they find themselves, and to exploit the rich lode of wisdom which it contains. Thus the explanations of some of the parables given by the Evangelists are in reality their application to the experiences of the Church in the apostolic age.[38] The fourth Evangelist, moreover, has not hesitated to present Jesus' teaching in his own way and has brought to perfection the dialectical method of instruction (which, of course, owes its origins to Jesus Himself).[39]

DIDACHE AND THE GOSPEL FORM

We come finally to answer our principal question: In what way can apostolic teaching be said to have influenced the form of our canonical Gospels?

It will be helpful here to recall one Evangelist's view of his own written work. St. Luke sums up his first volume as "an account of all that Jesus began to do and to teach" (Acts 1:1).[40] What Jesus *did* (His redemptive death and resurrection, the work of the public ministry) forms the basis of the apostolic kerygma. What Jesus *taught* (understood by the apostles in the light of Pentecost) forms the basis of the apostolic teaching. We have already remarked on the place of honor which all the Evangelists give to Jesus' teaching and on their care to explain the meaning of the more significant actions of His life. This all comes under the notion of *didachē*. But over and above that, the very form which the Gospels take is determined, to a large extent, by the Evangelists' preoccupation with teaching the believer the inner sense of the substance of the kerygma. Matthew uses five discourses which he has carefully constructed as his method of commenting upon the meaning of the kingdom of heaven as it has come in Jesus Christ. Luke employs the travel story[41] to bring out the meaning of Jesus' death and resurrection, which he conceives as an *exodos*, a passing from this world to the Father (Lk 9:31). St. John sees in the Cross as well as in the glorification of Christ the *doxa,* the divine glory, the definitive revelation of the divinity of Jesus. Accordingly, he portrays the actions and words of Christ as a series of minor Christophanies which prepare the believer for the final Christophany of Good Friday and Easter Sunday. Mark's Gospel is nearer the kerygma than any of the others. Still, as we have seen, his work also manifests the influence of the apostolic teaching—that of Peter, the chief of the apostles. Mark seeks to give his reader the answer to the question "Who is Jesus?" and he has accordingly presented the works of Jesus' public life and the events which form its climax as the revelation of the mystery of the God-man.

We may conclude, therefore, that if, on the one hand, the preaching of the apostles certainly played a major role in the creation of the evangelical *genre littéraire,* it is no less clear, on the other, that the teaching of the apostolic Church was also an essential factor in its emergence. The kerygma has provided the basic blueprint for the Gospel form in the quadripartite plan which includes the major events from the appearance of the Baptist to the resurrection of Christ. To the *didachē,* however, must be attributed the undeniable *cachet personnel* with which each of the four Evangelists has impregnated the basic material so as to give his own characteristic version of the Good News of Jesus Christ.

8

Salvation in the Synoptic Gospels

IN A previous study[1] an investigation was made into the origins of the Christian notion of salvation, which was shown to have stemmed principally from the pentecostal experience of the first disciples and which was expressed in a somewhat rudimentary fashion in the apostolic kerygma. In the course of that preliminary study it became evident that the first specifically Christian soteriology was the direct result of the revelation of the divine personality of the Holy Spirit, whose descent had inaugurated "the last times" and had transformed the disciples into the Messianic *qahal* of the new Israel, and of the disclosure of the divinity of Jesus of Nazareth, whose enthronement at God's right hand, publicized by His sending of the Spirit, proved His identity "as prince and saviour, in order to give repentance to Israel, as well as remission of sins" (Acts 5:31). Since this was the psychological process by which the apostolic community arrived at their belief in Jesus as divine saviour, it was natural that their kerygma should have been centered primarily upon the fact that God had raised Him from the dead and seated Him in glory as copartner in the divine governance of the universe. It was also due to this realization of Jesus' divinity that His passion and death were proclaimed as universally salvific. To these two principal articles of the Christian faith the apostolic preachers added some of the incidents of Jesus' public life and certain examples of His teaching, which He had given in preparation for the final accomplishment of salvation.[2]

When one attempts, as we propose to do in the present study, to assess the advance which the Gospels bearing the names of Matthew, Mark, and Luke represent over this primitive salvation doctrine, two fundamental points must be constantly borne in mind. In the first place, one is no longer dealing immediately with the oral preaching of the apostolic age, but with a literary genre, the written Gospel, which we have elsewhere termed *didachē*[3] and which is distinguishable from the kerygma by two qualities. First, these written accounts of the Christian history of salvation were aimed, not at the conversion of the non-Christian world, but at the Christian reading-public, already professing faith in Christ as the *Kyrios*, yet requiring further instruction in the meaning of the events of His earthly career which culminated in His *sessio ad dexteram Patris*.[4] Second, the primary principle governing the selection, arrangement, and mode of narration of the events and teaching of the Master was the interpretation, in function of the new-found Christian faith, of the data of the kerygma. This interpretative function of the inspired writers must not be passed over in any proper evaluation of the stage of dogmatic development represented by the Synoptics. Such a disregard, in the case of some exegetes and theologians, led to a somewhat naive attitude towards what are termed the *ipsissima verba Christi*, as well as to the deplorably uncritical tendency to "harmonize" the divergent Synoptic records of Jesus' words or miracles by ignoring or minimizing those discrepancies in detail which often represent the personal signature of the Evangelist or constitute the easily recognizable hallmark of oral tradition.

The second major factor which should be operative in any judgment of the Synoptic contribution to New Testament soteriology is the substantial dependence of each of the first three Evangelists upon the primitive kerygma as regards the general schema which remains at the basis of his written work, as also upon oral tradition and earlier written evangelical "essays."[5] However the Evangelist may arrange, interpret, or narrate the sayings and doings of Jesus Christ, his theological presentation is subordinated to the facts, historical and meta-historical, of the sacred history which he is narrating. He may redistribute the various logia of Jesus by grouping them into discourses of his own construction, just as he may reconstruct the setting of incidents only sketchily transmitted to him by tradition. He does not, however, create these sermons or miracles out of whole cloth. The materials which he works upon are the data furnished him by apostolic eyewitnesses.[6]

In our study of the Synoptic doctrine of salvation, we wish to discuss the individual purpose of each writer insofar as it is discernible in his book and then to examine the principal texts of each Gospel dealing with our subject. We shall begin with Mark, since it is closest in time and in spirit to the apostolic preaching. Then we shall investigate the modalities of the soteriology found in Matthew and Mark.

GENERAL CHARACTERISTICS OF SYNOPTIC SOTERIOLOGY

Broadly speaking, the outline followed by each of the first three Evangelists in his written account of the salvation accomplished by God in Jesus Christ coincides with that found in the primitive preaching. The Synoptic Gospels take the ministry of John the Baptist as point of departure,[7] recount incidents and report the main points of teaching which occurred in the Galilean ministry, and, after noting the last journey of Jesus from Galilee to Jerusalem, bring their story to its climax in His passion, death, and resurrection.[8] Moreover, many of the titles applied to Christ in the primitive preaching as well as certain characterizations of Him derived from Old Testament typology (the suffering-glorified Servant, the new Moses, the new David) recur in the Synoptic Gospels, as is evident from the references to the parousiac return of the risen Christ, to the final judgment, and the use of apocalyptic imagery borrowed from the Old Testament.[9]

At the same time, the soteriology of the Synoptic Gospels represents a more developed stage than that found in the primitive preaching.[10] To confine ourselves to generalities for the moment, this development may be most clearly seen in the Synoptic use of the materials concerning the public life of Jesus. In the earlier period of theological thinking, mainly through the efforts of the Hellenistic element in the Jerusalem Church,[11] the Old Testament history of salvation had been reinterpreted in function of the Christ-event. The great discovery at this stage had been the typological significance of the great Old Testament figures and events, which were quickly pressed into service in presenting the kerygma to the Jews of Palestine. By the time the Synoptic Gospels were written, however, there is evidence of a new current of thought. These Evangelists have learned to employ the sayings and doings of Jesus during the Galilean ministry to shed light upon the mystery of His divinity and, conversely, to interpret these facts in function of His subsequent death and resurrection. Their awareness of the salvific significance of the events which climaxed Jesus' earthly mission provided the sacred writers with the key to the meaning of His miracles and to His teaching concerning the proximate advent of the kingdom of God. They also found in the happenings of Jesus' earthly ministry an explanation for the experiences through which the apostolic

Church of their day was passing.[12] It is the fruit of such theological reflection which is enshrined in the Synoptic Gospels and which constitutes perhaps their most salient feature.

PURPOSE AND PLAN OF ST. MARK'S GOSPEL

We have already stated that in some respects the second Gospel stands nearer than any other to the primitive preaching. Tradition tells us, and recent criticism is more ready than formerly to accept it as genuine,[13] that Mark wrote down the Petrine catechesis "as well as he could remember it." Thus the soteriology of this Gospel is basically that worked out by St. Peter, who is depicted in Acts as the principal author of the schema of the apostolic preaching.[14]

One characteristic of Mark's Gospel which reveals a point of view akin to that found in the kerygma is the close bond which exists between its soteriology and its Christology. In the first days of Christianity, the initial insight into the mystery of Jesus provided by the pentecostal revelation gave rise to the earliest soteriological formulations. "By raising His servant, God has sent Him to you, first of all, to bless you, by turning each of you from your iniquity" (Acts 3:26; cf. also Acts 2:36; 5:31). For Mark, the mystery of the kingdom of God or of the divine definitive salvation is inseparable from the mystery of Jesus. He expresses the theme of his book in its opening words: "the Good News of Jesus Christ, Son of God" (1:1). The question which Mark seeks to answer in his Gospel is "Who is Jesus?"[15] The first section of his work sketches the mystery; the second section presents its unfolding through Jesus' death and resurrection.[16]

It is to be noted that Mark's answer to his question is given in the existential order: Jesus is a man who acts like God. Such a statement, which confines itself to the order of activity rather than that of essences, is typical of the Semitic mind. For the Israelite, Yahweh was the only existing God because He was the only God who had ever done anything for Israel. When Mark depicts Jesus of Nazareth as a man who acts like Yahweh, he is affirming the reality both of Jesus' human nature and of His divinity.[17] This characteristically Marcan viewpoint, which is reminiscent of Peter's pentecostal discourse,[18] may be illustrated by two series of texts.

The first series consists of texts which show Jesus acting in a way which in the Old Testament was an inalienable prerogative of Yahweh. When the Scribes ask: "Who can forgive sins but God alone?", Jesus replies by healing the paralytic "in order that you may know that the Son of Man has power to forgive sins upon earth . . ." (2:7–10). The dispute between the disciples and the Pharisees about the plucking of grain on the Sabbath is settled by Jesus' remark: "So the Son of Man is Lord even of the Sabbath" (2:23–28).[19] After the calming of the storm, Mark, through the disciples, puts the question to his reader: "What sort of man is this, since even the wind and the sea obey Him?" (4:41). It is by means of incidents like these that Mark sets before the reader the divinity of Jesus.[20]

The second series contains those texts in which the title "Son of God" is applied to Jesus. When it occurs in the title line of the Gospel, addressed to the believer, it retains its full theological meaning (1:1). On the other hand, it is only vaguely Messianic when put in the mouth of the demons who scream out: "You are the Son of God!" (3:11; 5:7). In asserting the ignorance of "the Son" concerning the date of the destruction of the Temple, Jesus refers to Himself in His role of revealer of God's plan of salvation to men (13:32). Mark intends that the Christian reader shall recognize in Jesus' affirmative answer to the question put to Him by the Highpriest and Sanhedrin, "Are you the Christ, the Son of the Blessed?", a solemn affirmation of His divinity (14:61–62). The last text provides an interesting illustration of the way Mark uses the data of tradition. The remark "This man must surely have been a Son of God" (15:39) in the mouth of a pagan centurion could have meant no more than a kind of superstitious admiration.[21] Its function, at the very climax of the Marcan Gospel, however, is to provide the reader with an expression of faith in Christ's divinity as he finishes the book. Thus it is clear that the title "Son of God," taken in relation to the faith of the Church at the time when this Gospel was written, is intended to be understood in its full Christian sense, even though in its original context it may have signified much less. It is Mark's way of answering the question which is central to his whole exposition.

SOTERIOLOGY OF THE SECOND GOSPEL

The doctrine of salvation presented by Mark has not the theological finesse which characterizes the fourth Gospel or the Pauline letters. Still, the supreme value of Jesus' redemptive death and the importance of His resurrection in the history of salvation are clearly asserted. In the first place, Jesus' entire mission in this world is related to sin and its destruction. Second, His sufferings, death, and resurrection are shown to be no mere chance occurrences, but form an integral part of the divine salvific plan. As such, they are foretold by Jesus in the course of His public ministry. We wish now to examine the texts which illustrate these two points in Marcan soteriology.

The Connection between Jesus' Mission and Sin

Mk 2:17: And Jesus hearing says to them: "The healthy have no need of a doctor, but the sick [do need one]. I have not come to call the just, but sinners."

Jesus here uses a proverb which was a commonplace with the Cynic philosophers but which is natural enough in this context.[22] Besides, it may contain a reference to the Deutero-Isaian Servant (cf. Mt 8:16–17). The call to repentance is directed to those who acknowledge themselves sinners rather than to the self-righteous like the "scribes and the Pharisees," whose criticism appears to have occasioned this remark (2:16).

More generally, Mark depicts Jesus' mission as a struggle against Satan, to which the Holy Spirit "drives" Jesus immediately after His baptism (1:12 f.). From the very beginning of His public life, Jesus, refusing to remain in Capharnaum, tours the Galilean villages, preaching "and casting out the demons" (1:39). The first miracle related in the second Gospel is an exorcism (1:23–26). Mark expressly notes that in choosing the Twelve Jesus' purpose is "that they might be with Him and that He might send them to preach and to have power to cast out the demons" (3:14–15). The conferring of this power (6:7) is recorded, as well as its exercise by the apostles (6:13).

Christ's Passion, Death, Resurrection, Prophesied by Him, Are Not Fortuitous Events but Part of the Divine Plan of Salvation

Mk 2:20: "But days will come when the bridegroom will be taken from them, and then they will fast on that day."

The use of the rare word *aphairesthai* is, according to M.-J.

Lagrange,[23] a reference to the Servant in Is 53:8: *hairetai apo tēs gēs hē zōē autou,* and consequently a prophecy of Jesus' death. V. Taylor[24] agrees that there is no mere allegory here. The application to Jesus is, of course, made necessary by the question in v. 18b.

The most celebrated of Jesus' references to His approaching death and resurrection are the three predictions (Mk 8:31; 9:31; 10:33–34) which recur in each of the Synoptic Gospels and are there transcribed with remarkable fidelity.[25] The triple repetition is simply a device to indicate how frequently Jesus must have taught His disciples about what would happen to Himself. In each Gospel the third account is much more detailed, and there is no difficulty in admitting that Jesus' prophecy was, in posterior tradition, made more explicit.[26] While these prophecies are couched in terms of the Suffering Servant,[27] each of them concerns "the Son of Man" described in Daniel. The coupling together of these two Old Testament types of the Saviour-Messiah most probably goes back to Jesus Himself.

Mk 9:12: "Granted that Elijah must come first to restore all things, then why does Scripture say of the Son of Man that He must suffer much and be treated with contempt?"

The general sense of this obscure verse appears to be that while Jewish tradition (cf. Mal 3:22–23; Sir 48:1–11) is substantially correct in assuming that Elijah's function, performed already by John the Baptist, is essentially ordained to God's final act of salvation, still it is through his unjustly merited death that John fulfils his principal role as type of Christ.[28] Thus Jesus answers the question in His disciples' minds ("What does resurrection from the dead mean?", 9:10) by showing them the connection between His own death and "the restoration of all things."

Mk 10:39: "You will drink the cup which I am drinking and will receive the baptism with which I am being baptized. . . ."

This logion refers to Jesus' redemptive sufferings under two Old Testament symbols for suffering and calamity: the cup and water. E. Lohmeyer is likely right in assuming that in Mark's mind there is some connection with the sacraments of the Eucharist and baptism,[29] which both derive their efficacy and their symbolism from Jesus' passion and death. An interesting feature of this verse is the conception that Christ's Messianic sufferings have already begun in His public life. It is this reinterpretation of the meaning of the Galilean ministry in function of Jesus' death and resurrection which, as has already been stated, is the hallmark of the Synoptic soteriology.

Mk 10:45: "Now the Son of Man has not come to be served but to serve, and to give His life as a ransom for many."

Vincent Taylor remarks that this saying is one of the most important in the Gospels, and he accepts it as genuine despite the arguments which liberal criticism has long urged against it.[30] In the context of the last journey to Jerusalem, such a precise statement is what one would expect.[31] Jesus describes His passion and death as a service and a gift; for it is through His undertaking the role of the Suffering Servant that He will inaugurate the kingdom of God, that divine sovereignty over men imparted to them as a grace. By employing the word *lytron,* which expresses the notion of expiation found in Is 53 (cf. the Septuagint of Is 52:3 where the verb *lytroun* is found), Mark evokes the Servant theology. Thus the verse is a most explicit affirmation of the redemptive value of Jesus' suffering and death: He is come for no other purpose but to redeem sinners at the price of His life, offered for their sins.

Mk 12:10: "Did you never read this text, 'The very stone which the builders rejected has become the cornerstone: this is the Lord's doing, and it is a marvel in our eyes'?"

This reference to Ps 117(118):22–23 is attached to the parable of the Wicked Husbandmen (12:1–9; *item* Mt 21: 33–46; Lk 20:9–19) and was likely added by our Lord Himself. As Vincent Taylor remarks, it is probable that the popularity of this conception of Christ in primitive Christianity, as the *lithos* rejected by men but selected by God as cornerstone of a new temple, was due to the apostolic recollection of the use Jesus made of this Psalm in His polemic against the Jewish religious leaders.[32] At any rate, the theme follows the same pattern as that of the Servant theology: God has glorified His Christ, whom His people have rejected and slain.

Mk 14:24: "This is my blood, covenant blood, which is about to be shed for the sake of many."

Mark's formula of the words of institution over the chalice, probably adopted by him from the Roman liturgy,[33] recalls both Is 53 and the logion he recorded earlier (10:45), as well as the words of the Sinaitic pact (Ex 24:8) with which they were connected in apostolic Christianity.[34] Thus the words of Jesus as reported by Mark refer the meaning of the Eucharist to the atoning sacrifice of the Deutero-Isaian Servant, as well as to the Sinaitic rite of the sprinkling of blood, signifying the solidarity of the people in the covenant blessings, type of the Messianic blessings. The Gospel use of the word *diathēkē* to translate *berith* is akin to the usage found in the Septuagint, but also suggests, as Lagrange has noted,[35] that this covenant is, properly speaking, Jesus' last will and testament (He is about to die and disposes of His lifeblood).[36] The phrase "about to be shed for the sake of many" indicates the atoning significance of the sacrifice of Jesus' life in the vocabulary of the Servant soteriology.[37]

Conclusions

By concentrating the attention of his reader upon the mystery of Jesus, Mark continues the thought found in the primitive preaching, where Christology and soteriology were complementary conceptions. In proportion as the expression of the Christological dogma becomes more exact and explicit, the soteriological values of Jesus' death become more obvious. Thus we have, in the second Gospel, affirmations concerning the redemptive nature of Jesus' death which disclose an already carefully-worked-out theology of salvation, especially in Mk 10:45 and 14:24.

MATTHEW'S VIEW OF THE CHRISTIAN PLAN OF SALVATION

In contrast with Mark, the writer of Greek Matthew portrays Jesus principally as the Prophet, who is doctor of the new law, i.e., as the new Moses. Instead of drawing attention to the acting Christ, he has collected from tradition as many of Jesus' logia as possible and has erected them into five great discourses, by means of which he articulates the various sections of his Gospel.[38] Israel expected a Messiah who would explain the law, since Moses (Dt 18:15) had promised it. The Deutero-Isaian Servant is a doctor of the law: "Faithfully shall he publish justice; He shall not flicker or bend, till he establish justice on the earth, and the coastlands wait for his teaching" (Is 42:3c–4). Reflections of such a Messianic expectation recur throughout the New Testament: the words of Moses are cited in Acts 3:22; 7:37; and Jn 1:21; 6:14; 7:40 also contain references to the same text. In the Matthean Sermon on the Mount, Jesus reveals Himself as the very incarnation of the law, its perfect fulfilment. Such a delineation of Christ has been dictated by the Evangelist's central interest, which is ecclesiological. In his book, more than in any other piece of New Testament writing, soteriology is elaborated in function of one fundamental insight: the kingdom of God, or the divine sovereignty over mankind, is established in this world through the death and resurrection of Jesus Christ by means of the institution and development of the Church.[39]

This is clear from the main theme of the first Gospel, which is that Jesus' rejection by Israel, which resulted in His death, forms part of God's redemptive plan for all humanity, since thereby the pagan peoples are called to inherit the kingdom.[40] Jesus' death and resurrection, moreover, have brought about the creation of the new heavens and the new earth. This eschatological view of the redemption is emphasized in Matthew, which includes, in addition to the discourse on the fall of Jerusalem, a series of texts which describe the central act of Christian redemption in the language of the Old Testament apocalypses. We wish to review the principal texts which illustrate this characteristically Matthean soteriology.

Relation of Jesus' Earthly Life and Death to the Destruction of Sin

The Matthean Infancy Gospel is carefully constructed by the author in order to give a kind of preview of his main theme. In a first section, Matthew shows the *continuity* which exists between the Gospel message and the religion of Israel by highlighting the solid links which bind Jesus to the past of His nation (cf. the genealogy, 1:1–17). At the same time he draws attention to the complete *novelty* of the Gospel through the narration of Jesus' virginal birth (1:18–25), an occurrence undreamed of by the liveliest Jewish expectations, which however does not break with the prophetic traditions of authentic Messianism. After these points are demonstrated within the cadre of family life,[41] a second section sketches a kind of public life of the Infant Messiah, whose royalty is revealed to the Gentiles but is rejected by the Jews (2:1–12), and who, through suffering persecution from His own people (2:13–18), receives His Messianic vocation from God (2:19–23).

Mt 1:21: "She will bear a son, and you shall call His name Jesus. He it is who will save His people from their sins."

From the opening scene of the Gospel, the Child Jesus is presented as the saviour of Israel. The theophoric name which by divine command is to be imposed on Him by Joseph means "salvation of Yahweh" or "Yahweh saves." The words of the divine message present Him as the Davidic Messiah and describe His work in terms which recall Old Testament prophecy of Yahweh's future redemption of Israel (Ps 129[130]:8). Thus the Evangelist announces that Jesus will bring the salvation which Israel awaited from Yahweh.

Mt 4:14–16: "Land of Zabulon and land of Nephthalim along the road by the sea; land beyond the Jordan, Galilee of the Gentiles! The people dwelling in darkness have beheld a great light, and over the dwellers in the land overshadowed by death light has arisen."

Matthew cites Is 8:23 and 9:1 as a kind of prologue to the Galilean ministry, which enables him to inform the reader that with Jesus' public life the era of salvation is inaugurated. After the depredations of Tiglath-Pileser in Nephthalim (cf. 4 K 15:29), the prophet announces that the district which has suffered most will be the first to attain glory. Matthew transposes the Isaian prophecy in order to show its fulfilment through the coming of Jesus in Galilee: this most despised region was the first to receive God's word of salvation. Thus "the road to the sea," which in Isaiah means the route from Damascus to Carmel, becomes for Matthew the road along the lake of

Galilee near Capharnaum. Matthew is, however, faithful to the fundamental Isaian scheme: the Messianic hope is proclaimed as realized for the parts of Israel which have been most tried. It is here that Jesus first preaches the advent of the kingdom of heaven.

It is perhaps Matthew's miracle theology which most strikingly reveals Jesus' mission against the power of sin. For the Evangelist, Jesus' miracles are the initial attack upon the Satanic dominion over the world of men. As the pledge of Satan's future definitive overthrow by Jesus' death and resurrection, these "signs and wonders" are the first step in the establishing of the kingdom of heaven (8:29; 10:1). Matthew insists upon this original theme by a new application of the Servant theology, employed by the primitive preaching to express the salvific character of Jesus' death and resurrection, to the miracles of healing (8:16–17). He uses this motif also to explain Jesus' insistence upon the avoidance of publicity in connection with His cures (12:17–21).

Mt 15:24: "My mission is exclusively to the lost sheep of the house of Israel."

The great contrast between the work of Jesus and that of the Church in the period towards the end of the apostolic age, when Greek Matthew was written, is the difference in audience. Jesus' message was addressed only to the Jews; the Church, predominantly Gentile by the time our canonical Gospel was published,[42] was to preach to pagans, the mission reserved for her by her divine Master.

Matthew Refers Jesus' Passion and Death to the Redemption

In addition to the various logia, repeated by Matthew, which we have already noted in Mark, there is one striking transformation of the Jonah-logion in the first Gospel which deserves attention.[43] Mt 12:39–40: "A perverse and adulterous generation demands a proof of my claims! Still, proof will not be granted it, except the proof which Jonah gave. Just as Jonah spent three days and three nights in the belly of the sea monster, so the Son of Man will spend three days and three nights in the heart of the earth."

As described in this text, the sign of Jonah is analogous to that given to Achaz (Is 7:10–25): it is at once a divine threat of the judgment visited upon incredulity, and also a sign, like the sign of the maiden pregnant, of salvation. Thus Jesus proposes prophetically the central object of the future Christian faith, His own death and resurrection, to His adversaries as the sign of salvation.

Christ's Rejection and Death an Essential Part of God's Salvific Plan

It is chiefly in the parables recounted towards the end of the Gospel that we see this characteristically Matthean view of Christian salvation illustrated. More specifically, it is in parables peculiar to Matthew (or at least re-edited by him) that we find insistence on this theme, which provides such telling evidence of the fact that the Church (at least that section of it with which the author was familiar) had already become predominantly Gentile in origin by the time the Gospel was composed.[44]

The parable of the Day Laborers in the vineyard (20:1–16), found only in this Gospel, has its point underscored in the concluding remark: "The last shall be first, and the first last." The Jews have been rejected in favor of the pagans; moreover, this is due to Israel's rejection of her Messiah. The brief parable of the Two Sons (2:28–31) teaches the lesson that the man who changes his attitude to the will of the Father (cf. the call to *metanoia* in the kerygma) is alone worthy of membership in the Church. This, the parable points out, is true, not of the first-born (the Jew) but rather of the Gentile. The Matthean version of the parable of the Wicked Vinedressers (21:33–43) makes a clear allusion to the death of Jesus "outside the camp" (v. 39; cf. Heb 13:13) and underscores its connection with the divine rejection of the Jews (vv. 41–46). The Matthean addition to the parable of the Wedding Feast (22:11–14) is meant as a warning to the non-Jewish converts against presuming unduly upon the divine favor. The danger of such a sin of presumption could arise only in a church predominantly Gentile and conscious of supplanting the chosen people in the kingdom of heaven. Yet v. 14, a reference to the Remnant doctrine of the prophets, assures the reader that Matthew has not forgotten that only a small fraction of Israel has been deemed worthy of the kingdom. With the Woes-discourse (23:1–36), the theme of the rejection of the Jews reaches its terrible climax. Canon Osty has remarked[45] how the first Gospel depicts in an ascending progression Jesus' beneficent activity towards the Jews on the one hand, and on the other the machinations of His enemies, until a deep-seated anger finally bursts in a flood in this magnificent passage.

Eschatological Orientation of the Matthean Salvation Doctrine

The first Gospel, by a special series of texts, seeks to emphasize the fact that with Jesus' death and resurrection the *eschaton* has finally entered human history.

Mt 10:23: "When you are persecuted in one city, flee to another; and when you are persecuted in that other, flee to still another. I can assure you with certainty that you will not make the round of the towns of Israel before the Son of Man comes."

The second half of the missionary discourse (10:17–23), in which this text occurs, enjoys a much broader perspective than the first part, which contains Jesus' recommendations to the Twelve on their first preaching tour. Here there is question rather of the persecution directed against the Church in the apostolic age. Jesus assures the apostles that He will make a divine visitation (the destruction of the Temple in 70 A.D. is meant)[46] by means of a historical event which will be an external sign of the divine rejection of Israel. This is clear from the close connection in this logion between the Jewish rejection of the gospel and their persecution of the apostles, and this "coming" of the glorified Son of Man.

Mt 16:27–28: "The Son of Man is to come [hereafter] wrapt in His Father's glory and escorted by His angels, when He will repay every man in accordance with his conduct. I tell you truly that some of those present here will not taste death before they see the Son of Man coming in His royal state."

These two verses, which Matthew has juxtaposed so closely, refer to two different events, as Lagrange points out.[47] The Evangelist distinguishes, like Paul (cf. 1 Cor 15:24 ff.; Col 1:13 ff.), between the earthly phase of the kingdom, the kingdom of Christ or the Church, and the celestial phase, the kingdom of the Father, inaugurated at the final judgment. Jesus' coming "wrapt in His Father's glory" refers to the end of the world, while His coming "in His (own) royal state" most probably refers to the destruction of the Temple, which for Matthew means the externalization of the risen Christ's triumph over Judaism.[48]

Mt 19:28: "In the final regeneration, when the Son of Man takes His seat on a throne befitting His glory, you, my followers, will, in your turn, be seated on twelve thrones and have jurisdiction over the twelve tribes of Israel."

The term *palingenesia,* used only one other time in the New Testament (cf Tit 3:5), denotes "the restoration of all things" to be accomplished through Jesus' death and resurrection. In virtue of His *sessio ad dexteram Patris,* the apostolic college will assume the hierarchical direction of the new Israel, the kingdom of heaven upon earth. Such an ecclesiastical view of Christian salvation is typical of the first Gospel.

Mt 23:37–39: "Jerusalem, Jerusalem, murderess of prophets, stoner of the messengers sent to you, how often did I wish to gather your children, as a mother bird gathers her brood under her wings—and you refused! Mark well, you will find your House abandoned, a prey to desolation. Yes, I tell you: you will not see me again till you cry out, 'A blessing on Him who comes in the name of the Lord!' "

Despite his insistence upon Israel's rejection, our author recalls the apostolic doctrine, based on Jesus' own teaching, concerning the final conversion of Israel (cf. Acts 3:19–21; Rom 11:25–26). Here Jesus refers to Himself in His risen state as the new Temple, source of salvation for all in the Messianic times. As Feuillet has pointed out,[49] since the cry of the Jews is one of conversion, the coming to which Jesus refers cannot be that of the final judgment. Nor can it be His triumphal entry into Jerusalem, which, in this Gospel, has already occurred (21:8 ff.). It is with the eyes of Christian faith that Israel will one day behold her risen Messiah.

Conclusions

Writing at a much later date than the author of Mark, when the nature of the Church had become predominantly Gentile in membership, the inspired writer of the first Gospel emphasizes the significance of salvation for the pagan world of his time. Where Mark conceives his soteriology from a Christological viewpoint, Matthew shows how important, for an understanding of the New Testament doctrine of salvation, is an awareness of the function of the kingdom become Church. At the same time, he underlines the eschatological overtones which held such an important place in the soteriology of the primitive preaching.

THE LUCAN GOSPEL OF SALVATION

One may say that the third Gospel is the Gospel of salvation par excellence. Luke is the only one of the Synoptics in which the terms *sōtēria* (1:69, 71, 77; 19:9), *sōtēr* (1:47; 2:11), *to sōtērion* (2:30; 3:6) occur. The author is the only Evangelist to apply the term "saviour" to Christ (2:11). It is interesting also to observe the Lucan additions to traditional logia which are the common property of the three Synoptics: the explanation of the parable of the Sower, "The devil comes and steals the gospel from their minds, with the result that they do not believe *and are not saved*" (8:12); "For the Son of Man has come to seek *and to save what is lost*" (19:10; cf. Mt 15:24); "When these things begin to happen, look up and raise your head, for your redemption is at hand" (21:28).[50]

Luke's special contribution to New Testament soteriology lies in his highlighting of the universalist nature of the salvation wrought by Jesus Christ. He portrays Jesus' death and resurrection as an "assumption" (9:51; cf., re Elijah, 4 K 2:9, 10, 11), as an *exodos* (9:31). This viewpoint designates the third Evangelist as a member of the Johannine school of theology, in which the central mystery of salvation is thought of as a "passing from this world to the Father" (Jn 13:1). Luke's use of the travel-story genre in the large section of his Gospel devoted to Jesus' journey up to Jerusalem for the denouement of this story (9:51—19:27), as has been suggested elsewhere,[51] is perhaps due to this characteristic view of salvation. In his Gospel the story is thus seen to move towards Jerusalem with a mysterious dynamism; for Jerusalem is not only the scene of Jesus' death, resurrection, and ascension, but also of the descent of the Holy Spirit, who will transform the timid, narrow-minded disciples into the preachers of universalist salvation to the whole world.

Relation of Jesus' Public Ministry to Salvation

Lk 4:13: "And having exhausted every kind of temptation, the devil left Him until the time appointed by divine Providence."

The additional phrase *achri kairou* is a typically Lucan device which directs the reader's attention to the sequel. Here it refers to the agony in the garden, thus linking up the temptations of Jesus at the beginning of His public life with His passion.

Lk 12:49–50: "To throw a firebrand upon earth—that is my mission! And oh, how I wish it were already ablaze! But then I have yet to undergo a baptism—and how frustrated I feel until it be carried out!"

In view of the third Evangelist's interest in the Holy Spirit, it is probably correct to see a reference to Him in this symbolic fire (a view held by many of the Fathers of the Church). But the necessary preamble to the gift of the Spirit is, of course, the "baptism" of Jesus' passion and death.

Lk 19:11: "While they were listening to these words, He

added a parable, since He was near Jerusalem and they thought that the kingdom of God was going to be revealed imminently."

As Père Lagrange remarks,[52] the point of the parable of the King, who travels to a distant land "to receive a kingdom and return" (v. 12), is directed against the apocalyptic enthusiasm which was gaining control of Jesus' disciples at the thought of the proximity to Jerusalem, where they expected a sudden manifestation of the divine sovereignty. The thinly-veiled allegory of the story indicates that Jesus must be separated from His disciples by His passion and death before He comes into His kingdom. It is the reader's final preparation for the drama which is to be unfolded in the rest of the Gospel.

Conclusions

This, the most literary of all the Gospels, has not only a carefully-worked soteriology, comparable in some respects with the Johannine and Pauline theologies; its author has, in addition, made a lasting contribution to the expression of New Testament soteriology by providing the technical terms for the doctrine of salvation, found at least in no other Gospel: *exodos* (9:31), *analēmpsis* (9:51), *apolytrōsis* (21:38). More important still, by sketching Jesus' work of salvation as a passing from this earth to the Father, Luke makes clearer than either Mark or Matthew how Jesus' passion and death must be closely linked to His resurrection in any adequate theology of the atonement. Twice in the closing chapter of this Gospel the risen Jesus states this in unequivocal terms: "Was it not necessary that the Messiah should undergo these sufferings and enter into His glory?" (24:26). "This is the gist of the Scriptures: the Messiah must suffer and on the third day rise from the dead" (24:45–46).

THE SYNOPTIC CONTRIBUTION TO NEW TESTAMENT SOTERIOLOGY

1) The most significant advance made by the Synoptic Gospels over the soteriology of the primitive preaching is to be found in their development of the meaning of Christ's death "for our sins." In Mark it appears as a *lytron,* the ransom offered by the Suffering Servant "for the many" (10:45; 14: 24). Matthew presents Jesus' death and resurrection as the efficacious establishing of the kingdom upon earth. As such, in his Gospel the double act of man's salvation is manifested as the link between the kingdom preached by Jesus and the Church instituted in the apostolic age. As Mt 28:18 makes plain, it is in virtue of His universal sovereignty over the whole of creation, acquired by Christ through His death and resurrection, that He issues the command to "make disciples of all the nations." Thus Matthew explains how the kingdom has passed by divine decree from the chosen people to the pagans "who will produce its fruits." The Lucan characterization of Jesus' saving work as an *exodos* or *analēmpsis* underscores the complementary nature of His passion, death, and resurrection, and thus adumbrates a theme which will be carried to its perfect expression in Hebrews and in the fourth Gospel.

2) Moreover, this Synoptic theology has succeeded in effectively incorporating into its conception of Christian salvation the work of the Galilean ministry, through the exploitation of the soteriological value of Jesus' miracles. Mark gives to the exorcisms of Jesus and His disciples a special prominence in His work among His people, which reveals the author's awareness of its fundamental character as an attack upon Satan.[58] Matthew's miracle theology, which is much more highly developed, discloses that liberation from sickness and infirmity,

as well as from sin, is in point of fact deliverance from the power of the devil, and hence the inaugural act of Christian salvation.

3) In the Infancy Gospels which Matthew and Luke have prefixed to their written Gospels, we can observe the first attempts at sketching a soteriology of the Incarnation, which will be the main preoccupation of the fourth Evangelist. Jesus' virginal birth, which constitutes the theological center of each of these Infancy narratives, prepares for the Pauline doctrine of the pre-existent Christ.

4) The eschatological resonances which were so inextricably interwoven into the kerygma retain their force in the Synoptic tradition, as can be seen by the triple reporting of Jesus' prophecy upon the ruin of Jerusalem and its Temple. In Matthew and Luke, the two Gospels most probably written after Titus had put an end to the old world of Israel and its centralized cultus, there is perceptible a deeper theological interpretation of the disaster as a divine "visitation" of the risen Christ, which thus becomes a "sign of the Son of Man," proof of His definitive liberation of Christianity from the swaddling bands of the ancient religion. There is, as yet, no formulation of the "realized eschatology" which is characteristic of the fourth Gospel, but the eschatological texts, particularly those in Matthew, give promise of a trend in that direction.

9

The Gospels As Salvation History

FOR some time now, it appears, a new breeze has been blowing in the domain of Catholic biblical studies. "The breeze blows wherever it pleases," St. John informs us; and the breeze, which for well over a decade has sprung up to revivify Catholic scholarly endeavor, has been felt in almost every branch of scriptural research. Biblical inspiration and inerrancy, the Mosaic authorship of the Pentateuch, the "prehistory" of the first eleven chapters of Genesis, all exemplify the type of question which has received quite new solutions. Among the problems that have undergone a reorientation in New Testament studies, that of the historical character of the Gospels has enjoyed a certain pre-eminence. Catholic exegetes are now permitted to voice opinions upon this difficult question which fifty, even twenty-five, years ago would have caused considerable concern, if not explicit censure.[1]

While the professional student of Scripture rejoices at the new impetus thus given his work through the present-day liberal attitude of the magisterium, he is also conscious that, on the part of some within the Church, there has already been a reaction to many of the views he now feels free to express. He would be foolish indeed to ignore the fact that a certain malaise has manifested itself on the part of some theologians. They are not quite so sure as their biblical colleagues that the effects of the twentieth-century scriptural renaissance can be called progress. There are undoubtedly some who feel, even though perhaps they do not express their fears too openly, that the old ghost of Modernism, which Pius X was thought to have laid within the household of the faith, has staged a reappearance, this time as a poltergeist. As John L. McKenzie recently observed, "At the present writing, fifteen years after the publication of the encyclical [*Divino afflante Spiritu*], opposition to creative biblical scholarship speaks only in whispers, and it no longer inhibits original work which goes beyond commonly accepted theological opinon."[2]

The publicity which this divergence of views on scriptural interpretation among Catholics has received in our day may indeed serve a useful purpose, if it convinces non-Catholic scholars that on "many very important questions," to cite a phrase of Pius XII, there is room in Catholic scholarship for freedom of opinion about the meaning of biblical passages, that there is not, in other words, a "party line" which all are obliged to follow unthinkingly.

Nowhere, perhaps, is this difference of viewpoint so strikingly exemplified as it is with regard to the exegetes' new conception of what has always been known as the "historicity" of the Gospels. Even some of those who have come to recognize the validity of certain principles of Form Criticism, when they are applied to the Old Testament books, hesitate to permit these same principles to operate in the study of the Gospels. The truth is, of course, that if these principles have real, universal validity, then it ought to be not only possible but necessary to apply them (due regard being had for the variety that obtains in biblical historical narrative) no less to the New than to the Old Testament.

Let me say at once, on the other hand, that there is some reasonableness in this somewhat conservative attitude. It is only too obvious, for instance, that between the antiquity and folkloric character of many oral traditions incorporated in the

Old Testament and the relatively short-lived and well-substantiated oral traditions forming the basis of the written Gospels, there is a vast and easily discernible difference. Anyone can surely see that there were no human eyewitnesses to the creation. By contrast, the Evangelists could have found a not inconsiderable number of serious-minded, sincere men to testify to the sayings and doings of Jesus of Nazareth during his public life. That they actually succeeded in doing so has been convincingly demonstrated by C. H. Dodd in his *History and the Gospel*.[3]

We do not wish to minimize this attitude of reserve which, though rarely vocal, is certainly present in some Catholic minds. It is based really upon a fear that, because certain familiar props have been pulled out from under the structure of Catholic apologetics by the new methods, the whole edifice is in danger of collapse. I find no difficulty in granting that such a fear (undoubtedly unfounded, as I believe) has been partly caused by a few of the Catholic exegetes themselves. It is most regrettable that occasionally the Scripture scholar has, in the exuberance of his new-found freedom, displayed an entirely too negative attitude in approaching the question of the Gospels' historical character. Fr. Thomas Worden, editor of the English Catholic periodical *Scripture*, gives a balanced and penetrating criticism of such a regrettable outlook in his article "Is Scripture to Remain the Cinderella of Catholic Theology?"[4]

Certainly what is needed, if the work of demolition of certain outmoded solutions to scriptural difficulties is to be helpful, is the stressing of those positive values which are to be found in the explanations which modern biblical science is capable of offering and must offer. The New Testament critic must shoulder his new responsibility of developing a much-needed New Testament biblical theology.

FUNDAMENTALISM

Still, when we speak of the need of delicacy and prudence in promoting the new Catholic approach to Gospel criticism, we do not mean to suggest that the biblical scholar can take refuge in a conservatism which borders upon obscurantism. J. Cambier described the proper method to be adopted in a paper read at the Louvain Biblical Week some years ago:

> The judicious, nuanced application of this literary method . . . for the study of the Synoptic Gospels demands that we admit the existence of certain liberties which the Evangelists have taken with history in the critical and modern sense of that word. We feel that, both for a more balanced understanding of the sacred history and also to assist the seminary student or the educated Catholic to avoid an unnecessary lapse into skepticism, we must attempt to provide them with a clearer insight into the problem.[5]

This sane, very Catholic view has also been serenely expressed by Luis Alonso Schökel, professor of Old Testament biblical theology at the Pontifical Biblical Institute of Rome. I refer to his trenchant review of a certain Introduction to the Old Testament, whose author, to say the least, has not managed to move with the times:

> The author appears to feel that progress consists solely, or at least principally, in the fact that those opinions which he is pleased to call "traditional" should receive confirmation. He is doubtless convinced that he is serving the Church more faithfully by teaching safer doctrine. Actually, the more rigid opinion is not always the safer one. Pupils formed according to the spirit of this book will approach their priestly work armed with the arguments which it contains. They will propose them to the faithful, among whom will be educated, intelligent laymen, who will be told that these opinions, thanks to such arguments, form part of the faith. Will not their own belief be endangered, or at least will they not be afflicted with doubts which might easily have been avoided?[6]

As splendid examples of modern Catholic work on the Gospels, I might mention here the commentaries in the collection *La sainte Bible*, issued under the direction of the Dominicans of Jerusalem—particularly that on Matthew by Pierre Benoit and that on John by Donatien Mollat. The remarks of the present rector of the Pontifical Biblical Institute of Rome, R. A. F. MacKenzie, in his review of several Old Testament fascicules in this series, apply also to these New Testament studies: "These Catholic scholars, free of polemical preoccupations, are going about their own proper work, in the calm assurance that they are carrying on the centuries-old exegetical tradition of the Church, and that, in the light of faith, they can safely and profitably use modern discoveries, to achieve that fuller understanding of Sacred Scripture which the Holy See hopes and expects of them."[7]

The antithesis of such a serene and scholarly spirit of inquiry is an attitude which, while more characteristic perhaps of certain Protestant groups, is also operative in the thinking of not a few Catholics. I mean, of course, biblical fundamentalism. The adherents of fundamentalism have been found chiefly among certain non-Catholic sects, for the very good reason that Bible reading has been more commonly practiced by them than by Catholics. In addition, the fundamentalist viewpoint has developed partly as a corollary of the Protestant view of "private interpretation" of Scripture, partly as a repudiation by sincere (often uneducated) Christians of that "historicism" to which nineteenth-century liberal Protestantism lent its patronage. Historicism, which, applied to the Gospels, was known as the "quest of the historical Jesus," never won any support in Catholic scholarship.

The revolt against historicism and the demand for a biblical theology in the Protestant churches has had a parallel in the Catholic Church. Here there was no revolt against historicism, because there never had been any historicism against which to revolt. But there was a stout affirmation of the "historical character" of the Bible without any attention to the study of literary forms. The purely defensive and almost entirely controversial scholarship of the era of the siege mentality had by 1943 proved its sterility beyond all question.[8]

John L. McKenzie has defined the phenomenon known as biblical fundamentalism as "the crass literal interpretation of the Bible without regard for literary forms and literary background."[9] Indeed, it consists essentially of a conscious and deliberate "literalmindedness" in accepting the affirmations of biblical writers without regard to the idiom, the context, or the literary form through which they are expressed. I use the terms "conscious" and "deliberate" in order to exclude the simple faithful who, despite an often unconsciously ingenuous attitude towards much in the Bible, do reach *the real message* of the sacred text. The fault inherent in fundamentalism is the result of a misguided determination to cling to a superficial meaning of the Bible at all costs—even the cost of real understanding. A form of anti-intellectualism, this viewpoint is quite out of harmony with that spirit of religious inquiry (*fides quaerens intellectum*) which the Catholic Church has always sought to inculcate and encourage in the faithful, and which is the ideal and the guiding principle of Catholic theology.

One pernicious effect of the fundamentalist mentality is to expose the Scriptures to serious misunderstanding and even ridicule by those who do not possess Christian faith. It can, moreover, create a harmful dichotomy between faith and reason among Christians in whom a well-developed literary or scientific education is combined with religious instruction that is uncritical and intellectually deficient.

Indeed, fundamentalism has been known to lead to a kind of "illuminism." I am thinking of the injudicious attack by an Italian priest, Dolindo Ruotolo, made in 1941 upon Catholic biblical scholarship through a pamphlet which had to be censured by the Biblical Commission. In this tract, *Un gravissimo pericolo per la Chiesa e per le anime: Il sistema critico-scientifico nello studio e nell'interpretazione della Sacra Scrittura, le sue deviazioni funeste e le sue aberrazioni* Ruotolo (or "Dain Cohenel," as he signed himself), advocated giving free rein to the Spirit for a proper comprehension of the Bible, "as though," to cite the official condemnation of his ideas, "all were in personal communion with the divine Wisdom and received from the Holy Spirit special personal illumination. . . ."[10]

DIVINO AFFLANTE SPIRITU

In his Encyclical of 1943, *On Biblical Studies and the Opportune Means of Promoting Them,* Pius XII "unequivocally repudiated fundamentalism in Catholic exegesis."[11] This statement by John L. McKenzie requires some amplification, since the fundamentalist attitude had, over all too long a period, become firmly entrenched in Catholic thinking. And this was particularly true where the Gospels were concerned. Accordingly, it may not be out of place here to recall briefly those directives of Pius XII which provide a new orientation for the desirable, indeed necessary, Catholic approach to Gospel studies.

Pius XII lays down two principles of paramount importance, which run directly counter to the fundamentalist position: (1) "the supreme law of interpretation is that by which we discover and determine what the writer meant to say";[12] (2) there are only very few texts of the Bible "whose meaning has been declared by the authority of the Church, nor are those more numerous about which there is a unanimous opinion of the holy Fathers."[13] It may be useful to examine the scope of these two norms, which are applicable to the study of the Gospels, in greater detail.

How, in the opinion of Pius XII, does one determine the sacred writer's meaning? "Let the interpreter therefore use every care, and take advantage of every indication provided by the most recent research, in an endeavour to discern the distinctive genius of the sacred writer, his condition in life, the age in which he lived, the written or oral sources he may have used, and the literary forms he employed. He will thus be able better to discover who the sacred writer was and what he meant by what he wrote."[14] The Pope's insistence upon the human character of the Bible is noteworthy. Also to be noted is his repeated emphasis upon the primacy of what he calls the *sensus litteralis*.

In fact, in his later Encyclical *Humani generis* the Pope added a further important nuance: "Indeed, it is useless for them [certain writers whose attitude the Pope condemned] to speak of the human meaning of the sacred books, under which their divine meaning, the only one in their opinion which is infallible, lies hidden."[15] "And moreover, the *sensus litteralis* of Holy Writ and its exposition, which has been elaborated by so many and such great exegetes under the eye of the Church, must, according to their erroneous views, give way to a new exegesis which they call symbolic or spiritual."[16] In commenting on this papal document, Gustave Lambert observed: "The Encyclical *Divino afflante Spiritu* had, however, insisted with all the clarity that could be desired upon the *only meaning* which is found *everywhere* in Scripture: *the literal sense.* This literal sense, which is also *the theological sense* of the sacred texts, is that which was known and willed *conjointly* by the principal author, God, and by the intelligent, free, instrumental cause, the human hagiographer. . . . The hagiographer, by writing in a human fashion, has expressed a divine way of thinking."[17]

Divino afflante Spiritu makes it abundantly clear that belief in God's primary authorship of the sacred books must not be misunderstood, so that, for instance, we attempt implausible "harmonizations" of various Gospel accounts of the same episode, forcing them to agree where they actually differ in details. We shall cite here two examples of such a mentality.

While the Synoptics agree in placing Jesus' cleansing of the Temple at the close of His public life, indeed in its last week (Mt 21:12–13; Mk 11:15–17, where it occurs the day *after* Jesus' Messianic entry into Jerusalem; Lk 19:45–46), Jn 2: 13–22 employs the episode as the inaugural act of Jesus' ministry in Jerusalem. There are various ways of explaining these inconcinnities. The Synoptic writers, who depict Jesus' public life as chiefly a Galilean ministry, bring him to Jerusalem only in the last ten days before His death. John, on the other hand, whose Gospel might be considered a kind of commentary on the saying found in Lk 13:34 and parallels, may well be following the chronological order. In any event, however, to postulate two cleansings of the Temple is nothing but a refusal to see or explain the problem, a refusal to understand what the sacred writers are attempting to tell us.

The second example concerns the two accounts of the death of Judas (Mt 27:3–10; Acts 1:18–19), which differ strikingly in three important details. Did Judas commit suicide (Mt), or did he die of some mysterious accident or disease (Acts)? Did the Sanhedrin purchase the "potter's field" (Mt), or did Judas himself buy it as a farm (Acts)? Whose blood led to naming the area Haceldama, Jesus' (Mt) or Judas' (Acts)? It seems unreasonable to ignore the fact that two quite independent versions of how a bad man came to a bad end have been preserved in the New Testament. Nor does any ingenious harmonizing, like that of the Vulgate version for Acts 1:18, "suspensus crepuit medius" ("and being hanged, burst asunder in the midst": Douay), really resolve the difficulty.

The proper method of handling these questions, we are told by Pius XII, entails careful research into the background and culture, as well as the manner of writing (sources used, literary forms employed), of the sacred writer. We must not allow ourselves to overlook the profound differences separating our modern, Occidental point of view from that of the ancient Near East. "Frequently the literal sense is not so obvious in the words and writings of ancient Oriental authors as it is with the writers of today"[18]—an admirable example of papal understatement. A good illustration of what is meant here is provided by Mt 23:9: "And do not call anyone on earth your father. Only one is your Father, and He is in heaven." This text, which causes some people to scruple about addressing a Catholic priest as "Father," probably is a warning to the disciples not to imitate the scribes and Pharisees in their pretensions. These men delighted in assuming high-sounding titles and assimilating themselves to "the fathers," i.e., the patriarchs and other famous forebears of Israel.

If, then, we are to grasp the mind of authors of an age so remote from, and of a culture so alien to, our own, it is not enough to study the rules of grammar and philology which govern their languages. We must invoke the aid of history, archeology, ethnology, and even psychology. "For what they [the sacred writers] intended to signify by their words is not determined only by the laws of grammar or philology, nor merely by the context; it is absolutely necessary for the interpreter to go back in spirit to those remote centuries of the East and make proper use of the aids afforded by history, archeology, ethnology, and other sciences, in order to discover what literary forms the writers of that early age intended to use and did actually employ."[19] As examples of studies of the psychological differences between the Western and the biblical mentalities, we might cite the book by Gregory Dix, *Jew and Greek*,[20] or the article by Célestin Charlier, "Méthode historique et lecture spirituelle des écritures."[21]

The importance which Pius XII attached to the study of the literary types surviving in Near Eastern literary remains for mastering the thought of the sacred writers deserves to be borne in mind:

> For to express what they had in mind, the ancients of the East did not always use the same forms and expressions as we use today; they used those which were current among the people of their own time and place; and what these were the exegete cannot determine a priori, but only from a careful study of ancient Oriental literature. This study has been pursued during the past few decades with greater care and industry than formerly, and has made us better acquainted with the literary forms used in those ancient times, whether in poetical descriptions, or in the formulation of rules and laws of conduct, or in the narration of historical facts and events.[22]

As regards the variety of historical writing to be found in the Bible, the interpreter must constantly bear in mind "the special purpose, the religious purpose, of biblical history." As we shall return to a consideration of this remark when we discuss the special character of the Gospels as salvation history, it may not be out of place to cite the Pope's remarks in full.

> This same study has now also clearly demonstrated the unique preeminence among all the ancient nations of the East which the people of Israel enjoyed in historical writing, both in regard to the antiquity of the events recorded and to the accuracy with which they

are related—a circumstance, of course, which is explained by the charisma of divine inspiration and by the special purpose, the religious purpose, of biblical history.[23]

Speaking more generally of the great riches of biblical literary forms, Pius XII states that "the sacred books need not exclude any of the forms of expression which were commonly used in human speech by the ancient peoples, especially of the East, to convey their meaning, so long as they are in no way incompatible with God's sanctity and truth."[24] Thus that ingenuous apriorism habitually found in the fundamentalist interpretation of the Bible is effectively ruled out. The exegete "must ask himself how far the form of expression or literary idiom employed by the sacred writer may contribute to the true and genuine interpretation."[25]

The second basic principle of Catholic hermeneutics, namely, that only a tiny sector of the many affirmations in the Bible has received any authoritative interpretation, has been called "perhaps the most important statement of the Encyclical."[26] The Pope asserts that the Catholic exegete must be given full liberty in his search for solutions to "many important questions" which admit of free discussion within the limits of orthodoxy. Not infrequently we meet the tendency on the part of some Catholics to cling doggedly to what they imagine to be the "traditional" interpretation of a scriptural passage. They sincerely feel that in this way they are being most orthodox, when in point of fact no such tradition—I mean, theologically significant tradition—exists. To cite one example of this sort of thing, Stanislas Lyonnet has pointed[27] out in his interpretation of the pentecostal "gift of tongues," which he claims is a form of mystical or ecstatic prayer, that the rather commonly accepted view (that it was a gift of speaking foreign languages in a miraculous way) was based upon the demonstrably erroneous view that the charism was given for preaching. As he ably shows, it was a question not of preaching but of prayer.

This is but one instance of the vast quantity of "unfinished business" which Pius XII urges the Scripture scholar to deal with courageously.

> This state of things must in no wise daunt the Catholic interpreter; prompted by a practical and ardent love of his science, and sincerely devoted to Holy Mother Church, he must grapple perseveringly with the problems thus far solved . . . to find an explanation which will be faithfully consonant with the teaching of the Church, particularly with the traditional doctrine of the inerrancy of Scripture, while being at the same time in due conformity with the certain conclusions of profane sciences.[28]

Another point clarified by this papal directive is the concept of "private interpretation." Provided it does not conflict with Catholic doctrine, any explanation of the great bulk of scriptural texts is as good or bad as the reasons given for it, and this holds good equally for the majority of the patristic opinions or those given by theologians, however ancient, as for the suggestions of modern exegetes. Indeed, today's biblical scholar may quite conceivably provide a far more satisfactory explanation of a scriptural difficulty than his predecessors.[29] Moreover, he is informed through *Divino afflante Spiritu* that this is the direction in which his duty lies, while those who differ are warned by Pius XII not to employ the term "new" as if it were a stigma.

> And let all other children of the Church bear in mind that the efforts of these valiant laborers in the vineyard of the Lord are to be judged not only with fairness and justice, but also with the greatest charity; they are to avoid that somewhat indiscreet zeal which considers everything new to be for that very reason a fit object for attack or suspicion. Let them remember above all that the rules and

laws laid down by the Church are concerned with the doctrines of faith and morals; and that among the many matters set forth in the legal, historical, sapiential, and prophetical books of the Bible there are only a few whose sense has been declared by the authority of the Church, and that there are equally few concerning which the opinion of the holy Fathers is unanimous. There consequently remain many matters, and important matters, in the exposition and explanation of which the sagacity and ingenuity of Catholic interpreters can and ought to be freely exercised. . . .[30]

With the insights provided by these hermeneutical norms, we must now examine what is meant by the historical character of the Gospels.

HISTORICAL CHARACTER OF THE GOSPEL NARRATIVES

The modern concept of history goes back ultimately to the Greeks, who classed it among the arts under the patronage of the muse Clio. "The concept of history," as Erich Dinkler has remarked, "has been given to us by Greek science and to this very day is employed by us in a Greek sense. From Thucydides to Toynbee, the common and connecting assumption has been that history is a rational, intelligible continuity, an integrated nexus or concatenation, operating in a unified world, capable of investigation and illumination by historical method."[31]

In our day, inasmuch as it is the product of the historical method, history is classed as a social science. However, the writing of history remains an art, involving, as it inevitably does, the selection and interpretation in some literary form of the "remembered past."[32]

More basically, history in the modern sense of that word is to be identified with the ancient Greeks' view of it, because the intelligibility sought by the contemporary as by the classical historian is a *human* intelligibility. Both share the conviction that there is a pattern discernible in the events of the past which sprang ultimately from the mind of man, a pattern, consequently, which is recoverable by the application of the historical method (a process invented by the mind of man) and which can be represented by the art of historical writing.

"Historical writing," says C. H. Dodd, "is not merely a record of occurrences as such. It is, at least implicitly, a record of the interest and meaning they bore for those who took part in them, or were affected by them. . . ." And he concludes: "Thus the events which make up history are relative to the human mind which is active in those events."[33] Later, Dodd defines history "as consisting of events which are of the nature of occurrences plus meaning."[34]

If we accept Dodd's definition, it becomes clear that the task of selecting and interpreting the facts to be chronicled is an essential part of the historian's function. While the exercise of these two will vary according as he writes cultural, political, or economic history, the historian must choose and he must interpret. Assuming, for instance, it were possible to film a battle in its entirety, such a newsreel record would not be history, but only a source for history.

Selection and interpretation, of course, presuppose some criterion of judgment. The very choice, indeed, will be governed by the type of history written. The political historian will find much of his data in government archives; the cultural historian discovers valuable material in folklore, local customs, family traditions, even legends. It is the fashion, at least in clerical circles, to smile superiorly at the stories occasionally found in the lives of the saints commemorated in the Roman breviary: e.g., the heroic fasts of the infant St. Nicholas, or the marvelous prayer feats of St. Patrick. While in the future revision of the Divine Office we can expect that many of these legends will be excised, it should be remembered that these stories constitute (and this not despite, but precisely because of, their incredible character) the essential proof of the people's belief in the holiness of these saints. Thus, in this respect, the stories do represent historical reality. *Vox populi, vox Dei*, in the age before official canonization, was the principle which justified the cultus paid to the saints. These legendary tales are the popular expression of a solid faith in the heroic sanctity of these ancient Christian heroes.

The historian's work will ultimately be judged by the correctness of his interpretation of the evidence he has unearthed. In some instances he will be led to highlight an event which in itself, or at the time of its occurrence, may have been almost insignificant. Thus, the historian of the Counter Reformation will direct attention to the battle of Pampeluna, a tiny incident in a series of border skirmishes, because an impoverished Basque nobleman, Iñigo de Loyola, there received the wound which led to his "conversion" and eventually to the founding of the Society of Jesus.

But before he selects and interprets the events about which he intends to write, the historian must satisfy himself as to their situation in space and time. "When" and "where" are two of the historian's most elementary queries. Chronology and geography have been called "the eyes of history." "If the modern historian cannot tell you when and where something happened, he will not call it a historical event, although he does not thereby deny that it happened."[35]

It is of considerable significance for any understanding of what is meant by the historical nature of the Gospels to be aware that the Evangelists show a strongly marked tendency to dissociate most of the episodes of Jesus' public life which they record from both time and place. While some explanation of this phenomenon will appear later in this essay, it must be noted here as one indication of the distance which separates the Gospels from modern historical writing. The Evangelists' lack of interest in the specific geographical or chronological settings of many of their narratives unquestionably sets a limitation upon our attempts to prove these events "historical" in the modern sense.

We might note, as one consequence of this fact, that the historicity of the Gospels is not as simple as some apologetics manuals would lead us to think. Their authors' purpose was quite different from that of the modern historian. Their primary aim was to testify to the divine-human fact of God's intervention in human history which brought man salvation in Jesus Christ. In order to express this fundamental fact, the Evangelists have chosen narratives of varying type, from parables to eyewitness accounts. Attention to this point will reveal the supreme importance of studying the many subsidiary literary forms found in the Gospels. If an apologetic is to be valid, it must face the fact that the Magi story, for example, is not "historical" in the sense in which the narrative of the Crucifixion may be said to be "historical." Jesus' earthly life, to be sure, is located in Palestine; His birth occurred "in the days of King Herod," His death "under Pontius Pilate." The dates of both events, however, are known only approximately. As for the period of His public ministry, the impression given by the first three Gospels is that it lasted about six months.

What, then, is the biblical conception of history, and how do our Gospels differ from "history" in the modern acceptation of the word? The biblical notion of history rests upon the belief that God has, in the past, revealed Himself in a special way within the cadre of human affairs. "This is in fact the assertion," says Dodd, "which Christianity makes. It takes the series of events recorded or reflected in the Bible, from the call of Abraham to the emergence of the Church, and declares that in this series the ultimate reality of all history, which is the purpose of God, is finally revealed, because the series is itself controlled by the supreme event of all—the life, death and resurrection of Jesus Christ."[36]

Through specific events, personalities, and human utterances, God has intervened in the world of man. From this point of view, it is clear that the intelligibility to be seen in the biblical narratives is essentially that of a divine, not a human, pattern. It is this viewpoint which distinguishes all biblical history from the profane, or so-called scientific, history, and indeed constitutes its superiority vis-à-vis "history" as we understand it today. It is best described as "a mystery," in the Pauline and Johannine sense, namely, as God's revelation, in time, to men of His eternal plan for the salvation of the world.

This mystery was disclosed to mankind in two stages: one incomplete and rudimentary, to God's chosen people in the Old Testament; the second, complete and definitive, through His only Son Jesus Christ, to the Church of the New Testament. This genre of history, which we call salvation history or *Heilsgeschichte*, is the story of God's self-revelation to us; and its purpose is obviously very different from that modern scientific history which is written without reference to the divine point of view.

Here, in fact, we have touched upon one of the profound differences between the *Weltanschauung* of modern man, the product of a distinctively Greek culture, and the ancient Semitic mentality. Where we moderns habitually discuss the meanings of happenings in terms of secondary or finite causality, the Semitic genius interested itself principally in God, first cause of all things. The attitude may, now and then, strike us today as somewhat naive. How many Christians, for instance, after smiling indulgently at the explanation offered by

Psalm 28 of the thunderstorm as the "voice of Yahweh," turn to the newspaper or television broadcast for an analysis of the weather? They find, we must admit it frankly, that the meteorologist's pronunciamentos, couched in the mythological terms of "high-and-low-pressure areas," are eminently more satisfying than the insight of the Psalmist. Yet if, as the Christian surely believes, God causes the weather as He causes everything else, which explanation touches the reality more profoundly? At any rate, the example provides a useful illustration of the radical difference between the two viewpoints of which we are speaking.

Before we proceed further, one may well ask upon what grounds the validity of this suprahuman interpretation rests, if, as we have asserted, salvation history is simply God's revelation of Himself. Obviously, it cannot be proven (or disproven) *solely* by the use of modern historical method. For while it is quite possible to demonstrate scientifically the "historical" (in our modern sense) character of the Gospel, still the fact that God has spoken to man by means of books written by human beings is an object of faith. Faith's guarantee that these writers have infallibly expressed the revelation of Jesus Christ as incarnate Son and universal Redeemer is founded upon the supernatural fact of scriptural inspiration. Thus, for an adequate comprehension of the Evangelists' testimony, we must realize that it possesses not merely the authority of reliable eyewitnesses, but also the authority of God Himself.

The Evangelists do indeed propose, in the written accounts of Jesus' life upon earth, to give their reader a narrative that is based upon ocular testimony. It is of paramount importance, however, to appreciate the fact that they aim principally at writing salvation history, which entails testimony to something that lies beyond the competence of any eyewitness. They offer, that is, an insight into the meaning of the mystery of Jesus Christ. They disclose to the reader (in whom they presuppose Christian faith) something which cannot be seen with the eye or perceived by the ear, namely, the *propter nos et propter nostram salutem*. A careful reading of 1 Jn 1:1–2 will substantiate this statement.

And this, we should not forget, is these sacred authors' primary intention. They claim to represent not only eyewitnesses, but witnesses of the Good News of salvation, since their message, like the rest of the Bible, is addressed not simply to man's mind for his information, but to the whole man for his redemption.

We see this twofold nature of the apostolic testimony to Jesus Christ already consciously present in Peter's sermon to Cornelius and his household at Palestinian Caesarea (Acts 10: 34–43). The apostolic preachers are, in the first place, "witnesses of all He [Jesus] did in the country of the Jews and Jerusalem" (v. 39), or "witnesses appointed beforehand by God, who ate and drank with Him after His resurrection from death" (v. 41). But they have the office of witnessing in a deeper, more important sense, because they have received a mandate from the risen Lord "to preach to the people and to bear witness that He is the judge of living and dead, constituted by God" (v. 42).

This same twofold purpose is manifest also in our written Gospels. Mark, whose account reflects, perhaps more strikingly than any other Gospel, the influence of an observant eyewitness, has entitled his book "The Good News of Jesus Christ, Son of God" (Mk 1:1). A study of this Gospel reveals that its author, while providing us with some of the most vivid and detailed scenes of Jesus' public life, was innocent of anything like literary art or a creative imagination. This strange combination of two seemingly contradictory qualities happily vouches for the authenticity of the early testimony of Papias, namely, that while Mark was not himself a disciple of Jesus, he "wrote down accurately all that he remembered" of Peter's preaching. Thus the liveliness of the Marcan narratives, so rich in minute detail, goes back to Peter's all-seeing eye.

Mark's intention, expressed in the title of his book, of providing us with a profounder realization of Christ's divinity, with a grasp, that is, of a supernatural truth which does not fall under the observation of the senses, implies something more than ocular testimony. Even Luke, whose prologue reveals a spirit not unacquainted with "historical method," manifests to his aristocratic convert Theophilus his aim of writing salvation history. True, he has "investigated it all carefully from the beginning"; he has "decided to write a connected account of it." But both the thorough examination of his sources and the ordering of his narrative have been carried out "in order that you may more clearly grasp the authentic character of the oral instructions you have received" (Lk 1:4). The term we have translated "the authentic character" (*asphaleia*) meant "security" in the contemporary commercial and military usage. Since he is writing for a man who is already a believer in Christianity, Luke aims at more than establishing the historical character of the events and sayings he records. He means to interpret their Christological significance, as indeed the whole of his two-volume work reveals.

The author of the fourth Gospel declares, as he reaches the conclusion of his book, that "these things have been written in order that you may persevere in your belief that Jesus is the Messiah, the Son of God, and that persevering in this belief you may possess life in His Name" (Jn 20:31). John's use of the present subjunctive with the Greek verb (usually materials that have gone into the making of his book, and finally (3) by determining the manifold literary types[37] through which he has expressed what he wishes to tell us.

Before we attempt to illustrate our answers to these three aspects of the problem by means of concrete examples, however, several observations of a general character are in order. First, it must be evident that to treat these questions thoroughly demands exact and detailed literary and historical analysis, which would be out of place here. Second, we must not allow ourselves to forget that there is no rule-of-thumb solution to the question of the historicity of the Gospels: each narrative must be examined for itself and for the problems it presents. Third, if we are to avoid the fundamentalist mentality, we must be on our guard against the superficial conclusion that, because one may be led to admit that certain details in an Evangelist's narrative (or even its general framework) are due to the literary form used or to his specific purpose, the whole story has been invented. Such a black-or-white attitude stems simply from the failure, on the part of a modern, Occidental mind, to comprehend the Semitic viewpoint evinced by the inspired author. Finally, it will not infrequently happen that, after the most patient and painstaking literary analysis, we cannot decide with any certainty "what did actually happen," and we must content ourselves with such imprecision. The phrase "what did actually happen" (*wie es eigentlich gewesen ist*) implies, of course, the modern point of view. For the early Christians and the biblical writers, "what did actually happen" was what was recorded upon the sacred page. The term *dabar* in Hebrew means both "word" and "event." It is quite true that we can, by an investigation of the original life-situation (*Sitz im Leben*) in which a scriptural passage was created or produced, satisfy the curiosity of the modern mind. Still, it must be recalled that, however use-

Such a Christological interpretation of the history of Jesus is seen already operative in the Marcan Gospel, in many respects the least artistically presented of the four, adhering as it does so closely to the scheme provided by Peter for the apostolic preaching. Mark's principal theme is that the incarnate Son of God, Jesus Christ, has, in His public life, death, and resurrection, realized the prophetic fulfilment of His vocation as the Servant of God. It is in terms of the Deutero-Isaian suffering and glorified *'Ebed Yahweh* that Mark has couched the Gospel message. At Jesus' first appearance in his book, on the occasion of His baptism by John, the heavenly Voice proclaims Him the Son of God, who is also the Suffering Servant: "You are my beloved Son: in you I take delight" (Mk 1:11). The words contain an allusion to the first Servant Song (Is 42:1 ff.). Rightly called the Gospel of the Passion, Mark's book announces Jesus' death as early as the third chapter (Mk 3:6); and the Passion account occupies a proportionally large place in this shortest of the Gospels. Jesus' statement of the purpose of His life's work, a theologoumenon which is taken as typical of Mark, is expressed in terms of the Servant theme: "Why even the Son of Man has come to act as a servant, not to be served, and to lay down His life as a ransom for many" (Mk 10:45; cf. Is 53:5–8). Another echo of this same motif is perceptible in the Transfiguration episode, which forms the literary center of Mark's Gospel: "This is my beloved Son: pay heed to Him" (Mk 9:7).[40] Moreover, the threefold prophecy by Jesus of His future passion is expressed in terms of the Servant's mission (Mk 8:31; 9:31=Is 53:10–11; Mk 10:33=Is 50:6).

Since it is as the *incarnate* Son that Jesus acts as the Servant in the eyes of Mark, his narrative underscores the reality of Jesus' human nature to the point where the Christian reader is almost disconcerted. Indeed, it would seem that the author of Greek Matthew, who would appear to have re-edited many of Mark's narratives (compare Mk 4:38 with Mt 8:25; Mk 6:5–6 with Mt 13:58; Mk 5:30–31 is omitted in Mt 9:22), was also disedified by such candid realism. In Mark's Gospel Jesus can become impatient, angry, sharp in His rebukes, sensitive to His hearers' reactions, surprised at the turn of events. Yet Mark presents undeniable evidence of Jesus' divinity, while stating implicitly that the reality of Jesus' adoption of the Servant's role hid this profound truth during His public life from all, even His chosen followers, until, at His death, even a pagan centurion could be moved to confess "This man was really God's Son!" (Mk 15:39).[41] Mark provides his Christian reader with incontrovertible evidence that Jesus is the Son of God: by His power to forgive sins (Mk 2:1–11), His assertion of authority over the Sabbath (Mk 2:28), His control even of inanimate nature (Mk 4:35–41). Thus the second Gospel provides an unmistakable picture of the Son of God incarnate, who "despoiled Himself by taking on the Servant's character" and "carried self-abasement, through obedience, right up to death" (Phil 2:7–8).

Matthew, in contrast with Mark, presents a conception of Jesus and His redemptive work which is intimately bound up with the mystery of the Church which He came to found. For it is in the Church, the divine or "heavenly kingdom," that Matthew discovers the realization in this world of God's dominion or sovereignty over all creation. Matthew's characteristic title for Jesus is Emmanuel, a name foretold by Isaiah in his prediction of Jesus' virginal conception (Is 7:14), as Matthew informs us, and explained at the outset of this Gospel as meaning "with us is God" (Mt 1:24). As he brings his story to a close, Matthew refers once again to this image of Jesus Christ, when he records the promise of the glorified Christ at His departure from this world: "And remember,

I am with you all the time until the end of the world" (Mt 28:20). Thus we have an example of the Semitic *inclusio*, which enunciates the theme which dominates the whole book. In the center of his Gospel, Matthew also reminds us of Jesus' role as Emmanuel by recording a logion of the Master not found elsewhere. It is instructive to observe that this saying concerns liturgical prayer, the prayer proper to the community as such: "Where two or three have gathered in my Name, there am I among them" (Mt 18:20).

Matthew's version of Jesus' public life is so constructed as to bring home to us the truth that in His Galilean ministry—particularly in His preaching (Matthew's chief interest is in the logia of Jesus, while the event is of importance mainly for the doctrinal message it contains)—Jesus has begun to found that Church through which He will remain with us until the end of time. Behind the immediate reality of five long instructions, into which Matthew has grouped Jesus' sayings, we are given a glimpse of the future Church. The Sermon on the Mount (Mt 5–7) is an expression of the spirit and function of the Church as the perfect fulfilment of Old Testament religion. The missionary discourse (Mt 10), particularly its second half, is a prediction of the evangelizing activities of the Church in the apostolic age (cf. Mt 10:17–42). The wider perspective of this second part of the discourse can be seen in the heightened opposition to the Christian gospel (vv. 16–17) both in Palestine itself (v. 17) and in the Diaspora (v. 18). The disciples are now endowed with the pentecostal Spirit (v. 20). The divine visitation of the glorified "Son of Man" in the destruction of the Temple in A.D. 70 is mentioned (v. 23), and the apostolic kerygma is pictured as already being preached universally (v. 27), since the apostles have now, in the primitive Christian Church, been entrusted with the office of prophet (v. 41).

The instruction in parables (Mt 13) discloses the mystery involved in the supernatural character of the Church. Matthew's appended explanations of the Sower (Mt 13:19–23) and of the Cockle (Mt 13:36–43) reflect the experiences of the apostolic Church. The point of the Sower centers upon the harvest, a symbol of the eschatological judgment: the future judgment will reveal what is decided already in the present (represented by the varying fortune of the seed). In the explanation of this parable, however, the original point is overshadowed by a psychological allegorization, which dwells upon the reception of the *logos* (the apostolic kerygma) by various classes of men. One type of hearer is characterized as *proskairos* ("inconstant," v. 21), a term otherwise found only in the writings of Paul. Such a "lack of perseverance" or inconstancy can be judged only in relation to an organized and permanent community, a conception implied also in the reference to persecution (*thlipsis, diōgmos*) directed against it. Another type of listener is led to abandon the Christian faith by what is called the *merimna tou aiōnos* or the *apatē tou ploutou* (v. 22). The classic example of this category may be seen in the story of Ananias and Sapphira (Acts 5:1–11). Accordingly, it appears to be not implausible that we are dealing here with applications of the Lord's teaching made by the apostolic Church as a result of her own experiences in the early years after Jesus' death.

Matthew is the only Evangelist who records the explanation of the Cockle. Here again, while the point of the parable, the eschatological judgment, indicated by the command (which contradicts normal Palestinian agricultural practice) to collect the cockle *first* (v. 30), has been preserved in the explanation, still it appears that we are dealing with an allegorical application to the Church of the apostolic age. Jesus' habitual custom of addressing His message only to his fellow Jews during

His lifetime has here been abandoned for the universal Gentile mission (v. 38: *ho de agros estin ho kosmos*). Moreover, the good seed is construed as symbolizing the members of the Christian Church (v. 38b: *hoi huioi tēs basileias*), here distinguished (v. 43) from heaven (*basileia tou Patros mou*), a distinction reminiscent of the letters of Paul.

The importance of recognizing that these explanations (which, in Matthew's Gospel, appear on the lips of Jesus) are *in their present form* the creation of the apostolic Church, must not be lost sight of. They provide a most valuable piece of evidence that the primitive Christian community was already doing what the Church in every age has claimed the right to do, namely, render explicit the doctrinal implications of her Master's teaching.

The community discourse (Mt 18) prescribes the mutual relations, to be governed by brotherly love, which must obtain among the members of the Church. The prophetic description of the fall of Jerusalem and the ruin of the Temple (Mt 24–25) gives a preview of the ultimate liberation of the Church from the Judaism in which she was born. This essential autonomy of Christianity vis-à-vis the Mosaic code and cult, which includes the *visible* character of the Church, is depicted as a necessary consequence of Jesus' exaltation through His passion and resurrection. André Feuillet has convincingly demonstrated[42] that this discourse applies directly and *in toto* to the events of A.D. 70, and hence only in a typical sense to the end of the world.

For Luke, Jesus is primarily the Saviour. He alone of the Synoptic Evangelists gives Jesus the title *sōtēr* (Lk 2:11; cf. also 1:68, 71, 77; 2:30; 3:6; 19:9). The Gospel is the message of mercy and salvation which provides the God-given answer to the religious aspirations of that Hellenistic world for which Luke writes. Jerusalem, the principal scene of man's redemption, is the focal point of the third Gospel, which describes all the events of Jesus' life as orientated toward the Holy City. The Infancy Gospel and its narrative revolves about Jerusalem and its Temple; and almost ten chapters of Luke's book are devoted to Jesus' last journey to the arena of His passion and resurrection (Lk 9:51—19:27). Once the disciples arrive there, Luke insinuates, they "tarry in the city" constantly (Lk 24:49) until the coming of the Holy Spirit.

The Gospel of John is markedly different in spirit and style, as in the episodes narrated, from the first three. John is absorbed in the contemplation of God's Son, the divine Word incarnate, or perfect expression of the God "no man has ever seen" (Jn 1:18). It is, above all, the sacramental quality of Jesus' actions during His public life which has impressed John, for the Logos has become man in order to interpret to us the invisible Father. Christ speaks to men of the Father, not only by what He says, but even more forcibly by the symbolic character of His actions. His miracles are "signs" (*sēmeia*), which have a supernatural significance for the eyes and ears of faith. They are so many symbols of the Christian sacraments. Baptism, for instance, is symbolized by the cure of the blind man (Jn 9:1–41), who washed in a pool bearing Christ's name, "the One sent" (Jn 9:7). The author employs popular etymology for the place name Siloe (which actually means a conduit), in order to indicate that the pool in which the man is cured of blindness (symbol of a lack of Christian faith) is a type of the baptismal font. The miracle of the multiplication of loaves (Jn 6:1–13) is narrated in such a way as to reveal its Eucharistic significance.[43] In brief, John's message, directed, as we have seen, to those Christians who have believed without having seen Jesus upon earth, is that the glorified Christ, who lives on in the Church and in her sacraments, is the same Jesus of Nazareth whose "signs" revealed to men the character of His unseen Father.

THE EVANGELISTS' USE OF THEIR SOURCES

An examination of the manner in which the Evangelists have employed the data about Jesus furnished them by tradition will reveal their utter fidelity to the reality of sacred history. At the same time, it will be seen that they employ considerable freedom in their expression of the meaning of the *Heilsgeschichte*. Thus, while Matthew and Luke present Jesus' temptations in the desert as a rejection of the false Messianic ideals current in contemporary Judaism, Mark, who devotes but a single verse to the episode, portrays Jesus in this event as the new Adam in the new Paradise. The Lucan account of Jesus' visit to Nazareth, which appears to be a synthesis of three visits, or of three distinct scenes, forms the solemn introduction to Jesus' public life in the third Gospel. Matthew, in fact, mentions two visits: one at the beginning of the public ministry (4:12–13), another later (13:54–58). In addition, Luke has in his well-developed travel story of the last journey to Jerusalem (Lk 9:51—19:27) assembled together the bulk of those materials which his own independent research has unearthed.

Matthew has his own characteristic method of dealing with narratives. Since he is primarily interested in highlighting their religious meaning, he habitually compresses these episodes by eliminating such details as he considers superfluous. Matthew appears also to have abbreviated his description of events, in order to leave room for the inclusion of the many logia of Jesus, with which he is principally concerned. At times this Matthean brevity can lead to obscurity: to understand Mt

9:2b ("Jesus seeing their faith"); one must read Mk 2:4; similarly, the incomprehensible "I repeat" of Mt. 19:24 (Jesus has not made the remark before) is clarified by Mk 10:23–24. Matthew will suppress secondary characters in an episode when he considers it unnecessary to mention them. Thus, the centurion seeking a cure for his sick "boy" comes in person to make his request (Mt 8:5–13), which according to Luke's version was actually made through two groups of intermediaries (Mk 7:1–10). This same technique may be seen to operate in Matthew's story of the raising of Jairus' daughter (compare Mt 9:18–24 with Mk 5:21–43). By having Jairus himself announce to Jesus that his daughter "has just died," Matthew can tell his story without introducing the messengers who appear in Mark, where they bring to Jairus (who had already informed Jesus that his daughter "was dying") news of the little girl's death. Matthew described the fig tree which Jesus cursed as withering up "instantaneously" (Mt 21:19), while the Marcan version of this parabolic event is notably lengthier (Mk 11:12–14, 20–25).

Occasionally we see an Evangelist create a new literary unit out of materials gathered from different traditions. In the first chapter of the fourth Gospel, for example, the author presents a series of testimonies given by Jesus' disciples, in which we can discern a Christological rather than a simple historical purpose. John wishes to provide, at the outset of his book, a fairly complete record of the disciples' conception of their Master and His work; and he does this by means of seven titles given to Jesus (the Prophet, the Lamb of God, the Son of God, Rabbi, the Anointed, King of Israel, Son of Man). A comparative study of the other Gospels will reveal that these titles were given at various times throughout the earthly or the risen life of Christ and that the realization of their significance was the result of a long evolution. At the same time, an examination of this chapter shows that John has recorded much valuable historical data, namely, that Peter, Andrew, John, Nathanael, and Philip, even Jesus Himself, had all originally been for some time followers of John the Baptist, or that the change of Simon's name to Peter probably occurred at quite an early stage of Jesus' public ministry (as Mk 3:10 and Lk 6:14 also attest), and hence not as late as the event at Caesarea Philippi, where Mt 16:18 places it.

THE EVANGELISTS' USE OF LITERARY FORMS

Each of the four Gospels, if they be considered as a whole, belongs to a type of literature which took shape from the oral tradition represented by the apostolic preaching. The kerygma was a proclamation to nonbelievers of Jesus' work of universal redemption through His passion and resurrection, to which certain episodes and sayings from His public life were added. On the other hand, the written Gospel, as we asserted earlier, was intended for readers already possessed of the Christian faith, to provide them with a more profound understanding of the mysteries of the faith. Thus it may be classified as a particular genre of that religious history of which the Encyclical *Divino afflante Spiritu* speaks. Like the preaching, however, the written Gospel attempts to express that reality which surpasses the limits of our time-space world and its experiences. Indeed, it would be no exaggeration to say that the external historical events which the written Gospel records are subordinate to the infinitely more important, less easily perceptible fact that God has, in Jesus Christ, personally entered our human history. It should never be overlooked that the historical happenings which form the warp and woof of our Gospels are not introduced solely (or even primarily) for the sake of the "history" (in our modern sense) which they con-

Catholic critic when he is discussing the literary form of certain Gospel narratives: "Where do you stop?" If we accept the incarnational view of Sacred Scripture which has been proposed by *Divino afflante Spiritu,* then the answer to this question is clear enough. For Pius XII has stated that "just as the substantial Word of God became like to men in all things, 'without sin,' so the words of God, expressed in human language, became in all things like to human speech, except error."[45] Now just as the Word became incarnate to reveal to men some understanding of the unseen God, so the scriptural Word contained in the Bible was intended, in the divine plan, *to be understood* by man's intelligence aided by faith. Accordingly, we "stop" when we have been satisfied that we understand the words of the inspired writer, since then we know that we have grasped the divine message contained in a particular biblical passage. In addition, we might draw attention here once again to the false implication contained in such a question, namely, that the attempt to understand the Bible by the use of literary criticism calls in question or destroys the historical character of the events recorded in the Bible.

Among the subordinate literary forms in the Gospel narratives, we might enumerate the genealogy, the eyewitness account, popular traditions, family reminiscences, externalized representations of interior experiences, and, finally, midrash. The biblical genealogy, it is to be noted, is an art form, and hence it is not to be confused with those family trees found in modern histories or biographies, which profess to trace all the ancestors of a given individual back through many generations. The biblical genealogy has some doctrinal significance: in the Old Testament and in the New, it is frequently put at the service of the Messianic idea. Matthew's genealogy testifies that Jesus is an Abrahamid, and also of the royal Davidic dynasty. Luke's purpose in employing an ascending genealogy underscores the universality of the Christian religion, by tracing Jesus' lineage back to Adam, "who was of God." This last phrase, whose significance is so clearly different from the others in this series, attests the divine filiation of Jesus.

It is perhaps Mark's Gospel which contains the greatest number of eyewitness narratives, since that Evangelist is the faithful recorder of what Peter's observant eye had noted. Striking examples of the genre are to be found in Mk 1:23–27; 2:1–12; 3:9–11, etc.

The popular tradition is that type of story told, especially in the ancient Near East, among the people. By the nature of things, there are many more examples of this form to be found in the Old Testament than in the New. However, the two accounts of Judas' death (Mt 27:3–10; Acts 1:18–19), to which we have already made reference, provide an instance of it. Possibly, the same genre is to be seen in the story of the slaughter of the Innocents (Mt 2:16–18). For those who boggle at the suggestion that God has condescended to use "the story" as vehicle of His revelation, we commend John L. McKenzie's masterly discussion in *The Two-edged Sword*.[46]

Certain elements in Matthew's and Luke's Infancy Gospels belong to the class designated as family reminiscences, as does also perhaps the strange story preserved only in Mk 3:21–22.

There are certain scenes in the Gospels which may be best described as externalized descriptions of some inner experience. The account of Jesus' triple temptation (Mk 4:1–11; Lk 4:1–13) or of Joseph's dream (Mt 1:20–21) belongs in this category. Related to this genre also are those attempts by the sacred writers to describe some supernatural phenomenon which defies description in human language. We might cite the description in Acts of the first Pentecost, with its "sound *like that* of a violent wind blowing," or the "tongues *as if* of fire" (Acts 2:2–3). Here, as in Luke's statement concerning Jesus' agony in the garden—"His sweat became *as it were* clots of blood . . ." (Lk 22:34b)—it is to be observed that the writer does not say there *was* a violent wind, or fire, or blood.

The midrash is a literary form much cultivated in Old Testament biblical literature. It is also found in noninspired Jewish writings. Its distinctive character consists in supplementing with scriptural language or passages the description of some event about which usually little detailed information is available. The principle operative in this form of literature, particularly in biblical accounts, appears to be the continuity and consistency of God's actions throughout the course of sacred history. It is important to remember that at the base of any midrashic account there is always a historical nucleus of some kind, even though the nature and extent of the original happening may be difficult to determine. René Laurentin, in his interesting book *Structure et théologie de Luc* I—II,[47] discusses several examples of this type of writing in the Lucan Infancy narratives.

With regard to the sayings and sermons of Jesus, there are undoubtedly certain logia which retain the very form and idiom of their author. These can often be determined quite accurately by a comparison of the varying forms in which a logion is recorded in the evangelical tradition. The simplest and most obvious example perhaps is Mt 5:40, which represents the *ipsissima verba Jesu* (cf. Lk 6:29b).

There are, however, discourses which the sacred writer himself has constructed from Jesus' utterances and sermons; and these can even be expressed (as frequently in the fourth Gospel) in the author's own style and terminology. There are parables which, in the course of oral tradition, have undergone a certain historicization. The Wedding Feast (Mt 22:1–14) exemplifies this development. The detail in v. 7 is probably a reference to the destruction of Jerusalem under Titus, which has borrowed from the actual occurrence. The Matthean epilogue concerning the guest without a wedding garment (vv. 11 ff.), intended as a warning to the Gentile Christians, probably reflects the changed complexion of the Church by the year 80, when the Greek edition of the first Gospel was written. Again, there are parables which appear, in the form in which we possess them, to have been allegorized. While it is a delicate question to determine how much or how little allegory was present in Jesus' own version of certain parables, it is not implausible that three Matthean parables—the Steward (Mt 24:45–51), the Virgins (Mt 25:1–13), and the Talents (Mt 25:14–30)—reflect the ecclesiastical organization of the apostolic Church in the author's day, and portray respectively the hierarchical authorities, groups of consecrated women, and the body of the faithful.

At times it is possible to discern liturgical texts which enshrine the pronouncements of Jesus dealing with the ritual or sacramental life of His future Church. An instance of this literary type may be seen in Mt 28:18–19 and Jn 9:35–48; and Acts 8:34 ff. appears to reflect the prebaptismal instructions given in the early Church, as we have pointed out elsewhere.[48]

While this list of literary genres found in the Gospels is by no means exhaustive, it exemplifies sufficiently the great variety of types of literature which they contain. It should also serve to demonstrate the truth of the statement by Pius XII already referred to, that prescinding from divine inspiration, the preeminence of the Israelites in historical writing lies in the *religious* character of the history they wrote. Indeed, it is this quality which so sharply distinguishes the literature of Israel from that of her neighbors and explains the remarkable way in which the sacred writers, at least in the Old Testament, were able to take over literary forms and even myths from their pagan contemporaries and transform them into suitable media for the expression of divine revelation. With regard to the Evangelists, it is clear that while they were concerned with the historical and employed eyewitness accounts where these were available, they were always engaged upon their predominating purpose, the recording of the Good News of Jesus Christ, which is the supreme example of salvation history.

CONCLUSION

In closing this essay, I wish to refer to an episode in the fourth Gospel which, I believe, illustrates in a very striking way the conception of salvation history which we have been discussing in these pages. I have in mind the scene in which a baffled Sanhedrin is resolving to put Jesus effectively out of the way. "If we permit Him to go on this way, everybody will find faith in Him. Besides, the Romans will intervene and do away with both the Temple and the nation" (Jn 11:48). To them in their quandary Caiphas, "as high priest of that year" (of the accomplishment of man's redemption), addresses an inspired pronouncement: "You have completely misunderstood the case. You do not realize that it is better that one man die for the people, and that the whole nation should not perish" (Jn 11:50). This remark is designated as "prophecy" by the sacred author. The term is not used in the sense of a mere prediction of Jesus' approaching death which the supreme council of Judaism was at that very moment discussing. Rather, it is meant in the sense of an utterance which voices the divine verdict about the saving nature of that death. In John's view, Caiphas here has become God's official spokesman. Accordingly, the high priest gives expression (whether unwittingly or not, John does not tell us) to the *propter nos et propter nos-*

tram salutem which is the principal preoccupation of the Evangelist himself.

John's reflections upon the true significance of Caiphas' words are germane to our study, since they imply not only his own awareness as an inspired writer of the nature of salvation history, but also a conviction that, to deliver such a statement, a special divine charism was at work. John immediately adds: "He did not say this on his own. But as high priest of that year, he prophesied that Jesus was destined to die for the nation—indeed, not only for the nation, but that He might reunite God's dispersed children" (Jn 11:51–52).

IV

The Apostolic Church among the Gentiles

IN HER origins the Church was Jewish. Her founder was a Jew; her original leaders, the Twelve, were formed within the ancient religion of Israel; her place of origin was the Jewish land of Palestine—she was born, in fact, in Jerusalem upon the mount of Sion, the very heart of Judaism in the first century. Moreover, when the Church as a consequence of Jesus' death and exaltation sprang to life under the quickening impulse of the Holy Spirit, whom her Lord had sent from heaven, she retained the Scriptures of Israel as part of her heritage.

Accordingly, the problem of the salvation of the Gentiles, the *goiim* or pagans, was an important piece of unfinished business committed to the Church by her departed Master. During His earthly ministry Jesus had insisted that His own mission was restricted to "the sheep that are lost of the house of Israel" (Mt 15:24), and in His own teaching on this important problem He does not seem to have advanced beyond the rather vague doctrine of the Old Testament prophets. The statement in Mt 8:11–12 may well be considered characteristic of His veiled predictions concerning the Gentile mission.

Thanks to the insight of a man like Stephen and to the

initiative of that "Hellenistic" branch of the primitive Christian community of which Stephen was an outstanding representative, the pagans were to be favored with the hearing of the gospel first at Antioch (Acts 11:19 ff.). From Antioch, under the clear guidance of the Holy Spirit, Barnabas and Saul inaugurated a more extensive tour of evangelization in Asia Minor. Finally, when Saul attained his majority as the Apostle Paul, the apostolic preaching would resound throughout the ancient Mediterranean world. It was, indeed, mainly the religious genius of Paul which provided the Greco-Roman world of the first century with the grace of receiving and assimilating the truths of the Christian faith.

What was the gospel of Paul? If we can believe his own attestation, his preaching faithfully mirrored that of the apostolic kerygma (cf. 1 Cor 15:3–4); and the samples of Paul's sermons which Luke, companion of the Apostle's travels, provides in Acts appear to bear out Paul's own assertion of his fidelity to apostolic tradition (Acts 13:16–41). On the other hand, the teaching of Paul as we can recover it from his extant letters has its own cachet of individuality.

As a result of his unique experience at the moment of his conversion on the Damascus road, when Paul saw the exalted Christ surrounded by the light of glory, he was led to represent our Lord as the new or last or second Adam. At the heart of Pauline soteriology lies the twin mystery of Jesus' death and resurrection. In contrast with John, the Apostle of the Gentiles does not seem to have thought of the Incarnation as part of Christ's work of redemption. For Paul, the coming of the Son of God into history was "in the likeness of sinful flesh" (Rom 8:3). He was "born of a woman, born under the law" (Gal 4:4). "Being rich, He became poor for your sakes" (2 Cor 8:9). Thus, in assuming human nature the pre-existent Christ entered—as far as was possible for one who was sinless—the sinful solidarity of the first Adam. By His redemptive death He destroyed this old sinful solidarity under which humanity had so long been enslaved. He did this, however, not as a private individual, but as the one representative of the whole race: "One died for all—therefore all have died" (2 Cor 5:14). By His resurrection Christ created a wholly new family, the supernaturally endowed "Israel of God." "And He died for all, in order that the living might no longer live for themselves, but for Him who died and was raised for them" (2 Cor 5:15). "He was handed over for our sins and raised for our justification" (Rom 4:25). Accordingly, we are all part of this new Adam (Gal 3:26–29) and sons of God by participation in His unique divine Sonship. We are—as members of the Church—simply "His body" (Col 1:18; 1 Cor 12:12–27).

As the new Adam, the risen Christ, on Paul's view, presents in His glorified human nature the spectacle of the first redeemed man. Through that glorified humanity as instrumental cause, the glorified Lord endows all Christians with the Spirit, the life of grace, uniting them with His risen body as members of it. Accordingly, they constitute corporately "that new Man," Adam, who has been "created according to God in justice and genuine holiness" (Eph 4:24). Christ's death and resurrection, moreover, impart to the Christian sacraments their basic character (cf. Rom 6:3–5; 1 Cor 11:26). They also control the primordial rhythms of the Christian life (cf. 2 Cor 4:10; Phil 3:10–11). Indeed, they have imposed their pattern upon the whole of Christian salvation history (cf. Rom 11:15).

Since Paul was not himself an eyewitness of Jesus' earthly life and had not shared with the earlier disciples in the public ministry, one might ask, what right had Paul to give testimony to Christ? Paul was, as he himself reminds us, also an apostle:

he had met the risen Christ at the moment of his own conversion (1 Cor 9:1); and his witness to the apostolic Christian faith is, perhaps after that of Peter, the most important of all the great *martyres* of the first age of the Church.

The first study in this final section is devoted to an analysis of the threefold account of Paul's conversion given us by Luke in the Acts of the Apostles. No study of Pauline theology can be adequate or even accurate without taking this great experience of the Apostle into careful consideration. Paul's approach to the Christian mystery was through the glorified Christ, who identified Himself with the humble rabbi Jesus of Nazareth. The risen Lord also revealed that He was still active in history through the work of His followers—in fact, that it was through men (like Ananias, who made Saul a member of the Church) that He willed to save other men. Finally, Paul learned in the hour of his conversion to Christ that his vocation to be a Christian was at the same time a call to be an apostle (cf. Rom 1:1).

The second essay is devoted to one aspect of Paul's apostolic vocation which he always considered of paramount importance. His task of witnessing to Christ, of suffering for the gospel, was simply a prolongation of Jesus' own role as the suffering and glorified Servant of Yahweh. In the preaching and the liturgy of Palestinian Christianity, the characterization of Jesus Christ as the Servant of God of whom the Deutero-Isaiah had sung became a favorite soteriological theme. In such circumstances it is striking indeed that Paul should essay to apply these Isaian texts to himself and his own apostolate.

The third study attempts to correct the exaggerated view that Paul did not know, or even deliberately ignored, the evangelical traditions which had preserved the logia and the teaching of Jesus. There is sufficient evidence to be found in the Pauline letters, from the citations of and references and allusions to Jesus' sayings, to correct such a one-sided view of Pauline theology.

The last essay presents some reflections upon Paul's seemingly strange advocacy of the imitation of himself by his Christian converts. This doctrine of imitation, confined almost exclusively in the New Testament to Paul's writings, provides a valuable insight into the Apostle's understanding of the significance of apostolic tradition and the manner in which it is to be transmitted to successive generations of Christians. Thus this conception rightfully has a place in any study of the Church in the New Testament.

10

Paul's Conversion in Acts

THAT the meeting of Paul with the glorified Christ upon the Damascus road is essential to the understanding of the Apostle's very personal conception of Christianity, of what he loves to call "my gospel," is today an accepted theorem amongst students of Pauline theology.[1] The triple narrative of that supremely critical hour in a life fraught with crises deserves to be studied from another aspect: the function assigned it in the exposition of his theme by the author of the book of Acts.

Indeed, it is noteworthy that in the past decade or so, when much has been written upon primitive Christianity and upon the veritable web of problems woven into the tissue of Luke's second volume, relatively little attention has been devoted to the puzzling repetition of Paul's conversion in a book otherwise notable for its rigid economy of narrative detail.[2]

No doubt this is largely due to the concentrating of the scholar's attention, within or without the Church, upon the harmonization of apparently contradictory data provided him by the three versions of Paul's first encounter with Christ. And surely such a method has been rightly judged by critics[3] to have long since yielded its scientific lode. Nor, for the Catholic exegete, was the problem ever a serious one from the viewpoint of inerrancy. For even were it granted that minor discrepancies might defy the harmonizer's subtlest efforts, two of the three accounts are explicitly set down as the reporting of speeches made on two very different and very difficult occasions.

As a matter of fact, however, the details which at first sight seem to conflict can be quite satisfactorily accounted for.[4] The author's statement[5] that Saul fell down while the rest of his company "stood amazed" need not be at variance with Paul's own assertion[6] that the whole band fell to the ground. That the companions, in Luke's words, "heard the voice, but saw no one" is not irreconcilable with Paul's observation that "my companions saw the light, but did not hear the voice speaking to me."[7] And even if it be urged that Paul, in the address to Agrippa, puts into the mouth of Christ a proverb found only in Greek literature,[8] such a view would scarcely provide an irrefragable argument against the historical credibility of this speech or against Luke's faithfulness in recording its substance. Indeed, the origin of Paul's apostolic commission as emanating immediately from Christ Himself, the problem which Kirsopp Lake[9] considers a most serious difficulty against Acts' historicity, seems capable of a fairly obvious solution.[10]

The main question to be answered, however, and one we feel will shed new light upon Luke's plan in the writing of Acts, is that envisaged in the present study: *why the three accounts?* To state the question adequately involves the asking of three other questions.

ASKING THE QUESTIONS

To suggest that Luke's purpose in repeating the account of Paul's conversion in Acts has some relation with the general scheme of his presentation of the first years of Christianity after Christ's ascension, demands the keeping in mind of a threefold problem. There is, first of all, the problem that confronted the apostolic Church in the critical first years of her development: the gradual severing of the ties which naturally bound her to Judaism. There is, in the second place, the problem for the author of any book like Acts: the development of a theme, conditioned by the sources at his disposal, so as to provide his public with that insight into the interplay of personality and event which is his *raison d'être* as a historian. Finally, we have the reader's problem, which can be stated most simply as the problem of the *genre littéraire*, or as "grasping the mind of the writer."

The investigation of the series of events that led to the Church's full autonomy of the religion she came to supersede is a path beset with pitfalls for the unwary, and hence it is not to be wondered at, regrettable though it may appear to our spirit of inquiry, that the Catholic historian, by and large, seems to have shied away from a discussion of this thorny question.[11] Yet to consider that a writer of Luke's competence and honesty could have written even a sketch of those meaningful years without taking cognizance of and coping with this central problem is inconceivable. That the author of Acts was not only aware of the fact, but that he gave its explanation a primary place in the little book he wrote as companion volume to his Gospel, is shown by his enunciation of its *theme* and by the *literary form* he adopted as the best means for its development. This is only as it should be; for to perceive how Luke handles his "author's problem" and to grasp the literary form in which he presents it to the reader, puts us in a position to appreciate his portrayal of how the little Christian community rose from a position where it seemed almost[12] a sect of Judaism to complete independence of the outmoded religion of Israel.

The Theme of Acts

The theme, all are agreed, is contained in the announcement of the ascending Christ to His apostles: "You will receive the power of the Holy Spirit coming upon you, and you will be witnesses of mine in Jerusalem and in the whole of Judea and Samaria, and to the end of the earth."[13] Yet if such be clearly the theme of Acts, it is no less clear what a relatively small part the apostolic college, listed in the very first chapter (1:26), plays in Luke's story. And Matthias brings the group to its complement of twelve, only to disappear immediately after his election. St. John, who preaches with St. Peter in Jerusalem,[14] accompanies him to Samaria, and assists on the return journey with the evangelization of "many Samaritan villages" (8:25), is heard of no more. The several Jameses mentioned in the course of the narrative never seem to depart from the Holy City,[15] while even Peter himself, portrayed in the first half of Acts as head of the apostles, never gets further than Judea and Samaria, if we except the enigmatic remark that upon his release from prison "he went off to another place."[16]

The theme of Acts, however, includes the extension of the Church "to the end of the earth," and the author does not fail to let his reader know that in his story the carrying out of this part of Christ's prophecy regarding the universal character of the Church is left to Paul. Paul, according to Luke, is aware of this mission almost from the opening of his apostolic career. At Pisidian Antioch, upon the rejection of his message by the Jews, he and Barnabas announce, *as applied by Christ Himself to their apostolate,* the words of the Isaian Servant Song: "I have constituted you a light to the Gentiles, in order that you may be a source of salvation *to the end of the earth*" (13:47).[17] That it is principally in Paul's journey to Rome that

Luke finds these words fulfilled, implying as they do that Paul's work is somehow an extension of the Redeemer's,[18] will become evident in the course of our study of the conversion narratives.

It remains to point out here the problems confronting Luke, who, because of his interest in Paul and of the sources for a history of the primitive Church at his command, develops his theme as he does. The apostles are commissioned as Christ's *witnesses* for the spread of Christianity. Paul quite evidently does not come up to the standard of a "witness" according to Peter's definition, and hence is ineligible for the role of apostle as described in Acts 1:21 ff.[19] In consequence, it becomes clear that Luke is scarcely justified in bestowing, as he twice does,[20] this title upon Paul, unless he shows that the notion underwent some kind of evolution in the very early Church.

The Literary Genre

The late Wilfred L. Knox has shown[21] that, like the third Gospel, the book of Acts has been written as a travel story, a literary form much in vogue in the ancient world. Luke's Gospel as a travel story illustrates his aim—that of showing how the central figure, Jesus Christ, comes to Jerusalem, seat of the ancient true cult of God, to accomplish there, by His passion and resurrection, the redemption of mankind. It is not accidental to his theme that Luke insists upon the scene of these events as a significant *terminus ad quem*: Christ comes to the center of the religion of Israel to found the religion which is its consummation.[22] We have, in Acts, a story of the same genre whose theme is developed by a movement "beginning from Jerusalem,"[23] which comes to a conclusion in the reaching of Rome by the protagonist, St. Paul.[24] This insight of Knox's is one of the finest contributions of his stimulating little book on the Acts of the Apostles; for it solves the "reader's problem" with respect to Acts, in that it discovers to us Luke's literary method of dealing with the theme of Acts and thereby enables the reader to grasp the meaning Luke has seen in his story. For by casting the theme of the expansion of primitive Christianity into the form of a travel story, the author of Acts tells us that the realization by the Church of her founder's promise of universality is ultimately accomplished by a journey of one of her foremost personalities from Jerusalem to Rome.

The method is not unfamiliar to the reader of the third Gospel: by displaying Christ's work as a journey from Galilee to Jerusalem, Luke has shown how the old religion finds its perfect consummation in that which the Redeemer has founded by dying and rising for our salvation. The story begins and ends with the worship of God in the Temple. Yet what an infinite distance separates the religion of a Zachary from that of apostles who, adoring their risen Lord upon Mount Olivet, return to the Temple to worship the Father through Jesus Christ![25]

Similarly in Acts, a journey makes it clear that in the course of the first decades of her existence the Church has ceased to look to Jerusalem as the center of religious interest and turns her gaze to another city, which, as seat of world empire, better expresses her catholicity. The book has repeated references to the Christian's worship in the Temple. (On his last pilgrimage to Jerusalem Paul, on the advice of James, associates himself with sacrificial rites.) But in the person of Paul and by means of his last journey, Luke discloses to us that this stage in Christianity's development is come to an end. The definitive severing of the Apostle's relations with the theocracy of Israel occurs with his divinely inspired "appello ad Caesarem,"[26] by which he effectively withdraws himself forever from the power of high priest and Sanhedrin, and begins the long odyssey with which the story is to end.

Thus we see Luke's purpose in highlighting this journey. We perceive also a reason for his curious unconcern with the outcome of Paul's trial. With Paul established in Rome, Luke's theme is played out to its conclusion: the apostolic Church has broken out of the narrow compass within which its links with Israel's religion inevitably tended to confine it and has carried out the Master's command to reach "the end of the earth."

But for the author of Acts, the adoption of the same literary form he used in writing his Gospel raises a new problem: the choice of a protagonist—a task much less easy than in his first volume. The journey Luke follows is not, as the first half of Acts would lead us to expect, that of Peter. It is in Paul's travels that Luke sees the illustration of the most significant part of his theme.[27]

This choice is no doubt imposed by our historian's acquaintance with the events of early Christianity; it is dictated also by his interest (and his public's interest) in the Apostle of the Gentiles. It may be that his story stops where it does because Luke is unaware of the sequel or is anxious to spare the sensibilities of his Roman readers. Yet when all this is conceded—indeed, it is to Luke's credit as a historian that it should be so—the coming of Paul to Rome is the completion of his narrative; for Luke, though aware that Christianity has already preceded Paul to the city of the Caesars,[28] wishes to draw attention to Paul's advent as bestowing upon the Roman Church something which it had not hitherto possessed.[29]

One of the most important devices Luke uses in his narrative to stress the importance of Paul's Roman voyage and to discover its meaning to the reader is, we venture to suggest, the repetition of the story of the Apostle's first meeting with

Christ. It is in view of ascertaining the function of these three accounts in the story told in Acts that we wish to examine their distinctive features.

A SYNOPSIS OF THE THREE ACCOUNTS

For the reader's convenience we include here a synopsis[30] in which we have tried to reproduce the original in English as faithfully as possible, using the same word or phrase to bring out a corresponding repetition in the Greek so that similarities and divergencies may be at once evident.

Acts 9:3–19	*Acts* 22:6–16	*Acts* 26:12–18
	INTRODUCTORY	
3 Upon the journey, as he drew near Damascus, suddenly a light from heaven flashed round him, 4 and having fallen to the earth, he heard a voice saying to him:	6 Upon my journey as I was nearing Damascus about noon, suddenly a great light from heaven flashed round me, 7 and I fell to the ground and heard a voice saying to me:	12 . . . journeying to Damascus . . . 13 at midday along the road, I saw, Sire, a light from heaven beyond the brightness of the sun shine round me and my companions, 14 and when we had all fallen to the earth, I heard a voice saying to me in Aramaic:
	THE ENCOUNTER	
Saul, Saul, why do you persecute me? 5 And he said: Who are you, Lord? He: I am Jesus, whom you are persecuting.	8 Saul, Saul, why do you persecute me? And I replied: Who are you, Lord? And He said to me: I am Jesus the	Saul, Saul, why do you persecute me? It is hard for you to kick against the goad. And I said: 15 Who are you, Lord?

	Nazarene, whom you are persecuting . . . 10 I said: What shall I do, Lord? Then the Lord said to me:	The Lord said: I am Jesus, whom you are persecuting.
6 But get up, and enter the city, and you will be told what you have to do.	Get up, and go to Damascus, and there you will be told all that is determined for you to do.	16 But get up and stand on your feet: for I have appeared to you in order to constitute you a servant and a witness of the fact you have seen me, and of what I shall, in future appearances, reveal to you, choosing you from the people and from the Gentiles to whom I shall send you, 18 to open their eyes, to turn [them] from darkness to light, and from Satan to God, so that they may receive remission of their sins and an inheritance among those conse- crated by faith in me.

THE EFFECT ON PAUL AND ON COMPANIONS

7 Now his companions stood speechless, for they heard the voice, but saw no one. 8 Saul was raised up from the earth, but	9 (Now my compan- ions saw the light, but they did not hear the voice speaking to me.) 11 Since I could not see because	

though his eyes were
open, he saw nothing.
And leading him,
they brought him into
Damascus. 9 And he
was three days
sightless; and he did
not eat or drink.

of the glory of that
light, being led by my
companions, I came
to Damascus.

ROLE OF ANANIAS

10 There was a
disciple in Damascus
by the name of
Ananias; and the
Lord said to him in
a vision: Ananias!
He replied: Here,
Lord! 11 The Lord
said to him: Arise,
go into the lane
called Straight; and
seek in the house of
Judas, Saul called the
Tarsian. For lo, he
is praying, and 12
he has seen in a
vision a man named
Ananias come in and
lay his hands upon
him that he may
recover his sight. 13
But Ananias replied:
Lord, I have heard
from many about
this man and of the
harm he did to your
saints in Jerusalem;
14 and here he has

12 Now Ananias, a
man whose devotion
to the law is attested
by the resident Jews,

power from the high
priests to shackle all
who call upon your
Name. 15 And the
Lord said to him:
Go! A vessel of
election
is the man to me:
to carry my Name
to the Gentiles and
kings and to the
sons of Israel. 16
For I shall show him
what he must suffer
for my Name's sake.
17 And Ananias went
to the house, and
laying his hands
upon him said: Saul,
brother, the Lord has
sent me—Jesus, who
appeared to you on
the road you were
traveling—that you
may recover your
sight and be filled
with a Holy Spirit.
18 And straightway a
kind of scales fell
from his eyes, and he
recovered his sight;

13 came to me:
and standing by me,
said to me:
Saul, brother,
recover your sight.

And I at once
recovered my sight.

14 Then he said: The
God of our fathers
has selected you
to learn His will:
to see the Just One
and hear from His
lips 15 that you are
to be a witness for

and rising up, he
was baptized;
19 and when he had
eaten, he regained
his strength.

Him before all men
of what you have seen
and heard. 16 And
now, why delay?
Get up and be
baptized, and be
washed free of your
sins by invoking
His Name.

The One Constant Element in the Accounts

A cursory reading of this synopsis will reveal the striking fact that only in the dialogue between Christ and Paul is there full verbal agreement among the three accounts. "Saul, Saul, why do you persecute me?" "Who are you, Lord?" "I am Jesus, whom you are persecuting." Such word-for-word repetition is no chance occurrence in accounts which display such a wealth of variation. It brings out the force of the tremendous impact upon Paul of the identity revealed as existing between the exalted Christ and His Church. That Luke, even in his own historian's narrative, has carefully reproduced this revelation verbatim, shows how basic to the scheme of his whole story is the mystery of the oneness of Christ and the Church, and how essential to it is Paul's awareness of that mystery. For Luke will take care to show that, *in a very special manner,* Paul is himself identified with the Lord. To appreciate how our author does this, it will be necessary to examine the accounts in turn.

THE HISTORICAL NARRATIVE OF THE CONVERSION

A glance at the account Luke gives in chapter 9 reveals such a close similarity to Paul's speech to the Jews in chapter 22 that this discourse may be regarded as one of the primary sources for Luke's historical narrative. The additions made to the data given by Paul point to the possible existence of another source, perhaps Ananias. What is here most revealing, however, is that Luke has omitted certain details in Paul's description—a fact that provides a precious clue to our author's purpose in writing up the first notice he gives upon Paul's conversion.

Details Added by Luke

The evidence that Luke has carefully made use of almost each detail from the speech in chapter 22 is quite impressive.[31] Our first introduction to the young Saul at Stephen's trial is a mosaic of items selected from Paul's apologia. This is particularly striking where Luke observes that "Saul entirely approved his being put to death"—an insight that can only have come from Paul himself.[32] The description of Paul's part in the subsequent persecution of the Church is from the same source.[33]

Luke introduces his account with Paul's departure for Damascus armed with letters from the high priest "to the synagogues" (Paul says "to the brethren": 22:5). This more precise information about the relations of Church to synagogue in the Diaspora, as well as the summary of the contents of the decrees, may well have come from Ananias.[34] Luke's phrase "to the synagogues" shows that the heads of Judaism were considered to have jurisdiction over Christians, who were looked upon as merely a recalcitrant, if highly devout, sect of that religion. It may well be that in places like Damascus they still frequented the synagogues, as in Jerusalem they worshiped in the Temple. An interesting sidelight on social relations in the remote cities, where antagonism was apt to be less acute between Christian and Jew, is given in Ananias' being able to visit Saul in the house of Judas.[35] Such hints, together with the recounting of the visions of Paul and Ananias, enable Luke's story to run more smoothly and logically than either of Paul's subsequent relations.[36] Ananias' recorded reaction to Saul gives an idea of the persecutor's notoriety and of the attitude of mistrust which Christians as well as Jews would subsequently display toward the converted Paul.[37]

Most important for Luke's narrative at this turning point in his book are the contents of Ananias' vision and his announcement to Paul of the purpose of his visit.[38] Christ has characterized Paul's vocation in His words to Ananias: Paul is to preach to Gentiles as well as Jews; his apostolic career is to be noteworthy for suffering.[39] To Paul Ananias explains that he is sent not only to restore his sight but also that he might "be filled with a Holy Spirit." This last phrase is the same used in Luke's description of the first Pentecost: "and all were filled with a Holy Spirit."[40] Thus his reader is made aware that this occasion is in a sense the Pauline Pentecost, and is prepared to some extent to discover later on that the result in Paul's case is not unlike the effect on the apostles: "and they began to speak with other tongues, just as the Spirit was giving them *to prophesy*." Canon Cerfaux has drawn attention to the portrayal of the Twelve, in the beginning of Acts, as prophets of the New Testament.[41] He has perhaps not so clearly adverted to a like characterization in the case of Paul—necessary for Luke's demonstration that the Apostle of the Gentiles ranks with the Twelve.[42]

Lastly, it is Luke, as a good historian, who alone states explicitly the fact of Paul's being baptized (9:18), who sounds the keynote of the Pauline kerygma: "and forthwith in the synagogues he began to preach Jesus by saying: 'This man is the Son of God.' "[43]

Apart from some minor points,[44] there are two important

omissions in Luke's narrative. The first of these is the absence of any reference to Paul's religious interpretation of his blindness, to be seen in the next section. Instead Luke gives a sober, almost[45] a diagnostician's account: the eyes were covered with a sort of scaly substance (9:18). This matter-of-fact attitude shows the impression Luke will convey: he is content (as he promised in the Gospel prologue, Lk 1:3 f.) to set forth *the facts* so far as his evidence permits, without giving anything like a mystical interpretation of them, although he recounts the Elymas incident, where Paul deems blindness a symbolic punishment for spiritual blindness (13:10 ff.).

The other event omitted in Luke's narrative is the vision in the Temple which tells Paul how he must witness to Christ. Since Jews and perhaps even Christians refuse to accept his testimony, he is to leave Jerusalem with all speed.[46] That Luke does not refer to the incident in chapter 9 proves fairly certainly that it was separated from the events in Damascus by some period of time. Else it is difficult to see why he does not include here a vision which reveals the gradual revelation to Paul of his role as a witness and explains why Paul was created Apostle of the Gentiles.[47]

Function of Luke's Account in Acts

It is by appreciating the contrast between Luke's description of the effect upon Paul and upon the rest of the travelers, and that given later by Paul himself, that we get a clue to the function of chapter 9 in the whole story. Paul will describe the scene by saying that his companions saw the light, but did not "hear" the words of Christ (22:9). Luke puts it very differently (9:7): "His companions stood speechless; for they heard the voice, but saw no one." Why attempt a description which apparently contradicts what Paul has to say? To answer this question, which has not perhaps received the attention it deserves, is to divine Luke's purpose in furnishing his own account of the meeting between Christ and Paul.

For this, it is essential to grasp the meaning of the New Testament phrase "to hear the voice," when the object is put in the genitive case rather than in the accusative. It means to recognize that a person is speaking, without necessarily understanding what is said.[48] Consequently, Luke here means to single out a difference between Paul's experience and that of his companions, important for his narrative. The other travelers "heard the voice," that is to say, they recognized the fact that a person was speaking, but they were prevented from seeing who the person was. They were, however, sure that someone was present. Here is the point of Luke's remark: he wishes to insist that Paul did see Christ. His experience was, then, specifically the same as that of the apostles on the various occasions of Christ's postresurrection appearances. That this gave Paul the right to the title "apostle," Luke undoubtedly learned from Paul himself,[49] and where his story becomes almost a biography of the great missionary, Luke suggests that Paul has basis for such a claim.

For the same reason, the detailed description of Ananias' part in the story is inserted here. Christ, who had told His apostles that they would be His witnesses "even to the end of the earth," now appears to Ananias in order to apply this prophecy to him who is chosen as "a vessel of election . . . to carry my Name to the Gentiles and kings . . ." (9:15).

Similarly, Luke is also enabled, by the inclusion of this Ananias section, to show Paul's sufferings as a part of the divine plan. Suffering is a characteristic, Luke knows, of the apostolic calling, as may be gathered by a remark of his with reference to the apostles: "They then went on their way, rejoicing, from the audience with the Sanhedrin, because they had been considered worthy to suffer dishonor for the Name" (5:41). One feels that such a remark is the result of a profound impression made on the writer very early perhaps in his own Christian life by the apostles' conduct under persecution. At any rate, throughout the rest of his book Luke will draw attention to Paul's sufferings as a part of Christ's designs.[50]

Thus the impression made by Luke's own version of the Damascus-road event is that from the first he wishes to show the convert Saul as one to whom the name "apostle" rightly belongs. He has truly "seen the Lord"; he is to be formed by suffering on the pattern of the Twelve; and Christ Himself appears to Ananias in order to reveal a new and deeper meaning in the notion of "witness" than Peter's speech before Matthias' election would lead us to believe.

PAUL'S ARAMAIC ACCOUNT OF HIS CONVERSION

This second record of Paul's conversion figures in his own speech on the occasion of his arrest in the Temple. Its purpose, so far as that occasion is concerned, is apologetic.[51] What is of greater moment to us here is the reason why the author of Acts, who already made great use of the facts it furnishes, should include it in his narrative.

Paul's Purpose

From the beginning, Paul is anxious to conciliate the infuriated Jerusalem mob by identifying himself as closely as possible with the Jews of the Holy City. He speaks to them in their own language;[52] he insists on his Jewish blood, upon his rabbinic training at the feet of the revered Gamaliel, upon his zeal for God that rivals their own. He introduces Ananias by pointing out that he is a Jew noted for observance of the Torah and one whose integrity any Damascene Jew will vouch for. Perhaps even his mention of Christ's order to depart for "nations afar" is a gentle hint that they will soon be rid of him. This apology of Paul's serves the general purpose of the story of Acts inasmuch as it underlines the unreasonableness of Jewish opposition to the Apostle.

But there is another theme, characteristic of this speech, which best explains its inclusion here by Luke: the religious significance Paul sees in his own blindness. Such an aspect, as we have already observed, was carefully omitted from Luke's own historical account; and indeed, in Paul's speech before Agrippa, any hint of his blindness is lacking. This theme, then, here merits our attention.

Religious Significance of Paul's Blindness

In the first conversion-account, we observed the historian's hand. Content to allude to Paul's blindness and recovery as historical events, Luke wishes by a sober narration of carefully selected facts to make it clear that Paul's meeting with Christ is not to be classed with other visions however supernatural, but is to be accepted on a par with the other appearances of the risen Lord.

At the same time, Christ's appearance to Paul, Luke knows, differs in one very notable respect from His visits with His own in Jerusalem or Galilee: it is the Christ exalted in divine glory who appears to Saul. We possess no record of any such revelation of His glorified humanity to the Twelve during the forty days before the Ascension. In fact, as Père Benoit has rightly observed,[53] Luke's description of the Ascension is rendered remarkable by the absence of any light of glory, and thus differs from the *caelestis exaltatio* described elsewhere in the New Testament. This distinctive feature of the appearance to Paul we owe to Paul's own testimony here.

He depicts his experience rather as a revelation of *seeing* than of hearing;[54] and the difference of the effect produced in himself and in his companions is described in terms of the sense of sight. Thus he says his companions see the light (they hear nothing); but they are not affected, as he himself is, by this wondrous illumination. They are neither blinded, nor do they receive the gift of supernatural insight, the virtue of faith. The cause of his blindness Paul ascribes, not to the mere light, but to "the glory of that light." And it is this "glory,"[55] manifestation of divinity no less in the New than in the Old Testament, which ever remains, for Paul, the characteristic quality of his experience near Damascus. Years later, to the Corinthians, he will describe the infusion of faith as a divine act of the "new creation": "The God who said 'Light, shine out of darkness' is He who shone in our hearts to illuminate our knowledge of the glory of God reflected in the face of Christ" (2 Cor 4:6).

Thus Paul is well aware of the religious meaning that underlies the fact of his blinding. It is not, like that of Elymas, a symbol of that spiritual blindness which is the awful consequence of a refusal to believe. Rather it represents the lesson which, once learnt, made the essential difference between Saul the Pharisee and Paul the servant of Christ: the impotency of the natural man in face of the supernatural, a lesson Paul will dwell on so graphically in his letter to the Philippians.[56] Paul is probably not unaware of the similarity of his own experience to that of Ezekiel in his inaugural vision, when he too saw the "glory of the Lord" and fell upon his face.[57]

Yet, though Paul wishes here to point out the spiritual significance of this event, he does not neglect its historical character.[58] Thus it is from this account, for instance, that we first learn the time of its occurrence, a factor which, as Loisy has noted, brings home its reality.[59]

That Luke has refrained until now from recording these two theologically paramount aspects of Paul's conversion, despite the fact that he used this speech as primary source of his own account in chapter 9, is evidence not only of his artistry but also of his awareness of the important turn his story is now to take. His narrative is reaching its final phase: the journey of Paul to Rome. That Paul should now declare that he has enjoyed a meeting with Christ wholly unprecedented in the experience of the Twelve is surely reason enough for the author of Acts to represent the establishment of the apostolic Church at Rome in the person of his hero. Likewise, it is appropriate that at this juncture, where Paul stands at the beginning of a series of events behind which Luke never tires of pointing out the finger of God,[60] and whose unfolding contains the denouement of the whole book, Paul should describe his blindness as a kind of parable in action. His insight into the triumph of grace over nature has already formed the theme of a letter written to the Roman Church,[61] and is the most striking facet of his apostolic character as divinely chosen herald of "the mystery," the admission of the Gentiles into the Church.

PAUL'S ACCOUNT OF HIS CONVERSION IN GREEK

In contrast with the two preceding, the third account of his conversion, given by Paul in his speech before Agrippa, Bernice, and Festus, is strikingly brief. Once the reader has passed the introductory details, which are almost[62] identical with those in Paul's first speech, he is made aware of the distinctive character of this final narrative. All but the essentials have been shorn away here in an effort to highlight the most momentous meeting of his life. There is no hint of his blinding, or his baptism, no reference to Ananias, nor—but for a passing remark[63]—any mention of his companions' reaction. Paul clearly wishes to center his audience's whole attention upon Christ and the words He addressed to His future apostle.

Two references give this speech verisimilitude as an address to his Hellenistically-educated audience. Paul notes that the voice he heard spoke "in the Hebrew tongue," that is, in Aramaic, the lingua franca of the Palestine of that day. And then, to make the meaning of Christ's first question clear to his royal listeners, Paul puts into His mouth a proverb, current, it would seem,[64] only in the Greek-speaking world. While its meaning here is much disputed, the maxim has almost certainly the same function as the religious significance Paul assigned to his blindness in the speech to the Jews: it underscores the transcendence of the divine, the supernatural.[65]

It is, however, with verse 16 that the role assigned here by Paul to the story of his conversion becomes clear. It is not accidental that the words Christ is reported as using are an echo of those addressed to Ezekiel in that prophet's inaugural vision. Like the omission of any reference to his loss of sight and to the intervention of any other human being, the reference to Ezekiel's vision which introduces the most lengthy speech of the risen Lord reported in any of the three conversion-accounts is Paul's manner of describing his encounter with Christ as his own inaugural vision. A few verses further on, indeed, he will refer to it in a manner altogether unique either in Acts or in his letters,[66] as "the heavenly vision" (Acts 26:19) which is the beginning of his apostolic activity.

Paul in the Role of a Prophet

The primary purpose[67] of this address to Agrippa is to induce him to see in Paul a prophet like those of the Old Testament, in whom, Paul hopes against all appearances, Agrippa still believes, or at any rate, whose function this half-pagan potentate can understand. The conversion of Saul the zealot is carefully set forth, not so much as the commencement of the Christian life into which the neophyte is initiated by baptism, as rather the beginning of Paul's career as a prophet. The content of this message is described in words used by the Evangelists to describe the kerygma of the last great prophet of the old dispensation, the fearless John the Baptist, of whom this Herod may be expected to have heard.[68] "I preached repentance and a turning to God by doing works worthy of repentance" (26:20). But not content with such passing references to Ezekiel or the Baptist, Paul explicitly identifies his message with that of the prophets of the Old Testament, declaring it contains "nothing beyond what the prophets had declared would come to pass—and Moses: namely, that the Christ was to suffer, was, as first of the resurrection of the dead, to proclaim light both to the people and to the Gentiles" (26:22).

Whether or not Paul's self-characterization as a prophet was doomed to failure on this occasion, its importance in his story is not lost upon the author of Acts, and he includes two other bits of dialogue which further delineate the prophetic role of the Apostle. When Festus remarks that Paul is "raving" (an expression used to describe the frenzied ecstasy of the *mantis* of Hellenistic mystery cults), the answer he receives does not assert that his impression is entirely false. Rather, Paul corrects it to bring out the true reason for his exalted utterances: "I am *not raving*, Your Excellency, I am prophesying" (26:24 f.).[69] That Paul had a ready reply to such an objection is proven by a remark he had already made in writing to the Corinthians on the subject of such charismata: "If, then, the whole church be assembled together and strangers or unbelievers come in, will they not say 'You are raving'?" (1 Cor

Paul's own apostolic career the words of a prophecy, indisputably Messianic by the witness of the most primitive Christian tradition, are clearly applied, can lead but to a single conclusion: that the work of Christ as Redeemer is carried on "to the end of the earth," is most strikingly exemplified, in the missionary activity of the Apostle of the Gentiles. If Peter is unquestionably portrayed in the Gospels and in Acts as head of the apostolic college, Paul is revealed in the New Testament as the apostle specially selected to continue the work of the Servant of Yahweh. In his person, then, the exalted Christ from the right hand of the Father carries on His work of the redemption. If the book of Acts constantly portrays the invisible Christ at work directing His young Church at each important turn in her first beginnings, so that it underscores the essential Christian dogma that the Church and Christ are one, it lays special stress upon this truth in the case of the convert Saul. He thus becomes the apostolic missionary par excellence, the disciple in whose person this union is patently manifested—so that it would not seem an exaggeration to say that when Paul goes to Rome, Christ, in Paul's person, goes to Rome. And Luke, by his recording of Christ's words that identify Paul's work with His own as the Servant of Yahweh, is not unconscious of their momentous import.

In Is 42:6 f., the first of the Servant Songs, Yahweh says to Jacob "my servant," to Israel "my chosen one": "I the Lord am the God who called you in justice and who will grasp you by the hand and fill you with strength, who gave you as a covenant of the people, as a light to the Gentiles to open the eyes of the blind, to rescue from bonds those who are prisoners and those who sit in darkness, from their jail." In his Gospel Matthew (12:18 ff.) has cited this passage and applied it to Christ. Luke does not refer to it, but quotes a passage of Isaiah (61:1 ff.) in the scene in the Nazareth synagogue, which is very similar to it and which several commentators have regarded as an additional Servant Song: "The spirit of the Lord is upon me; wherefore He has anointed me: to preach the good news to the poor He has sent me, to herald to captives forgiveness, and to the blind sight. . . ." J. S. van der Ploeg,[73] who refuses to include this passage among the four songs of the Servant of Yahweh (while asserting of course its Messianic character), points out "une différence profonde": the Servant's mission is to preach to all the nations the religion of Yahweh, whereas the personage in 61:1 ff. is to exercise his ministry among the Israelites. Christ had declared (Mt 15:24) that He was sent only to the lost sheep of the house of Israel, and indeed His personal ministry did not exceed the narrow limits of Palestine. It was in the person of His apostles, and particularly that of Paul, that He was to announce the good news of redemption to all the nations. Thus it is that we find, in the third account of Paul's conversion in Acts, Christ describing his apostolic commission to Paul in terms of the first of the Servant Songs.

SUMMARY

1) The question to which we sought an answer in this study of the threefold repetition in Acts of the conversion of St. Paul is one which appears to us most fundamental: why the three accounts?

2) The theme chosen by Luke as subject matter for his second volume, the gradual historical realization of Christianity's universal character, is the most acute problem, both historically and theologically, of the first decades of the apostolic Church.

3) This development of primitive Christianity Luke chose to present in the same literary form he had adopted in his

Gospel: the travel story. The choice of such a *genre littéraire* here, however, involves a problem not encountered in his earlier work: about whom is the narrative to revolve? Who plays the central role in this second travel story?

4) For Luke as a theologian, the answer is not hard to find: the risen Christ exalted at the Father's right hand is the personality who dominates the story at every turn through the Holy Spirit He sends.

5) As a historian, Luke must find some figure in the apostolic Church whose biography forms a suitable vehicle for the development of his theme. That figure he finds in the convert Saul of Tarsus, whose missionary activity and, especially, whose journey to Rome illustrate with singular vividness the growth of the early Church away from the ties binding it to Judaism.

6) Such a choice commits the author to the task of proving Paul an apostle in the full sense, and of showing in some way his identification with the risen Christ, the Redeemer.

7) One literary device in Acts to demonstrate this double role of Paul's is, we believe, the threefold insertion of his conversion at focal points in Luke's narrative. A comparative study of these accounts reveals the artistry, no less than the historical fidelity, of this first of Church historians, and gives us the answer to our initial question.

8) It is not accidental that the three versions agree verbatim only in the dialogue by which the glorified Christ identifies Himself with His Church. For Luke, the history of His Church is the extension of Christ's redemptive activity in the world.

9) On the other hand, further study of these three accounts reveals the fact that while substantially in agreement, they are carefully presented so as to pick out various aspects of Paul's apostolic character: (*a*) Luke's own account is prin-

cipally directed to proving that Paul *really saw* Christ (and hence in this is on an equal footing with the Twelve). (*b*) Paul's Aramaic address to the Jews reveals the unique character of this meeting: Paul alone of all apostles has seen the Christ *exalted in glory*. (*c*) The speech in Greek before Agrippa presents the meeting with Christ as Paul's *inaugural vision,* underscoring the role *as a prophet* (like that of the apostles in the beginning of Acts). Most important of all, it is in this version of Paul's apostolic commission from Christ Himself that the Apostle *is identified as the Servant of Yahweh,* thus proving beyond a doubt that Paul's career is, *in Christ's own eyes,* an extension of His redemptive activity here below.

10) Thus, with Paul established in Rome, Luke's theme attains the goal of its development. The Church has realized the promise of universality prophesied by her exalted Lord and contained in the phrase "to the end of the earth." Or rather, in the person of Paul, the second Servant of Yahweh, the glorified Christ Himself has come to the city, whose imperial dominion symbolizes the universal character of His Church.

11

Paul and the Christian Concept of the Servant of God

MORE than any other Old Testament theme, the Isaian writings concerning the fate of the Servant of Yahweh were destined to provide the primitive Christian community with a vehicle for their earliest theological presentation of Christ's redemptive death and resurrection. Several precious indications of the manner in which Deutero-Isaiah was laid under tribute by the first preachers of Christianity are preserved for us in the book of Acts; and the Gospels themselves also witness to the prominent place which the Servant soteriology enjoyed in the apostolic preaching.[1] In the light of this evidence, which we shall have occasion to review presently, the thoroughgoing transposition which the Servant motif seems to have undergone at the hands of St. Paul appears as a rather startling variation upon the original theme. For at least in the writings of his which have survived, the Apostle does not seem to have made any great use of the *primary* soteriological implications of the Deutero-Isaian prophecy. And what is more indicative of his attitude towards it than any mere argument *ex silentio*, Paul has, with an astonishing apostolic liberty, employed his creative genius to elaborate a completely new Servant theology in which he himself appears as the *'Ebed Yahweh*. As a result, this theme, hitherto uniquely employed to convey the meaning of the central events of Christ's redemptive mission among men, becomes under Paul's inspired pen the basis for his mystical conception of the Christian apostolate.

This Pauline transposition of a theme already integrated into the pattern of the apostolic kerygma emanating from Jerusalem may well be expected to provide an important clue to Paul's very personal presentation of the gospel. At any rate, it is, as far as I have been able to ascertain, a problem which has not thus far been expressly treated.[2] Consequently, the present article is an attempt at an investigation of the reasons behind such a transmutation of the Servant theme on the part of St. Paul, a transmutation which may well have appeared revolutionary in the apostolic Church.

IMPORTANCE OF THE SERVANT SOTERIOLOGY IN THE PRIMITIVE PREACHING

In his article on *euangelizomai*, contributed to Kittel's *Wörterbuch*, Gerhard Friedrich stresses the importance of the prophecies of Deutero-Isaiah for an understanding of the Christian term "gospel."[3] Not only does that author approach more closely than any other Old Testament writer the religious connotation of the word as current in New Testament usage;[4] he also dwells upon two themes which form the very essence of the gospel message as we find it in the apostolic writings: the notion of the kingdom of God and the delineation of the Messiah's person and work as the Servant of Yahweh.[5] The burden of the Isaian herald's message, the "good news" is summed up in the proclamation "Your God is King." (Is 52:7; 40:9; 41:27; 43:15).

Thus it is little wonder that in our canonical Gospels both Christ Himself and John the Baptist are depicted as beginning their preaching of the advent of God's kingdom in terms borrowed from Deutero-Isaiah.[6] We wish in this present section to review the monuments of early Christian prayer and preaching preserved for us by the New Testament writers, in order to form a judgment as to the importance of the *'Ebed Yahweh* theme in primitive Christianity.

The Apostolic Kerygma in Its Beginnings

For the beginnings of the apostolic preaching, we must turn to the first half of Acts, where we shall find three personalities whose recorded words offer matter for our investigation: Peter, Stephen, and Philip.

The Petrine Catechesis

The speech of St. Peter in Acts 3:12–26, judged one of the "most ancient sections of the New Testament,"[7] is dominated by the conception of Christ as the *'Ebed Yahweh*. The apostle bases his explanation of the healing of the crippled beggarman upon the exaltation of the Servant mentioned in Is 52:13—53:12. "The God of Abraham and Isaac and Jacob, the God of our fathers, has glorified His Servant Jesus, whom you handed over and denied before Pilate, when he had decreed His release. You denied the Holy and the Just One, demanding that a murderer be delivered up to you, whilst you slew Him who is source of life, and whom [subsequently] God raised from the dead" (Acts 3:13–15).

Peter has, however, revolutionized, theologically speaking, the conception of Deutero-Isaiah in bestowing upon Jesus of Nazareth the two names "the Holy" and "the Just." Of these characteristically Isaian epithets, only the second had ever been applied to the Servant by the prophet, and that but once.[8] As for the appellation "the Holy," Yahweh constantly vindicates it for Himself.[9] Thus the bestowal of these names upon Christ is not only evidence of the devotion to the Holy Name in the early Church,[10] but proof also of Peter's conscious faith in Christ's divinity, which had been the result of the Resurrection.[11]

At the close of his discourse, St. Peter again presents Christ, man's Redeemer from sin, as the Servant of Yahweh: "And all the prophets who spoke from Samuel onwards, also announced these days. You are the sons of the prophets and of the covenant which God struck with your fathers. . . . For you, first and foremost, God has raised up His Servant, and sent Him to bless you by converting each of you from your evil ways" (vv. 24–26).

It is not only in proclaiming the gospel to Israel that Peter employs the theology of the Servant. He makes reference to it also in catechizing the Gentile Cornelius (Acts 10:36 ff.).[12] "[Ours is] the message that [God] sent to the sons of Israel, gospeling peace through Jesus Christ. He it is who is Lord of all. You know the story that has spread throughout the whole of Judea. It began in Galilee after the baptism which John preached, and concerns Jesus of Nazareth, and how God anointed Him with a Holy Spirit and with power, and how He went about doing good and healing all those possessed by the devil, because God was with Him. And we are witnesses of all He did in the country of the Jews and in Jerusalem. Him indeed they took and hung upon a tree; Him God raised the third day, and permitted to appear, not indeed to all the people, but to the witnesses divinely chosen, to us, who have eaten and drunk with Him after His rising from the dead."

Here we have what may be termed the gospel in its most summary form.[13] Given the primitive nature of this sermon, the influence of Deutero-Isaian thought upon it is of the greatest interest. The description of the Christian kerygma as the "gospeling of peace through Jesus Christ," a recollection of Is 52:7 ("How beautiful upon the mountains are the feet of him who brings the good tidings, who preaches peace, etc. . ."), will shortly become a *terminus technicus* denoting the apostolic preaching.[14] Another important piece of evidence for the use of the book of Isaiah in the interpretation of Christ's public ministry is to be seen in the declaration that His anointing with the Spirit is the source of His miracles. Whether Is 61:1 ff. is rightly to be regarded as a fifth Servant Song or not,[15] this passage, which Luke's Gospel will set in sharp relief, was the *point de départ,* as we shall presently see, for the early dogmatic development with regard to the purpose of the miracles of Christ's public life.[16]

In connection with this discussion of Peter's preaching, reference must also be made to the liturgical prayer offered in the Jerusalem Church according to Acts 4:25 ff., which may reasonably be supposed to owe its origin to the Petrine circle of influence, if not to St. Peter himself, and which displays in its own way the conception of Christ as the Isaian Servant.[17] "O Lord, who hast made the heavens and the earth and the sea and all that be in them. . . . They have come together in this city against thy holy Servant Jesus, whom thou hast anointed . . . to do whatever thy hand and thy will foresaw would come to pass. And now, Lord, have an eye to their threats, and grant that thy slaves may with all freedom proclaim thy gospel, by stretching forth thy hand for healing and by the accomplishing of signs and prodigies wrought in the Name of thy holy Servant Jesus."

The Apologia of Stephen

The longest résumé of any of the speeches in Acts—a fact which undoubtedly demonstrates its great significance for

Luke's general theme—Stephen's fiery manifesto before the Sanhedrin is notable for its apparent lack of reference to the *'Ebed Yahweh*. A reason for this omission might be found in the fact that Stephen was interrupted before he could arrive at the final stage of his development. It might be also urged that Stephen was not here engaged in preaching the kerygma, in witnessing to the resurrection and to the miracles of the earthly life of Jesus, but rather in defending himself before his judges. Yet, in a very real sense this *apologia pro vita sua* was a *martyrion*, an act of witnessing to the truths of the gospel sealed by the testimony of his own blood;[18] and Stephen's death was not only the first but the greatest of those striking depositions on the part of "faithful witnesses" which subsequent ages would call martyrdom.[19]

One reference to Isaiah is to be found, however, just before Stephen is forced to terminate his defense. His impassioned denunciation of Judaism, at the close of his review of the history of Israel, is made in terms borrowed from that prophet: "You have always resisted the Holy Spirit. As your fathers have done, so do you. Which of the prophets did your fathers not persecute? Indeed, they slew the preachers of the proto-evangel concerning the coming of the Just One, whose betrayers and murderers you are now become" (Acts 7:51 ff.). Isaiah, proto-evangelist par excellence, had already described Israel's reaction to the Christ in similar terms: "But they revolted; and they grieved His Holy Spirit, and He was moved to enmity towards them, and He Himself warred against them" (Is 63:10).[20]

A profounder study of Stephen's speech reveals a conception of Christianity which bears striking analogies with Deutero-Isaian theology. The Exodus theme, with its promise of a new cult "in spirit and in truth" where the Temple appears to play no part,[21] is central to the prophet's message. An echo of this theme is to be perceived in Stephen's sketch of Israel's "displaced persons," which begins with Abraham and culminates in the characterization of Yahweh, who does not dwell "in buildings made with hands" (Acts 7:48). Moreover, both prophet and protomartyr insist upon the ephemeral character of the Mosaic code,[22] as also upon what Dom Charlier has termed *l'échec rédempteur.*[23]

And yet we find in Stephen's conception of the new religion the adumbration of a new theological conception.[24] Where the Servant theology tended to underscore the continuity existing between the Christian message and the religion of Israel, Stephen thinks of Christianity's supreme transcendence over the old worship of God. And when, at his life's close, Stephen is accorded a vision of Christ, not as the suffering and glorified Servant, but as the exalted Son of Man, one feels that Christian soteriology has in this moment received a new orientation. In the light of subsequent developments, it is perhaps not too much to say that the seed is being implanted in the mind of the young Saul who witnessed this martyr's death, a seed which will one day develop along lines calculated to express more completely the catholic character of the Christian faith.

The Gospel of Philip

The preaching of the deacon Philip, apostle of Samaria, is depicted in Acts as following the lines of the traditional Jerusalem kerygma. His conversation with the eunuch of the Queen of Ethiopia (Acts 8:26 ff.) revolves about the identity of the Suffering Servant described in Isaiah 53 as being "led like a sheep to the slaughter." To the chamberlain's query Philip replies by "gospeling Jesus to him, beginning with this passage" (Acts 8:35). It is to be observed that it is no mere chance that St. Luke includes this sample of early Christian evangelization based on the theology of the Servant, however fortuitous the reading of Isaiah, on the part of the eunuch, may have been. Philip's preparedness to expose the gospel in terms of the Suffering Servant surely presupposes a previous thinking-out of the kerygma along the lines of the Isaian theme. Moreover, Luke would appear to indicate by the inclusion of this episode that in the Hellenistic branch of the Palestinian Church the Servant motif, which had originated with St. Peter, was being thoroughly exploited, particularly in connection with prebaptismal instruction.[25] Indeed, it would not be unreasonable to suppose that about this period in the Antiochian Church, the fairest fruit of early Hellenistic evangelization,[26] certain modalities of the Servant theme would have a prominent place in the new Eucharistic "liturgy," which it was that Church's privilege to create.[27]

The Servant Theme in the Gospel Record

When we turn to our four Gospels, we discover, as might be expected, a fuller elaboration of the Servant theology. What appears in the primitive sources as often no more than a passing reference emerges in the Synoptics and in St. John as a more completely assimilated doctrine. In the Synoptic tradition particularly, while each Evangelist will add his own personal variations to the theme, there are observable a number of Servant episodes which form a common heritage. These will be noted in discussing the Gospel of St. Mark, which may in some respects be considered the literary parent of Greek Matthew no less than of the third Gospel.[28]

Mark's Version of the Petrine Preaching

The Papias tradition of the origin of Mark's Gospel as deriving essentially from St. Peter's preaching seems solidly probable; and as Vincent Taylor has recently pointed out, there is no reason to question it.[29] The point is of particular interest for our inquiry, as it points to Peter as one of the main early Christian authors of the Servant soteriology. There are four episodes recorded by St. Mark where reference is made to our theme, and in which he is followed with minor variations by Matthew and Luke: Christ's baptism, the Transfiguration, the Passion prophecies, and the Last Supper. We shall treat these first, leaving for final study the one passage proper to the second Gospel (Mk 10:45) which is redolent of the Servant theme.

Mark's version of the heavenly utterance at Christ's baptism combines a reference to Isaiah 42 with a reminiscence of the second Psalm.[30] "And a voice came from the heavens: 'You are my beloved Son: in you have I taken my delight' " (Mk 1:11).[31] "Behold my Servant," Isaiah had written, "whom I uphold; my Chosen One, my soul takes delight in Him." The use of the third person in the Matthean account underscores the allusion to this first of the Servant Songs: "This is my beloved Son, in whom I have taken my delight" (Mt 3:17). Luke, on the other hand, transforms the proclamation (at least according to certain important textual witnesses[32]) into an explicit citation of Psalm 2: "You are my Son: this day have I begotten you" (Lk 3:22). The fourth Gospel, though omitting the account of the baptism, has included a reference to the celestial voice in the Baptist's reference to the baptism theophany: "Yes, I have seen and I testify that He is the Chosen One of God."[33]

The divine voice at the Transfiguration recorded by Mark as "This is my beloved Son: hear Him" (Mk 9:7) is again referred more explicitly by Matthew to Isaiah: "This is my beloved Son, in whom I have taken my delight: hear Him" (Mt 17:5). In the third Gospel there is yet another echo of the first Servant Song: "This is my Son, the Chosen One: hear Him" (Lk 9:35 f.).

The Synoptic tradition contains three predictions by Christ of His coming passion and resurrection. The first reminds us of the Servant's rejection, sufferings, and exaltation:[34] "And He began to teach them that the Son of Man must suffer greatly, be rejected by the elders and the chief priests and the scribes, and be put to death, and rise after three days" (Mk 8:31). The second prophecy, "The Son of Man must be delivered over into the hands of men; they will put Him to death and three days after His death He will rise" (Mk 9:31), recalls Is 53:10 ff. The final prediction, according to Mk 10:33, states that "The Son of Man will be handed over to the chief priests and the scribes; and they will condemn Him to death, and will hand Him over to the pagans, and they will strike Him and spit upon Him and scourge Him and kill Him, and after three days He will rise." In the Septuagintal version of Is 50:6, the Servant cries: "I have submitted my back to the scourges, and my cheeks to blows; I have not turned away my face from the shame of being spit upon." To this brutally explicit picture of the Passion, another Isaian touch has been added by Luke: "He was despised" (Lk 18:32; cf. Is 53:3).[34a]

In the opinion of Oscar Cullmann,[35] the clearest reference made by Christ in the Gospels to His role as the Servant is contained in the words uttered over the chalice at the Last Supper: "And He said to them: 'This is my blood, the blood of the covenant, poured out for many'" (Mk 14:24). The notion of a death "for many" is the dominant theme of Isaiah 53: "Of a truth, he has assumed our infirmity, our woes has he borne (v. 4). . . . He was transpierced for our sins, he was bruised for our crimes. The chastisement he bears is our peace: his bruises are our weal (v. 5) . . . our collective sin Yahweh has made to fall upon him (v. 6). . . . He has been cut off from the land of the living because of the sin of my people (v. 8). . . . My Servant, the Just One, will justify a great number: he will himself bear their sins (v. 11). . . . He has borne the sin of many, and has made intercession for sinners (v. 12)."

This verse of Mark concerning the chalice will appear with some slight alterations in Greek Matthew, Luke, and Paul, but always with the unmistakable reference to the Servant. So, too, will the notion of the covenant be repeated in each account, the re-establishment of which is considered by Isaiah as the principal achievement of the Servant (Is 42:6; 59:6).

There remains to consider the much controverted logion which Mark alone reports: "The Son of Man is come not to be served, but to serve; and to give His life as a ransom for many" (Mk 10:45). Alfred Loisy, together with a great number of the critics, maintained that the second half of this statement betrays the influence of Paul upon the second Gospel.[36] While it is even possible that the first part of the verse contains an allusion to the Servant role of Christ,[37] it is abundantly clear that the remainder is a summary of the Isaian theme described in Is 53:5–8. If, indeed, in the Septuagintal rendering of this chapter the word *lytron* does not occur, still the offering of his life by the Servant is designated an *āšām* in the Masoretic text.[38] The Servant gives his life in sacrifice (v. 10), thereby justifying many sinners (v. 11), because he has borne the sins of many (v. 12). Such a thoroughly Isaian picture of the atonement as the words of Christ in Mk 10:45 display will be found, in the second section of this study, to be completely absent from the soteriology of St. Paul. Accordingly, Loisy could not have been more unfortunate, in his attempt to prove the inauthenticity of this saying, than by ascribing it to the Apostle's influence upon Mark.

The Servant Theology of Greek Matthew

We have already remarked upon the tendency of Greek Matthew to develop the characterization of Christ as the *'Ebed Yahweh* which was insinuated by the second Evangelist. It will, then, not be surprising to discover that in the sections proper to Matthew there is evidence of a more thoroughgoing reflection upon this theme than perhaps in either of the other Synoptic Gospels.[39] In fact, considering that the first Gospel more than any of the others centers about the notion of the kingdom of God, a conception nowhere so fully developed in the Old Testament as with Isaiah,[40] such a preoccupation as Matthew evinces for the Servant theme is only what was expected.

In the Sermon on the Mount, Matthew's first great discourse, there are two references to the Servant. The Beatitudes are in part inspired by Is 61:1, where the Servant is said to "preach to the poor," to "comfort all that mourn."[41] In the same chapter there is a saying of Christ whose literary dependence upon Is 60:6, 8 has been demonstrated by William Manson:[42] ". . . resist not the evil man. On the contrary, if a man strikes you on the right cheek, turn the other also to him. If a man wishes to hale you into court and take your tunic, give him your cloak also."[43] If one accepts Manson's view of the Isaian coloring of an authentic logion of Christ, then we have here an instance of the adaptation of the Servant theology, not, as in the examples previously studied, to the Christian soteriological teaching, but to parenetic purposes.

Matthew's two most striking Servant passages have to do with the Galilean ministry of Christ. The first of these occurs as a conclusion to the account of the day of miracles at Capharnaum (Mt 8:16 f.), where the Evangelist cites Is 53:4: "He has assumed our infirmities; our woes has he borne."

This reflection on the part of the Evangelist holds a twofold interest for our investigation. In the first place, it manifests a new insight into the implications of the Servant soteriology. Not only does Christ assume the role of the Servant in His passion and resurrection, but on Matthew's view this activity can be traced back into His public life.

It will be remembered that for Matthew the significance of Christ's miracles is their connection with the advent of the kingdom of heaven. If it is through His death and resurrection that the definitive overthrow of the devil's domination in this world is effected, the miracles of the public life are the initiation of the victory over Satan.[44] If this be so—and Matthew has seen that it is—then these thaumaturgical activities of Christ are also the initial phase of Jesus' salvific role as the *'Ebed Yahweh*.

This theological transposition of the purpose of Christ's miracles by Matthew just at this point of his Gospel has a second highly interesting corollary. In chapters 8–9, the Evangelist has grouped together ten miracles in order to prepare the answer for the question put to Christ by John the Baptist's disciples in chapter 11: "Are you He who is to come, or must we await another?" (Mt 11:3). Thus Jesus is able to reply simply by pointing to what He has (in the Matthean account) already done: "The blind see, the lame walk, the lepers are cleansed, the deaf hear, the dead rise, the gospel is proclaimed to the poor." If, moreover, we recall that these are precisely the miracles predicted throughout the book of Isaiah as signs of the Messianic age,[45] and if, granted the superb pedagogy of Christ everywhere manifest in the Gospels, the disciples of John would seem to have received from Him an answer which their schooling had best fitted them to understand, then Matthew would seem to imply that it was the precursor himself who had first adopted the Servant theme in proclaiming the advent of "Him who is to come."[46] Indeed, as we shall have occasion to observe, the fourth Evangelist makes at least one explicit statement about the Isaian coloring of the Baptist's teaching.

The second reference to the Servant theme in connection with the public ministry of Christ is made by Matthew in the course of another summary of His Galilean activity. In Mt. 12:17 ff. we have what Joseph Schmitt has termed "une glose de l'évangéliste,"[47] a citation from the first Servant Song (Is 42:1 ff.). Matthew here dwells upon the final cause of Jesus' public life: "in order that what Isaiah the prophet had said might be fulfilled: 'Behold my Servant, in whom I have taken my delight. . . . I shall set my Spirit upon him, and he will proclaim judgment to the pagans. He will not strive nor cry out, etc. . . .' "

It is to be noted that these two loci in Greek Matthew (Mt 8:16 f.; 12:17–21) are the only two instances in the Synoptic Gospels where the writer refers to the Servant theme on his own initiative. In all other cases it is Christ Himself (or the heavenly Voice) who draws the analogies. These facts permit us to conclude that, on the one hand, Christ certainly employed the Servant theme to teach His disciples the meaning of His redemptive death, and on the other, the apostolic Church was engaged in reflection upon the *sensus plenior*[48] of this Isaian motif, extending its meaning to embrace more of His activities than those involved in the central act of the redemption.[49]

The Third Gospel

St. Luke, convert from paganism and probably a member of the Antiochian Gentile Church, writing for the Hellenistically-educated reading public of his day, does not employ the Old

Testament Scriptures to the same extent as Matthew. In the light of this fact it is significant that the only two lengthy citations in his Gospel are both taken from the Deutero-Isaiah.[50]

To form a kind of prologue to Jesus' public life, Luke has conflated three different episodes, all concerned with a visit or various visits of Christ to Nazareth.[51] This fusion of *récits* which constitutes the Lucan rejection at Nazareth has its *raison d'être* in that Evangelist's interpretation of the Galilean ministry. On this view, the presentation by Jesus of His Messianic credentials is doomed to end in His becoming "a sign which provokes contradiction" (Lk 2:34) for the Galileans, and consequently this phase of the public life is but a prelude to the last journey to Jerusalem, which occupies such a proportionally prominent place in the third Gospel.[52] In his description of the scene in the Nazareth synagogue, Luke, alone of the Evangelists, gives us the text of Christ's discourse—and it is a passage of Isaiah which describes the work of the *'Ebed Yahweh*. Hence, for Luke, it is as the Servant that Christ is rejected by His own townfolk, and ultimately by all of Galilee and Judea; and such a characterization serves as a kind of preview of the drama to be unfolded in Jerusalem.

In the Lucan account of the discourse after the Last Supper, Christ makes an allusion to Is 53:12, which is not mentioned in the other Gospels.[53] "For I say to you: it is necessary that this word of Scripture be fulfilled in my regard: 'He has been placed among the number of wrongdoers' " (Lk 22:37). And when, in his account of the Passion, Luke brings Jesus to Calvary, the first detail to be mentioned is the fulfilment of this prophecy: "Arrived at the place called Calvary, they crucified Jesus there together with the criminals, one on His right, the other on His left" (Lk 23:33).

Finally, in the scene upon the road to Emmaus, the day of

Christ's resurrection, it is the third Evangelist who records Jesus' words to the disillusioned disciples: "You stupid blunderers! Hearts so slow to find faith in all that the prophets announced! Was it not necessary that the Messiah undergo these sufferings in order to enter into His glory?" These words are a kind of summary of the Isaian predictions concerning the sufferings and glorification of the Servant. They contain, moreover, in germ a conception which in the fourth Gospel will be erected into a *thèse magistrale.*

St. John and the Glory of the Servant

The fourth Gospel, written sometime after the others were finally edited, witnesses to further reflection by its author upon the theme of the Servant. Both at the beginning and at the end of his Gospel, St. John has combined it with another theme, dear to him as it was to Deutero-Isaiah, that of the Exodus. Twice in the opening chapter John the Baptist points out Jesus to his disciples: "Behold the Lamb of God, Him who takes away the sin of the world" (Jn 1:29, 37). M.-J. Lagrange and Ferdinand Prat have maintained that here it is the innocence of Christ which is alluded to, and not His character as victim.[54] However, Paul Joüon has, I believe, successfully answered their arguments,[55] while Gerhard Kittel has observed that the expression "Lamb of God" in Aramaic might also be translated "Servant of Yahweh."[56] If John the Evangelist meant to underscore the expiatory role of Christ by thus recording the Baptist's testimony, it remains for us to investigate the source or sources of this representation of the Redeemer as a lamb. (It will be recalled that already the Apocalypse [5:8] had designated Him in His salvific activity as "the Lamb that was slain.")

There are two biblical sources which explain the use of this image: the paschal lamb (Ex 12:3 ff.) and the Servant of Yahweh (Is 53), who is compared to a lamb and who offers his life as an *āšām*. Moreover, as has been already noted,[57] the Servant is compared in this chapter to a leper (v. 3), at whose cure the law prescribed an *āšām*, consisting of two lambs and a sheep. Indeed, it must be confessed that, since the paschal lamb was not a sacrifice of atonement, it is rather as the *'Ebed Yahweh* compared to a lamb that Christ "takes away the sin of the world." This interpretation receives a confirmation from the words of John the Baptist cited in this very passage: "I saw and I have testified that He is the Chosen One of God"—a reference, as we already have seen, to the first Servant Song (Is 42:1).

In the account of the Passion in the fourth Gospel, there is a reference to Christ as the new Pasch (Jn 19:14), where Pilate passes the sentence of death on Him at the very hour when the paschal lambs are being sacrificed in the Temple. There is, however, another indication in John's Passion story which insinuates that the Evangelist has once again combined the idea of the paschal lamb with that of the Suffering Servant. "All this came about," John remarks (19:36), "in order that the Scripture might be fulfilled: 'Bone of his will not be broken.' " As Père Mollat points out,[58] this citation is a combination of Ex 12:46 (the reference is to the paschal lamb) and of Ps 34:20. In this latter passage there is question of God's protection of the just man in time of persecution, of whom the Suffering Servant is the classical type. The most striking passage in the fourth Gospel, because it gives an insight into John's very personal interpretation of the Servant theology, is that found in 12:37 ff. Apropos of the miracles of Jesus, John remarks that "although He had worked so many signs in their presence, they did not believe in Him, in order that the word which the prophet Isaiah spoke might be fulfilled, 'Lord, who has believed our report, and to whom has the arm of the Lord been revealed?' " (Is 53:1). It may seem strange, at first sight, that John should have referred to this passage of Isaiah, particularly in view of the very clear reasons for the Jews' lack of faith given in Is 6:9 f., which he will immediately quote. At the conclusion of these citations, however, the Evangelist makes a remark which is more enigmatic still: "Isaiah said these things because he had seen *His glory* and he *spoke* of Him" (Jn 12:41). On John's view, both these remarks of the prophet were the result of his seeing the "glory" of Christ! Two questions must be answered before the meaning of this pericope can be perceived: What does John mean by the "glory" of Christ? What does John mean when he says that Isaiah "had seen His glory"?

What does "glory" mean in the fourth Gospel? It has already been pointed out by A. M. Ramsey[59] that the "glory" or exaltation of Christ for St. John means His passion as well as His resurrection. It remains for us here to point out another modality of this important Johannine term which it derives from its Old Testament associations. In the Old Testament, *kābōd Yahweh* signifies the sensible manifestation of the divine Presence and Power in such theophanies as the burning bush or the passage of the Red Sea. Indeed, as Père Boismard has observed, the miracles of the Exodus are attributed by the sacred writer to the intervention of this divine "glory."[60]

In his account of the miracle of Cana, John has established a similar relation between the "signs" wrought by Jesus and His "glory": "Such was the first of Jesus' signs. . . . He manifested His glory, and His disciples began to believe in Him" (Jn 2:11). Here, then, in the fourth Gospel, we obtain a new insight into the meaning of the miracles of Christ: they bear a relation to Christ's "glory," i.e., to His passion and resurrection. Why? Because, for John, passion and resurrection are the supreme theophany, the definitive manifestation of the divinity of Christ;[61] and the "signs" or miracles are a first glimpse of that "glory" which the divine Pedagogue grants to His own to prepare them for the revelation of the central mystery of Christianity, the Incarnation. Only after His resurrection will they fully comprehend the "Messianic secret," the divine personality of Jesus of Nazareth; meanwhile, during the ministry of Jesus, they are accorded "signs" to assist the growth of their faith in Him. One day they will assert, as John does in his Prologue: "we have beheld His glory, the glory [He receives] from the Father as the only-begotten Son" (Jn 1:14).

What does John mean, then, when he says that Isaiah "had beheld His glory"? First of all, the Evangelist makes it clear that he has in mind *both* citations of Isaiah when he makes this remark ("Isaiah said these things") and that *both* passages refer to Christ ("for . . . he spoke of Him"). The author of the fourth Gospel, then, for whom "glory" is a consecrated term, refers here at once to the inaugural vision of Isaiah recounted in the sixth chapter;[62] and also to the passion and glorification of Christ which is the theme of Isaiah 53.[63] John points out that the seer had beheld the mystery of Christ's divinity, manifested to him not only in the "glory" he had beheld at the beginning of his prophetic career, but also in the vision of the passion and resurrection of Christ, Servant of Yahweh, which for the Evangelist reveals the secret of the same mystery.

Further Developments[64] *of the Servant Theme in the New Testament*

St. John's Gospel attained its final form somewhere between the year 70 and the final decade of the first century.[65]

Still, it must be remembered that it was the fruit of long years of ministry, and that the notions contained in it had, before its final redaction, influenced other New Testament writings, such as the third Gospel[66] and the Epistle to the Hebrews.[67] Before closing this section, we must touch briefly upon two documents contained in the *corpus epistolare* of the New Testament anterior to the fourth Gospel, which reflect the influence of the Servant soteriology. First Peter was, in the opinion of E. G. Selwyn, composed about 63 A.D.;[68] Hebrews was most probably written in the year 69 A.D., on the eve of the destruction of Jerusalem.[69] The cloud of mystery which surrounds the identity of the author of each of these letters does not bear directly upon the use we shall make of them, and hence that obscure question need not detain us here. Suffice it to say that the influence of St. Peter upon the former, and of St. Paul upon the latter of these writings is today unquestioned by sound exegesis.[70]

The Servant Concept in First Peter

In the first chapter of this letter, we find a passage in which the idea of the paschal lamb of the Exodus has been combined with the redemptive act of the Isaian Servant. To urge his addressees to zeal in the pursuit of holiness, the author remarks: "And since you invoke as Father Him who judges each man impartially according to his works, live out in all reverence the time of your pilgrimage. For you are well aware that it was not with that wealth which perishes, gold and silver, that you have been redeemed from the shoddy existence, your legacy from your parents, but by the precious blood of Christ, the Lamb without spot or blemish, designated from the foundation of the world and made known to you in these latter days. Through Him it is that you have found faith in God, who raised Him from the dead by bestowing glory on Him so that God might be the object of your faith and hope" (1 Pt 1:17–21).

Here the reminiscences of the Exodus are manifest: this life is a "time of pilgrimage," Christ is the spotless Lamb of the paschal supper. At the same time, the mention of God's "giving Him glory" recalls Peter's phrase in his discourse recorded by Acts 3:13: "He has glorified His Servant Jesus." He who has been "made known to you in these latter days" as the Lamb is the Christ Peter had heard described by the Baptist's "Behold the Lamb of God, who takes away the sin of the world" (Jn 1:29), the Lamb of Is 53:7. It is highly interesting that both St. John and St. Peter combine in their writings the two Lamb-motifs which they had first heard juxtaposed by John the Baptist.

The second Servant passage occurs in the second chapter of this epistle, in the discussion of the duties of servants towards their masters. "What glory is there in enduring blows for a fault you have committed? No; what pleases God is the bearing of suffering when you have done your duty. For that is your vocation, since God also suffered for you, leaving you an example, that you might follow in the footsteps of Him who never committed sin and whose lips have never known deceit, who though abused did not render insult in return, maltreated made no threat, but handed Himself over to the just Judge; He who upon the tree has Himself borne our sins in His body, that we, dead to our sins, might live to justice; He whose bruises have held your healing. For you were gone astray like sheep, but now you have been turned around to [face] the watchful Shepherd of your souls" (1 Pt 2:20–25).

Here, as Selwyn has well observed, we have the recollections of Christ's passion, or of such scenes as Peter himself witnessed. The allusions to Isaiah are remarkably frequent:

Christ as the *'Ebed Yahweh* suffers on our behalf, "in whose mouth deceit is not found"; of Him the term *paredidou* is predicated, key word of Servant terminology;[71] He "Himself bore our sins"; "by His bruising" were we healed, "who had gone astray like sheep." Whatever we may discover in our next section about the abandonment of the Servant theology in the writings of St. Paul, it is certain that this soteriology was constantly preached within the Petrine sphere of influence.[72]

The Evangelical Heritage of Hebrews

In his monumental study of Hebrews, Ceslaus Spicq has traced the evidence for its author's use of "la catéchèse évangélique,"[73] and has concluded that the preponderant influence from this quarter is Johannine. We might, then, expect some reference to the Servant theme in this epistle, even though its *idée maîtresse* is that of the priestly function of Christ, an idea entirely absent from Deutero-Isaiah. There is, however, but one clear reference[74] to the Servant role of Christ: "And just as it is the fate of men to die once . . . so Christ offered Himself once to take away the sins of many, and He will appear a second time having nothing to do with sin, for the salvation of those who await Him" (Heb 9:27–28).

At His first appearance Christ wore the guise of the Servant: at His parousia He will be manifested, not this time to "take away the sins of the world," but as a glorious sign of salvation for the believer in His resurrection. In this development we perceive a new current of thought, which, as we shall see, stems from Pauline theology: the exaltation of Christ is not primarily for His own glory, but for those who are *solidaires* with Him.[75] This verse of Hebrews may well be considered a *trait d'union* between the two great apostolic soteriologies, one stemming from the Palestinian community, which we may designate as Petrine, and the other enucleated by the Apostle of the Gentiles, the Pauline.

Some Conclusions

From our investigation of the passages in the New Testament (exclusive of our Pauline writings) which derive their inspiration from the Deutero-Isaian theme of the Servant of Yahweh, three conclusions may be drawn at once:

1) As to *the sources of the Servant theology and the milieu* in which it flourished: Two main spheres of influence seem indicated by the evidence of the New Testament: the Palestinian Church and that of Asia Minor, i.e., the Petrine circle and the Johannine. One reason for the popularity of the Servant theology with the preachers of Christianity to Jewish hearers can be found in the problem which, as the first half of Acts repeatedly testifies, confronted them continually: the difficulty of explaining the stumbling block of Christ's passion and death. In the prophecies of the Suffering Servant they found proof beyond question that the humiliations borne by Jesus of Nazareth were "according to the settled purpose and foreknowledge of God" (Acts 2:23). St Peter, first of all, who had personally felt so strongly, even in anticipation, the scandal of the sufferings of His Master (Mt 16:22 ff.), and who had been witness of so much of His passion (1 Pt 2:20 ff.), accorded the Servant theme a privileged place in his catechesis, as the Petrine sermons in Acts, the Gospel of St. Mark, and First Peter testify. St. John also, so closely connected with the sufferings of his beloved Lord, had meditated deeply upon His role as the Servant, and it has left its mark upon his Gospel as well as upon the Apocalypse and also upon Hebrews, where his thought had impressed itself upon the author.

Where did Peter and John derive this characterization of Christ as suffering and glorified Servant? The answer is not far to seek: from the instructions of the Master Himself concerning the death He was to undergo. Had we no other proof of this than Mark 10:45, the thing would be clear enough. But the Marcan résumé of Peter's preaching shows us that at every important episode in the earthly life of Jesus, He was proclaimed to the disciples as the *'Ebed Yahweh*: at His baptism, His Transfiguration, in the predictions of His death, at the Last Supper. Is it possible to discover another source for this doctrine prior to Christ Himself? All the Evangelists draw attention to the use of the Deutero-Isaian prophecy by John the Baptist; and we have seen that both John and Luke, whose Gospel bears so many analogies to the fourth Gospel, give evidence of this fact. And it can be no mere accident that precisely the two apostles who had previously been the Baptist's disciples, John and Peter, are the two who appear to have made particular use of the Servant theme.

2) As to *the development of the Servant doctrine*: If Peter and John remain as the two most important representatives of the preaching of Christ as the Suffering Servant, it was left to St. Matthew particularly to develop the characterization and to apply it to the earthly life of Christ. Not that he was the only one to do so (indeed, we saw that the fourth Gospel carried this evolution to its most perfect expression: Jn 12:37 ff.), but it is in his Gospel first of all that we discover an application of the motif which comes, not from Christ's mouth, but from the Evangelist's own intuition. Such a development was only to have been expected, given the psychological approach of the first disciples to the mystery of Jesus of Nazareth. It was the teaching and the miracles of the public life which had formed their introduction to Him. When then, as was only natural, they turned in the course of their preaching

for proofs of His Messianic vocation and examples of His doctrine in those wonderful years spent with Him in Galilee or Judea, they discovered a new application of the Servant theology. Like the anointed *'Ebed Yahweh,* Christ had been anointed with the Spirit at His baptism; like *'Ebed Yahweh,* He had carried man's infirmities, healed and comforted men, recalled them from sin. The precious proof of such an evolution in doctrine is provided for us by the Gospels of Matthew and John; and it was prompted by their experience of the earthly life of the Master. The contrast is striking between such a viewpoint and that manifested in the writings of Saul of Tarsus, whose knowledge of Christ came in almost inverse fashion. And it is a well-known fact that, in the pages of Paul, the preresurrection phase of Christ's earthly career appears to play no primary role.

3) As to *the nature of the Servant theme:* The theme of the *'Ebed Yahweh* is an emphatically Jewish theme, and in the Judaism just prior to our era it had been commonly related to the fate of Israel itself, and became the inspiration of upsurging nationalism.[76] Indeed, as Joachim Jeremias has recently shown, it was possibly interpreted in a Messianic sense by the rabbis of the same period.[77] With the advent of Christianity, Messianic implications of the Isaian message had been taught by Jesus Himself; and when we recall that His personal mission was confined to those "that are lost of the house of Israel" (Mt 15:24), we realize how admirably the role of the predominantly Jewish Servant of Yahweh became Him. Hence it is not surprising that we find in Matthew, in some respects a consciously Jewish Gospel, the only two references to the Isaian Servant which are not quotations from Christ or the heavenly Father.

4) Finally, it should be noted that the soteriological synthesis developed under the influence of Deutero-Isaiah places the

Yahweh. Not that Paul was unaware of the Jerusalem Church's interest in and use of the motif, or that he neglected it entirely in his earlier preaching: the opening lines of the fifteenth chapter of First Corinthians prove the contrary. "I remind you, brethren, of the gospel which I have preached to you, and which you accepted. . . . For I handed on to you as of paramount importance that which I also received [from tradition], that Christ died for our sins according to the Scriptures, and that He was buried, and that He has risen, the third day, according to the Scriptures . . ." (1 Cor 15:13). The satisfactory death of Christ described with its aspect of substitution (Is 53:4, 5, 6, 11, 12), His burial (Is 53:9), and His exaltation (Is 52:13, 15; 53:10, 12) are described nowhere so clearly in the Old Testament as in the Servant passages of the Deutero-Isaiah; and it is to these passages, as has been shown, that the apostolic Church had had recourse above all. Yet, when Paul gives us a glimpse of his own Christology in the course of his greater epistles, he never develops the Servant aspect of the data of the apostolic tradition. Indeed, apart from the passage just cited, there are only two other places in the entire Pauline corpus where, in treating of the act of man's redemption, the Apostle refers to Christ as *'Ebed Yahweh*.

Rom 4:25 may be considered one such passage. Paul there declares that the object of Abrahamitic, no less than Christian faith is the Jesus "who was handed over for our sins, and raised for our justification." The first half of the verse is a reminiscence of the Seputuagintal version of the closing phrase of Is 53:12: "and for their sins was he handed over."[80] But already in the second clause ("He was raised for our justification") a new (and typically Pauline[81]) theological conception makes its appearance: the finality of the exaltation of Christ is primarily "for our justification," and not merely for Jesus' glorification, as in the Isaian prophecy (Is 52:13; 53:

12). Here Paul is evidently thinking of Christ as the second Adam, whose transfigured humanity is at once the gauge and, ultimately, the instrument of man's own redemption and glorification.[82] Indeed, it might be noted in passing that even in a passage like Rom 5:12 ff., where so much emphasis is laid upon the obedience of the Redeemer, it is not the Servant theme which dominates Paul's thought, but the conception of Christ as antitype of the first man, through whose agency sin and death came into the world.[83]

The second and most striking reference to the Christology which stems from Deutero-Isaiah is the celebrated passage in Phil 2:5 ff. There can be no doubt but what it owes its entire inspiration to Is 52:13—53:12. Since in many respects this pericope presents a character that is unique in the writings of St. Paul, we shall devote to the discussion of it a section at the end of this article, contenting ourselves here with a single remark, which is, we believe, an important prolegomenon to any study of this controverted passage. Is it merely some accident of transmission that the Pauline theology of the redemption, as handed down to us by Romans, Galatians, Corinthians, or the captivity epistles, appears to have sought its inspiration, not, as had the Jerusalem kerygma, in the theme of the Servant, but by preference in the thesis of the second Adam? There are grounds for thinking that Paul's extant letters represent his actual preference for the second-Adam theme.[84]

Paul in the Role of the Servant

If, as has been shown, Pauline soteriology owes its inspiration to a conception of Christ's redemptive work other than that employed most commonly in the apostolic preaching, it is not to be thought that the passages cited in the preceding section are the only references to the Servant passages of Deutero-Isaiah that can be found in his writings. There are, on the contrary, a considerable number of more or less explicit quotations which reveal an entirely novel application of the Servant theme. In this group of texts, it is the Apostle himself who appears in the role of the *'Ebed Yahweh*, and one has only to recall the prominent and quite exclusive application of this motif to Christ as Redeemer by the earlier kerygma to realize how significant is this transposition of a theme already traditional in the apostolic Church.

First of all, Paul is conscious that in the hour of his conversion he received the divine vocation to be Apostle of the Gentiles. In the autobiographical introduction to Galatians, he refers to the great grace given him by the Damascus road as the moment "when it pleased Him who set me apart from my mother's womb and called me through His love to reveal His Son in me, that I might gospel Him among the Gentiles . . ." (Gal 1:15). In the second of the Servant Songs, the *'Ebed Yahweh* describes his call by God (according to the Septuagintal version): "From the womb of my mother, He bestowed on me my name . . . and He said to me: 'You are my servant, O Israel, and in you shall I be glorified. . . . Lo! I have set you a covenant of the race, as a light of the Gentiles, that you may be my salvation even to the end of the earth'" (Is 49:1–6).

Another echo of this Pauline parallel between the call of the Servant and his own vocation is to be found in Acts, when the jealous opposition of the synagogue in Pisidian Antioch merits condemnation from the two missionaries, Paul and Barnabas. "It was necessary that the word of God should be spoken to you first. But since you reject it . . . behold we turn now to the Gentiles. For the Lord has commanded us: 'I have set thee as a light to the Gentiles, that thou mayest be a means of salvation to the end of the earth'" (Acts 13:45 ff.).[85]

Throughout his missionary career Paul, while ever conscious that Christ Himself is the Servant par excellence,[86] repeatedly reminds his listeners that in his own apostolic labors the work of the Servant is being carried forward. He urges the Philippians to perfection, that they may one day be his boast, a proof "that I have not labored in vain" (Phil 2:16), a phrase which in Greek clearly recalls a remark of the Servant:[87] "I have labored in vain: I have spent my strength without cause and to no purpose" (Is 49:4). Again, in the section of Romans which deals with the problem of Israel's salvation, Paul recalls his own dealings with the Jews of the Diaspora; and here two Servant passages are pressed into service. First, he reveals his consciousness of the lofty vocation which he shares with other apostles: "How beautiful upon the mountains are the feet of those gospeling the good news" (Is 52:7). Then he remembers the reception which his message almost invariably met with in the synagogues of the Dispersion: "Lord, who has believed our report?" (Is 53:1).

There are, however, two passages in his epistles where Paul dwells at some length upon the meaning of Christian apostleship, and where his development is indebted to his characterization of himself as the Servant of Yahweh. Towards the end of one of these sections, Rom 15:7–21, Paul finds in the Septuagintal text of Is 52:15 a reason for his invariable practice of preaching only "where Christ has never been invoked." As Canon Cerfaux has noted,[88] Paul's insistence upon always seeking completely new mission fields is not merely a point of honor with him. He has a profounder motive which he has derived from the nature of the ministry of the Servant: "They to whom the good news about Him has not been announced shall see: and they who have not heard will understand" (Is 52:15).

The other pericope devoted to the apostolic calling is

found in 2 Cor 4–6. The first section which has a certain Deutero-Isaian coloring is 5:17–21. Here Paul first describes the effects of the redemption in terms borrowed from the description of the new Exodus in Is 43:18–19: "Do not recall the former events, nor consider the ancient order of things. Lo, I am making a new order that will spring to light and you shall know it. . . ." Paul describes the results of man's sanctification by remarking that "if a man be in union with Christ, he is a new creation. The ancient order of things has passed away; lo, it is become new" (2 Cor 5:17). The announcement of this divine message of salvation was, in Deutero-Isaiah, described as the work of the Servant: "How beautiful upon the mountains are the feet of him gospeling the good news of peace, announcing the good tidings . . ." (Is 52:7). Paul is aware that this office has been bestowed upon himself: "We are therefore ambassadors on behalf of Christ. It is as if God were exhorting (you) through us. We beg of you in the Name of Christ: be reconciled with God." This passage gives an insight into Paul's conception of his Servant vocation: it is "on behalf of Christ," "in the Name of Christ," and God uses the Apostle, as He had used Christ His Servant par excellence, to carry His revelation to men. Paul is able to call himself *the* Servant because he is an "ambassador" of the Servant, to continue His ministry among men.

The first verses of chapter 6 contain a citation of the second Servant Song. "And since we are Christ's collaborators, we also exhort you not to receive the grace of God in vain. For He says: 'At a providential moment I have heard thee, and on the day of salvation I have called thee.' Behold, now is the propitious moment! Lo, now is the day of salvation!" (2 Cor 6:1–2). In his exhortation to the Corinthian Church Paul does not overlook the possibility of a refusal of the divine grace offered to his neophytes: they *can* "receive the grace of God in vain." The Apostle reminds them of the import of his own vocation: to him have been addressed the words which Yahweh had spoken to His servant: "At a providential moment I have heard thee," i.e., Paul; "on the day of salvation" God has called Paul to Corinth. His presence among his Corinthians, then, means the dawning of their salvation, a grace which is conditioned by their submission to their apostle as the Servant of Yahweh.[89]

In concluding this section, we might say a word about the use of Paul's favorite title for himself, that of *doulos*.[90] Given the importance of the Deutero-Isaian Servant theme for the expression by Paul of his conception of his own apostolate, it may well be that this appellation implies another reference to his own role as Servant of Yahweh. In the second of the Servant songs, which, as we noted, Paul quotes in Gal 1:15 where he is describing his own vocation, the Septuagintal version uses the word *doulos* twice.[91]

The Origin of This New Conception

What authority had St. Paul for thus casting himself in the role of the Servant of Yahweh? The answer to this question is to be found in the Apostle's account of his conversion rendered to Agrippa II: "I have appeared to you," Paul quotes the risen Christ as saying to him during his Damascus vision, "in order to constitute you Servant and witness . . . . selecting you from the people and from the Gentiles, to whom I am sending you, to open their eyes, to convert them from darkness to light and from the power of Satan to God" (Acts 26:12 ff.). The glorified Christ gives Paul his apostolic commission in terms borrowed from the first Servant Song, words taken from a section which, we saw, St. Matthew had applied to Jesus Himself. Consequently, it was made clear to Paul from the moment of his conversion that in being chosen for the apostolate he was destined to prolong in his own person the salvific work of Christ, the *'Ebed Yahweh.*[92]

Conclusions

1) The appointment by Christ to continue His work as the Servant of Yahweh led Paul to rethink the theology of the redemption along lines quite different from that of the primitive preaching. Where Palestinian Christianity tended to follow the lead given them by the Master during His earthly life and construct a soteriology based upon Christ's fulfilment of the prophecy of Deutero-Isaiah, St. Paul preached the work of the redemption as a new creation. On his view, Christ was regarded rather as the second Adam.[93] As we have seen, the theme of the new creation also owed its existence to the writings of Deutero-Isaiah. And it is important to remember that the Pauline no less than the Palestinian explanation of Christ's redemptive activity derives its inspiration from the same Old Testament source.

At the same time, there were other influences at work which concurred in shaping the thought of Paul. For if the second-creation motif be Deutero-Isaian, the characterization of Christ as second Adam is found nowhere in that book. One contact which undoubtedly left its mark upon the mind and heart of Paul, and which probably prepared the way for his future theological conception of Christ as Redeemer, was the contact with Stephen the protomartyr, one of the great personalities of the Jerusalem community. Stephen's dying vision of the glorified Son of Man, which young Saul had beheld reflected upon the martyr's countenance (Acts 6:15), must have helped the persecutor of the Church, in the hour of his conversion, to identify the heavenly *Kyrios.* And Christ's declared solidarity with the Christian Church on that occasion had added the final touch to the delineation of Himself as the second Adam. The fact that later on in the course of his ministry Paul would develop this theme rather than that of the *'Ebed Yahweh* may also have been due to the fact that it was his vocation to preach the gospel to pagans rather than to Jews. In the freedom-loving Greek communities to which Paul was apostle, the notion of the Servant would scarcely have the same appeal as in Jewish Palestine, while the second-Adam theme with its universalist interest provided a more suitable approach to Gentile audiences. Moreover, it was precisely in these pagan communities that Christianity appeared in all its novelty and freshness as "a new creation." Where the Jewish Christian remained conscious of the continuity between his new-found beliefs and the religion of Israel, the Gentile Christian was equally aware of the unbridgeable chasm separating his new religious life from the old: it was simply a new creation.

2) However, I believe the ultimate reason why Paul's theology of the redemption developed along such distinctive lines lies in his personal approach, unique amongst the apostles, to Jesus of Nazareth. The fact that it was the *risen Christ* whom Paul first knew gave him an insight into the meaning of the Master's death that went beyond the divine necessity of prophetic declaration, and enabled him to grasp the more positive aspects of that death's efficiency. As second Adam, Paul perceived, Christ had perforce to break the old sinful solidarity that bound man to his first parent. The significance of Christ's death, then, was as a dying to sin (Rom 6:10), to the law (Gal 2:19–20), to death itself (1 Cor 15:26; Rom 6:9). To create a completely new unity of grace and life, Christ had risen from the dead and had bestowed upon man the Spirit, whose operations through grace were identified

with those of the risen Lord (2 Cor 3:17;[94] Rom 8:9–11). Accordingly, His resurrection was conceived by Paul not so much as a vindication of His death or as a reward for His transcendent obedience—a view suggested by the Servant theology—but rather "for our justification" (Rom 4:25). To express this higher synthesis, which may be considered Paul's chief contribution to apostolic Christianity, the theme of the *'Ebed Yahweh* was not sufficient. There was needed the more mystical intuition of Christ as Head of a new creation.

3) On the other hand, Paul's utilization of the Servant theme as applied to his own missionary activity led to a new dogmatic development, which in its turn was of the greatest importance. It produced a characteristically Pauline thesis: the mystical conception of the apostolic vocation. Aware of his divine appointment as the Servant of Yahweh, Paul perceived, more deeply perhaps than any other inspired New Testament writer, that in carrying on the work of his Lord as the Servant in gospeling to the Gentiles, he was in a very real sense identified with Him.

THE ORIGIN OF THE HYMN IN PHILIPPIANS 2:5–11

The Epistle to the Philippians is one of the most personal as well as one of the simplest of those found in the Pauline corpus, "un entretien coeur à coeur,"[95] or, as Père Huby has styled it, "la plus 'lettré' " of all the Pauline epistles.[96] In sharp contrast with the general tone of the epistle, the section in 2:5–11 is remarkable for its theological density, its elevated tone and rhythmic character, and the number of Pauline *hapax legomena* found therein.[97]

Modern commentators concur in recognizing the hymnological nature of the passage. J. Weiss speaks of "der vorhandene Rhythmus";[98] Hans Lietzmann has called it a "Lied";[99] M. Dibelius has remarked that "eine Art Rythmus liegt zweifellos vor";[100] E. Lohmeyer terms it "ein carmen Christi im strengen Sinne";[101] Canon Cerfaux has seen in it a hymn, probably composed for the Eucharistic liturgy;[102] Pierre Benoit refers to it as "le magnifique cantique sur la 'Kénôse' du Christ."[103]

That it is a hymn then may be taken for granted here. What interests us particularly is the theological conception which it sets forth, and the divergencies of that conception from the usual viewpoint of St. Paul.

Theological Conception Exhibited in the Hymn

As has been already remarked,[104] the hymn derives its inspiration primarily from the Servant passage in Is 52:13—53:12. The general pattern followed by Phil 2:5–11 is that set forth by Deutero-Isaiah. The prophet had depicted the Servant as humiliated, as burdened with the sins of the multitude, suffering even death for their sakes and in their stead; and this heroic conduct, springing from his perfect submission to God, is the very reason for his exaltation. In Philippians, Christ's career is similarly characterized as a *kenōsis* that provides the divine motive for rewarding Him with the Name *Kyrios.*[105]

Moreover, the terminology adopted in the hymn betrays its Isaian inspiration. By His incarnation, Christ assumes the *morphēn doulou,* the role of the Servant.[106] The *heauton ekenōsen* of Phil 2:7 may have been suggested by the *kenōs ekopiasa* of Is 49:4.[107] There is a close parallel between the *hyperypsōsen* of the exaltation in Phil 2:9 and the *hypsōthēsetai* of Is 52:13. The causal connection between the *kenōsis* of Christ and His glorification, expressed by *dio*[108]

(Phil 2:9), corresponds to the *dia touto* of Is 53:12 and shows how closely the conception of the hymn is patterned upon that of the Servant Song, where the exaltation of the *'Ebed Yahweh* is bestowed as a reward for his submissive obedience to God.

Contrast with the Characteristic Pauline Viewpoint

We have already seen that the Servant theme is not employed by St. Paul to express the redemptive work of Christ, either in his epistles or in the sermons which Luke ascribes to him in Acts, with the exception of the passing allusion in Rom 4:25 and here in Phil 2:5–11. Consequently, the question arises as to whether St. Paul is author of this hymn which he quotes, or whether he is citing a composition which arose in the milieu where the Servant theology was constantly employed, in the Palestinian Christian Church.

Apart from the references to Isaiah 53, there are other expressions which seem to indicate a point of view not found elsewhere in Paul. There is the use of *echarisato* (Phil 2:9): "God gave Him the Name as a pure favor." That the exaltation of Christ should be regarded as a grace to the sacred humanity is an idea that is unparalleled in the Pauline writings.[109] The reason more usually assigned by Paul for the Resurrection is found in the beginning of Romans, where Jesus' glorification is declared to be "in accordance with the spirit of holiness," that is, as a result of the hypostatic union.[110] On the other hand, we miss in this hymn certain notions which are hallmarks of Pauline soteriology: the love of Christ for men, the primacy of the glorified Lord over all creation, the redemptive value of His death and resurrection.[111] In connection with this last point, it is to be noted that while in Paul's letter the exaltation of Christ is considered primarily in its effects upon the rest of humanity and not as a personal reward to the Redeemer for His obedience and sufferings, in this hymn it is precisely this aspect of the *meritum Christi,* so characteristic of Isaiah 53, which is underscored.

The contrast between this conception and that found in Paul can be appreciated by a consideration of a text like 2 Cor 8:9, often quoted as a parallel to our hymn: "You recall the favor of our Lord Jesus Christ, who for you became poor whereas He was rich, in order that you might become rich through His poverty." Here the kenotic quality of Christ's earthly career forms the central thought. But the difference of accent is seen in the use of *di' hymas:* it is "with you in mind," to enrich mankind, that Christ died and rose. 2 Cor 13:3–4 reveals the same point of view: "You wish a proof of the fact that Christ speaks in me. He is not weak in your regard, but He displays His power among you. Indeed He was crucified by reason of His weakness, but He lives [now] by the power of God. Similarly with us: we are weak in Him indeed; but we shall live with Him by the power of God [through our apostolic activity] in your regard." Texts like 1 Cor 15:45; 2 Cor 5:21; Gal 3:12; 4:4 ff., and Col 1:18 manifest the same teleology for the glorification of Christ: *propter nos et propter nostram salutem.*

Thus the soteriology of Phil 2:5–11 is not in Paul's usual style. Moreover, in citing the hymn, Paul's purpose is not to outline the doctrine of the redemption, but to provide a motive for the practice of Christian humility and charity, proper to "him who is in union with Christ Jesus."[112] On the other hand, the theology displayed by this hymn is clearly the same as that represented by the discourses of Peter in Acts, by the baptismal catechesis of Philip, and by an important section of the Gospel traditions which stem from Petrine or Johannine centers of influence.

Conclusions

As a corollary to the general thesis established with respect to the use of the Servant theology in Palestinian Christianity to express the mystery of the redemption and its transposition by St. Paul, which resulted in the adumbration of his mystical conception of the Christian apostolate, we are warranted in drawing the following conclusions concerning the authorship of the hymn in Phil 2:5 ff.

1) This passage is unique in all the Pauline epistles as one in which more than a passing reference is made to the Christology which derives its inspiration from the Servant Songs of Deutero-Isaiah. On the other hand, it belongs to the same circle of ideas which we saw propagated in the Jerusalem kerygma as reflected in Acts or in our Gospels.

2) When we recall Paul's customary avoidance of this soteriology, remembering at the same time the transposition of the Servant theme in his writings where he himself appears as the Servant, it seems clear that this hymn is not a Pauline composition, but one which originated in the theological milieu of Palestinian Christianity. Paul, who may have learned it at Antioch, during his long stay there prior to his missionary activities in Asia Minor (Acts 11:26), probably used it in his earlier attempts at catechizing at Philippi. Thus, in his letter to that Church he cites an ode already familiar to them, not indeed to teach the redemptive nature of Christ's death and resurrection, but to inculcate a much-needed lesson in Christian humility.

3) Given the admittedly liturgical nature of the hymn,[113] it is very likely that it formed part of the liturgy in use at Philippi, which Paul would have introduced there from Antioch. Whether it pertained to the Eucharistic or to the baptismal liturgy is difficult to decide,[114] although Luke's *récit* of

the baptism of Candace's eunuch by Philip might possibly hint at the origin of just such a baptismal hymn, familiar at the time of the writing of Acts to Christians like himself of Antiochian origin.

12

Pauline Allusions to the Sayings of Jesus

IN STUDYING the Pauline epistles, I have been struck, not infrequently, by the presence of certain metaphors and illustrations which recall those employed by Jesus in His teaching as it is recorded especially in the Synoptic Gospels. The most interesting examples, perhaps, are those which reveal a familiarity with certain parables. There are, in addition, a number of passages in Paul whose doctrinal content appears to reflect some logion of Jesus. The present study is an attempt to review some of those parallels in the hope that some light may be shed upon Paul's use of these materials in his preaching and teaching, as well as upon the history of Jesus' sayings before their redaction in our canonical Gospels.

It is to be noted that it is not a question of *literary* allusions or references. The Gospels, at least in their present form, were written at a period subsequent to Paul's letters. Some years ago Dom Bernard Orchard asserted a literary dependence of the eschatological passages in the epistles to the Thessalonians upon the Matthean discourse on the destruction of the Temple (Mt 23:31—25:46).[1] The evidence he advanced, however, in support of his conclusion is not entirely convincing; yet it does indicate Paul's acquaintance with data which were embodied in the Gospels.

PAUL AND THE APOSTOLIC TRADITION

Actually, Paul himself testifies constantly in his writings that he preached the traditional gospel which had emanated from the apostolic community.[2] He asserts categorically in Galatians that "there is no other gospel" than that which he preached (cf. Gal 1:7–9). In another letter he implied that there can be no orthodox kerygma which proclaims "another Jesus, whom we have not proclaimed . . . or another gospel, which you have not received" (2 Cor 11:4).

In addition, there are several passages in which reference is made to Christian traditions which can only be of apostolic origin. Paul states that while he adheres to them faithfully in his preaching, they did not originate with him. "I handed on to you, as of primary importance, that which I also had received, viz., that Christ died for our sins in accordance with the Scriptures, and that He was buried, and that He was raised the third day in accordance with the Scriptures, and that He appeared to Kephas, and later to the Twelve . . ." (1 Cor 15: 3–5). He introduces his account of the institution of the Eucharist by saying: "I received from the Lord that which I also handed on to you, viz., how the Lord Jesus on the night He was betrayed . . ." (1 Cor 11:23). Indeed, how carefully, even to the expression, Paul relayed these traditional data, we may gather by comparing this narrative (vv. 23–25) with those found in the Synoptics. That Paul considered exactitude in this matter of paramount importance can be seen from a remark which he makes earlier in this same chapter: "I congratulate you upon remembering *all my* teaching and holding fast to the traditions *just as* I handed them on to you" (1 Cor 11:2).

That Paul was conscious of adhering closely to the apostolic kerygma in his preaching as well as in his letters can be seen from a remark he makes to the Thessalonians: "Consequently, brothers, stand firm and preserve the traditions which you have learned either by our gospel or by letter" (2 Th 2:15).[3]

SPECIFIC ALLUSIONS TO SOME LOGIA OF JESUS

In his discourse at Miletus (Acts 20:35) Paul is represented as citing a saying of Jesus. The rather impressive number of express references in his letters to some specific teaching of our Lord shows that he was in the habit of citing such sayings in his preaching and teaching. Thus, he repeats Jesus' prohibition of divorce: "I command those who have been married (indeed, it is not my command but the Lord's): a wife must not separate from her husband . . ." (1 Cor 7:10). Jesus' saying is found in all the Synoptic Gospels (Mt 5:32; 19:5–6; Lk 16:18; Mk 10:11–12), although the Marcan version of it is perhaps closest in form to Paul's.[4]

Paul bases his right to be supported by the faithful upon an injunction of Jesus: "Thus, moreover, did the Lord ordain that those who proclaim the gospel live by the gospel" (1 Cor 9:14; cf. also 9:4; 2 Th 3:9). This appears to be a recollection of Jesus' remark, which Matthew includes in the missionary instructions to the Twelve: "The worker is worthy of his keep" (Mt 10:10b).

When, in his letter to the Roman Church, Paul asserts that the old distinction between clean and unclean has been abolished, he does so, aware that Jesus had already proclaimed the same truth. "I know this (I have it on the word of the Lord Jesus): nothing is unclean of itself". (Rom 14:14). In Matthew's Gospel, Jesus states this principle to the crowd after a discussion with the Pharisees and scribes from Jerusalem: "It is not what goes into his mouth that makes a man unclean . . ." (Mt 15:11, 20; cf. Mk 7:1–23).

In Eph 4:20–21, Paul takes it for granted that his addressees, whom he did not personally evangelize, have heard the apostolic kerygma. "As for you, you did not learn Christ in this way, if at least you heard Him, were instructed in Him, in accordance with the truth there is in Jesus." By the phrase "the truth there is in Jesus" Paul probably means the episodes and sayings connected with Jesus' public ministry. At any rate, this would seem to be the meaning of a similar remark which Paul makes to the Thessalonians: "You know what instructions we gave you through the Lord Jesus" (1 Th 4:2). Shortly afterwards, in the same chapter, Paul makes reference to two sayings of Jesus. The first alludes to the command to "love one another" (Jn 13:34; 15:12, 17): "Concerning brotherly love, you have no need that I write to you, since you yourselves are divinely instructed about loving one another" (1 Th 4:9). The second reference is perhaps somewhat difficult to trace. Paul is seeking to reassure the Christian community, which is disturbed over the deaths of some of its members. "We make this assertion to you, based upon a saying of the Lord: we the living, who are left at the Lord's parousia, will not get ahead of those who have fallen asleep" (1 Th 4:15). I suggest that this is an inference Paul makes from a remark of Jesus in His debate about the resurrection with the Sadducees: "He is not the God of the dead, but of the living" (Mt 22:32). On this principle, Paul may well argue that the dead Christians will not be at any disadvantage when the moment comes for Christ's parousia, for they are regarded not so much as dead, but as living. Another saying of Jesus which may be Paul's source is that found in Mt 12:41–42: "The men of Nineveh will rise at the judgment with the men of today . . . the queen of the south will be raised at the judgment with the men of today." In this text, the dead rise to be with Jesus' contemporaries, who represent probably "the living" in the Pauline text.

DOCTRINAL PARALLELS TO LOGIA OF JESUS

We shall first discuss certain statements found in Paul's letters which echo sayings of Jesus found in the Gospels. We have grouped them together for convenience in several categories. There are, in the first place, three passages in Paul which contain Old Testament citations, which appear to have been influenced by Jesus' own references to the same texts.

Paul urges the Philippians to remain "blameless children of God in the midst of *an erring and perverse generation,* among whom you appear as luminaries in the world"[5] (Phil 2:15b). Paul here describes the nonbelieving world in terms of Dt 32:5, which speaks disapprovingly of the Israelites during their wandering in the desert as "an evil and perverse generation." Jesus had applied this same expression to his incredulous fellow countrymen: to the scribes and Pharisees who seek "a sign" from him (Mt 12:39; 16:4; cf. 12:41); to the crowd accompanying the man with the lunatic son (Mt 17:17). It occurs also in Mark's version of the logion: "whoever is ashamed of me and of my words before this adulterous and sinful generation" (Mk 8:38), as also in the Lucan eschatological discourse: "But first He [the Son of Man] must suffer greatly and be dishonored by this generation" (Lk 17:25). It will be recalled that Paul, like the Old Testament prophets,[6] customarily regards the *ekklēsia* of Israel in the desert as a type of the Church.[7] This pejorative reference to them as "a wicked generation" by Paul is probably a borrowing from Christ himself.

Paul's uncompromising condemnation of the Jew for his false religious spirit in Romans contains a citation of Ps 62(61):13 in a context which strongly resembles a saying of Jesus: "By your hardheartedness and impenitent spirit, you are storing up for yourselves wrath on the day of wrath and of the revelation of the just judgment of God, *who will repay every man according to his works*" (Rom 2:5–6). In Mt 16:27, Jesus declares: "The Son of Man is surely coming with His Father's glory, and then He *will repay every man according to his works.*" Paul's animadversion on the necessity of "works" in a section where he insists so strongly (cf. Rom. 3:28) upon the primacy of faith in justification appears to have been inspired by a realization of the necessity of presenting Jesus' teaching in its totality.

In Jesus' discussion with the Pharisees and scribes about various practices of contemporary Judaism, recorded in Mk 7:1–23 and Mt 15:1–20, He castigates them severely for insisting upon casuistry to the detriment of the basic aims of the law, and he cites Is 29:13, which contains the phrase "instilling as doctrine mere human precepts." Paul warns the Colossians of the dangers attendant upon certain Judaizing practices by remarking: "If you have died with Christ to the elements of the world, why do you follow certain prescriptions as if you lived in the world? 'Do not handle,' 'do not taste,' 'do not touch' all the things doomed to perish by use—that sort of thing is *according to mere human precepts and teaching*" (Col 2:20–21). It seems clear that Paul is here summarizing Jesus' criticism of the Judaism of the period, just as Paul's phrase to the Jew, "you are convinced you are a leader of the blind" (Rom 2:19), a phrase employed by Jesus on various occasions (Mt 15:14; 23:16–24) towards the Pharisees, probably comes from the same source.

Here we may note several Pauline affirmations in Romans

about the fulfilment of the law by Christ. He asserts that "Christ is the fulfilment of law" (Rom 10:4); "Christ became servant of the circumcision for the sake of God's faithfulness, to accomplish the promises made to the patriarchs" (Rom 15:8). In Mt 15:24, Jesus is represented as saying: "I have been sent only to the sheep of the house of Israel that have been lost," while in Mt 5:17 He states: "Do not think I have come to destroy the law and the prophets. I have come to fulfil, not to destroy." Paul insists that he maintains the same attitude towards the Mosaic legislation, despite his trenchant criticism of his fellow Jews for their superstitious practice of the "law of works": "Are we then invalidating law by faith? God forbid. On the contrary, we are establishing law on a firm basis" (Rom 3:31). He sums up the purpose of Christ's redemptive death and resurrection as being "in order that the justice of the law might be fulfilled in us" (Rom 8:4).

The Pauline Doctrine of Prayer

Repeated examples of prayers throughout Paul's letters indicate how deeply he had assimilated Jesus' teaching that His followers "must always pray without ever giving up" (Lk 18:1). Paul urges the Thessalonians: "Pray ceaselessly. Give thanks in every vicissitude. This is God's will in Christ Jesus for you" (1 Th 5:17). He reminds another community to "keep praying at every opportunity in the Spirit with every sort of prayer and petition. Be vigilant about it with every sort of intercession and petition on behalf of all the saints and myself . . ." (Eph 6:18).

At least three of Paul's remarks about the importance of the Holy Spirit in the Christian life appear to be inspired by Jesus' sayings. When he discusses charismatic gifts with the Corinthians, he begins by recalling that they are the effects of the

Spirit: "I tell you that no man speaking with the Spirit can say 'Cursed be Jesus,' and no man can say 'Jesus is Lord' except by the Holy Spirit" (1 Cor 12:3). Jesus had expressed the same truth in slightly different terms to John, after he had tried to stop a strange exorcist who was using Jesus' name: "There is no man who can, after performing a miracle in my Name, immediately speak evil of me" (Mk 9:39b).

Speaking of his imprisonment and pending trial, Paul tells the Philippians: "I know that this will count for my salvation, thanks to your prayers and to the aid of the Spirit of Jesus Christ which will be given to me" (Phil 1:19). Paul is aware that Jesus had promised His disciples that when they were tried by "governors and kings," "it is not you who are the speakers, but the Spirit of my Father in you who is the speaker" (Mt 10:20).[8]

When Paul warns the Thessalonians of the danger of disobeying his commands, he transposes a logion of Jesus in terms of the Holy Spirit: "Now the man who rejects [this] is not rejecting man but the God *who gives you His Holy Spirit*" (1 Th 4:8). In Lk 10:16, Jesus states: "He who listens to you listens to me; he who rejects you rejects me. Now he who rejects me rejects Him who sent me."

The Pater Noster being the Christian prayer par excellence, it is not surprising to find references to it in the Pauline epistles. The proof of the Christian's adoptive sonship is expressed through the voice of the indwelling "Spirit of His Son crying 'Abba' " (Gal 4:6); "because you have received the Spirit of adoptive filiation in whom we cry 'Abba' " (Rom 8:15). It is probable that Paul is alluding here to the Pater.

The central petition of the whole prayer, in which we ask that God's kingdom may descend upon earth, is expressed also by means of the two variant phrases, "May thy Name be sanctified" (the coming of the kingdom being represented as a consecration of men to God), and "May thy will be carried out."[9] Paul appears to allude to these two petitions when he tells the Thessalonians: "This is God's will: your sanctification" (1 Th 4:3).

The petition for forgiveness in the Pater is made contingent upon our forgiving our fellow men. It is recalled twice in the captivity epistles: "forgiving one another as the Lord forgave you. So must you forgive" (Col 3:12b–13); "forgiving one another just as God forgave you in Christ" (Eph 4:32).[10]

The final petition, "deliver us from evil" (or "from the Evil One"), is alluded to in 2 Th 3:3: "The Lord is faithful. He will make you strong and guard you from evil" (or "the Evil One").

Christ's Second Coming

Paul warns the Thessalonians of the unexpected character of Christ's parousia: "You yourselves know full well that the Day of the Lord is coming like a thief at night" (1 Th 5:2). The reason they know this is that Jesus had already foretold it, employing the same bold metaphor: "This you know: if the householder were aware at what time of night the thief were coming, he would remain awake . . ." (Mt 24:43–44; cf. Ap 3:4; 16:15; 2 Pt 3:10; Lk 12:39–40). In the preceding verse of this same letter Paul had said: "But as regards dates and times, brothers, it is not necessary to write you" (1 Th 5:1). There is a saying of Jesus which Luke has incorporated into the Ascension scene in Acts: "It is not your business to know the dates and times which the Father has retained under His own jurisdiction" (Acts 1:7). In the Matthean discourse on the destruction of the Temple, Jesus remarks: "But as regards that day and time no man knows, not even the heavenly angels—only the Father alone" (Mt 24:36; cf. 24:42; 25:13; Mk 13:32).

Paul has also borrowed the figure of "birth pangs" from the sayings of Jesus in order to suggest the suddenness of Christ's second coming: "When men say '[We have] peace and security,' then suddenly destruction comes upon them as the birth pangs upon a pregnant woman" (1 Th 5:3). In Rom 8:22, Paul pictures the whole of creation as being one in "suffering the birth pangs" in preparation for the eschatological glory. Matthew represents Jesus as saying, in His apocalyptic description of the ruin of Jerusalem: "All these things are the beginning of the birth pangs" (Mt 24:8).

The Christian Attitude towards Others

Jesus had declared that love of God and love of neighbor were the most important commandments of the law (Mt 22: 34–40; Mk 12:28–34; Lk 10:25–28). He asserted that the whole aim of "the law and the prophets" was realized by acting towards others as one would wish them to act towards oneself (Mt 7:12). Two Pauline passages allude clearly to this doctrine: "The whole law is fulfilled in one saying: 'Love your neighbor as yourself'" (Gal 5:14). "Owe no man anything except mutual love. The man who loves his fellow man has fulfilled the law. 'Do not commit adultery,' 'Do not kill,' 'Do not steal,' 'Do not covet,' and any other commandment, are summed up in this: 'Love your neighbor as yourself.' Love causes no evil to one's fellow man. Thus love is the fulness of the law" (Rom 13:8–10).

Paul tells the Galatians: "Carry one another's heavy loads. It is thus you will fulfil the law of Christ" (Gal 6:2)—an obvious allusion to Jesus' commandment in the fourth Gospel:

"A new commandment I give you: 'Love one another as I have loved you' . . ." (Jn 13:34; 15:12, 17). When, a few verses later on, Paul remarks: "Each man must carry his own burden" (*phortion*) (Gal 6:5), he is alluding to a logion which appears in varying forms in the Synoptics. In Mt 16:24, Jesus asserts: "If a man wishes to come after me, he must deny himself and *take up his cross*. . . ." It may well be that, in the original sayings of Jesus, "burden" (*phortion*) was used instead of "cross" (*stauron*), the change in terminology being the result of the apostolic doctrine of the redemptive death of Christ. It is to be noted that the term *phortion* is retained in the Matthean saying, "My yoke lies easy, my *burden* is light" (Mt 11:30).

Jesus' warning, "Do not go on judging lest you be judged; you will be judged by the standards by which you judge" (Mt 7:1–2), is echoed by Paul in his apostrophe to the Jew in Rom 2:1: "Accordingly, you, sir (anyone who judges), are without defense. By the fact that you judge another, you condemn yourself."

Jesus had said: "Love your enemies. Do good to those who hate you. Bless those who curse you. Pray for those who abuse you" (Lk 6:27–28). Paul tells the Romans: "Bless those who persecute you. Bless them; do not curse them" (Rom 12:14). He tells the Corinthians: "When men insult us, we bless them. When men persecute us, we endure it. When men calumniate us, we offer consolation" (1 Cor 4:12b–13a). He warns the Thessalonians: "Watch for fear anyone repay another evil for evil. Always pursue good with regard to one another and to all men" (1 Th 5:15). And he reminds them in a second letter that "persecutions and tribulations" are "a proof of God's just judgment, in order to make you worthy of the kingdom of God" (2 Th 1:5). This doctrine had been promulgated in the Beatitudes: "Happy those who have been persecuted for religion: the kingdom of heaven is theirs. Happy are you whenever they abuse you and persecute you and utter every sort of evil calumny against you for my sake. Rejoice, be overjoyed. Your reward is great in heaven" (Mt 5:10–12).

Paul's command, "Give to all men what is due them . . . taxes to whom taxes are due" (Rom 13:7), is a repetition of Jesus' saying, "Give to the emperor what belongs to the emperor" (Mt 22:21).

The rules for fraternal correction given by Jesus (Mt 18: 15–17) are followed faithfully by Paul in his advice to the Thessalonians: "If anyone does not obey our command in this letter, make an example of him. Do not have anything to do with him, in order that he may learn reverence. Yet do not treat him as an enemy, but correct him as a brother" (2 Th 3: 14–15). In issuing orders for the "excommunication" of the incestuous Christian at Corinth, Paul says: "When you have assembled together in the Name of our Lord Jesus Christ . . . with the power of our Lord Jesus, hand this man over to Satan" (1 Cor 5:4–5). This seems to be an application of the saying, "Where two or three are gathered together in my Name, I am there among them" (Mt 18:20).

PAULINE ALLUSIONS TO JESUS' PARABLES

We come now to treat of the second category of Pauline allusions to Jesus' teaching: those indicated by Paul's use of similar metaphors and illustrations, some of which seem to be references to Jesus' parables.

It is customary for commentators who draw a contrast between the writings of Paul and the sayings of Jesus to observe that while our Lord employs figures and illustrations suited to a rural audience (the Galilean crowds), Paul's comparisons reflect the cosmopolitanism or city culture of the Hellenistic world.[11] Paul's metaphors, it is said (and quite rightly), are taken from the Greek games (Phil 2:16; 3:12–14; 1 Cor 9:24–27; 2 Cor 4:8–9), from Greek political terminology (Phil 1:27; 3:20; Eph 2:19), from commercial or financial language (Phil 3:17; Phm 18; Col 2:14), from legal vocabulary (Gal 3:15; Gal 4:1–2; Rom 7:1–3), from the slave market (Rom 7:14),[12] from army terms (1 Cor 9:7; 14:8; Rom 6:23), from popular Stoicism (Col 2:8; Eph 1:23), from Hellenistic festivals and the emperor cult[13] (1 Th 2:19; Phil 4:1).

But what perhaps is not so frequently remarked is the number of Pauline metaphors that bespeak an agrarian culture (again, like that of Galilee): agricultural metaphors (1 Cor 3:6, 9b; 9:7b) like ploughing (1 Cor 9:10b), the vineyard (1 Cor 9:7a), sowing (1 Cor 9:11; 15:36–37, 42–44; 2 Cor 9:6, 10; Gal 6:7–8), harvesting (1 Cor 9:11; 2 Cor 9:6; Gal 6:7–9), fruit (Phil 1:22; 4:17; 1 Cor 9:7; Gal 5:22; Rom 1:13; 6:21; 7:4–5; 15:28; Col 1:6; Eph 5:9).

As an explanation of this relatively frequent use of such symbolism in one who by birth and career was certainly "a city man," I venture to suggest Paul's familiarity with Jesus' logia, particularly with Jesus' parables. Before discussing the probable Pauline allusions to specific parables, however, I should like to mention certain metaphors or illustrations which appear to be borrowings from Jesus' sayings.

In his development on charity, Paul speaks of "all the faith [it takes] to move mountains" (1 Cor 13:2b), a fairly clear reference to Jesus' remark to the disciples: "if you have faith as big as a mustard seed, you will say to this mountain, 'Move from here to there,' and it will move" (Mt 17:20).

Paul describes his apostolate in Corinth by means of the metaphor of building: "Like a wise (*sophos*) architect, I laid a foundation . . . no man can lay any other foundation than that laid, which is Jesus Christ" (1 Cor 3:10–11). The passage is reminiscent of the conclusion of the Matthean Sermon on the Mount: "Now everyone who hears these words of mine and does them may be compared to a wise (*phronimos*) man who built his house upon rock . . ." (Mt 7:24). In the Lucan version of this saying, we have mention of the foundation: "he is like a man building a house, who excavated and dug deep and set a foundation upon rock" (Lk 6:48).

Paul calls the Corinthian community "God's cultivation" (*geōrgion*) (1 Cor 3:9b). Jesus had used a similar figure: "every planting (*phyteia*) which my Father has not planted will be rooted up" (Mt 15:13).

The Faithful Steward

In endeavoring to make the Corinthians understand his role (and that of others, like Apollo) as apostle, Paul makes a rather clear allusion to Jesus' parable of the Faithful Steward. "Thus let a man consider us as servants of Christ and stewards (*oikonomous*) of God's mysteries. Now what one looks for in stewards is one who will prove faithful (*pistos*). To me it is of little concern that I be judged by you or by any merely human 'day' (*hēmera*) . . . he who judges me is the Lord. So do not judge prematurely until the Lord returns, who will also illuminate what is hidden in the darkness . . . then praise will come to each man from God" (1 Cor 4:1–5).

In Mt 24:45–46, Jesus asks: "Who, then, is the faithful (*pistos*) and wise servant (*doulos*) whom his lord put in charge of his household (*oiketeias*) to provide food for them at the proper time? Happy that servant whom his lord upon his return will find thus employed." The point of this Matthean parable, directed towards the hierarchical section of the Christian Church, is fidelity to one's responsibilities within the household of the faith, the precise point Paul makes in the paragraph cited above. The parable, like the Pauline passage, connects the judgment with the "Lord's return": praise (or blame) "comes to each man from God." Paul's use of "day" to symbolize the tribunal of judgment is borrowed from the term "Day of the Lord," which denotes Christ's parousia, when He will judge all men. The term, however, occurs also in the last section of the parable, which depicts the fate of an unfaithful steward whose "lord will return *on a day* and at an hour when he is not expecting him . . ." (v. 50), to judge him.

Parable of the Vineyard

There appears to be an allusion to the parable of the Vineyard (Mt 21:33–43; Mk 12:1–12; Lk 20:9–19) in Paul's question to the Corinthians: "Who plants a vineyard and does not eat its fruit?" (1 Cor 9:7b). The man who "planted a vineyard" tried repeatedly to obtain his share of the fruit, which thus forms the focus of interest in the parable. The owner "sends out his slaves to the tenant farmers to get his share of the fruit" (Mt 21:34). The tenant farmers kill the owner's son to "possess his inheritance," viz., the vineyard with its fruit (v. 38). Jesus' auditors, in answer to His question about what "the owner of the vineyard will do to these tenant farmers," assert that after punishing them "he will rent out the vineyard to other tenant farmers, who will give him its fruit at the proper season" (v. 41). Jesus Himself concludes by applying the parable to the religious leaders of Judaism: "God's kingdom will be taken from you and given to a people producing its fruit" (v. 43). Thus Paul's question is a neat summary of the whole parable.

The Parable of the Virgins

In his second extant letter to Corinth, Paul compares the Corinthian community to a virgin in a way which recalls Jesus' parable of the wise and foolish virgins (Mt 25:1–13): "I have betrothed you to one husband like a pure virgin, to present to Christ" (2 Cor 11:2b). Paul's unusual expression "to *one* husband" becomes understandable when we recall that in the parable all the virgins "go to meet" the single bridegroom, and are thus intended collectively to symbolize the bride, who is not mentioned in the story. In the development which follows (vv. 3–4) in the Pauline passage, the Apostle expresses a fear that, like Eve,[14] some of the community may be deceived by Satan through false preachers; in the parable, the foolish virgins are found unworthy of the marriage with the bridegroom (Mt 25:12).[15]

The Owner of the Vineyard

The Matthean parable of the Owner of the Vineyard (Mt 19:30—20:16) describes a man who hires various groups of workmen. The "inclusion" at the beginning and end of the story ("the first will be last, the last first") makes it clear that it illustrates the gratuitous nature of the "kingdom of heaven." It is a kind of symbolic history of the call of the Gentiles to the Church in place of God's chosen people. Paul exemplified the same point in Rom 4:1–17 by means of the history of Abraham. One remark in this development appears to be an allusion to this parable: "For the man who works, his pay is not considered as a favor, but as his just due. But to the man who does not work but puts his faith in him who justifies the sinner, that faith of his is considered as justice" (Rom 4:4–5).

It will be observed that, in the parable, the question of pay is only raised with the first two groups hired (who represent the Jews): "after agreeing with the workers for the usual daily wage" (v. 2), and "I shall give you what will be just" (v. 4). When the owner engages the last group, he merely says: "You too must go into my vineyard" (v. 7). When those who had worked all day object to their pay, the owner reminds them of their contract (v. 13), and then points out that he does not offend against justice by giving the late-comers what amounts to a gratuity: "Am I not permitted to do what I wish with what belongs to me? Or are you taking a jaundiced view of the fact that I am generous?" (v. 15). Thus these "last" who "do not work" except very briefly, but who had "put their faith" in the owner's kindness, rank "first"; the others "who worked" receive strict justice, and "their pay is not considered as a favor, but as their just due."

The Prodigal Son

In Eph 2:1–22, Paul addresses the predominantly Gentile Christian community to which he writes, contrasting their former condition with their present status. Several phrases in this paragraph will recall the Lucan parable of the Prodigal Son (Lk 15:11–32). Paul describes God as "rich in mercy" (v. 4), a phrase which also characterizes the father in the parable, who, upon seeing his wayward son "while he was yet a long way off," "was filled with pity" (v. 20). The verse which forms a kind of refrain in the parable, "this son of mine was dead and has come back to life, was lost and is found" (Lk 15:24, 32), is echoed in Paul. He refers to the Gentile Christians as "dead through transgressions" (v. 1), repeating the expression a little later: "He brought us back to life when we were dead through transgressions" (v. 5). Like the prodigal son (Lk 15:13, 30), the Gentile converts, "formerly a long way off, have come near" (Eph 2:13). Like the prodigal, they are now "fellow citizens of the saints and members of God's household" (v. 19): he had his filial rights, symbolized by the robe and ring (v. 22) restored to him, despite his request to be only a hired man (vv. 19, 21). The father in the parable attempts to reconcile the elder son, who represents the Jews, to the younger, erring son, who represents the Gentiles (vv. 28–32). Paul calls Christ "our peace," because He has reconciled Jews and Gentiles in the Christian Church, so that they become "one new man" (vv. 14–16).

The Leaven

In the Matthean discourse in parables, Jesus compares the "kingdom of heaven" to "yeast which a woman took and kneaded into three measures of flour until the whole was leavened" (Mt 13:33). He uses the same figure to warn his disciples to "beware of the yeast, that is, the hypocrisy, of the Pharisees" (Lk 12:1). When Paul reprimands the Corinthians for their indifference to the evil example of the incestuous man, he asks: "Do you not know that a little yeast leavens the whole batch?" (1 Cor 5:6b). This same allusion to Jesus' parable occurs in Paul's warning to the Galatians about their acceptance of circumcision and other Judaizing practices: "a little yeast leavens the whole batch" (Gal 5:9).

Possible Allusion to a Marcan Parable

When speaking of the work accomplished by himself and Apollo at Corinth, Paul underscores God's part in the supernatural results: "I did the planting, Apollo the watering, but God made it grow" (1 Cor 3:6). The point of the little parable, which is characteristic of Mark's view of the mystery of the kingdom and is found only in his Gospel, is similar: "A man scatters seed upon the earth. He goes to bed at night, gets up in the morning, while the seed sprouts and grows without his knowing how" (Mk 4:26–27).

CONCLUSION

These are some of the allusions found in the Pauline epistles to the sayings of Jesus which we possess in our written Gospels. While admittedly some are less clear and convincing than others, still they occur in sufficient numbers to warrant the conclusion that Paul was familiar with the materials preserved in the oral evangelical tradition, and that, moreover, he must have made use of these illustrations and metaphors (even perhaps of the parables) in his own preaching and teaching. To appreciate the value of such allusions as we find, however brief, it must be remembered that they are not references in the literary sense, and that, moreover, they have been incorporated by Paul into the exposition of themes which differ markedly in scope and in vocabulary from the type of literature to which our Gospels, especially the Synoptic Gospels, belong.

13

"Become Imitators of Me": Apostolic Tradition in Paul

THE expression *mimētēs ginesthai* and the verb *mimeisthai* are found, in the New Testament, almost exclusively in the Pauline letters.[1] Nor, in the Septuagint, where their appearance is late and rare, do the terms have any semantic prehistory which is significant for their meaning in Paul.[2] In the Greek literature of the classical and postclassical periods, there are numerous instances of the use of these words, but they provide no real parallels to Pauline usage.[3] This can be seen from a remark of Xenophon, frequently if inaccurately adduced as an illustration of the Pauline sense: *hoi didaskaloi tous mathētas mimētas heautōn apodeiknuousin.*[4] The notion of collecting a group of disciples around his own person is so foreign to Paul's mind that the word *mathētēs* is found nowhere in his letters.[5] It is also instructive to observe that the verb *akolouthein,* which in its derived sense might be considered a synonym of *mimeisthai,* is employed by New Testament writers only with respect to the immediate disciples of Jesus.[6] This suggests that Paul conceives the situation in which he recommends "imitation" as quite different from that of Jesus' public ministry. In the eyes of the various New Testament authors, those who followed Jesus personally—as also the first Christians who formed the Jerusalem community—appear to have held a privileged position vis-à-vis those who in a later age, or at least in more remote parts of the world, accepted the Christian faith.[7]

In Paul's own case, this impression—that he holds a position of privilege with respect to the communities he founded—is continually conveyed by the fact that with but two exceptions[8] it is always the imitation of himself which he proposes to his converts. Indeed, of these two exceptions, one is only so in appearance,[9] while the other (Eph 5:1) is easily explained by Paul's lack of acquaintance with his addressees. This habit of putting himself forward as an example to be imitated, in a man as self-effacing as Paul, surely requires some explanation. It would appear to indicate that, on his view, a special relationship exists between himself and those who accepted his kerygma.

But the importance which Paul attaches to this "imitation" of himself would seem to be out of harmony with what is nowadays regarded as the characteristic note of Pauline morality. Oscar Cullmann holds that the dynamic of Christian conduct, for Paul, springs from the indwelling Spirit, conferring on the Christian the power of *dokimazein,* "the capacity of taking, in each given situation, the moral decision conformed to the gospel."[10] This conception would minimize or eliminate the force of example. Stanislas Lyonnet gives a more nuanced picture.[11] The Christian being called to liberty (Gal 5:13, 18), all extrinsic norms of conduct have been per se abolished. The Christian, ideally speaking, is guided interiorly by the "law of the Spirit" (Rom 8:2). Thus in Paul's eyes the "law of Christ" (Gal 6:2; 1 Cor 9:21) excels the Mosaic law, not as a loftier moral code excels a more primitive one, but as the living Spirit excels the "letter" which "kills" (2 Cor 3:6; Rom 7:6). Pauline realism, of course, recognizes that this is the ideal, rarely attained. Because the majority of Christians are sinners (1 Tim 1:9) and because even the holiest of them are in constant danger of falling from grace (Gal 5:17), some external rules of Christian conduct are normally a practical necessity. Such laws, however, always remain secondary to the "law of the Spirit"; moreover, they have a reason for existing only insofar as they are somehow the expression of Christian love (Gal 5:13–14; Rom 13:8–9).

These principles of Pauline morality enable us from the start to exclude from Paul's conception of imitation any idea of a mechanical reproduction in word or gesture of the Apostle's life and conduct. Moreover, they would lead us to expect that this imitation is something pertaining to the supernatural order and is somehow an expression of Christian charity.

Wilhelm Michaelis[12] finds that the words *mimētēs ginesthai* or *mimeisthai* are employed by Paul in three senses, signifying (1) a simple comparison (1 Th 2:14; perhaps also 1 Th 1:6); (2) the following of Paul's own example (2 Th 3:7, 9; Phil 3:17); (3) obedience to Paul's commands (1 Cor 4:16; 1 Cor 11:1; 1 Th 1:6; Eph 5:1). Since the texts classified under (2) also imply obedience to Paul, Michaelis denies categorically that there is any foundation in Paul's writing for the doctrine of the *imitatio Christi.*[13] This is no less true of Christ in His glorified existence than in His earthly life. Heinrich Schlier[14] considers that this opinion of Michaelis is founded less upon the Pauline texts than upon a Protestant prejudice against the notion of *Vorbild*, and Charles Masson[15] would concur in this judgment. Jean Héring[16] asserts that it is impossible to deny Paul's intense interest in Jesus' earthly life and its force as an example.

It must be admitted, I believe, that the Pauline letters rarely propose Jesus' earthly career as a model for Christian behavior (cf. Phil 2:5 ff.; Rom 15:7; Col 3:13). On the other hand, the conception of Christian life as an inchoative and graduated assimilation to the "image" of the glorified Christ is indisputably

Paul's (2 Cor 3:18; Col 3:10–11). This process is foreordained by God (Rom 8:29), begun through baptism (Rom 6:5), and will be consummated by the resurrection of the just (1 Cor 15:49). Paul's celebrated use of certain verbs compounded with *syn* to describe the Christian supernatural association (through the agency of the Father) with Christ in the principal mysteries of the redemption is further evidence for this same Pauline viewpoint.[17]

However, whether it is this doctrine which Paul attempts to express through the terms *mimētēs ginesthai* and *mimeisthai*, or whether by "imitation" he means something quite different, can only be decided by an investigation of the texts in the Pauline letters which contain these expressions.

1 THESSALONIANS 1:3–8

Paul begins his letter with a paragraph of thanksgiving in gratitude to God for the dynamic efficacy of his preaching in Thessalonica, attested by the marvelous receptiveness of the first converts and their perseverance in the Christian way of life:

(We give thanks to God . . .) 3 because we retain the memory of
the active quality of your faith, the labor of your love, and the persevering nature of your hope in our Lord Jesus Christ, before God
our Father. 4 We are well aware, brothers whom God so loves, that
you have been chosen. 5 Our gospel reached you not as a matter of
mere words, but with the power of the Holy Spirit—and that in generous measure. You know, of course, what we meant to you while we
were with you. 6 *You* in your turn *became imitators of us and of the
Lord,* by having despite great tribulation accepted the Word with
joy, a gift of the Holy Spirit. 7 As a consequence, you became an
example for all the faithful in Macedonia and Achaea. 8 From your
community, the Word of the Lord has re-echoed—and that, not only

in Macedonia and Achaea. Everywhere, in fact, your faith in God has spread, so that we have no need to speak of it.

In v. 3, Paul gratefully recall his converts' practice of Christianity in terms of the theological virtues. It is not a mere generalization, however, but a description of these virtues as exercised in the concrete situation in which these Christians find themselves. Their faith directs all their actions;[18] their love undertakes painfully difficult tasks; their hope in the Lord's parousia makes them persevere despite the trials which they experience.[19]

In vv. 4–5, Paul expresses his thanks for the divine election of the Thessalonians which has made them part of God's new "chosen people." Paul himself has evidence of this in the outpouring of those charismatic gifts bestowed on the Jerusalem community at the first Pentecost and repeatedly given to the churches founded by Paul (1 Cor 2:4–5; Gal 3:3). Moreover, as Père Rigaux has pointed out,[20] by the term "gospel" or "the Word" Paul understands not his effort of preaching but rather the interior divine communication of God's mysteries, which effects through faith the salvation of the believer (Rom 1:16). Thus it is in a context which stresses the supernatural aspect of the Thessalonians' conversion and continued living of the faith that Paul speaks of "imitation."

Yet I believe it is significant that Paul speaks of "*our* gospel." While he is aware that the effective preaching of the Word of God necessarily entails Christ's operative presence through the Holy Spirit, still he never forgets (cf. Rom 10:14) that the function of the preacher is a necessary, if subordinate one. While the kerygma is primarily God's speaking to men in Christ, it is by God's design that it reaches men through the mediation of other men.[21] Throughout his missionary career Paul always felt that there was a special bond uniting him with the communities he had evangelized[22]—a relationship he frequently compares to that of a father towards his children (1 Th 2:11; 1 Cor 4:15; 2 Cor 6:13; Gal 4:19).[23]

Thus, on Paul's view, if the divine truth of the gospel is unique and invariable (cf. Gal 1:6–9), yet in its transmission it appears incarnated, so to speak, in the preacher's own Christian faith. This personal character of his own manner of preaching the Word makes Paul refer to it as "our gospel." This same quality may be discerned in the various spiritualities prevalent in the Church, as also in the inspired writings of the Bible.[24] Paul's preaching not only provides an occasion for the operation of the Spirit by faith in the hearts of his hearers; by its own characteristic modalities, which mirror Paul's own spirituality, it provides an objective norm against which the neo-Christian can measure his own experience of the Spirit of God.

"You in your turn became imitators of us—and of the Lord." The passive force of the verb (*egenēthēte*) is to be noted. As Masson remarks,[25] the turn of expression indicates that God is the unnamed agent here, which excludes any ordinary kind of conscious imitation. Nor is any similarity with the circumstances of Paul's own conversion to be sought.[26] As Rigaux remarks,[27] this imitation of Paul lies rather in the conduct of the Thessalonian community since conversion.

The precise point of comparison is suggested by v. 6b. These Christians have imitated Paul "by having despite great tribulation accepted the Word with joy." Jesus had taught His disciples that persecution was a sign, in the Christian dispensation as in the lives of the prophets, of God's predilection, and He commanded His followers to rejoice in suffering (Mt 5:13; Lk 6:23).[28] Joy in the face of persecution had characterized the Jerusalem community (Acts 5:41), strengthened by repetitions of the miracle of Pentecost (Acts 4:31). This same attitude is characteristic of Paul himself (Phil 1:18–20; 2:17; 2

Cor 6:10; 13:9; Col 1:24). Indeed, as is abundantly clear from his letters, Paul conceived his apostolic vocation as a prolongation of Jesus' role as the Suffering Servant of Yahweh.[29] There can be no doubt that in his kerygma Paul made use of this Deutero-Isaian theme in presenting the redemptive character of Christ's passion (cf. Phil 2:5 ff.). It is instructive to recall that, in his summary of Paul's preaching at Thessalonica, Luke suggests the prominence of this very motif: "He discussed the Scriptures with them, explaining them and showing that the Messiah had of necessity to suffer and rise from death" (Acts 17:3).

Paul's reason for asserting that the Thessalonians have become imitators of himself (and of Christ) is then clear. They have accepted his version of the gospel and proven by their own lives its efficacious force by their perseverance and fidelity "despite great tribulation, with joy." They have been given the grace of sharing in Paul's vocation as the Suffering Servant, and so have come to resemble Jesus Himself, the Suffering Servant par excellence.

One final nuance is not to be overlooked. Paul describes the Thessalonians as "imitators of us," and only as a kind of afterthought[30] does he call them "imitators of the Lord." This remarkable way of expressing himself is not accidental. It is "*our* gospel," as Paul has remarked, which the Thessalonians accepted; and by means of it they have found faith in Christ, whose representative as apostle and Suffering Servant Paul is.

Vv. 7–8 again reveal this Pauline concept of the gospel as a personal living testimony to Christ. The Thessalonians add their attestation to that of Paul, and so become "an example" to others. "The Word of the Lord" is thus increased in volume and now "re-echoes," because their "faith in God" has been added to the witnessing of their apostle.

1 THESSALONIANS 2:11–15a

After devoting a paragraph in chapter 2 to the attitude which he and his coworkers displayed to their converts at Thessalonica (2:1–12), Paul once more gives thanks for the courage these new Christians have displayed under persecution (13–16):

. . . 11 As you know, like a father towards his children, each of
you 12 have we exhorted, encouraged, adjured to live a life worthy
of the God who calls you to His kingdom and glory. 13 That is why,
on our part, we give thanks to God unceasingly that, in receiving the
Word of God preached by us, you have accepted not a human word,
but as it is in reality, God's Word. And it is rendered active in you
who possess the faith. 13 *You indeed have become imitators*, brothers,
of the churches of God in Judea, the Christian communities that is,
since you yourselves have endured the same sufferings from your own
countrymen as they did from the Jews, 15 who killed the Lord Jesus
and the prophets, and persecuted us. . . .

Although Paul here introduces a new point of comparison into his description of the Thessalonians' "imitation," the passage enables us to confirm some of our notions about it and to gain new insight into its meaning.

Paul's description of himself as a father to the Thessalonians in v. 11 recalls the personal character of Paul's preaching, as well as how essential in his eyes is the role of the apostle in the conversion of others. This idea is amplified in v. 13, where Paul's kerygma is called "the Word of God preached by us." While it is "no human word," but truly "God's Word," it is Pauls' own personal testimony to the gospel; hence it retains something of Paul himself, his reaction of faith to the divine message, and so he is in a real sense the father in the faith of those who accept God's gospel.

However, the Thessalonians are not called imitators of Paul

here, but of those Christian Palestinian communities which constituted the primitive Church and which by their unique privilege of being the first depositaries of the Christian message are an example for all the later churches, such as those founded by Paul.[31] Still, the "imitation" of which there is question here is not mere comparison, as Michaelis believes.[32] As in the last passage considered, it is to be explained in terms of the acceptance of "God's Word" by the Thessalonians, even under the impact of persecution. It is the working-out in them through divine grace of what constitutes the object of Paul's kerygma, their assimilation to Christ, who has attained glory through suffering.

Why does Paul express this as an "imitation" of the persecuted Palestinian churches? It seems evident, from the fact that Paul connects it with his own sufferings at the hands of the Jews of Palestine, that the persecution of which he thinks is chiefly that mentioned in Acts as following Stephen's martyrdom (Acts 8:1). This persecution was of paramount importance in Paul's eyes, leading as it did to the foundation of the Antiochian Church (Acts 11:19) of which he was a member. Luke's view that this early period in the life of the apostolic Church is to be included in Christian salvation history (and so forms an integral part of the gospel)[33] was undoubtedly Paul's own viewpoint. In fact, he implies that these sufferings of the Palestinian communities are to be regarded as a complement to Jesus' own passion by remarking that they were persecuted by "the Jews who killed the Lord Jesus" (vv. 14–15). Accordingly, it is reasonable to assume that the experiences of these Jewish Christians and their testimony to Christ were included in Paul's version of the kerygma, and the "imitation" of which he speaks is intended to be understood in the same sense in which he already used it in the preceding passage.

2 THESSALONIANS 3:6–9

In the concluding line of his second brief note to the Thessalonian community, Paul shows concern over the immoral effects which an exaggerated anticipation of Christ's parousia has had upon some of its members. They shirk their own duties to meddle with things that are not their concern ("doing nothing but busy with everything," v. 11), with the result that they live like parasites upon the charity of other Christians.

6 Now we beg you brothers, in the name of our Lord Jesus Christ,
to have nothing to do with any Christian whose behavior is unprincipled and contrary to the tradition they received from us. 7 For
your part, you know *how you are to imitate us.* We did not while with you live an unprincipled life. 8 We did not eat anyone's food
gratis. No, we worked hard and long, day and night, so as not to burden any of you. 9 Not that we do not have the right [to support],
but rather to give you an example in ourselves *for you to imitate.*

Paul interposes his apostolic authority, as the solemn formula in v. 6 ("in the name of our Lord Jesus Christ") indicates. Moreover, he appeals to the apostolic "tradition" which he has handed on to them himself as the source of those principles which must regulate Christian conduct. The acceptance of the kerygma, as we have already seen, implies much more than an intellectual assent to certain abstract doctrines; it involves a way of life in conformity with the gospel which Paul has preached and which is exemplified in his own life. The complete acceptance of the gospel demands some very practical, down-to-earth applications to Christian living (v. 10 contains a sample: "If anyone refuses to work, he must not eat").

This is also to be regarded as the "imitation" of Paul—on a less heroic scale, no doubt, than the earlier examples given in his Thessalonian correspondence, but no less necessary. In

v. 7, Paul reminds the community that they know how necessary this "imitation" is and that they know how they are to carry it out. They have an example in his own life during his stay with them (vv. 8–9). His working to support himself was motivated by fraternal charity in a twofold way: "so as not to burden any of you," and "to give you an example in ourselves for you to imitate." When in the sequel (vv. 14–15) Paul prescribes a kind of "excommunication" for the recalcitrant, this principle of fraternal charity is still operative ("reprimand him as a brother").

The importance of this passage for our present study lies in Paul's presentation of himself as a concrete example of Christian tradition, which is handed on to the community which he founded. It is by "imitation" that this tradition, which comprehends the whole range of Christian faith and morality, is kept alive in the Church.

PHILIPPIANS 3:15–17

In chapter 3 of his letter to Philippi, Paul renews his exhortation to preserve unity in that church (cf. 2:3 ff.) by avoiding certain Jewish influences which inculcate individualism or confidence "in the flesh." Paul's own past life illustrates the necessity of repudiating such reliance upon natural merits. His Jewish ideals (vv. 4–7) were changed by his experience on the Damascus road (vv. 7–9). His new Christian life is a striving to "know" Christ, in the biblical sense of experiencing the dynamic operation of the risen Lord (vv. 8–14). Christian existence can be described as a "fellowship in His passion," the effect of "the power of His resurrection" (v. 10). God the Father is the source of this "power," operative in Jesus' resurrection and also in Paul's life and that of every Christian. God will bring them, like Jesus, through suffering and death to a future resurrection (cf. also 1 Th 4:14; 2 Cor 4:10–11; Rom 14:7–9; Eph 2:4–6).

15 All of us, then, who are mature must adopt this attitude. And if
on any point you have a different attitude, God will reveal this attitude
to you. 16 Only no matter what we have attained, we must keep on
making progress with the help of the same [ideal]. 17 *Remain united
in becoming imitators of me,* brothers; and keep your eye on those
who live according to the example you have in us.

Verse 15 explains that the Christian who has attained to a spiritual maturity must adopt the attitude exhibited in the life of Paul, as described in vv. 8–14, if unity in the Philippian Church is to be safeguarded. This is, however, not merely a matter of human effort, but depends primarily upon divine revelation. The opposite viewpoint is displayed by the "enemies of the Cross of Christ," whose perspective is limited to "the things of earth" (vv. 18–19). That the adoption of this attitude entails suffering is clear from Paul's description of his own life as a "fellowship" in Christ's passion (v. 10).

This method of living up to the Christian principles which have guided Paul's own life is once again designated by the technical term "imitation" (v. 17). By slightly varying the consecrated phrase (*symmimētai*), Paul suggests—it would appear[34]—that such "imitation" is a true source of unity, since all will live "with the help of the same" ideal.[35]

Earlier in this letter (Phil 2:2 ff.) Paul had begged the Philippians to avoid any partisan spirit and remain united in fraternal charity by imitating the redemptive career of Christ, reviewed by a citation from a hymn probably familiar from its use in the liturgy.[36] The phrase *touto phronōmen* which Paul employs (3:16) recalls his *touto phroneite* (2:5). The parallel between these two passages implies that the "imitation" of himself is implicitly or indirectly imitation of Christ the Redeemer. Still, it is, I believe, significant that Paul does not employ the word "imitation" in connection with the earlier passage.

1 CORINTHIANS 4:14—17

This passage forms the conclusion to a rather lengthy discussion of the friction which has arisen in the Corinthian Church, caused by exaggerated loyalty to certain leaders: Paul, Peter, or Apollo (1 Cor 1:12). There are two causes of such division: a false idea of Christian wisdom (1 Cor 1:18—3:4) and a misconception of the apostolic vocation (1 Cor 3:5–17). True Christian wisdom consists in realizing the oneness of the whole Church in Christ and in the Father (3:18–23). The proper view of an apostle is an essentially supernatural one, which considers him as "a servant of Christ and a steward of God's mysteries" (4:1). If one were to take a natural view of the apostle's life, it is one of obscurity, hardship, and sufferings (4:9–13).

14 It is not to embarrass you that I write this, but to educate you as
my beloved children. 15 You may have thousands of guides in Christianity. You have not a plurality of fathers, since, as regards your
union with Christ, it was I who fathered you through the gospel. 16
Consequently, I beg you, *become imitators of me.* 17 It was for this
purpose I sent you Timothy, my beloved child and a faithful Christian, to help you keep in mind my Christian way of life according to
my teaching everywhere in each community.

Paul claims as his paternal right the duty of educating the Corinthian Church, because it was he and no other who "fathered" them in the faith by means of his kerygma. It is this spiritual paternity which gives a unique quality to his relationship with them. No matter how many *paidagōgoi*[37] they may have, they have only one father; and it is natural that children should resemble their father. Consequently, it is Pauline spirituality that they should adopt as their Christian way of life, since they received the faith through Paul's version of the gospel.

It is upon this line of reasoning that Paul here bases his exhortation to "become imitators" of himself (v. 16). He does not stop to explain the nature of this "imitation," because he has sent Timothy to do this. As one of Paul's own "children" in the faith, he will be quite capable of recalling to them Paul's view of the "Christian way of life."

The passage shows how the Pauline notion of "imitation" is built upon the Apostle's awareness of the personal nature of his gospel and of the close ties which bind his converts to himself. It is noteworthy that this notion of "imitation" of himself is put forward only in those letters which Paul wrote to churches of which he was the founder and apostle: Thessalonica, Philippi, Corinth, and Galatia.[38]

Here, as in Phil 3:15–17, this "imitation" of himself is proposed by Paul as a pledge of the unity of the Church. To recognize the real nature of their relation to Paul, that of children to a father, is the one great remedy for party strife.

1 CORINTHIANS 10:31—11:1

One of the cases of conscience which Paul dealt with in this letter concerned the eating of meat that had been used in the worship of pagan idols (8:1—11:1). Paul's solution is based on three principles. The Christian is per se at perfect liberty to eat such food, since idols have no power to affect it for better or worse (8:1–6). Fraternal charity, however, can limit the Christian's freedom, as Paul's apostolic practice of earning his own living shows (8:7—9:17). Christian prudence also may modify the actions of those who seek to secure their own salvation (10:1–13).[39] After giving his solution of the problem (10:14–30), Paul adds the following lines of exhortation:

31 Whether, then, you eat or drink, or whatever you do, do everything for God's glory. 32 Strive not to be an obstacle either to Jews or Greeks of God's Church, 33 just as I for my part render service to all in everything. I seek, not what benefits myself, but what benefits everyone else, so that they may be saved. 11:1 *Become imitators of me,* just as I am an *imitator of Christ.*

This passage may be regarded as a well-balanced statement of Christian liberty as Paul envisages it. Verse 31 expresses the motive that must dominate Christian living: "everything for God's glory," ultimately achieved by the winning of one's own salvation (cf. Phil 1:11; 2 Cor 4:15; Col 3:17).[40] Verse 32 puts the same idea more concretely: the Christian must avoid in his conduct whatever might hinder the conversion of Jews or pagans, as well as anything that might scandalize his fellow Christians. The negative form which Paul's statement takes suggests the primacy of divine grace in Christian conduct.

Paul states in verse 33 that this ideal has motivated his own apostolic conduct. The phrase *panta pasin areskō* is an epitome of his whole apostolic career.[41] His assertion that he puts the spiritual profit of others ahead of his own is simply a paradoxical way of saying that he aims at saving his own soul by saving others.[42]

Paul resumes what he has said in verses 32–33 by saying: "Become imitators of me, just as I am an imitator of Christ." Two points in this statement are worthy of comment. In the first place, Paul does not urge the Corinthians to imitate himself *because* he imitates Christ, but "just as" he imitates Him. Secondly, he does not command them to imitate Christ, but to imitate himself. There is an essentially hierarchical structure in this Pauline conception of "imitation," which shows how important he considers his function of transmitting the apostolic faith to others. His own mediatorial role is highly necessary. He is not merely a mouthpiece through which the gospel is handed on mechanically to other men. Not only *what* he says, but *how* he says it, as well as *what he is,* have a part to play in the Christian formation of those he evangelizes. The gospel of Christ which Paul preaches is also his gospel, in a real if subordinate sense. The Corinthians are not called upon to imitate Christ *directly,* but to imitate Paul, in whom they possess a concrete realization of the imitation of Christ. By insisting upon this necessarily mediated *imitatio Christi,* Paul is simply witnessing to the necessity of apostolic tradition in the life of the Church.

GALATIANS 4:12

In chapter 4 of this letter Paul gives a sketch of true Christian liberty. By their union with Christ, the Galatians have become adoptive sons of God and heirs together with Christ of God's kingdom (vv. 1–7). To adopt the program proposed by Judaizing Christians would be tantamount to a return to a state of slavery (vv. 8–11). Paul halts his development at this point to introduce a paragraph of a more personal tone, since he fears that his work in Galatia may become fruitless (v. 11). He begins this passage, which recalls the specific circumstances of the Galatians' reception of his kerygma and of himself, by a plea that they imitate his own way of life.

12 *Become like me,* because I for my part have become like you. . . .

W. Michaelis[43] denies that this verse exemplifies the Pauline notion of "imitation." While it is true that the technical term *mimeisthai* is wanting (a sign perhaps of Paul's agitation),[44] still, when we consider the whole context of this letter and the references immediately following to Paul's preaching in Galatia and the reception of his gospel by the Galatians, it appears much more probable that there is question here of the same notion of the "imitation" of himself which we have seen in the earlier letters.[45]

As he has stated in chapter 3, the Mosaic law, its traditions and observances, have no longer any part to play in the divine economy of salvation. While Paul recognizes that in the gospel as preached by Peter among the Jews some concessions may legitimately be made to Mosaic legal observance (Gal 2:8), he himself in his vocation as Apostle of the Gentiles (1 Cor 9:21) has discarded the practice of the law (he is *hōs anomos*) and follows solely "the law of Christ" (*ennomos Christou*).

Since it is Paul, not Peter, who has converted the pagans of Galatia to Christianity, their Christian life must be based upon his personal version of the gospel, in which Mosaic observances have no part. The apostolic traditions, as represented by Paul's kerygma and his own life, provide the Galatian community with the necessary example for "imitation." No other type of Christian life is to be admitted among them.

EPHESIANS 4:32—5:2

In chapter 4 of this letter to a community which Paul does not appear to have known personally (Eph 1:15; 4:21) and which consequently is unacquainted with himself (Eph 3:2–4),[46] Paul makes a strong plea for the preservation of unity, based upon his conception of the Church as Christ's body (Eph 4:1–16). At the conclusion of the passage, he urges his addressees to observe fraternal charity as the principal means to union with one another:

32 Be good to one another, tenderhearted, forgiving one another, just as God the Father has forgiven you in Christ. 5:1 Therefore, *become*

imitators of God the Father like dear children. 2 Live a life of love, just as Christ has loved you and handed Himself over for us as a sweet-smelling offering and sacrifice to God.

Here we have an instance unparalleled in Paul's letters of the use of the technical phrase *mimētēs ginesthai* where there is no question of the "imitation" of Paul, but of God the Father. More precisely, Paul proposes that this community, in whose conversion and Christian formation he himself has had no part, imitate God the Father as He has revealed Himself through the principal object of the gospel, viz., God's definitive, universal act of redemption in Jesus Christ. Since Paul, as a remark of his in this same chapter (4:21) reveals, does not know the special modalities of the gospel as preached to these Christians, he must content himself with proposing some essential datum of the kergyma for "imitation." We have two other instances of this procedure in letters written to churches unfamiliar to Paul (Rom 15:7; Col 3:13).

If his addressees cannot be considered Paul's "children" in any sense, they are nonetheless God's "dear children" by their acceptance of the Christian message. They can, therefore, be exhorted to "become imitators of God the Father." As a guide in the pursuit of this ideal they have the example of Christ's own life of love, summed up in his "handing Himself over for us."

CONCLUSIONS

Our inquiry has yielded the following data. (1) Paul urges this "imitation" of himself only to those communities which he has founded. (2) It is the necessary result of having accepted "his" gospel, which creates a special relationship between himself and the churches he founded personally. While Paul insists that his kerygma is essentially the same as that preached by other apostles, he is also aware that, as his personal testimony to Christ, his preaching and way of life have their own characteristic modalities, determined chiefly by his conviction that he carries on the role of Christ as the Suffering Servant of God. (3) Thus the *imitatio Christi* which Paul proposes to his communities is a mediated imitation. It springs both from Paul's apostolic authority as an authentic representative of Christian tradition, and from the recognized need of those he has fathered in the faith to have an objective, concrete norm against which they can "test" (*dokimazein*) the influence of the Spirit upon themselves. W. Michaelis is surely right inasmuch as obedience is certainly one element in this "imitation" of Paul by other Christians. It involves in addition, however, the help provided by a concrete *Vorbild*, the specific examples and lessons contained in Paul's own version of the gospel as preached and lived by him.

Consequently, this "self-imitation" proposed by the Apostle, so necessary in his eyes as a vehicle for the transmission of apostolic tradition, must not be overlooked in any systematic presentation of Pauline moral theology.

Conclusion

We have endeavored in these pages to present a picture of the principal ways in which the primitive Church succeeded in arriving at a self-consciousness of her own proper character, her peculiar mission, and her ultimate destiny: One of the most important means through which the apostolic Church expressed this self-awareness, I believe, was the preaching of the Word of salvation—that "good news" proclaimed with Christian hope to a world already despairing of being saved. Of equal significance with the kerygma was undoubtedly the Christian public worship of the risen Lord. Therein the early Church, like the Church of today, experienced a deeper realization of Christ's redemptive work through His saving gestures, the Christian sacraments, and above all through the Eucharistic liturgy. It was during the "breaking of the Bread," as we learn from the New Testament (Acts 13:1–3), that the Antiochian community was taught by the Holy Spirit the meaning of the historical period between the first and second comings of the Lord Jesus: her missionary vocation. In the third place, by the creation of a body of inspired Christian literature, the Church at once gave testimony to the faith she possessed in Jesus Christ and also expressed her own interior knowledge of her role in history. The missionary experiences in the Greco-Roman world of the first several decades of the Church's existence added a new dimension to her membership through the admission of the Gentiles, as well as to the formulation of her doctrinal beliefs through the language and thought patterns of Hellenistic culture.

It will be obvious to the reader that no attempt has been made in this small study to express all the facets of the "personality" of the apostolic Church as we find it reflected in the pages of the New Testament. Very little has been said concerning the ecclesiology found in the writings emanating from the school of John, one of the greatest New Testament theologians. One will find no essay on the Pauline conception of the Church as the body of Christ. There are several interesting questions concerning the early Church which have merely been touched on in passing, e.g., the somewhat rapid disappearance of the concept of "the Remnant" so very prominent in the Old Testament prophets. No chapter has been expressly devoted to the notion of the Church as the people of God, which has been stressed with so much reason during the Second Vatican Council. Perhaps some may miss that apologetic orientation which is usually found in discussions on the Church. The present writer feels that much more is to be gained by simply presenting the Church's own picture of herself.

From what has been said, however, we can catch a hint at least of the process by which in New Testament times the Church achieved the essential knowledge of her own nature and purpose among men. At the beginning the primitive community thought of itself as the *qahal* of the new Israel, being basically Jewish in complexion and in heritage. This characterization is to be seen in the early chapters of Acts and even to some extent in the Gospel of Matthew. Like the Israel of their ancestors, these Jewish Christians believed themselves to be the people of God—a notion that was to persist throughout the writings of Paul. He speaks of the Christians as "the Israel of God" (Gal 6:16), as the *segullah*, or people of God's acquisition (1 Th 5:9). This latter idea recurs in those writings which bear the imprint of Pauline theology (Eph. 1:14; Heb 10:39; 1 Pt 2:9).

A prominent feature of the theological viewpoint in Paul's earlier letters is, of course, the expectation of the Second Coming. In Paul's correspondence with Thessalonica, Philippi, and even Corinth, the Church might be characterized as "the Church of the Parousia." As the result of certain experiences in the course of his missionary career, Paul's view is modified with respect to his hope of a proximate Second Coming. Accordingly, he comes to concentrate upon the nature of the Church as an institution in this world, a prolongation "in mystery" of the exalted Christ, whose body the Church truly is. A prominent Christological feature of the "great" Pauline letters is the presentation of the risen Lord as the last or second Adam. And in the captivity epistles, which represent Paul's mature ecclesiology, the Church appears as "the Church of the New Man," as the body of her glorified Head.

Where Paul discovers the genesis of the Church in Jesus' death and resurrection, and Matthew traces her beginnings back to the words and actions of our Lord during His Galilean ministry, the writers of the Johannine school provide the insight that the origins of the Church go back to the very moment when "the Word became flesh and pitched His tent among us" (Jn 1:14). The Son of God made man, "full of grace and truth," is the incarnation of the new covenant (Jn 1:14–18). Consequently, the Church is thought of as the extension of the Incarnation; for it is in the incarnate Son that all Christians "have received the power to become God's children" (Jn 1:12). This conception of the Christian people as "the Church of the Incarnation" is already operative in the Apocalypse.

In his efforts to expose to his persecuted people the Christian significance of their sufferings, the author of the Apocalypse represents the Church as the affianced bride of "the Lamb who has been slain"—the risen Christ. Since her Spouse is master of human history, such persecution cannot harm her members. From a more positive point of view, these sufferings form an integral part of "the just deeds of the saints" with which the bride must be adorned for her celestial nuptials with the Lamb. It is thus that she becomes likened to her glorified Lord, who still wears the badges of His sacred passion. It is, however, in the great symbolic tableau which forms the heart of this book of revelation, in chapter 12, that the Church is pictured as the mother of the Messiah (Ap 12:1–6). Here again we learn that the Incarnation holds the secret of the Church's mysterious nature for John. He may rightly be regarded as the theologian of "the Church of the Incarnation."

One final observation is perhaps in place here. As one pages through the New Testament in search of the picture which the Church provides of herself, it becomes clear that the Christians of the apostolic age advanced in their knowledge and appreciation of the role and character of the Church in proportion as they grasped the significance of Jesus Christ, His person and His redemptive work. With their first intuition of Jesus' exaltation at God's right hand on the first Pentecost came their initial awareness of their own identity as the new Israel. During the first years of their existence as the Christian community, their reflections upon Jesus' public ministry and His redemptive death brought the realization of how definite had been His intention of founding His Church—even though during His public ministry they had been unable to perceive it. Through the theological genius of a Paul and a John, the Christians of the apostolic age were taught the more profound meaning of the Church. These inspired writers bequeathed to the Christian people a rich collection of images expressive of the Church's character, which throughout subsequent centuries would yield ever new insights into the mystery of the Church. The declared purpose of Pope John in summoning the Second Vatican Council shows us that we have not yet plumbed the depths of meaning which the New Testament offers regarding this mystery.

Thus we are led inevitably to the conclusion that while our comprehension of the nature of the Church has been deepened and perhaps broadened with the passage of time and the continuing experiences of the Christian people, we must always return to the New Testament to rediscover for ourselves the meaning of the Church in our own day. If this series of studies has reawakened in the reader a desire to reread these most hallowed pages of Christian literature, this little volume will have achieved its primary purpose.

Notes

Kingdom to Church

Editor's Note.—This originally appeared in *Theological Studies* 16 (1955) 1–29.

NOTES TO CHAPTER 1

[1] One of the principal aims of the treatise *De ecclesia* is to establish a relationship of identity between the kingdom of God proclaimed by Jesus and the Church. The bibliography by W. G. Kümmel shows the contemporary interest in this problem among non-Catholics; cf. "Jesus und die Anfänge der Kirche," *Studia theologica* 7 (1953) 1–27. Among more recent studies of the New Testament conception of the Church, we wish to mention: Krister Stendahl, "Kirche: II. Im Urchristentum," *Die Religion in Geschichte und Gegenwart* 3 (2nd ed.; Tübingen, 1959) 1297–1304; Barnabas Mary Ahern, "The Conception of the Church in Biblical Thought," *Proceedings of the Society of Catholic College Teachers of Sacred Doctrine*, 1961, pp. 32–54; D. M. Stanley, "The Witness of the Church: The Manner of Recording Salvation History in the New Testament," in *The Gospel of Jesus the Christ* (Seton Hall, N.J., 1962) pp. 35–51; *id.*, "Reflections on the Church in the New Testament," *Catholic Biblical Quarterly* 25 (1963) 387–400.

[2] A. Loisy, *Les évangiles synoptiques* (Ceffonds, 1908) p. 9; *Les Actes des apôtres* (Paris, 1920) p. 153.

[3] For this reason the tendency of some treatises on the Church to express the relation of kingdom to Church in a neatly conceptualized equation based on a text like Mt 16:16–18 cannot be regarded with complete satisfaction. What must be demonstrated is that, on the view of the writers of the New Testament, the coming of the kingdom coincides with the developments which resulted, toward the latter part of the apostolic age, in the organization of the Church.

[4] Arthur Michael Ramsey, *The Resurrection of Christ: An Essay in Biblical Theology* (2nd ed.; London, 1946) p. 80.

[5] Cf. the remarks of L. Cerfaux in his *Introduction* to *Les Actes des*

apôtres (*Bible de Jérusalem*; Paris, 1953) p. 11; also Stanislas Lyonnet, *Le récit de l'annonciation et la maternité divine de la sainte Vierge* (Rome, 1954).

[6] Pierre Benoit, "L'Ascension," *Revue biblique* 56 (1949) 191.

[7] L. Cerfaux, *La communauté apostolique* (2nd ed.; Paris, 1953) pp. 26 ff. I wish to acknowledge my indebtedness to this unpretentious but excellent little study of the Jerusalem community. Many of the ideas which I have developed in this essay are the result of Msgr. Cerfaux's insights.

[8] A. Wikenhauser, *Die Apostelgeschichte* (2nd ed.; Regensburg, 1951) p. 30.—The apostolic group's preparations for Jesus' return to execute the great eschatological judgment are significant. They remain together; they pray constantly together; they feel the necessity of preserving the full complement of the Twelve. No adequate explanation of this phenomenon can be found except in the disciples' conviction that in so acting they were carrying out the will of Jesus, manifested to them during His public life. He had promised to be present in any group of disciples united in prayers (Mt 18:20). He had Himself constituted the Twelve (Mk 3:14). His sending them on a preaching tour had suggested their close association with Himself and His mission (Mk 6:7 ff.). It appears clear that some special significance was attached to the number twelve itself—although the texts cited in Acts 1:20 from the *OT* do not explain it. We may say that the significance of this incident derives (1) from Jesus' own action during His public ministry, (2) from the *Sitz im Leben* of the story itself, (3) from Matthew's technique in narrating it, which underlines his conception of its importance, and (4) from the constant references to "the Twelve" throughout the *NT*. Jesus' decision to permit the Twelve to share in His mission indicates His intention to have men assist Him by preaching and working miracles in places which He personally cannot visit. This extension of His influence in space, so to speak, implies an intention to extend Himself also in time, so long as the kingdom of God is not perfectly realized in history.—The life-situation in which the narrative took form, viz., the doctrinal instruction of the apostolic Church, reveals the significance perceived by the primitive community, for its own coming-to-be, of Jesus' choice of the Twelve.—The fact that, in his redaction of Jesus' instruction to the Twelve on the occasion of their mission in Galilee, Matthew has included (cf. Mt 10:17–42) materials which actually refer to the experiences of the Church

in the apostolic age (the other Synoptics set these logia in a different context: cf. Mk 13:9–13; Lk 12:2–9, 51–53; 14:26–27; 17:33) is proof of Matthew's realization that Jesus' selection and sending of the Twelve demonstrated our Lord's desire to found a Church directed by this group.—The paramount importance of "the Twelve" in apostolic Christianity is evident from the fact that all three Synoptics preserve this narrative (Mk 3:13–19 retains it, even though the Sermon on the Mount is omitted from the narrative; cf. Lk 6:12–16; Mt 10:2–4), that the fourth Gospel alludes to this action of Jesus (Jn 6:67–70), that Acts 1:13 repeats the list at a critical point. Paul (1 Cor 15:5) and the author of the Apocalypse (Ap 21:14) also testify to the role of "the Twelve" in the early Church.

[9] The meaning of *kathōs* is difficult to determine. It may signify causality: the disciples began to speak with other tongues *because* the Holy Spirit was giving them the grace to prophesy. In this hypothesis, there is question of two distinct charismata bestowed upon the group: ecstatic prayer and also prophecy. The first was exhibited by the disciples' actions (cf. v. 4) and attracted the crowd (v. 6); the second was exercised by Peter in the speech attributed to him (vv. 14 ff.). *Kathōs* may, on the other hand, mean "how" here: the disciples began to tell in other tongues *how* the Spirit was giving them the grace to prophesy (cf. Acts 15:14 for this usage of *kathōs*). In any event, it is to be noted that the verb *apophthengesthai* means "to prophesy" both here and in v. 14, as it does in Acts 26:25.

[9a] It is not a question here of the charism of "other tongues," which was essentially a form of ecstatic prayer of divine praise (cf. the accounts of a repetition of the phenomenon at Caesarea, Acts 10:46, and at Ephesus, Acts 19:6). In composing his narrative of the events which occurred at Pentecost, Luke has so closely interwoven the data of two sources (one describes the gift of tongues, another provides the substance of the Petrine discourse) as to give the (unwarranted) impression to not a few readers, especially among the Fathers of the Church, that when Peter preached he spoke in various foreign languages.

[10] The "speaking with other tongues" is interpreted as being ecstatic prayer by two prominent Catholic exegetes of the present day: cf. S. Lyonnet, "De glossolalia Pentecostes eiusque significatione," *Verbum domini* 24 (1944) 65–75; A. Wikenhauser, *op. cit.*, pp. 34 ff., "Das Reden in Zungen ('Zungenreden')."

[11] J. Schmitt, "L'Eglise de Jérusalem ou la 'restauration d'Israël," *Revue des sciences religieuses* 27 (1953) 209–18.

[12] A. Causse, "Le pèlerinage à Jérusalem et la première Pentecôte," *Revue d'histoire et de philosophie religieuses* 20 (1940) 120–41.

[13] The word *diamerizomenai* (Acts 2:3) used to describe the tongues is borrowed by Luke from the LXX translation of Dt 32:8, where allusion is made to the Tower of Babel or Babylon.

[14] Cf. the account in Ex 20:18 ff. A patristic tradition, represented by Severus of Antioch (cf. Cramer, *Catenae*, p. 17), points out this parallelism also. Pierre Benoit refuses to attribute this signification to Luke's account; cf. *art. cit.*, p. 193, n. 2.

[15] J. Schmitt, *art. cit.*, pp. 212–17, has reviewed this evidence provided by the first five chapters of Acts. The results of his investigation are most impressive.

[16] Pierre Benoit, "Remarques sur les 'sommaires' de Actes 2.42 à 5," in *Aux sources de la tradition chrétienne: Mélanges offerts à M. Maurice Goguel* (Paris, 1950) pp. 1–10.

[17] This *didachē tōn apostolōn* is the full fruit of a deeper understanding of the mysteries of Jesus' earthly career which was promised to the Twelve in the discourse after the Last Supper (Jn 14:26; 16:25). For a fuller discussion of this important aspect of early Christian doctrine, cf. "*Didachē* As a Constitutive Element of the Written Gospel," infra pp. 199 ff.

[18] The connection between the *fractio panis* and the post resurrection repasts shared by the disciples with the risen Christ is suggested by O. Cullmann, "La signification de la sainte cène dans le christianisme primitif," *Revue d'histoire et de philosophie religieuses* 16 (1936) 1–22. Cf. also Yves de Montcheuil, "Signification eschatologique du repas eucharistique," *Recherches de science religieuse* 33 (1946) 10–43.

[19] Stanislas Lyonnet, "La 'koinōnia' de l'église primitive et la sainte eucharistie," *Actas del XXXV Congreso Eucarístico Internacional—Barcelona 1953, Sesiones de estudio* 1, 511–15.

[20] The discourse credited to Peter on Pentecost (Acts 2:14–36) shows that the disciples first discerned the saving character of Christ's passion, death, and resurrection as a consequence of the descent of the Holy Spirit. The coming of the Spirit, they realized, was the result of Christ's exaltation to the right hand of the Father (Acts 2:33). This attested His constitution as *Kyrios* and Messiah (v. 36) and, moreover, His *new*

mission, through the activity of the Spirit, as *Saviour of Israel* (Acts 3:26). As far as I can ascertain, the importance of this last text has not been noted hitherto. It sheds much light upon the psychological process by which the Twelve arrived at their conception of Christ's death and resurrection as redemptive. They first recognized Him as Redeemer through His sending of the Holy Ghost, i.e., in His exaltation *ad dexteram Patris*. Further reflection revealed the saving character of the two greatest actions of His life, His death and resurrection. But for a fully-thought-out presentation of such a soteriology we must await the genius of Paul.

[20a] J. Schmitt, "Les sources et les thèmes de la naissante foi apostolique au Christ Sauveur," *Lumière et vie* 15 (1954) 39 f.

[21] Wilfred L. Knox, *The Acts of the Apostles* (Cambridge, 1948) pp. 72 ff.

[22] E. G. Selwyn, *The First Epistle of St. Peter* (London, 1949) p. 93.

[23] It is surely one of the conundrums of early Church history that, although the Jewish Christians knew that these charges had been expressly declared as cause of Christ's death by the Jews, still they were so slow in realizing that to follow Christ entailed the abandonment of the Temple and the law.

[24] It is impossible to decide the chronological order of the events subsequent upon the persecution of the Hellenist Christians in Jerusalem. However, Luke clearly indicates the literary (and hence, on his view, theological) sequence by the use of the phrase *hoi men oun diasparentes* in Acts 8:4 and 11:19.

[25] The apostles were aware that, upon emerging from the Jordan after His baptism by John, Jesus had received the Holy Spirit, who descended upon Him (Mt 3:13 ff.; Mk 1:9 ff.; Lk 3:21 f.). Moreover, in the fourth Gospel, it is instructive to observe the marked connection between John's identification of Jesus by the descending Spirit and the antithesis, John—water: Christ—Spirit, we have mentioned; cf. Jn 1:33. Thus the New Testament seems to indicate that the institution of the sacrament of baptism was begun in the Jordan but was only fully completed at Pentecost. The intuition of some of the Fathers of the Church (*Sum. theol.* 3, q. 66, a. 3) that Christ somehow instituted baptism at the Jordan is substantially correct.

[26] The meaning of the name is explained in Acts 4:36 as "clever at encouragement (or, exhortation)."

[27] It may be that this experience of Rome's protective might is the origin

of Paul's doctrine about the "obstacle" to the appearance of "the man of lawlessness" and the great apostasy (2 Th 2:6). At any rate, a most ancient Christian tradition has long identified this "obstacle" with the Roman Empire. Johannes Munck, *Paulus und die Heilsgeschichte* (Copenhagen, 1954), has recently revived this theory.

[28] C. H. Dodd, "The Mind of Paul: A Psychological Approach," *Bulletin of the John Rylands Library, Manchester* 17 (1933) 104.

[29] The phrase is that of Msgr. Cerfaux, *La communauté apostolique*, p. 96.

[30] Although this parable is common to all the Synoptics, it has a special Matthean conclusion, v. 43: "Thus I declare to you: the reign of God will be taken from you and given to a people who will produce its fruits."

[31] This parable is found also in Luke, but without the particular detail (v. 7) about the slaying of the murderers by the king and the burning of their city, and without the strange appendix (vv. 11–14), which would appear to be a warning to the Church of the Gentiles against presuming too much upon their vocation to the kingdom. Cf. D. M. Stanley, *The Gospel of St. Matthew* (*New Testament Reading Guide* 4; 2nd ed.; Collegeville, Minn., 1963) pp. 95 f.

[32] Cf. D. M. Stanley, *The Gospel of St. Matthew*, Introduction, pp. 13–15.

[33] A. Lemonnyer, "Le messianisme des 'béatitudes,'" *Revue des sciences philosophiques et théologiques* 11 (1922) 373–89.

[34] The missionary discourse, Mt 10:41; that in parables, 13:17; that of the sevenfold woes, 23:34.

[35] A. Feuillet, "Le discours de Jésus sur la ruine du temple," *Revue biblique* 56 (1949) 85, n. 2.

[36] A. Feuillet, "Le triomphe eschatologique de Jésus d'après quelques textes isolés des évangiles," *Nouvelle revue théologique* 71 (1949) 704–7.

Salvation in the Primitive Preaching

EDITOR'S NOTE.—This study originally appeared in the *Catholic Biblical Quarterly* 19 (1956) 231–54.

NOTES TO CHAPTER 2

[1] Cf. Joseph Bonsirven, *Théologie du Nouveau Testament* (Paris, 1951) p. 177.

[2] Paul preached the kerygma at Philippi (Phil 1:5) in its Palestinian form (Phil 2:6–11), at Thessalonica (1 Th 1:5; Acts 17:2-3), at Corinth (1 Cor 15:1 ff.), at Ephesus (Acts 20:20–21, 25), and even in Rome (Acts 28:30–31).

[3] Cf. Dom Gregory Dix, *Jew and Greek* (London, 1953) p. 5: "Christianity is the revelation of Divine Truth from beyond all history and all time, but it is so only because it is the only fully historical religion. It is the only religion which actually *depends entirely upon* history . . . it is Divine redemption given *from within* history . . . by the wrenching of one Man's flesh and the spilling of His blood upon one particular square yard of ground, outside one particular city gate during three particular unrepeatable hours. . . ."

[4] Cf. J. Pedersen, *Israel* 1 (London–Copenhagen, 1926) 330–35.

[5] Paul speaks only of "the redemption of our body" (Rom 8:23). The nearest approach to the modern theological (or psychological) viewpoint is perhaps Heb 10:39, *eis peripoiēsin psychēs.* By associating eschatological salvation with the resurrection of the body and refraining from affirmations about a *Zwischenzustand,* the New Testament authors avoided the embarrassment felt by many a Scholastic theologian in his attempts to explain the nature of that *beatitudo accidentalis* by which the *beatitudo essentialis* of the subsistent glorified soul is augmented upon its reunion with the body in heaven.

[6] Cf. R. Pautrel, "Jugement: dans l'Ancien Testament," *Dictionnaire de la Bible: Supplément* 4, 1321–44.

[7] Cf. W. Adams Brown, "Salvation, Saviour," *Hastings' Dictionary of the Bible* 4, 357–74.

[8] Cf. A.-M. Dubarle, *Les sages d'Israël* (Paris, 1946): for Prv, pp. 47, 53; for Qoh, p. 124; Jb, p. 91; Sir, p. 170.

[9] Wisdom does, however, introduce the conception of *aphtharsia* (Wis 2:23; 6:19; cf. 4 Mac 9:22; 17:12), which was incorporated into the primitive preaching as the theme of the incorruption of Jesus' body.

[10] Hence the difficulties about discovering the scriptural foundation for the Catholic doctrine of purgatory. Cf. D. M. Stanley, *The Gospel of St. Matthew* (2nd ed.; Collegeville, Minn., 1963) pp. 66–67, 82. C. Spicq, *Les épîtres pastorales* (Paris, 1947) p. 339, calls 2 Tim 1:18 "un exemple de prière en faveur des morts absolument unique dans le Nouveau Testament."

[11] Cf. Louis Bouyer, *La Bible et l'évangile* (Paris, 1951) pp. 166–67.

[12] Cf. P. van Imschoot, "Reich Gottes," Haag's *Bibel-Lexikon*, cols. 1412–18.

[13] H. Haag, "Rest (Israels)," *ibid.*, cols. 1427–28.

[14] On the authenticity of these Acts discourses, cf. the nuanced statements of P. Benoit, "Les origines du Symbole des apôtres dans le Nouveau Testament," *Lumière et vie*, fasc. 2, pp. 39–60; also Bertil Gaertner, *The Areopagus Speech and Natural Revelation* (Uppsala, 1955) pp. 7–36; C. H. Dodd, *The Apostolic Preaching and Its Developments* (2nd ed.; London, 1950) pp. 19–20.

[15] Cf. *Damascus Document* 1:6–9: "They recognized their iniquity and perceived that they were guilty men, and had like the blind been groping for twenty years . . ."; *Rule of the Qumrân Community* 1:25–26: "Then all who pass into the covenant must confess after them, 'We have committed iniquity, we have transgressed, we have sinned, we have done evil, we and our fathers before us, by walking contrary to the statutes of truth. But God is just, and His judgment upon us and our fathers is right, and the mercy of His persevering love He has accorded to us. . . .' " Cf. F.-M. Braun, "L'Arrière-fond judaïque du quatrième évangile et la communauté de l'alliance," *Revue biblique* 62 (1955) 21–22: "Par réaction contre le naturalisme des Sadducéens et la suffisance des Pharisiens, les gens de Qumran demeuraient partagés entre le sentiment de leur culpabilité et l'assurance du pardon. La tension entre les extrêmes n'est pas diminuée; le problème qu'elle pose est bien toujours celui qui opposait *l'Alliance* aux autres partis."

[16] Cf. J. Schmitt, "Les écrits du Nouveau Testament et les textes de

Qumran," *Revue des sciences religieuses* 29 (1955) 381–401; 30 (1956) 55–74.

[17] This is evident in the miracle theology of the Synoptics, which the fourth Gospel develops into a sacramental theology; cf. D. M. Stanley, "Baptism in the New Testament," *Scripture* 8 (1956) 48–50.

[18] Cf. M.-J. Lagrange, *Evangile selon saint Marc* (2nd ed.; Paris, 1947) p. 292.

[19] This is exemplified in the Sower, Mt 13:4–8; the Cockle, Mt. 13:24–30; and the Dragnet, Mt 13:47–50.

[20] Examples of this are the Mustard Seed, Mt 13:31–32; the Leaven, Mt 13:33.

[21] Cf. Célestin Charlier, "La présence dans l'absence," *Bible et vie chrétienne,* fasc. 2 (1953) 61–75.

[22] This point is often neglected in modern treatises on Christology. Yet each of the Evangelists is at pains to note how thoroughly Jesus' sufferings and death destroyed the disciples' faith in His Messianic mission (cf. Mt 28:16; Lk 24:21; Mk 16:13–14; Jn 20:14–25). Thus it is *psychologically* implausible that the disciples had ever, even momentarily, during Jesus' public life pierced the mystery of His divinity. When one recalls that to make such a supernatural act of faith the gift of the Holy Spirit is required (cf. Jn 7:37–39), then it becomes *theologically* impossible. Cf. Pierre Benoit, "La divinité de Jésus dans les évangiles synoptiques," *Lumière et vie,* fasc. 9 (1953) 43–74; D. M. Stanley, "Etudes matthéennes: La confession de Pierre à Césarée," *Sciences ecclésiastiques* 6 (1954) 51–61; also *The Gospel of St. Matthew* (Collegeville, Minn., 1963) pp. 81 f.

[23] Cf. Mt 28:17; Lk 24:32, 45; Jn 20:29; 21:7.

[24] The significance of the notion of presence will be dealt with shortly in this article (i.e., as it formed part of the pentecostal experience of the disciples). It is vital to the theology of the Eucharist, of sanctifying grace, of the conception of the Church as the "Body of Christ."

[25] Cf. Pierre Benoit, "L'Ascension," *Revue biblique* 56 (1949) 161–203.

[26] Cf. Oscar Cullmann, *Christ et le temps* (Neuchâtel–Paris, 1947) pp. 57–65.

[27] This problem was destined to preside over the development of much of the later New Testament theology of salvation, as it became the main preoccupation of Christian thinkers towards the end of the first century. It is poignantly expressed under one of its aspects in a line from the pen

of a second-generation Christian: "Still, for the present, not yet do we perceive all subject to His sway" (Heb 2:8b).

[28] On the evidence of the New Testament, it is only after, and as a result of, the descent of the Spirit that the disciples are permitted to collaborate in Jesus' mission of *teaching,* an office which during His public life He seems to have reserved exclusively for Himself; cf. the study further on in this book, "*Didachē* As a Constitutive Element of the Written Gospel," pp. 199–213.

[29] These were in part the result of a lack of the proper terminology, in part also of insufficient theological reflection upon the data of revelation.

[30] Henceforth it is true to say that the forward-looking Jewish Messianism is replaced by a retrospective contemplation of the historical acts of salvation accomplished in Jesus Christ. Not that the first Christians displayed any nostalgia for "the good old days," but this attitude of Christian faith distinguishes the Christian outlook not only from the Judaism which refuses to acknowledge Jesus as the Messiah, but from all forms of pseudo Messianism (Gnosticism, Renaissance humanism, the *Aufklärung,* nineteenth-century liberalism, and Marxism).

[31] Cf. J. Schmitt, "Les sources et les thèmes de la naissante foi apostolique au Christ Sauveur," *Lumière et vie,* fasc. 15 (1955) 309.

[32] "Tongues as if of fire" accompanied by "a sound like that of a violent wind blowing" (Acts 2:2–3); by something analogous to an earthquake (Acts 4:31).

[33] Cf. J. de Baciocchi, "Comment reconnaître la personnalité du Saint-Esprit?" *Nouvelle revue théologique* 77 (1955) 1025–49.

[34] Another incident, whose primitive character is admitted by the most radical critics (cf. Philippe-H. Menoud, "La mort d'Ananias et de Saphira (Actes 5:1–11)," in *Aux sources de la tradition chrétienne,* pp. 146–54), also indicates this same consciousness. Peter denounces the double-dealing of Ananias and Sapphira as an act of lying to the Spirit (Acts 5:3, 9). It is impossible to lie to an impersonal force. The essential malice of such acts implies their necessary relation to some person.

[35] In the Old Testament, where undoubtedly Yahweh revealed Himself primarily as a personal God, it was precisely by similar phenomena, similar manifestation of God's acting, so to speak, person to person, that this revelation was brought home to Israel.

[36] Cf. C. Spicq, "L'Esprit-Saint, vie et force de l'église primitive," *Lumière et vie,* fasc. 10 (1953) 9–28.

[37] *Art. cit.* (n. 17 above) p. 52.

[38] This is evident from the citation Peter makes from Joel at Pentecost. In the second half of Jl 3:5 (omitted by Luke in his Acts account) we have mention made of the remnant: "everyone who invokes the Name of the Lord will be saved, for upon the mountain of Sion there will be *some who escape,* as Yahweh has declared, and in Jerusalem *some survivors* whom Yahweh will call."

[39] Cf. J. Schmitt, "L'Eglise de Jérusalem ou la 'restauration' d'Israël d'après les cinq premiers chapîtres des Actes," *Revue des sciences religieuses* 27 (1953) 209–18.

[40] The references to Deuteronomy in Acts beyond the first five chapters: 7:5 = Dt 2:5, 49; 7:14–15 = Dt 10:22; 7:37 = Dt 18:15, 18; 7:45 = Dt 32:39; 10:34 = Dt 10:17; 10:39 = Dt 21:22–23; 13:18 = Dt 1:31; 13:19 = Dt 7:1; 20:32 = Dt 33:3–4; 26:18 = Dt 33:3–4. In the Synoptics we find the following parallels: Mt 5:48 = Dt 18:13; Mt 18:16 = Dt 19:15; Mt 22:37 = Dt 6:5; Mk 12:29–30 = Dt 6:4; Mk 12:33 = Dt 6:5.

[41] The italicized words draw attention to the borrowings from the two texts above.

[42] This seems clear from Acts 10:41, where Peter states that God allowed the risen Christ to manifest Himself, "not to all the people, but to those witnesses previously chosen by God, namely to us. . . ."

[43] Cf. Acts 3:19–21, which makes the Parousia dependent or consequent upon Israel's conversion, not its cause.

[44] Cf. also 1 Pt 3:22.

[45] Thus the pentecostal address of Peter states that, "having been exalted to God's right hand and having received from the Father the promise of the Holy Spirit, He has poured out what you both see and hear" (Acts 2:33), and, after citing Ps 110, he immediately concludes: "Therefore let all the house of Israel know for certain that God has made Him *Kyrios* and Messiah, this Jesus whom you have crucified" (Acts 2:36). Here again it is the presence of the Spirit which specifies Christ's new relationship to His people. This time, however, it is Christ's sovereignty, rather than His function as sanctifier, which holds the center of the stage. Elsewhere in the primitive preaching the simple assertion of Christ's continuous reign in heaven (Acts 3:21) suffices to express the idea of His kingly and divine status. It is this insight which was dominant in the ecstasy of Stephen (Acts 7:55–56).

[46] For further details, cf. pp. 104–6 and pp. 346–351.

[47] J. Schmitt, *Jésus ressuscité dans la prédication apostolique* (Paris, 1949) p. 204, discusses this important Semitic point of view.

[48] The term "metahistorical" is employed to designate realities or events of the divine or supernatural order which also pertain to the historical order; in a word, it denotes some entry of the divine into human history.

[49] It still retains its negative function, however, of demonstrating that the supernatural truth in question is not incompatible with reason.

[50] St Thomas, *Sum. theol.* 3, 55, 5–6, has an excellent treatment of this problem in his discussion of the resurrection of Christ.

[51] Cf. Gaertner, *op. cit.*, pp. 73–169.

[52] Cf. R. A. F. MacKenzie, "The Concept of Biblical Theology," *Proceedings of the Tenth Annual Convention, Catholic Theological Society of America* (New York, 1955) pp. 48–73.

[53] It might be said that the first three chapters of 1 Cor deal principally with a clarification of this distinction. In rejecting the pretensions of Greek philosophy, Paul does not adopt an anti-intellectual position. Cf. 1 Cor 1:17, where *sophia logou* denotes not merely rhetorical skill but that philosophy which was its basis and which was employed, in Paul's day, in the service of a rationalist mode of thought which denied supernatural mystery, or (what comes to the same thing) claimed to *explain* the divine mystery in such a way as to take away its character as God's self-revelation. Paul's principle, underlying this whole discussion, is that the insufficiency of mere proof must be supplemented by testimony (cf. 1 Cor 2:4).

[54] Cf. Schmitt, "Les sources et les thèmes . . ." (n. 31 above) pp. 310–11.

[55] Accordingly, it is not surprising that it recurs with such frequency in Acts: 2:32; 3:15; 4:33; 5:32; 10:40; 13:23; 30–31; 17:3; 18:31; 22:18; 26:22–23.

[56] Acts 2:23; 3:12–15; 4:10, 27; 5:28, 30; 7:53; 10:39; 13:28–29; 1 Th 2:15.

[57] Cf. Schmitt, *op. cit.*, *Jésus ressuscité* . . . (n. 47 above) p. 21.

[58] Mark's Christology follows the same pattern: Jesus shares in the uniquely divine prerogative of forgiving sin (Mk 2:1–12), of lordship over the Sabbath (Mk 2:27–28), as well as over inanimate nature (Mk 4:35–41). It is to be noted that we accept the view that "Son of Man" in these texts was intended by Jesus as a reference to Himself.

[59] Cf. W. L. Knox, *The Acts of the Apostles* (Cambridge, 1948) p. 72: "The primary prophecy on which the Church relied was that of Is. liii."

[60] Cf. Schmitt, "Les sources et les thèmes . . ." (n. 31 above) pp. 326–29.

[61] The hymn in Phil 2:6–11 contains a clear reference to Christ's preexistence in the first strophe. Whether this conception goes back to its original composer, or Paul himself has interpolated this doctrine into the ode, is very difficult to decide.

[62] It is perhaps more correct to say that this theology of the Incarnation was elaborated earlier than the composition of the fourth Gospel, but within the Johannine sphere of influence. It is already evident in Heb 10:5–10, whose author was demonstrably a disciple of John (cf. C. Spicq, *L'Epître aux Hébreux* 1 [Paris, 1952] 109–38).

[63] Cf. P. Lestringant, *Essai sur l'unité de la révélation biblique* (Paris, 1942) p. 68, n. 2, and (for a more balanced view) M. Goguel, *Les premiers temps de l'église* (Neuchâtel–Paris, 1949) p. 54.

[64] As Paul will do in masterful fashion in his letter to Rome.

[65] Cf. A. Causse, "Le pèlerinage à Jérusalem et la première Pentecôte," *Revue d'histoire et de philosophie religieuses* 20 (1940) 120–41.

[66] Despite Luke's attempts to universalize the crowds which assemble to hear the message of salvation on the first Pentecost (cf. Acts 2:5–11), the subsequent events in his narrative (e.g., Acts 10:1—11:18) show that until the Spirit manifested His will one day at Antioch (Acts 13:1 ff.) the mission to the Gentiles remained a puzzle to the apostolic community.

[67] For the importance of this distinction between "teaching" and "preaching" in the New Testament, cf. pp. 200–212.

[68] Cf. Yves de Montcheuil, "Signification eschatologique du repas eucharistique," *Recherches des sciences religieuses* 33 (1946) 10–43.

The Concept of Biblical Inspiration

Editor's Note.—This was originally read as the principal paper at the Thirteenth Annual Convention (1958) of the Catholic Theological Society of America and appeared in the *Proceedings* of that Society (New York, 1959) pp. 65–89.

NOTES TO CHAPTER 3

[1] Paul Synave and Pierre Benoit, *La prophétie* (*Somme théologique*, ed. Revue des Jeunes; Paris, 1947). Benoit has further clarified his ideas on inspiration in Robert–Tricot, *Initiation biblique* (3rd ed.; Paris, 1954) pp. 6–54. Further refinements of his view will be found in "Note complémentaire sur l'inspiration," *Revue biblique* 63 (1956) 416–422.

[2] Joseph Coppens of Louvain criticized Benoit's presentation in his review of *Initiation biblique* in *Ephemerides theologicae Lovanienses* 31 (1955) 671–73; cf. also his "Chronica," *ibid.* 32 (1956) 715–16. He gives a fuller and more balanced view of his own opinion in "L'Inspiration et l'inerrance bibliques," *ibid.* 33 (1957) 36–37.

[3] Karl Rahner, "Uber die Schriftinspiration," *Zeitschrift für katholische Theologie* 78 (1956) 127–68. This great German Jesuit theologian completed his presentation of the subject in the monograph *Über die Schriftinspiration* (*Quaestiones disputatae* 1; Freiburg, 1958).

[4] Bernhard Brinkmann, "Inspiration und Kanonizität der Heiligen Schrift in ihrem Verhältnis zur Kirche," *Scholastik* 33 (1958) 208–33.

[5] R. A. F. MacKenzie, "Some Problems in the Field of Inspiration," *Catholic Biblical Quarterly* 20 (1958) 8.

[6] J. B. Franzelin, *Tractatus de divina traditione et scriptura* (3rd ed.; Rome, 1882); cf. G. Courtade, "J. B. Franzelin: Les formules que le magistère de l'église lui a empruntées," *Recherches de science religieuse* 40 (1952) 317–25; also M.-J. Lagrange, "L'Inspiration des Livres saints," *Revue biblique* 5 (1896) 199–220; "L'Inspiration et les exigences de la critique," *ibid.*, pp. 496–518; "Une pensée de saint Thomas sur l'inspiration scripturaire," *ibid.* 4 (1895) 563–71; and his famous book *La méthode historique* (Paris, 1903).

[7] Célestin Charlier, "Méthode historique et lecture spirituelle des écritures," *Bible et vie chrétienne,* 18 (1957) 7–26.

[8] Cf. *ibid.,* pp. 10–11.

[9] *Ibid.,* p. 12: "Or la Bible appartient de toute évidence à un monde dont le génie humain est profondément différent du nôtre. La méconnaissance de ce génie propre est à l'origine des fantaisies rationalistes autant que des pusillanimités apologétiques."

[10] On this point cf. the remarks of Gregory Dix, "The Conflict of the Syriac and Greek Cultures," in *Jew and Greek* (London, 1953) pp. 1–18.—Liberal critics like Holtzmann, Beyschlag, Weiss, etc., produced books on comparative religion, apparently under the impression that they were writing biblical theology.

[11] The excellent studies by M.-J. Lagrange on each of the four Gospels are mainly apologetic in their orientation. Nowhere in the scholarly introductions to these volumes does one find anything like a really theological treatment of the religious message of the Evangelists.

[12] The theological thinking of some fifty or more years ago was conditioned by contemporary polemics and by the rather limited scientific knowledge of the period. It was probably something of the sort which Pierre Benoit was endeavoring to suggest when, after admitting Cardinal Franzelin's influence on the formulation of the statements by the First Vatican Council and by Leo XIII's *Providentissimus Deus,* he dubbed the Franzelin theory "une côte mal taillée" (*Initiation biblique,* 3rd ed., p. 13). Coppens criticized Benoit's remarks, insinuating (he subsequently withdrew the somewhat unfair charge) that they were an attack on the doctrinal affirmations of the magisterium. With this in mind, it is interesting to recall Coppens' remark in his own later article, already referred to: "Au reste, quel mal y aurait-il à mettre en lumière le caractère encore imparfait de la notion léonine d'inspiration et inerrance?" (*Ephemerides theologicae Lovanienses* 33 [1957] 39).

[13] Cf. Charlier, *art. cit.,* p. 14.

[14] For it was primarily interested in the presentation of reality and in testimony, rather than in the analysis of reality or in demonstrative proof. Cf. Austin Farrer, *A Rebirth of Images* (London, 1949) p. 19.

[15] Charlier, *art. cit.,* p. 16.

[16] *Ibid.* If we are to evaluate properly God's authorship of the Bible, we must set this divine activity into its context, which is God's particular providence over the history of the ancient Near East. In this way we can

do justice to what R. A. F. MacKenzie has called "the multiplicity of inspiration," by realizing that our sacred books are the product of an inspired tradition extending, for the Old Testament at least, over several centuries. John L. McKenzie has written a masterly article on this aspect of our topic: "The Social Character of Inspiration," *Catholic Biblical Quarterly* 24 (1962) 115–24.

[17] Cf. Benoit, *art. cit.* (n. 1 above), *Revue biblique* 63 (1956) 421.—I say "the spiritual sense" as understood in patristic exegesis, which recognized in the salvation history of the Bible the human expression of God's direction of history. To put it another way: the Fathers regarded the scriptural word as essentially related to the *Heilsereignis*, of which it was the infallible interpretation. Thus, "spiritual" in patristic thought is not opposed to "material"; it denotes that principle which orientates the whole man and all human history to the Spirit of God. Predicated of the sense of Scripture, it no more meant a slice of the biblical meaning in contradistinction to the "literal" sense than "spiritual" applied to man denoted for the Fathers a slice merely of human nature.

[18] *Enchiridion biblicum* (2nd ed.; Rome–Naples, 1954) no. 559.

[19] Cf. MacKenzie, *art. cit.* (n. 5 above) pp. 2, 4.

[20] The same holds good to a certain extent for the prophetic writings, the Petrine and Pauline letters, and the Gospel of Matthew, all of which have been aggregated to the biblical canon by the recognition of their *auctoritas* on the part of the synagogue or the Church.

[21] Cf. the view of C. Spicq regarding the question of Paul's authorship of Hebrews: *L'Epître aux Hébreux* 1 (Paris, 1952) 169–219.—"There were schools of writers, made up of disciples, in a wide sense, of great men; these successive generations of followers were consciously continuing the work of their respective masters, and so put their compositions under the master's name" (MacKenzie, *art. cit.*, p. 8).

[22] Cf. A. Barucq and H. Cazelles, "Les Livres inspirés," in *Introduction à la Bible* 1 (Tournai, 1957) 11.

[23] *Enchiridion biblicum*, no. 30.

[24] *Ibid.*, no. 40.

[25] A. Bea, "Deus auctor sacrae scripturae: Herkunft und Bedeutung der Formel," *Angelicum* 20 (1943) 16–31.

[26] Rahner, *art. cit.* (n. 3 above) p. 139, n. 1.

[27] *Ibid.*: "Wir lassen es also auch dahingestellt, ob die seit Franzelin übliche Betonung, dass es sich um einen literarischen Verfasser handle

und dieser Begriff mehr und Genaueres sage als irgendeine Urheberschaft (z.B. autoritativer Art) auch gegenüber einem Buch, nur eine Explikation des Dogmas von Gott als dem Urheber der Schrift ist, oder darüber hinaus etwas besagt, was nicht einfach als definiert gelten kann."

[28] *Ibid.*, p. 141, n. 5.

[29] Cf. Jean Levie, *The Bible: Word of God in Words of Men* (New York, 1961); G. Dejaifve, "Bible, tradition, magistère dans la théologie catholique," *Nouvelle revue théologique* 78 (1956) 135–51; Hans Urs von Balthasar, "Scripture as the Word of God," *Downside Review* 68 (1950) 1–20.

[30] Charlier, *art. cit.*, p. 22, puts the same idea in a different way: "Tout évènement dans l'écriture est Parole et toute parole rapporte l'Évènement. Ce que les Pères de l'Église, ce que la liturgie cherchent dans la Bible, c'est la marque tangible du fait essentiel, de l'évènement fondamental de l'Histoire, l'entrée de Dieu dans le monde, sa révélation aux hommes dans l'espace et le temps."

[31] Cf. J. de Fraine, "L'Encyclique 'Humani generis' et les erreurs concernant la sainte Ecriture," *Sciences ecclésiastiques* 5 (1953) 8–10.

[32] This being our Western view of truth, it is not to be wondered at that our treatises on scriptural inspiration treat of the inerrancy of the Bible as its principal (often, it would seem, its sole) effect. Scriptural inerrancy means for us a quality which is simply and solely intellectual.

[33] Not without reason has Pius XII bidden the would-be interpreter "go back in spirit to those far-off centuries of the East" (*Enchiridion biblicum*, no. 558).

[34] Pierre Benoit's first contribution to the subject took the form of a monograph on the Thomistic doctrine concerning prophecy and scriptural inspiration, which was appended to his re-editing of the late Paul Synave's commentary on the questions in the *Summa theologica* which treat of prophecy. We might add that this treatise deserves to rank very high among the classical works on scriptural inspiration.

[35] He remains, says Benoit, dependent like the pupil whose statements rest, consciously or unconsciously, upon the superior knowledge of the teacher.

[36] Karl Rahner criticized this description of the writer's instrumental activity, remarking that Benoit has not made it clear just why inspiration does not reduce the human author to the rank of secretary; cf. *art. cit.* (n. 3 above) p. 141, n. 5.

[37] Benoit accuses Franzelin's theory of being a compromise between the old and the new outlook, since in effect the Cardinal retained the dictation theory for the ideas, while abandoning it as far as the words were concerned; cf. *art. cit., Initiation biblique* (n. 1 above) p. 13.

[38] Benoit, *art. cit., Revue biblique* (n. 1 above) p. 420, n. 2; also *art. cit., Initiation biblique* (n. 1 above) p. 39.

[39] It is to be noted that for Benoit inspiration extends analogously to certain versions of the Bible, specifically the Septuagint; cf. "La Septante, est-elle inspirée?" in *Vom Wort des Lebens: Festschrift für Max Meinertz* (Münster, 1951) pp. 41–49; also Paul Auvray, "Comment se pose le problème de l'inspiration de la Septante?" *Revue biblique* 59 (1952) 321–36.

[40] Benoit subsequently adopted the term "énoncé"; cf. *art. cit., Revue biblique* (n. 1 above) p. 419, n. 1.

[41] Coppens believes Benoit to have come close to Newman's system, although he admits that *Divino afflante Spiritu* had anticipated Benoit's restriction of the "domain guaranteed by inerrancy," and he admits the real differences between Benoit's and Newman's positions. Coppens objects to the expression "objectively religious and supernatural truths" as equivocal; cf. *Ephemerides theologicae Lovanienses* 31 (1955) 673.

[42] Coppens, *art. cit., Ephemerides theologicae Lovanienses* (n. 2 above) 33 (1957) pp. 36–57.

[43] *Ibid.*, pp. 44–45.

[44] *Ibid.*, pp. 45–46.

[45] *Ibid.*, p. 44. I might add that Coppens' summary of points on inspiration which he feels are more or less settled today is worth a little study; cf. *ibid.*, pp. 52–55.

[46] Cf. also the essay by Rahner, "Zur Frage der Dogmenentwicklung," in *Schriften zur Theologie* 1 (Einsiedeln, 1954) pp. 49–90. This may also be read in English: "The Development of Dogma," in *Theological Investigations* 1 (Baltimore, 1961) 39–77.

[47] Rahner, *art. cit.* (n. 3 above) p. 158.

[48] Since the *Heilsgeschichte* is "God's own history," as Rahner (*ibid.*, p. 151) calls it, it is willed by Him in a more absolute manner than profane history. Hence God is Author of the Church in a more intimate way than of other things of which he is the transcendent cause. The historical divine activity which we call *Heilsgeschichte* reaches its climax in Jesus Christ and the Church. Before Christ entered human history, God's

dialogue with man had not received its definitive pattern. Whether it would issue in a judgment or in grace was not yet finally determined: the objective realization of the divine activity bore the possibility of being voided. The divine imperative of the positive Mosaic legislation contained from the beginning the potency to be abolished. It is only the character of the Old Testament as the prehistory of Jesus Christ and the Church which remains as permanent.

49 For a fuller discussion of this point, cf. the essay "The New Testament Doctrine of Baptism," in this volume, pp. 140–194.

50 Cf. the essay "Kingdom to Church," reprinted in this volume, pp. 5–37.

51 To deny this would be to deny any real authorship to the New Testament hagiographers and reduce them to mere mouthpieces of a heavenly message already "prefabricated." It would also be to deny an essential characteristic of the New Testament books: they are a manifestation of the faith of the authors and not only an epiphany of the divine Mystery in Jesus Christ.

52 Rahner, *art. cit.* (n. 3 above) p. 152.

53 *Ibid.*, p. 161, n. 28.

54 Most theologians are ready to admit, with Cardinal Bea, that "how and to whom this first revelation was made, we simply do not know"; cf. Rahner, *ibid.*, p. 163, n. 32.

55 Brinkmann, *art. cit.* (n. 4 above). The twelve-point *Zusammenfassung* at the conclusion of the article will be found very useful.

56 Franzelin, Pesch, Bea, Tromp, and Benoit all insist on an explicit revelation for inspiration and canonicity to be known, while Lagrange, Dewailly, and others hold this twofold fact to have been revealed by way of a theological conclusion (*conclusio theologica*), i.e., with the aid of reason.

57 Brinkmann, *art. cit.*, p. 209.

58 Jesus' teaching on the character of the apostolic office, and still more the pentecostal experience of the disciples, made it clear that, whether they spoke or wrote, the apostles were governed, in the exercise of their divinely conferred functions, by the Holy Spirit Himself.

59 Again, it is (so Brinkmann) theoretically possible that the Church could still accept as canonical some apostolic book, lost for centuries and then recovered, if it could be proven to be certainly authentic (i.e., of apostolic origin).

[60] How else explain the long hesitation on the part of the Church in accepting Hebrews into the New Testament canon, or the nonacceptance by the Church of that earlier Pauline letter to Corinth (1 Cor 5:9), or the final rejection by the Church (after a certain hesitant acceptance) of *1 Clement*, the *Epistle of Barnabas*, and the *Shepherd* of Hermas?

[61] There is perhaps still too much insistence in apologetics manuals upon the simple character (i.e., untheological) of the accounts by eyewitnesses found in the Synoptic Gospels.

[62] For an excellent discussion of the nature of Jesus' resurrection, cf. W. Grossouw, "Verrijzenis van Jesus Christus," *Bijbels Woordenboek* (2nd ed.; Roermond en Maaseik, 1954–57) col. 1777.

[63] R. A. F. MacKenzie, "The Concept of Biblical Theology," *Proceedings of the Tenth Annual Convention, Catholic Theological Society of America* (New York, 1955) p. 61, n. 14.

[64] Karl Rahner has hinted in what sense the Old Testament might be included in his theory as part of the prehistory of the Church; *art. cit.* (n. 3 above) pp. 146, n. 13, and 151, n. 17. He devotes a section of his monograph *Über die Schriftinspiration* (n. 3 above) to a discussion of this interesting question.

[65] The early Church acknowledged that word and pen were complementary media of the exercise of the apostolic office; cf. Eusebius, *Ecclesiastical History* 3, 37, 2. Since the preaching of the gospel had been entrusted to the apostles as a group, the Church sought the unique "gospel of God" in those writings which were endowed with *auctoritas apostolica*, since they were normative for the People of God; cf. Irenaeus (in *Patrologia graeca* 7, 803). Thus Irenaeus points out that Luke's Gospel was simply a written record of the preaching of Paul (*PG* 7, 845), and Papias asserts that Mark carefully reported the kerygma of Peter (Eusebius, *Ecclesiastical History* 3, 39, 15).

[66] Cf. 1 Cor 15:3; 11:23; Gal 1:6–9; Luke 1:1–2.—Many other questions in this area still beg to be discussed and solved: What relation does inspiration bear to the various senses of Scripture—in particular, to the "spiritual" and to the "fuller" senses? While theologians state that "revelation was closed with the apostles," why do we never find the assertion "inspiration was closed with the apostles"? Indeed, as G. Bardy points out, it appears that there was a rather consistent belief among the Fathers of the Church that each of them was inspired; cf. "L'Inspiration des Pères de l'église," *Recherches de science religieuse* 40 (1951–52) 7–26.

Carmenque Christo Quasi Deo Dicere

EDITOR'S NOTE.—This study originally appeared in the *Catholic Biblical Quarterly* (1958) 173–91.

NOTES TO CHAPTER 4

[1] The verb *ainein* which is found here is employed by the LXX to translate *halal*, the most common biblical meaning of which seems to be "to praise (God) in song." Cf. H. Schlier, *Theologisches Wörterbuch zum Neuen Testament* 1, 176.

[2] *Ibid.*, p. 164.

[3] For some evidence of this in the New Testament, cf. the study of 1 Pt 1:3–5 by M.-E. Boismard, "Une liturgie baptismale dans la Prima Petri," *Revue biblique* 63 (1956) 182–208; 64 (1957) 161–83.

[4] The phrase *logos tou Kyriou* (*tou Theou*) designates the kerygma; cf. Acts 8:25; 13:5; 15:36; 2 Cor 2:17; Phil 1:14; 1 Th 1:8; 2 Th 3:1.

[5] H. Schlier, *art. cit.*, pp. 164–65: "Das geistliche Lied der Kirche ist das im Kultus in der Form wechselseitigen und gegenseitigen Zuspruches laut werdende Wort Christi. In diesem Sinn erfüllt es die Gemeinde mit Geist."

[6] There is somewhat of a parallel with the Psalms: those in praise of God's saving activity, which commemorate the *mirabilia Dei* or *gesta Dei*, are hymns to God no less than those in which God is directly addressed.

[7] *Epistularum liber* 10, 96.

[8] The term *depositum* reminds us of the use of *parathēkē* in 1 Tim 6:20, and its meaning is probably similar.

[9] Alfons Kurfess, "Plinius und der urchristliche Gottesdienst," *Zeitschrift für neutestamentliche Wissenschaft* 35 (1936) 295–98.

[10] *Ibid.*, p. 297.

[11] Balthasar Fischer, "Le Christ dans les psaumes," *Maison-Dieu* 27 (1951) 88.

[12] For other examples of New Testament hymns, cf. H. Leclercq, "Hymnes," *Dictionnaire d'archéologie chrétienne et de liturgie* 6, 2826–2928.

[13] For evidence of this, cf. Mt 28:16; Lk 24:21; Mk 16:13–14.

[14] Cf. "Salvation in the Primitive Preaching," reprinted in this volume, pp. 38–66.

[15] Joseph Schmitt, *Jésus ressuscité dans la prédication apostolique* (Paris, 1949) p. 202.

[16] *Ibid.*, p. 175, where a splendid description of this process is given.

[17] Cf. Vincent Taylor, *The Gospel according to St. Mark* (London, 1952) pp. 444–46.

[18] Cf. "Paul and the Christian Concept of the Servant of God," reprinted in this volume, pp. 312–51.

[19] Oscar Cullmann, *Die Christologie des Neuen Testaments* (Tübingen, 1957) pp. 50–81: "Jesus der leidende Gottesknecht."

[20] This latter title is often given to Yahweh in the Old Testament: Zeph 3:15; Za 9:9; 14:9; Mal 1:14; Is 32:1; 33:22; 41:21; 44:6; 52:7.

[21] The Servant theology appears to have been developed largely in the Palestinian Christian communities.

[22] Cf. Pierre Benoit, *Les épîtres de la captivité* (Paris, 1949) pp. 18–19.

[23] L. Cerfaux, *Le Christ dans la théologie de saint Paul* (Paris, 1951) pp. 288–98.

[24] Cf. the LXX version of Is 53:11, where the Servant is called *dikaios* and *eu douleuonta.*

[25] Cerfaux, *op. cit.*, p. 296.

[26] Cf., e.g., Paul Henry, "Kénose," *Dictionnaire de la Bible: Supplément* 5, 35.

[27] To appreciate the somewhat amazing character of this revelation, it is sufficient to read over Peter's pentecostal sermon (Acts 2:22–36), where he speaks of "Jesus . . . a man accredited to you by Yahweh . . . having been exalted to God's right hand and having received from the Father the promise of the Holy Spirit, He has poured out what you both see and hear. . . . God has made Him *Kyrios* and Messiah, this Jesus whom you have crucified."

[28] Cf. Rom 10:9; 1 Cor 12:3.

[29] Cf. Schmitt, *op. cit.*, pp. 199 ff.

[30] L. Cerfaux and J. Cambier, "*L'Apocalypse de saint Jean lue aux chrétiens* (Paris, 1955) p. 53.

[31] Cf. Johannes Behm, "*Kainos,*" *Theologisches Wörterbuch zum Neuen Testament* 3, 450–52.

[32] H.-M. Féret, *L'Apocalypse de saint Jean* (Paris, 1943) pp. 111 ff.

[33] Cerfaux–Cambier, *op. cit.*, p. 52.

[34] *Ibid.*, p. 135.

[35] Acts 2:33; 5:31; 7:56; Rom 8:34; 1 Cor 15:25 ff.; Eph 1:20; Col 3:1; 1 Pt 3:22, etc.

[36] Cf. "The New Testament Doctrine of Baptism," reprinted in this volume, pp. 140–194.

[37] Cf. Ceslaus Spicq, *L'Epître aux Hébreux* 2, 23.

[38] Cerfaux, *op. cit.*, p. 282.

[39] This suggests that the hymn, possibly of Ephesian origin, is inspired by the Christology of St. John, as exposed in the fourth Gospel. There the definitive revelation of the "glory" of Jesus Christ takes place through His passion, death, and resurrection.

[40] In other words, this is the opening of the era of salvation through the Church, which will continue until Christ's parousia, anticipated here by the use of the term "glory."

[41] The verse continues, "for you who through faith are fenced about with God's power." I have followed Boismard in his opinion that these words did not belong to the original hymn; cf. *art. cit.*, *Revue biblique* 63 (1956) 188–90.

[42] For one of the more recent defenders of this idea, cf. Ernst Käsemann, "Eine urchristliche Taufliturgie," in *Festschrift Rudolf Bultmann zum 65. Geburtstag überreicht* (Stuttgart–Cologne, 1949) pp. 133–48.

[43] This is the position adopted by J. Bonsirven, *L'Evangile de Paul* (Paris, 1948) pp. 86–88. I may add that it is not a common view among Catholic exegetes.

[44] Cf. Cerfaux, *op. cit.*, p. 298.

[45] Cf. Bonsirven, *op. cit.*, p. 88.

[46] Here we have the whole dispute about the meaning of *plērōma* in this passage. The interpretation given is adopted from Benoit, *op. cit.*, p. 56, note *e*.

[47] While it is impossible to prove the point apodictically, there is perhaps an indication that the hymn originally existed in two forms, one Palestinian and Semitizing, the other Hellenistic. The indication is to be found in vv. 12–13, which as they stand in the Gospel are almost certainly a conflation of two texts. Cf. M.-E. Boismard, *Le prologue de saint Jean* (Paris, 1953) pp. 54 ff.

[48] *Ibid.*, pp. 99 ff.

[49] The fourth Gospel lays great stress on the mission of Jesus Christ and describes Him most frequently as "coming into the world" (Jn 1:9; 3:19; 9:39; 12:46; 4:25; 6:14; 11:27; 16:28; 18:37). It also presents His work of salvation as an "elevation" or "lifting up" by the Cross and through His ascension, which constitute His passing to the Father (Jn 13:1, 3).

Liturgical Influences on the Formation of the Gospels

Editor's Note.—This essay, originally read at the first biblical session of the North American Liturgical Week in Cincinnati, August 18–22, 1958, was afterwards published in the *Catholic Biblical Quarterly* 21 (1959) 24–38.

NOTES TO CHAPTER 5

[1] Cf. Vincent Taylor, *The Formation of the Gospel Tradition* (2nd ed.; London, 1949) p. 12.

[2] Papias' statement is cited in Eusebius, *Hist. eccl.* 3, 39, 15, while that of Irenaeus may be found in *PG* 7, 845.

[3] Cf. "*Didachē* As a Constitutive Element of the Written Gospel," reprinted in this volume, pp. 199–213.

[4] Taylor, *op. cit.*, p. 16.

[5] S. Lyonnet, "La 'koinōnia' de l'église primitive et la sainte Eucharistie," *Actas del XXXV Congreso Eucarístico Internacional, Barcelona 1952*, Sesiones de Estudio 1, 511–15.

[6] Cf. the essay "*Didachē*" (n. 3 above).

[7] Augustin Bea, "The Pastoral Value of the Word of God in the Sacred Liturgy," in *The Assisi Papers* (Collegeville, 1957) p. 76.

[8] *Ibid.*, p. 77.

[9] Taylor, *op. cit.*, pp. 44 ff.

[10] Cf. "Carmenque Christo quasi Deo Dicere," reprinted in this volume, pp. 95–118.

[11] Cf., e.g., the opinion expressed by Pierre Benoit, *L'Evangile selon saint Matthieu* (Paris, 1950) p. 164: "Il n'est pas impossible que cette formule se ressente, dans sa précision, de l'usage liturgique établi plus tard dans la communauté primitive."

[12] Cf. Pierre Benoit, "Le récit de la Cène dans Lc XXII, 15–20: Etude de critique textuelle et littéraire," *Revue biblique* 48 (1939) 357–93.

[13] *Ibid.*, pp 384–86.

[14] Cf. Oscar Cullmann, *Baptism in the New Testament* (London, 1950) pp. 71–80.

[15] *Ibid.*, p. 78.

[16] Cf. "The New Testament Doctrine of Baptism," reprinted in this volume, pp. 140–194.

[17] Jesus' main purpose in citing these stories, of course, was to predict the vocation of the pagans to the Christian faith.

[18] Cf. Jean Daniélou, *Bible et liturgie* (Paris, 1951) pp. 151 ff.

[19] Oscar Cullmann, *Les sacrements dans l'évangile johannique* (Paris, 1951) pp. 25–28. Cf. also Bruce Vawter, "The Johannine Sacramentary," *Theological Studies* 17 (1956) 151–66; Raymond E. Brown, "The Johannine Sacramentary Reconsidered," *ibid.* 23 (1962) 183–206.

[20] D. M. Stanley, "Cana as Epiphany," *Worship* 32 (1958) 83–89. On the symbolism of the washing of feet, cf. E. C. Hoskyns, *The Fourth Gospel* (2nd ed.; London, 1948) pp. 436 ff.

[21] Hoskyns, *op. cit.*, pp. 532 ff.

[22] Vawter, *art. cit.*, pp. 151–66.

[23] *Ibid.*, p. 164.

[24] Benoit, *art. cit.*, has presented this impressionistic quality of Luke's account of the institution of the Eucharist.

[25] Note the use made of the liturgical motifs from the feast of Tabernacles in Ap 7:9–10 to describe the happiness in heaven of the Christian martyrs.

[26] Jean Daniélou, "Le quatre-temps de septembre et la fête des tabernacles," *Maison-Dieu* 46 (1956) 114–36.

[27] Daniélou also notes that in Za 14:4, 8, 16, 18 the Messianic age is depicted in terms of the feast of Tabernacles. Now it is a citation from this prophet (Za 9:9) which gives Jesus' triumphal entry into Jerusalem its Messianic significance (Mt 21:5; Jn 12:15).

[28] Daniélou, *art. cit.*, p. 118.

[29] René Laurentin, *Structure et théologie de Luc* I–II (Paris, 1957), pp. 103 ff. It is also to be observed that only in these two chapters do we have examples of hymns which may have been liturgical in origin (Magnificat, Benedictus, Nunc Dimittis). Nowhere else in the four Gospels are hymns to be found, except the prologue to St. John's Gospel.

[30] Cf. Donatien Mollat, *Evangile de saint Jean* (Paris, 1953) pp. 32–36.

[31] Cf. Karl Rahner, "Über die Schriftinspiration," *Zeitschrift für katholische Theologie* 78 (1956) 137–68.

The New Testament Doctrine of Baptism

EDITOR'S NOTE.—This originally appeared in *Theological Studies* 18 (1957) 169–215.

NOTES TO CHAPTER 6

[1] Ceslaus Spicq, *L'Epître aux Hébreux* 2 (Paris, 1953) 372.

[2] Cf. "Salvation in the Primitive Preaching," reprinted in this volume, pp. 38–66.

[3] Cf. Rudolf Bultmann, "Neues Testament und Mythologie," in H. W. Bartsch (ed.), *Kerygma und Mythos* 1 (Hamburg, 1951).

[4] L. Malevez, *Le message chrétien et le mythe* (Brussels–Bruges–Paris, 1954) p. 116.

[5] Cf. the passage from the rule of the Qumrân community (1 QS 8:12–16), tr. Millar Burrows, *The Dead Sea Scrolls* (New York, 1955) p. 382: "When these things come to pass for the community in Israel, by these regulations they shall be separated from the midst of the session of the men of error to go to the wilderness to prepare there the way of the Lord; as it is written, 'In the wilderness prepare the way of the Lord; make straight in the desert a highway for our God.' This is the study of the law, as he commanded through Moses, to do according to all that has been revealed from time to time, and as the prophets revealed by his Holy Spirit."

[6] The silence of the Evangelists concerning John's utterances about the observance of the law is, we believe, highly significant.

[7] Joseph Schmitt, "Les écrits du Nouveau Testament et les textes de Qumran," *Revue des sciences religieuses* 30 (1956) 55–74.

[8] "For my people have committed two crimes:
They have forsaken me, the fountain of living water,
To hew for themselves cisterns, broken cisterns,
That can hold no water."

[9] C. Lattey, "A Note on John VII. 37–8," *Scripture* 6 (1954) 151–53.

[10] Cf. "*Didachē* As a Constitutive Element of the Written Gospel," reprinted in this volume, pp. 199–213.

[11] The Infancy narratives of Mt and Lk may serve as an example of this.

[12] Thus Christ had to repeat in His earthly life the experiences of Israel as a people (cf. Jesus' temptations, Mt 4:1–11) as well as those of the great Old Testament figures (hence His characterization as the new Moses, new David, new Isaac, etc.).

[13] Jacques Guillet, *Thèmes bibliques* (Paris, 1951) p. 21.

[14] Thomas Aquinas, *Quodl.* 7, q. 6, a. 16 c; *Sum. theol.* 1, q. 1, a. 10.

[15] Hence an investigation of contemporary Jewish ablutional practices, e.g., those of the Qumrân community, will not help towards an understanding of the meaning of the Christian sacrament of baptism.

[16] D. M. Stanley, "Baptism in the New Testament," *Scripture* 8 (1956) 46.

[17] This is particularly true of the sacramental teaching in the fourth Gospel.

[18] Cf. the illuminating article by L. Bouyer, "Le symbolisme des rites baptismaux," *Maison-Dieu* 32 (1952) especially p. 15. He here points out what he calls a "capital distinction" concerning baptismal symbolism. While it is certainly natural symbolism (Christ was merely using water as symbol of initiation because, for the human mind, there is a real connection between water and life given by the mother), still a new significance has been superimposed upon this natural symbolism by the word of Christ. It now becomes a plunging into Jesus' own death in order to come forth possessed of His risen life. It is thus, he concludes, that the Word of God, both in the Bible as a whole and in the living tradition of the Church, reveals to us not only the material world and the body, but the spirit in the body and the invisible world beneath the visible creation.

[19] Thus, for instance, in the Johannine paragraph on the imparting of the power to forgive sins (Jn 20:19–23), the use of the verb *enephysēsen* is a literary reference to Gn 2:7; this work of the risen Christ is presented by the Evangelist as a "new creation."

[20] The miracle of the multiplication of the loaves plays an important role here; cf. Jn 6:26.

[21] This refashioning of the logia of Jesus, as found in the Synoptics, is characteristic of John's manner. In this same discourse we find similar references to the Synoptic accounts of Jesus' visit to Nazareth (Jn 6:42) and to Peter's profession of loyalty at Caesarea Philippi (Jn 6:68–69).

[22] This appears to be the meaning of this difficult section. The mention of Jesus' exaltation as the necessary preliminary to the gift of the Spirit (Jn 7:39) shows that John is well aware that the Eucharist is the sacrament of the glorified Christ in which He bestows the "life-giving Spirit." To think, as the Jews are here doing, of the Eucharist in terms of Jesus' mortal *sarx*, "profits nothing": such absence of faith renders a man incapable of receiving the sacramental doctrine of this Gospel.

[23] Cf. that of M.-J. Lagrange, *Evangile selon saint Jean* (7th ed.; Paris, 1948) pp. 171–96.

[24] J. van der Ploeg, "Old Testament Signs," *Scripture* 8 (1956) 33–44.

[25] Franz J. Leenhardt, "La signification de la notion de parole dans la pensée chrétienne," *Revue d'histoire et de philosophie religieuses* 35 (1955) 263–73.

[26] Cf. A. Humbert, "Le problème des sources théologiques au XVI° siècle," *Revue des sciences philosophiques et théologiques* 1 (1907) 90–91.

[27] Thus, for instance, J. Bellamy, "Baptême dans la sainte écriture," *Dictionnaire de théologie catholique* 2, 169; and A. d'Alès, "Baptême," *Dictionnaire de la Bible: Supplément* 1, 858, remarks that since Augustine, who held that the apostles administered Christian baptism before the Passion, this has become common theological opinion!

[28] Austin Farrer, *A Rebirth of Images* (Westminster, 1949) p. 15.

[29] Gerhard von Rad, *Das erste Buch Mose: Kap. 1–12/9* (2nd ed.; Göttingen, 1950) p. 34.

[30] C. R. North, *The Thought of the Old Testament* (London, 1948) pp. 25–26.

[31] R. A. F. MacKenzie, "Before Abraham was . . . ," *Catholic Biblical Quarterly* 15 (1953) 131–40.

[32] Gösta Lindeskog, *Studien zum neutestamentlichen Schöpfungsgedanken* 1 (Uppsala, 1952) 203.

[33] *Ibid.* 1, 236, 251.

[34] The aorist tense employed in the participles *apekdysamenoi* and *endysamenoi* shows that Paul is thinking of the single, past act of receiving baptism.

[35] On the characteristically Christian idea of newness expressed in the New Testament by *kainos* and its compounds, cf. Johannes Behm, "*Kainos*," *Theologisches Wörterbuch zum Neuen Testament* 3, 450–56.

[36] This apologetic interest appears in the author's omission of the names

for sun, moon, and stars, revered as deities in the cultures surrounding Israel.

[37] Vincent Taylor, *The Gospel according to St. Mark* (London, 1952) p. 164.

[38] Ap 22:1–2; Ez 47:1, 7.

[39] E.-B. Allo, *L'Apocalypse* (14th ed.; Paris, 1933) p. 353.

[40] I have followed the distinction of sources given by R. de Vaux, *Génèse* (Paris, 1951) p. 57.

[41] E. G. Selwyn, *The First Epistle of St. Peter* (London, 1949) pp. 333–34; Jean Daniélou, *Sacramentum futuri* (Paris, 1950) pp. 55–68.

[42] A. Feuillet, "La synthèse eschatologique de saint Matthieu," *Revue biblique* 56 (1949) 340–64; 57 (1950) 62–91, 180-211.

[43] This same letter contains a very interesting, though tantalizingly obscure reference to the role of water as instrument of the creation of the universe: 2 Pt 3:5.

[44] Paul Démann, "La signification d'Abraham dans la perspective du Nouveau Testament," *Cahiers Sioniens* 5 (1951) no. 2, 44–67.

[45] S. Lyonnet, *Les épîtres de saint Paul aux Galates, aux Romains* (Paris, 1953) p. 31.

[46] A. Grail, "Le baptême dans l'épître aux Galates III, 26–IV, 7," *Revue biblique* 58 (1951) 503–20.

[47] Yet it is difficult to see how Masson can conclude to the practice of circumcision by the Colossians on the evidence provided by this verse; cf. Charles Masson, *L'Epître de saint Paul aux Colossiens* (*Commentaire du Nouveau Testament* 10; Neuchâtel-Paris, 1950) p. 125.

[48] "He spread out a cloud as a screen,/And fire to give light by night."

[49] Guillet, *op. cit.*, pp. 22–23.

[50] C. Spicq, *L'Epître aux Hébreux* 1 (Paris, 1952) 269–80.

[51] *Ibid.* 2 (Paris, 1953) 78.

[52] *Ibid.* 2, 317.

[53] Louis Bouyer, *Le quatrième évangile* (2nd ed.; Tournai–Paris, 1955) p. 31.

[54] E. C. Hoskyns, *The Fourth Gospel* (2nd ed.; London, 1948) p. 394.

[55] A book, to which unfortunately I have not had access, defends this typology: Harald Sahlin, *Zur Typologie des Johannesevangeliums* (Uppsala, 1950).

[56] Jean Daniélou, *Bible et liturgie* (2nd ed.; Paris, 1951) pp. 136–44.

[57] Burkhard Neunheuser, *Taufe und Firmung* (*Handbuch der Dog-*

mengeschichte, ed. Schmaus–Geiselmann–Grillmeier, 4/2; Freiburg, 1956) p. 2.

58 G. F. Moore, *Judaism* 1 (Cambridge, 1927) 334.

59 The sobriquet "Baptist" is applied to John only by Matthew and Luke; Mark and John simply apply to him the participle *baptizōn,* as a general rule.

60 Schmitt, *art. cit.* (n. 7 above).

61 1 QS 4, 18–21, tr. Millar Burrows, *op. cit.* (n. 5 above) pp. 375 ff.: "But God in the mysteries of his understanding . . . has ordained a period for the ruin of error. . . . And then God will refine in his truth all the deeds of a man . . . cleansing him with a Holy Spirit from all wicked deeds. And he will sprinkle upon him a Spirit of Truth, like water for impurity."

62 H. Houbaut, "Jean-Baptiste (Baptême de saint)," *Dictionnaire de théologie catholique* 8, 653–55. We shall point out the misconception in this proposition further on in our study.

63 Albert Descamps, *Les justes et la justice dans les évangiles et le christianisme primitif hormis la doctrine proprement paulinienne* (Louvain–Gembloux, 1950) p. 115.

64 H. B. Swete, *The Gospel according to St. Mark* (London, 1898) p. 152.

65 Pierre Benoit, *L'Evangile selon saint Matthieu* (Paris, 1950) p. 126, considers that the wedding clothes represent "la pureté de vie (en théologie chrétienne, la Grâce) requise pour entrer dans la béatitude céleste." Is it not, however, a question here rather of entry into the Church?

66 In addition to the Synoptic data here presented, one might conjecture that the references to the widow of Sarepta and to Naaman's cleansing (Lk 4:25–27) are to be taken as vague hints about the doctrine of the Eucharist and baptism. This becomes plausible when we recall that the whole scene is a Lucan reconstruction which forms the prologue in his Gospel to Jesus' public ministry.

67 Cf. D. M. Stanley, "Baptism in the New Testament," *Scripture* 8 (1956) 48.

68 F.-M. Braun, *La mère des fidèles* (2nd ed.; Tournai–Paris, 1954) p. 69.

69 Donatien Mollat, "Le puits de Jacob," *Bible et vie chrétienne* 6 (1954) 83–91.

[70] Rudolf Bultmann, *Das Evangelium des Johannes* (11th ed.; Göttingen, 1950) p. 93.

[71] A. d'Alès, *art. cit.* (n. 27 above) col. 858, thinks it was: "Saint Augustin, aux prises avec le schisme donatiste, est heureux de pouvoir donner sa pleine valeur au principe théologique d'après lequel tout sacrement administré au nom du Christ est une œuvre du Christ." Theologians might well show more reserve towards Augustinian exegesis when it is pressed into service as a hammer of the heretics.

[72] M.-J. Lagrange remarks in his commentary on the fourth Gospel (n. 23 above, p. 91): "dire avec affectation qu'il ne baptisait pas, c'est éviter de donner à ce baptême le caractère du baptême chrétien, en parfaite conformité avec la doctrine de l'évangéliste que l'Esprit ne serait donné qu'après le départ du Christ (VII, 39; XVI, 7)."

[73] Mollat, *art. cit.* (n. 69 above) p. 88.

[74] Oscar Cullmann, *Les sacrements dans l'évangile johannique* (Paris, 1951) pp. 55–57, regards the scene at the pool of Bethesda also as baptismal.

[75] Even Père Lagrange admits the baptismal significance of this scene; cf. *op. cit.* (n. 23 above) pp. 256–71.

[76] D. Mollat, *L'Evangile de saint Jean* (Paris, 1953) p. 22.

[77] C. K. Barrett, *The Gospel according to St. John* (London, 1955) p. 71. The author continues: "To suggest that on certain occasions, however august and solemn, Jesus said, 'Baptize,' or 'Do this in remembrance of me,' might be misleading. No one, when John wrote, questioned that Jesus had willed, and thus instituted, the sacraments; what was important was to safeguard them from petty and partial explanations."

[78] Spicq, *L'Epître aux Hébreux* 2, 236.

[79] Hoskyns, *op. cit.* (n. 54 above) pp. 436–39.

[80] Bouyer, *op. cit.* (n. 53 above) p. 191.

[81] Cullmann, *op. cit.* (n. 74 above) pp. 173–76.

[82] J. Schmitt, *art. cit.* (n. 7 above), *Revue des sciences religieuses* 29 (1955) 394.

[83] P. van Imschoot, "Baptême d'eau et baptême d'Esprit saint," *Ephemerides theologicae Lovanienses* 13 (1936) 653–65.

[84] Thus, the Passion is spoken of in terms of *doxa*: Jn 12:41; 17:5, 24; of *doxazein*: Jn 7:39; 12:16, 28; 13:31; of *hypsoun*: Jn 3:14; 8:28; 12:32, 34.

[85] Mt 27:50: *aphēken to pneuma*, Mk 15:37 and Lk 23:46: *exepneusen*.

[86] Paul Gaechter, "Zur Exegese von Röm VI, 5," *Zeitschrift für katholische Theologie* 54 (1930) 88–92.

[87] Günther Bornkamm, "Taufe und neues Leben bei Paulus," *Theologische Blätter* 18 (1939) 235.

[88] Pierre Benoit, "L'Ascension," *Revue biblique* 56 (1949) 161–203.

[89] Cf. "Salvation in the Primitive Preaching," reprinted in this volume, pp. 38–66.

[90] The theological vagueness surrounding this primitive Christian view of the distinction between baptism and the imposition of hands makes it difficult to distinguish them *sine addito* (as some modern theologians appear to do) as the two sacraments of baptism and confirmation.

[91] The ancient tradition that the water in baptism must "flow" goes back either to the fourth Gospel's "living water," i.e., spring water (Jn 4:10, 14, etc.) or to the Johannine rite which was practiced in the "flowing water" of the Jordan. On the etymology of the word Jordan as "d. (immer) fliessende Strom," cf. Ludwig Koehler, in *Lexicon in veteris testamenti libros* (Leiden, 1953) p. 402.

[92] G. Jacquemet, "Baptême," *Catholicisme* I (Paris, 1948) 1207: "Jésus n'a donc pas eu à inventer le rite matériel du baptême. Mais c'est lui qui a décidé d'en faire le signe visible et efficace de l'entrée dans son royaume."

[93] *Sum. theol.* 3, q. 66, ad 1m, 2m.

[94] L. Lercher, *Institutiones theologiae dogmaticae* 4/2 (3rd ed.; Innsbruck, 1948) 121, makes "baptism in Jesus' Name" an objection to his thesis on the *forma baptismi.*

[95] Cf. "Salvation in the Primitive Preaching," reprinted in this volume, pp. 38–66.

[96] Acts' account of Philip's baptizing the Ethiopian eunuch makes this point clear (Acts 8:36–38). In this account in which the baptismal catechesis is reported in such detail, it is worth observing that no formula is recorded as used by Philip in the administration of baptism. Moreover, given the fact that v. 37 is an interpolation from some very early baptismal interrogation (both Irenaeus and Cyprian read the verse in their editions of Acts), it is odd that the interpolator did not interject the missing formula into v. 38—if at the time there were words pronounced by the minister.

[97] I owe this suggestion to my former colleague, R. A. F. MacKenzie (now Rector of the Pontifical Biblical Institute, Rome), whose untiring

help in the redaction of this article I should like to acknowledge here with deep gratitude.

[98] Cf. "Salvation in the Primitive Preaching," reprinted in this volume, pp. 38–66.

[99] S. Lyonnet, "S. Cyrille d'Alexandrie et 2 Cor 3, 17," *Biblica* 32 (1951) 25–31, has cited some texts of Cyril which indicate that he understood this passage in a baptismal sense.

[100] Cullmann, *op. cit.* (n. 74 above) pp. 26–27.

Didachē As a Constitutive Element of the Written Gospel

EDITOR'S NOTE.—This essay originally appeared in the *Catholic Biblical Quarterly* 17 (1955) 336–48.

NOTES TO CHAPTER 7

1 Among the questions asked during the interrogation of the consecrand is the following: "Vis ea quae ex divinis Scripturis intelligis, plebem, cui ordinandus es, et verbis docere et exemplis?" Later, during the ceremony, the consecrating prelate prays: "Sint speciosi munere tuo pedes ejus ad evangelizandum pacem, ad evangelizandum bona tua. Da ei, Domine, ministerium reconciliationis in verbo et in factis, in virtute signorum et prodigiorum. Sit sermo ejus, et praedicatio, non in persuasibilibus humanae sapientiae verbis, sed in ostensione spiritus et virtutis." When the consecrator delivers the Gospels to the new bishop, he says: "Accipe evangelium, et vade, praedica populo tibi commisso."

2 C. H. Dodd, *The Apostolic Preaching and Its Developments* (2nd ed.; London, 1950) pp. 7 ff.

3 Dodd's definition of preaching does not apply to John the Baptist's preaching (Christianity is still a future reality) and can only be applied to Jesus' own kerygma in an improper sense. Teaching, inasmuch as it is "ethical instruction," would not seem to be distinguished from preaching; the kerygma included a call to *metanoia* and to baptism.

4 For other synonyms cf. G. Friedrich, "*kēryssō*," *Theologisches Wörterbuch zum Neuen Testament* 3, 702.

5 André Rétif, "Qu'est-ce que le kérygme?" *Nouvelle revue théologique* 71 (1949) 910 ff.

6 The LXX uses the word *kērygma* in Jon 3:2. The only time the term is used in the Gospels (Mt 12:41; Lk 11:32), it is applied to the teaching of Jonah.

7 Cf. the LXX version of Is 42:9; 52:7; also 60:6; 61:1.

8 The reference to John's teaching (Lk 11:1) has been evidently over-

looked by G. Friedrich, *art. cit.*, p. 713, n .63: "Von Johannes dem Täufer wird niemals gesagt, das er gelehrt habe."

[9] Mt 9:14; 11:2; 14:12; Mk 2:18; Lk 5:33; 7:18; 11:1; Jn 1:35, 37; 3:25.

[10] The only exception is Lk 20:1, where, however, the teaching is given precedence over the preaching (as is the case also in Mt 11:1). Luke says: *didaskontos autou . . . kai euangelizomenou.*

[11] Thus, the angelic message to the shepherds at Jesus' birth is regarded by Luke as an example of preaching: *euangelizomai hymin charan megalēn* (Lk 2:10).

[12] The word is a favorite Johannine term for the preaching of the kerygma: cf. Jn 1:15; 12:44. It is used elsewhere of the proclamation made by the crowd on the occasion of Jesus' Messianic entry: Mt 21:9; Mk 11:9.

[13] Cf. the remark of A. Feuillet, "La synthèse eschatologique de saint Matthieu (XXIV–XXV)," *Revue biblique* 56 (1949) 361: ". . . le Règne de Dieu, qui dans son fond s'identifie avec Jésus . . . commence avec la venue même du Sauveur sur la terre, et plus particulièrement avec son ministère public, ses victoires sur la maladie, le péché et la mort et ses expulsions de démons; on oublie trop souvent que les miracles du Christ font présager le triomphe définitif du Bien sur le Mal et signifient que, d'une certaine manière, la fin des temps est arrivée."

[14] The text, which Jesus refers to His miracles of healing and of exorcism, speaks of *euangelisasthai ptōchois . . . kēryxai aichmalōtois aphesin kai typhlois anablepsin.* The whole episode, however, as Luke makes clear and as we shall have occasion to note later, is an example of teaching. Père Rétif (*art. cit.*, p. 916, n. 20) is mistaken in regarding it as a "cas du kérygme."

[15] Cf. L. Cerfaux's excellent study of the apostolic *martyrion*: "Témoins du Christ d'après le Livre des Actes," *Angelicum* 20 (1943) 166–83.

[16] For a convenient list of these kerygmatic discourses, cf. Rétif, *art. cit.*, p. 920, n. 31. The one exception is Paul's instruction at Miletus (Acts 20:18 ff.).

[17] Cf. E. Osty's introductory chapter to his *Les évangiles synoptiques* (Paris, 1947): "La naissance des évangiles," pp. x ff.

[18] 1 Cor 1:21; 2:4; 15:14; Tit 1:3; Rom 16:25. Apart from Paul, the word is only used twice in the Gospels, to refer to Jonah's preaching (cf. n. 6). Hence it appears to be a specifically Pauline term for the apostolic

preaching. Cf. W. Grossouw, "Evangelium," in H. Haag, *Bibel-Lexikon*, col. 456.

[19] The word *asphaleia*, here translated "the authentic character," signifies in the papyri "proof," "security," in commercial or military language; cf. Moulton-Milligan, *The Vocabulary of the Greek Testament*, p. 88. The security which Luke offers Theophilus is a well-authenticated account of Jesus' life and especially of His teaching, on which the apostolic *didachē* rests.

[20] Cf. D. Mollat, *L'Evangile selon saint Jean* (Paris, 1953) p. 195, n. *b*.

[21] Cf. Mt 4:23; 5:2; 7:29; 9:35; 11:1; 13:54; 21:23; 22:16; Mk 1:21; 2:13; 4:1; 6:6; 6:34; 8:31; 9:31; 10:1; Lk 4:15, 31; 5:3; 5:17; 6:6; 13:10, 22, 26; 20:1; 23:5; Jn 6:59; 7:14, 28; 18:20.

[22] The only instance of Jesus' preaching given at any length in the Gospels is the "Woes-discourse" (Mt 23:1–38).

[23] Three of these are expressly described as instructions given only to His own disciples: the missionary discourse (Mt 10:5-42), the ecclesiastical discourse (Mt 18:1–35), and the eschatological discourse (Mt 24:1—25:46). The parabolic discourse (Mt 13:3–52) is evidently an example of *didaskein* and is so denominated in Mk 4:2.

[24] P. Benoit, *L'Evangile selon saint Matthieu* (Paris, 1950) pp. 8 ff.

[25] W. Michaux, "L'Evangile selon Marc," *Bible et vie chrétienne* 1 (1953) 79–97.

[26] M.-J. Lagrange, "Le but des paraboles d'après l'évangile selon saint Marc," *Revue biblique* 7 (1910) 32–33.

[27] I have pointed out the implicit references to the Deutero-Isaian Servant in these Marcan Passion predictions in the essay "Paul and the Christian Concept of the Servant of God," reprinted in this volume, pp. 312–51.

[28] The Evangelists usually depict Jesus as teaching in the synagogues (Mt 4:23; 9:35; 13:54; Mk 1:21; Lk 4:15; 6:6; 13:10; Jn 6:59; 18:20) or in the Temple precincts (Mt 21:23; 22:16; Lk 19:47; Jn 7:14, 28). In either place Jesus would have the Old Testament Scriptures ready to hand.

[29] John is the only Evangelist to underscore the Eucharistic significance of this miracle by connecting it with the Jewish Pasch (Jn 6:4) and by relating the sequel to it, the Eucharistic discourse.

[30] Matthew is the one apparent exception to this: he tends to gloss over the ignorance of the apostles out of respect. Mark, however, insists on it

bluntly (Mk 4:13; 6:52; 8:14–21; 9:10; 9:32). Luke sees in this apostolic slowness to understand a design of Providence (Lk 9:45; 18:34). John points out that Christ's resurrection is the source of the apostles' supernatural intelligence of the facts of Jesus' earthly life (Jn 2:19; 7:37; 12:16; 13:7; 20:8–9).

[31] Such is the inference drawn by G. Friedrich, *art. cit.*, p. 713 and n. 64. Cf. also Rétif, *art. cit.*, p. 915, who follows Friedrich.

[32] Jesus' glorification, insofar as it has reference to men, consists primarily in His becoming Sender of the Spirit (cf. Jn 7:39).

[33] Luke also illustrates this in the Emmaus episodes (24:25 ff.).

[34] J. Dupont, *Les Actes des apôtres* (Paris, 1953) pp. 173 f.

[35] F. W. Grosheide, "The Pauline Epistles as Kerygma," *Studia Paulina* (Haarlem, 1953) pp. 139–45, maintains that "it is allowed to reckon the epistles of Paul to the apostolic kerygma" (p. 144). He holds that what he calls "the old kerygma" (the apostolic preaching) "was *didachē*", but the arguments advanced for this position are not convincing.

[36] By "the receiving" (*paralambanein*) Paul designates the correlative action of *kēryssein or euangelizesthai*: cf. v. 9 of this same chapter (*ei tis hymas euangelizetai par' ho parelabete . . .*).

[37] In translating this text and that of Eph 4:20 f., I have followed the interpretation of P. Benoit, *Les épîtres de saint Paul aux Philippiens . . .* (Paris, 1949) pp. 59, 96.

[38] Cf. P. Benoit, *Revue biblique* 55 (1948) 594–99.

[39] C. Charlier, "La présence dans l'absence," *Bible et vie chrétienne* 2 (1953) 61–75; cf. especially his illuminating remarks on John's development of a process already germinally present in Jesus' own teaching (pp. 67 f.).

[40] Does Luke, by the strange use of the verb *ērxato*, hint here that the apostolic teaching is simply a continuation and development of Jesus' teaching?

[41] Luke was, of course, led to employ this genre because of its popularity among the literati of his day. Still, there is a deeper purpose governing his choice, as Osty (*op. cit.*, p. lvi) has noted.

Salvation in the Synoptic Gospels

Editor's Note.—This study originally appeared in the *Catholic Biblical Quarterly* 18 (1956) 345–63.

NOTES TO CHAPTER 8

[1] Cf. "Salvation in the Primitive Preaching," reprinted in this volume, pp. 38–66.

[2] At this earliest stage, the miracles and teaching of Jesus were cited by the preachers in order to demonstrate His Messianic character, His "anointing by the Holy Spirit" (Acts 10:38), or to show that He was a "man approved by God" (Acts 2:22). Thus the only connection in the primitive preaching between Jesus' public life and His death and resurrection appears to have been an apologetic one.

[3] Cf. "*Didachē* As a Constitutive Element of the Written Gospel," reprinted in this volume, pp. 199–213.

[4] The phrase *essais évangéliques* is that of L. Vaganay, *Le problème synoptique* (Tournai, 1954).

[5] *Ibid.*, p. 342.

[6] Still, as is demonstrably evident (cf. Mt 5:40; Lk 6:29), each Evangelist strives to express Jesus' meaning or the sense of a particular event in his own characteristic way.

[7] To this essential schema both Mt and Lk have, of course, prefixed a group of *récits* concerning Jesus' infancy, in order to form a kind of prologue to the whole book.

[8] The first motives which led the apostolic preachers to create the kerygma was their sense of the consummation of Israel's religious history; cf. "Salvation in the Primitive Preaching," reprinted in this volume, pp. 38–66.

[9] The principal example of this eschatological interest in the three Synoptic Gospels is the so-called discourse on the ruin of the Temple: cf. Mk 13:5–37; Mt 24:4–36; Lk 21:8–36.

[10] We make this assertion regarding the primitive preaching as far as

it can be recovered from the speeches in Acts. Hence its validity is limited by the fragmentary nature of those discourses.

[11] That is to say, of Stephen and the group of Greek-speaking Jews who took such an active part in the early spread of Christianity. An example of their typological applications may be seen in Acts 7:2–53 and 13:16–22.

[12] This is illustrated by the Matthean missionary discourse (Mt 10:5–42) and in the explanations appended to the parables of the Sower (Mk 4:14–20) and of the Cockle (Mt. 13:36–42).

[13] Cf. Vincent Taylor, *The Gospel according to St. Mark* (London, 1952) pp. 1–8.

[14] Cf. F.-M. Braun, "Ecole de la Formgeschichte," *Dictionnaire de la Bible: Supplément* 3, 315.

[15] Cf. W. Michaux, "L'Evangile de Marc," *Bible et vie chrétienne* 1 (1953) 78–95.

[16] After a brief introduction (1:1–13), Mark sketches the mystery of Jesus (1:14—8:26). The literary center of the Gospel consists in a complex of *récits* and logia which Mark probably received in written form (8:27—9:32), showing the beginning of the revelation of the mystery. The last section of the Gospel (9:33—16:8) is devoted to the full unveiling of the mystery in Jesus' passion and resurrection; and the whole is concluded with an epilogue (16:9–20).

[17] Mark displays more vividly than the other Evangelists the full reality of Jesus' human nature, to the point where subsequent Evangelists will feel the need of toning down his realism in the interests of edification: cf. for instance Mk 6:5–6 and Mt 13:58.

[18] Cf. Acts 2:22–24.

[19] One of the chief pedagogical points in the account of the creation by the priestly writer (Gn 1:1—2:3) was to assert that Yahweh alone was Lord of the Sabbath.

[20] It is interesting to note in these narratives the recurrence of the title taken from Dn 7:13–14, "the Son of Man," applied by Jesus to Himself.

[21] What such an expression might have meant to a Roman centurion is of no interest to Mark—if indeed the question ever occurred to him.

[22] Cf. Taylor, *op. cit.*, p. 207.

[23] *L'Evangile selon saint Marc* (2nd ed.; Paris, 1947) p. 48.

[24] *Op. cit.*, p. 211.

[25] One notable change occurs where Mark's difficult phrase *meta treis*

hēmeras is replaced by *tē tritē hēmera* in Mt 16:21; 17:22; 20:19; Lk 9:22; 18:33.

[26] Such, e.g., are the additions made in the third prediction: *staurōsai* (Mt 20:19) and *kai hybristhēsetai* (Lk 18:32).

[27] The use of the term *paradidonai* in the second and third predictions is a technical term in the theology of the atonement, borrowed from the vocabulary of the Servant theology (cf. Is 53:12).

[28] Mt. 17:11–13 succeeds in ironing out the difficulties in the Marcan version, but as Taylor (*op. cit.*, p. 395) has noted, he has perhaps changed its meaning.

[29] *Das Evangelium des Markus* (2nd ed. Göttingen, 1951) p. 223: "Das Wort deutet zudem auf die beiden 'Sakramente,' Taufe und Abendmahl, mindestens für den Evangelisten."

[30] *Op. cit.*, pp. 445–46.

[31] Cf. J. Giblet, "Jésus Messie et Sauveur d'après les évangiles synoptiques," *Lumière et vie* 15 (1954) 333–70.

[32] Cf. Taylor, *op. cit.*, p. 477.

[33] Cf. Pierre Benoit, "Le récit de la Cène dans Lc XXII, 15–20," *Revue biblique* 48 (1939) 384–86.

[34] This is evident from Heb 9:20, where the Exodus text is quoted with the words of consecration in mind: *touto to haima tēs diathēkēs.*

[35] *Op. cit.*, p. 380.

[36] The only meaning assigned in the papyri to *diathēkē* is "testament, last will." The LXX writers used it because *synthēkē*, the usual Greek term for "covenant," implies equality between the two contracting parties and hence was unsuitable for denoting the Sinaitic *berith* between Yahweh and His people.

[37] The term *pollōn* is a reference to Is 53:12: in Hebrew idiom, "all in contrast with the one" is its meaning. Mt 26:28 makes the connection with sin more explicit by adding *eis aphesin hamartiōn*. The Pauline version contains a reference to the new covenant of Jer 31:31 in the word *kainē*.

[38] For the plan of Matthew, cf. D. M. Stanley, *The Gospel of St. Matthew* (2nd ed.; Collegeville, 1963) pp. 13–15.

[39] Cf. "Kingdom to Church," reprinted in this volume, pp. 5–37.

[40] Cf. Pierre Benoit, *L'Evangile selon saint Matthieu* (Paris, 1950).

[41] Cf. L. Soubigou, "L'Evangile de l'enfance selon saint Matthieu: structure du texte évangélique," *L'Année théologique* 9 (1948) 82–94.

[42] The evidence for this will be given presently. The celebrated Matthean insistence upon the fulfilment of Old Testament prophecy is no argument against the fact that the canonical Gospel was written for Christians of Gentile origin, but rather proof of the validity of tradition, which asserts that Matthew wrote an Aramaic Gospel (which, we believe, was incorporated into the Greek Gospel which bears his name).

[43] In Mt 16:1–4 (cf. Mk 8:11–13; Lk 11:29) there is another Jonah-logion which refers to "the proof which Jonah gave."

[44] In this connection we should like to call attention to the very valuable study by Krister Stendahl, *The School of St. Matthew* (Uppsala, 1954).

[45] Cf. *Les évangiles synoptiques* (Paris, 1947) p. 39.

[46] Cf. A. Feuillet, "Le triomphe eschatologique de Jésus d'après quelques textes isolés des évangiles," *Nouvelle revue théologique* 71 (1949) 701–22, 806–28.

[47] *L'Evangile selon saint Matthieu* (8th ed.; Paris, 1948) p. 333.

[48] "La synthèse eschatologique de saint Matthieu (XXIV–XXV)," *Revue biblique* 56 (1949) 340–64; 57 (1950) 62–91, 180–211.

[49] Cf. *art. cit.*, p. 809.

[50] This logion is added in Luke to the discourse on the destruction of the Temple. It is not found in either Matthew or Mark.

[51] Cf. "*Didachē* As a Constitutive Element of the Written Gospel," reprinted in this volume, pp. 199–213.

[52] M.-J. Lagrange, *L'Evangile selon saint Luc* (7th ed.; Paris, 1948) p. 492.

[53] A recent analysis of Mark's theological viewpoint, which is a fine example of post-Bultmannian *Redaktionsgeschichte*, is the small book by James M. Robinson, *The Problem of History in Mark* (London, 1957).

The Gospels As Salvation History

EDITOR'S NOTE.—This article, a slightly revised version of "The Conception of Our Gospel As Salvation History," published in *Theological Studies* 20 (1959) 561–89, appeared in the symposium *Christianity Divided: Protestant and Roman Catholic Theological Issues* (New York, 1961) pp. 111–45.

NOTES TO CHAPTER 9

1 Among recent studies on these subjects, the following are noteworthy: P. Synave and P. Benoit, *La prophétie* (*Somme théologique*, ed. Revue des Jeunes; Paris, 1947); P. Benoit, "L'Inspiration," in Robert-Tricot, *Initiation biblique* (3rd ed.; Paris, 1954) pp. 6–45; *idem*, "Note complémentaire sur l'inspiration," *Revue biblique* 63 (1956) 416–22; Karl Rahner, "Uber die Schriftinspiration," *Zeitschrift für katholische Theologie* 78 (1956) 127–68; *idem*, *Über die Schriftinspiration* (Freiburg, 1958); J. Coppens, "L'Inspiration et l'inérrance biblique," *Ephemerides theologicae Lovanienses* 33 (1957) 35–57; Johannes Schildenberger, *Vom Geheimnis des Gotteswortes: Einführung in das Verständnis der heiligen Schrift* (Heidelberg, 1950); R. A. F. MacKenzie, "Some Problems in the Field of Inspiration," *Catholic Biblical Quarterly* 20 (1958) 1–8.—Other studies which treat biblical questions in a new way are to be noted: Jean Levie, *The Bible: Word of God in Words of Men* (New York, 1961); C. Charlier, *The Christian Approach to the Bible* (London, 1958); Charles Hauret, *Origines de l'univers et de l'homme d'après la Bible* (2nd ed.; Paris, 1950); R. A. F. MacKenzie, *Faith and History in the Old Testament* (Minneapolis, 1963); also his article "Before Abraham was . . . ," *Catholic Biblical Quarterly* 15 (1953) 131–40; Bruce Vawter, *A Path through Genesis* (New York, 1956) and *Conscience of Israel* (New York, 1961); John L. McKenzie, *The Two-edged Sword* (Milwaukee, 1956); B. Rigaux, "L'Historicité de Jésus devant l'exégèse récente," *Revue biblique* 65 (1958) 481–522; Frederick L. Moriarty, *Introducing the Old Testament* (Milwaukee, 1960).

2 John L. McKenzie, "Problems of Hermeneutics in Roman Catholic

Exegesis," *Journal of Biblical Literature* 77 (1958) 197–204. However, within two years of this date a new storm of some proportions broke out, occasioned by an article of Luis Alonso Schökel, "Dove va l'esegesi cattolica?" *Civiltà cattolica* 111 (1960) 449–60. This scholar's remarks drew the fire of Msgr. Antonino Romeo, "L'Enciclica 'Divino afflante Spiritu' e le 'opiniones novae,'" *Divinitas* 4 (1960) 385–456. An informative account of this passage at arms is given by Joseph A. Fitzmyer, "A Recent Roman Scriptural Controversy," *Theological Studies* 22 (1961) 426–44. The June, 1962 suspension of two professors of Rome's Pontificio Istituto Biblico, Frs. Zerwick and Lyonnet, from the teaching of exegesis in that institution shows that certain voices have been effectively raised against the so-called "new approach" to the New Testament.

[3] London, 1938; cf. his chapter "The Historical Tradition in the New Testament," pp. 41–74.

[4] *Scripture* 8 (1956) 2–12. A very useful discussion of this question is to be found in Luis Alonso Schökel, *Understanding Biblical Research* (New York, 1963).

[5] "Historicité des évangiles synoptiques et Formgeschichte," in *La formation des évangiles* (Bruges, 1957) p. 196.

[6] *Biblica* 39 (1958) 502.

[7] *Theological Studies* 14 (1953) 465.

[8] John L. McKenzie, "Problems of Hermeneutics . . . ," p. 200.

[9] *The Two-edged Sword*, p. 105.

[10] *Acta apostolicae sedis* 33 (1941) 465–72.

[11] McKenzie, "Problems of Hermeneutics . . . ," p. 198.

[12] *Acta apostolicae sedis* 35 (1943) 314. Hereafter, citations from *Divino afflante Spiritu* will be taken from the translation of Canon G. D. Smith, published by the Catholic Truth Society (London, 1944).

[13] *Acta apostolicae sedis* 35 (1943) 319.

[14] *Ibid.*, p. 314.

[15] *Ibid.* 42 (1950) 569.

[16] *Ibid.*, p. 570.

[17] G. Lambert, "L'Encyclique 'Humani generis' et l'écriture sainte," *Nouvelle revue théologique* 73 (1951) 226.

[18] *Acta apostolicae sedis* 35 (1943) 314.

[19] *Ibid.*, p. 314.

[20] London, 1953.

[21] *Bible et vie chrétienne* 18 (1957) 7–26.

[22] *Acta apostolicae sedis* 35 (1943) 315.

[23] *Ibid.*, p. 315.

[24] *Ibid.*, p. 315.

[25] *Ibid.*, p. 316.

[26] McKenzie, "Problems of Hermeneutics . . . ," p. 198.

[27] Cf. S. Lyonnet, "De glossolalia Pentecostes eiusque significatione," *Verbum domini* 24 (1944) 65–75.

[28] *Acta apostolicae sedis* 35 (1943) 319.

[29] Cf. a recent and interesting instance of this in the interpretation of Mt 1:18–22 by Xavier Léon-Dufour, "L'Annonce à Joseph," in *Mélanges bibliques rédigés en l'honneur de André Robert* (Paris, 1957) pp. 390–97. There is also the brilliantly simple solution of the Matthean divorce logia by Alberto Vaccari, "La clausola sul divorzio in Matteo 5, 32:19, 9," *Revista biblica* 3 (1955) 97–119.

[30] *Acta apostolicae sedis* 35 (1943) 319.

[31] Erich Dinkler, *The Idea of History in the Ancient Near East* (New Haven–London, 1955) p. 172.

[32] McKenzie, *The Two-edged Sword*, p. 60.

[33] C. H. Dodd, *History and the Gospel* (London, 1938) pp. 26–27.

[34] *Ibid.*, p. 36.

[35] McKenzie, *The Two-edged Sword*, p. 62.

[36] Dodd, *History and the Gospel*, p. 30.

[37] For those who wish to gain a clear insight into the developments which constitute the modern Catholic scriptural movement, we recommend the book by Jean Levie, *La Bible: Parole humaine et message de Dieu* (Paris–Louvain, 1958). The English translation of this work is included in the bibliography under n. 1 above.

[38] J. Cambier, *art. cit.* (n. 5 above) p. 211.

[39] Oscar Cullmann, *Die Christologie des Neuen Testaments* (Tübingen, 1957) pp. 326–27.

[40] Cf. the plan of this Gospel proposed by Willibald Michaux, "Cahier de Bible: L'Evangile selon Marc," *Bible et vie chrétienne* 1 (1953) 78–97.

[41] On the significance of this confession, the reader may consult D. M. Stanley, "Balaam's Ass, or a Problem of New Testament Hermeneutics," *Catholic Biblical Quarterly* 20 (1958) 55–56.

[42] Cf. A. Feuillet, "La synthèse eschatologique de saint Matthieu (XXIV–XXV)," *Revue biblique* 56 (1949) 340–64; 57 (1950) 62–91, 180–211.

[43] Cf. D. M. Stanley, "The Bread of Life," *Worship* 32 (1957–58) 477–88.

[44] Cullmann, *op. cit.*, p. 328.

[45] *Acta apostolicae sedis* 35 (1943) 316.

[46] Cf. his chapter "The Hebrew Story," pp. 60 ff.

[47] Paris, 1957.

[48] Cf. D. M. Stanley, "Liturgical Influences on the Formation of the Four Gospels," *Catholic Biblical Quarterly* 21 (1959) 24–38. This article is also incorporated into the present volume, pp. 119–39.

Paul's Conversion in Acts

NOTES TO CHAPTER 10

[1] Cf. Joseph Bonsirven, *L'Evangile de Paul* (Paris, 1948) pp. 17–37. Maurice Goguel criticizes A. Schweitzer's *Die Mystik des Apostels Paulus* for omitting a study of Paul's conversion; see "La mystique paulinienne d'après Albert Schweitzer," *Revue d'histoire et de philosophie religieuses* 11 (1931) 185–210. Cf. also W. D. Davies, *Paul and Rabbinic Judaism* (London, 1948) p. 324.

[2] Cf. Jacques Dupont, *Les problèmes du Livre des Actes d'après les travaux récents* (Louvain, 1950); J. S. Lilly, "The Conversion of Paul: The Validity of His Testimony to the Resurrection of Jesus Christ," *Catholic Biblical Quarterly* 6 (1944) 180–204; and A. Wikenhauser, "Die Wirkung der Christophanie vor Damaskus auf Paulus und seine Begleiter nach den Berichten der Apostelgeschichte," *Biblica* 23 (1952) 313–23.

[3] Cf. Kirsopp and Silva Lake, *An Introduction to the New Testament* (London, 1948) p. 77.

[4] We cannot do better than refer to the late Fr. Lilly's competent article, n. 2 above.

[5] Cf. Acts 9:4 for the effect upon Paul; 9:7 for the effect upon his companions. The order followed here by Luke is that given by Paul's speech in Acts 22:6 ff.—though Luke has his own way of expressing it. Both Luke and Paul describe the effect of the appearance upon the companions in order to highlight different aspects of the occurrence in relation to Paul himself—and this according to the use made of the incident by Luke at the various points in his narrative.

[6] Cf. Acts 26:14. Here attention is centered completely on the dialogue between Christ and Paul; hence the speaker contents himself with a general reference to the effect of the light upon the whole group. Wikenhauser (*art. cit.*, p. 315) may be right in suggesting "dass der Schriftsteller in seinem Streben nach Verkürzung das Verhalten der Begleiter einfach dem des Saulus angeglichen hat."

[7] Compare Acts 9:7 with 22:9, which will be discussed in this study.

[8] For a brief account of evidence for the use of the proverb, cf. F. J. Foakes Jackson and Kirsopp Lake (eds.), *The Beginnings of Christianity* 4, 318. Future references to this work will designate it as *Beginnings*.

[9] Cf. Lake, *op. cit.*, p. 77. The problem is how to reconcile Ananias' remark in Acts 22:15 with Paul's insistence (cf. Gal 1:1, 11–12) that he had received his apostolic commission *immediately* from Christ Himself, not through any human intermediary.

[10] I suggest that the *hoti* of Acts 22:15 be translated simply "that," rather than "because"; hence it introduces a quotation of Christ's words, viz., "(to see the Just One and hear from His lips) *that* you are to be a witness for Him before all men. . . ."

[11] Cf. J. Lebreton and J. Zeiller, *L'Eglise primitive* (Paris, 1946) p. 128.

[12] The nicety of distinction is to be noted. P. Lestringant, *Essai sur l'unité de la révélation biblique* (Paris, 1942) p. 67, exaggerates when he asserts that Peter's sermons in Acts present only a slightly novel form of Judaism.

[13] The phrase "to the end of the earth" indicates the promise of the universalist character of Christianity. The LXX translator of Is 49:6 used the phrase in the second Servant Song, which is applied to Paul's ministry in Acts 13:47. Actually, the phrase in the context of Acts probably designates Rome. A. Wikenhauser, *Die Apostelgeschichte* (2nd ed.; Regensburg, 1951) p. 233, takes Luke's remark too literalistically when he observes that "Rom ist für Lukas nicht das Ende der Welt." The remarks of the commentator in *Beginnings* 4, 350 are nearer the truth: "We ought not to read into the author's expression of purpose too complete, too conscious, or too modern a plan. Perhaps the terminus he set himself was a place. . . . It was enough for him to have brought Paul to Rome to bear witness to the gospel there. The last sentence has a note of triumph, of triumph in chains. It is not a casual sentence. It may have been the author's deliberately chosen conclusion." Paul's arrival in Rome, it will be seen, brings to the promise of universalism in Christianity a particularly significant realization—not merely because imperial Rome was mistress of the then-known world, but because thus the gradual withdrawal of the Church from the sphere of influence of Judaism is for Luke fittingly symbolized.

[14] Cf. the accounts in Acts 3 and in 8:14.

[15] Acts 12:3 relates the beheading of James, "brother of John." There is a James also mentioned in 12:17; a James figures in the Council of

Jerusalem (Acts 15:13), and a James welcomes Paul and his companions to Jerusalem (Acts 21:18).

[16] Cf. Acts 12:17. The phrase may mean another town or merely another house. While agreeing that another place than Jerusalem is meant, commentators disagree as to its identification. All agree, however, that Rome is not meant.

[17] That these words were spoken *by Paul* with reference to himself may be gathered from the citation, in which "you" is singular. It is to be recalled also that Paul was chief speaker here, and generally on this missionary tour.

[18] The last six chapters are devoted to events culminating in Paul's taking up residence in Rome. Moreover, Luke has announced it beforehand: cf. Acts 19:21; 20:22 ff.

[19] Cf. L. Cerfaux, "Témoins du Christ (d'après le Livre des Actes)," *Angelicum* 20 (1943) 166–83.

[20] Cf. Acts 14:4, 14.

[21] W. L. Knox, *The Acts of the Apostles* (Cambridge, 1948) p. 55.

[22] Luke does not mention any Galilean appearance of the risen Christ and remarks that the preaching to all nations must begin "from Jerusalem" (Lk 24:47). Moreover, the apostles are to remain "in the city" until the promised Spirit comes (Lk 24:49). For Luke as for Paul, the gospel is offered "first to the Jew then to the Greek" (Rom 1:16). For Paul, the revelation of "the mystery" is contingent upon the Jews' rejection of the gospel (cf. esp. Rom 11:11 ff.): in Acts the reiterated refusal of Jews through the Diaspora to hear Paul's message becomes a sign of the gradual independence of the Church.

[23] The fact that Luke insists on this at the close of his Gospel and at the beginning of Acts (1:4) is proof of its close connection with his main theme.

[24] Cf. Acts 28:21.

[25] Cf. A. M. Ramsey, *The Resurrection of Christ* (2nd ed.; London, 1946) p. 80.

[26] Acts 25:11. That Paul has demanded trial before the imperial tribunal of Rome *under divine inspiration,* Luke is well aware: he has already recorded the vision in which Christ informs Paul he is to "be a witness" in Rome (Acts 23:11).

[27] Hence he stresses the direction of this journey by the exalted Christ: cf. Acts 20:22; 21:11; 23:11; 27:23.

[28] The Roman Christians come out to meet the prisoner (Acts 28:15).

[29] Thus we may abstract from the question of Peter's coming, which has no significance for Luke's story. If with the material he possesses he can show that *somehow* with Paul's arrival the apostolic center of Christianity has been shifted to Rome from Jerusalem, he has attained his objective.

[30] The "synoptic problem" here is more acute inasmuch as it occurs in one book: any shift in detail is the more significant because one author only is responsible. Hence it may be safely assumed that he had some purpose in placing details seemingly at variance with one another, other than a forlorn hope of tantalizing future commentators.

[31] It is likely that Luke actually heard this speech; cf. L. Pirot, "Actes des apôtres," *Dictionnaire de la Bible: Supplément* 1, 78.

[32] Cf. Acts 8:1 and its source in 22:20 (which also provides data mentioned in 7:58). This must surely be a genuine Pauline reminiscence.

[33] Cf. 8:3 with 22:19. For the detail "men and women," cf. 22:4. Luke has used his own writer's creativeness in filling out his descriptions: cf. 8:3, the remark that Saul *elymaineto*—a word related in popular etymology at least with *loimos*, which is what Tertullus calls Paul later (Acts 24:5).

[34] Or from Paul himself. In any event, the identification of the source is not important here.

[35] Judas' importance in the Jewish colony of Damascus is shown by the fact that Paul's companions took him there. They may have known him from instructions received in Jerusalem.

[36] Except perhaps for the more natural sequence in 22:8 ff.: "Who are you, Lord?" "I am Jesus. . . ." "What shall I do, Lord?" "Get up and go to Damascus. . . ."

[37] Cf. Acts 9:26 ff., and also the difficulties at Antioch (Acts 15:2 ff.). It is this type of reaction which directs Paul, under divine guidance, to his proper apostolate (cf. 22:18–19).

[38] Paul's conversion is the greatest event in primitive Church history after the events of the first Pentecost.

[39] Luke gives Paul's sufferings prominence throughout his book: suspicion on the part of fellow Christians (9:26); attempts on his life (9:29); abuse by the Jews of the Diaspora (13:45 ff.; 14:2 ff.; 14:19 ff.; 17:5 ff.; 18:6; 18:12 ff.; 19:9; 20:3; 21:27 ff.); differences with coworkers (15:37 ff.); scorn and persecution by pagans (16:19 ff.; 17:32 f.; 19:23

ff.). Luke depicts suffering as part of the divine plan for Paul (20:22; 21:11). In 23:11 it is linked with the role given Paul by Christ (repeated by an angel in 27:23). How central in Paul's own conception of the apostolate suffering is, may be seen from 2 Cor 4:7 ff.

[40] Note the omission of the definite article in each place (2:4 and 9:17).

[41] Cf. Cerfaux, *art. cit.*, p. 173.

[42] Cf. our remarks, later in this study, on the third account of Paul's conversion.

[43] C. H. Dodd, *The Apostolic Preaching and Its Developments* (2nd ed.; London, 1950) p. 25, omits an important characteristic of Paul's preaching. Paul does not seem to have used the Servant of Yahweh theme in his soteriological presentation of Christ's redemptive death.

[44] For example, the *time* when the meeting occurred (Acts 22:6), and the fact that Christ spoke Aramaic (26:14).

[45] Whether the terms in Acts 9:18 are medical or not is disputed. It is interesting to recall a similar description of the cure of Tobias (Tob 11:13).

[46] It is difficult to say to whom Acts 22:17 ff. refers. There is no doubt of the hostility of the Jews to this renegade Pharisee. Since, however, Luke shows that such opposition is active everywhere, it may be that he also refers here to suspicion on the part of Christians.

[47] Moreover, if we suppose that the vision occurred early in Paul's Christian life, it is hard to explain why he did not obey sooner—yet Luke apparently feels no need to give an explanation.

[48] With the accusative of *logos*, Luke shows clearly that the verb means "to comprehend, understand" (and since knowledge for a Semite is mainly experiential, it is equivalent of "to know so as to *do*"). Cf. Lk 8:21 and 11:28 in contrast with Lk 6:47, where the genitive is used in the same expression to signify "to hear ineffectually" (i.e., but not do). Cf. the similar examples in Mt 10:14 and Jn 5:37. Acts 17:32 illustrates the meaning with the accusative: once the Athenians had actually understood what Paul was talking about, i.e., the Resurrection, and not two new gods (cf. 17:18), they refused to listen any longer. Jn 10:3 illustrates the usage with the genitive: the sheep belonging to a good shepherd "*hear* his voice" as he calls to them; they follow him because "they *know* his voice," i.e., distinguish the sound of his voice from all others (they cannot understand the words he uses). Cf. also Jn 5:25, where the dead "hear" the voice of the Son of God, i.e., like the "sound of the last trumpet."

[49] Paul uses it to prove his apostolic vocation: cf. 1 Cor 9:1; 15:5.

[50] The references are given in n. 39 above.

[51] This purpose should not, however, be exaggerated; cf., as an instance of this, A. Loisy, *Les Actes des apôtres* (Paris, 1920) p. 817.

[52] How well this succeeded is evident from their silence (Acts 22:2).

[53] Cf. P. Benoit, "L'Ascension," *Revue biblique* 56 (1949) 161–203.

[54] Cf. G. Kittel, "*akouō*," *Theologisches Wörterbuch zum Neuen Testament* 1, 217–25. In contrast with Hellenistic mystery religions, where revelation is mainly a seeing, Old Testament revelation (except for apocalypses) is almost entirely a hearing, as befits an aniconic cult. Moses is the great exception, although the traditions are not in agreement as to his seeing God. The prophets of Israel were sent with the *word* of Yahweh, to which obedience is due: the Israelite is just because he *hears*, i.e., obeys God, not because he contemplates Him. In the New Testament, emphasis is laid also upon hearing (there is question of seeing where revelation is "eschatological," under which rubric Kittel includes the postresurrection appearances of Christ). Paul presents his meeting with our Lord first (22:6 ff.) as seeing, then (26:12 ff.) as hearing. The key to the meaning of these two accounts appears to lie in this distinction.

[55] The significance of this religious experience for an understanding of Paul's theology may be summed up in his seeing the *kabōd* of Yahweh upon the face of Christ. It was this which gave him his insight into the role of Jesus' resurrection in the twofold act of the redemption.

[56] Cf. Phil 3:7 ff. Paul here states that, as a result of his having been "seized" by the risen Christ on the Damascus road (3:12), what was gain for him as a Pharisee he now counts as loss.

[57] Cf. Acts 26:16 with Ez 2:1.

[58] There is no opposition between the historical and the supernatural. For Luke as a writer of religious history, the supernatural provides the events he records with their historical reality in the deepest sense.

[59] Cf. Loisy, *op. cit.*, p. 815.

[60] Luke shows that Paul goes to Rome under a special providence, and that his work is an extension of Christ, Servant of Yahweh.

[61] Cf. especially Rom 8, where Paul illustrates his theme that the gospel is "a power unto salvation" (Rom 1:16).

[62] Variant to be noted: Paul does not make any distinction between the effect of the light upon himself and his companions; the accent here

is rather on hearing; thus he says the light shone "round me and my companions, and when we had all fallen to the earth, *I heard. . . .*"

[63] Cf. Acts 26:14, which is noted immediately above.

[64] The only loci known to us are in Aeschylus (*Agamemnon* 1624), Euripides (*Bacchae* 795), and Pindar (*Pythian Ode* 2, 173).

[65] Is there evidence here of some psychological preparation for Paul's conversion? Probably not. That there was some preparation under grace is very likely; cf. James Brodrick, *St. Francis Xavier* (London, 1952) p. 49.

[66] Cf. H. B. Swete, *The Appearances of Our Lord after the Passion* (London, 1908) pp. 130 f.

[67] Subordinate aim: to prove to Festus that only a religious motive can be found for Paul's journey to Rome; cf. Acts 25:26 f. with 26:6 f.

[68] It was an aunt of his, Herodias, who contrived the death of John the Baptist for denouncing her attempted marriage with her uncle Herod Antipas.

[69] The word for "prophesy" here occurs only twice elsewhere in the New Testament, both times in connection with the pentecostal glossolaly (Acts 2:4, 14).

[70] Cf. n. 20 above.

[71] Cf. Knox, *op. cit.*, p. 72.

[72] Most striking instances: Acts 13:47 (Is 49:6); Acts 18:9–10 (Is 43:5); Gal 1:15 (Is 49:1); Rom 15:21 (Is 52:15).

[73] Cf. J. S. van der Ploeg, *Les chants du serviteur de Jahvé* (Paris, 1936) p. 201, for a list of recent exegetes who regard this passage as an additional Servant Song; cf. also his discriminating remarks on p. 203. Luke describes Jesus' personal mission to the house of Israel: He is "the comfort of Israel" (2:25), the "redemption of Jerusalem" (2:38), the One "destined to redeem Israel" (24:21). The Evangelist recognizes Jesus as the Suffering Servant (cf. Lk 2:32; 24:26; esp. 22:37); yet he does not, as Matthew does (Mt 12:18 ff.), refer to the synagogue scene where Christ applies to Himself the *first* Servant Song. This Luke reserves for Paul, Apostle of the Gentiles.

Paul and the Christian Concept of the Servant of God

EDITOR'S NOTE.—This study originally appeared in the *Catholic Biblical Quarterly* 16 (1954) 385–425.

NOTES TO CHAPTER 11

[1] Cf. W. L. Knox, *The Acts of the Apostles* (Cambridge, 1948) pp. 72 ff.; L. Cerfaux, "L'Exégèse de l'Ancien Testament par le Nouveau Testament," in *L'Ancien Testament et les chrétiens* (Paris, 1951) pp. 132–48; J. S. van der Ploeg, *Les chants du serviteur de Jahvé* (Paris, 1936) pp. 154 ff.; F. J. Foakes Jackson and Kirsopp Lake, *The Beginnings of Christianity* 1 (London, 1942) 384 ff.; C. R. North, *The Suffering Servant in Deutero-Isaiah* (Oxford, 1948) pp. 9 ff.; H. H. Rowley, "The Suffering Servant and the Davidic Messiah," in *The Servant of the Lord and Other Essays on the Old Testament* (London, 1952) pp. 59 ff.

[2] Cf. L. Cerfaux, "Saint Paul et le *serviteur de Dieu* d'Isaïe," *Studia Anselmiana* 27–28 (1951) 351–65. The question which the present study seeks to answer is: Why did Paul, who was very much aware of the kerygmatic use of the Servant theme in the primitive Church, transform it so radically?

[3] Cf. G. Friedrich, "*euangelizomai,*" "*euangelion,*" *Theologisches Wörterbuch zum Neuen Testament* 2, 705–34. He remarks (p. 706): "Für das Vorverständnis des nt.lichen Euangelionbegriffes ist Deutero-jesaja und die von ihm beeinflüsste Literatur am wichtigsten."

[4] *Ibid.* p. 707.

[5] The notion of Yahweh's kingdom or domination appears in Deutero-Isaiah combined with the theme of the new exodus or that of the new creation: cf. Is 43:14–21; 48:16–21; 49:6–13; 52:7; 51:16. Cf. the remarks of G. von Rad, "*basileus,*" *Theologisches Wörterbuch zum Neuen Testament* 1, 568. As A. Feuillet has pointed out, the eschatological note in the Evangelist's concept of the kingdom of God comes from Deutero-Isaiah; cf. "Isaïe," *Dictionnaire de la Bible: Supplément* 4, 701.

[6] Cf. the descriptions of the Baptist's preaching: Mt 3:2 ff.; Mk 1:2 ff.; Lk 3:3 ff.; Jn 1:23; that of Jesus: Mt 4:17; Mk 1:15; Lk 4:17 ff. In Mk 1:2, Mal 3:1 is also cited, but this prophecy was to be utilized rather to describe the *person* of John: cf. Mt 17:10.

[7] Cf. J. Schmitt, *Jésus ressuscité dans la prédication apostolique* (Paris, 1949) p. 185, n. 1.

[8] Is 53:11; cf. the LXX rendering of Is 45:21.

[9] Cf. Is 40:25; 41:20; 43:14; 47:4; 48:17; 49:7; 55:5 in the LXX.

[10] The devotion of the early Church to the Holy Name (cf. Acts 2:21; 4:12; 5:41) probably stems from Deutero-Isaiah (cf. Is 40:26; 41:25; 42:8; 47:4; 48:2; 51:15; 52:6; 54:5; 55:13—and especially Is 42:4; 49:1).

[11] Cf. Schmitt, *op. cit.*, p. 212; Pierre Benoit, "La divinité de Jésus dans les évangiles synoptiques," *Lumière et vie* 9, 58; D. M. Stanley, "Etudes matthéenes: La confession de Pierre à Césarée," *Sciences ecclésiastiques* 6 (1954) 51–61.

[12] If Cornelius were a proselyte of Judaism, he might be presumed to have some acquaintance with the Old Testament. The catechesis of a completely pagan audience was differently orientated: cf. Acts 14:15 ff.; 17:22 ff.

[13] Note the four points of the kerygma: the ministry of John, Jesus' public ministry (Galilean mainly for Synoptics, Judean for John), the journey to Jerusalem, the Passion and Resurrection.

[14] Cf. Friedrich, *art. cit.*, pp. 707, 724–28.

[15] Cf. van der Ploeg, *op. cit.*, pp. 201–5. In any event, the question would not have occurred to the Evangelists any more than that of the Deutero- or Trito-Isaiah. For the early Church, Isaiah was a prophet who had written of one Person, Jesus Christ, describing Him as the Servant of Yahweh.

[16] Each Evangelist has his own view of Jesus' miracles. For Mark, they prove his thesis, viz., that Jesus is Son of God. Matthew sees in them the initial attack on the satanic domination of humanity, and considers them characteristic of the work of the Servant. Luke employs them to illustrate the *mansuetudo Christi.* In John, the "signs" Jesus worked are an important pedagogical process which leads the believing disciples to the definitive manifestation of Jesus' "glory" through His death and resurrection.

[17] Peter's customary initiative and his return to the group with John

after being released from prison would suggest that on this significant occasion Peter led the community in a prayer which he improvised.

[18] Cf. L. Cerfaux, "Témoins du Christ (d'après le Livre des Actes)," *Angelicum* 20 (1943) 182–83.

[19] Cf. L. Cerfaux, *La communauté apostolique* (2nd ed.; Paris, 1953) p. 69.

[20] Cf. Feuillet, *art. cit.*, col. 717; also C. Charlier, "Le manifeste d'Etienne," *Bible et vie chrétienne* 3 (1953) 83–93.

[21] Cf. Cerfaux, *op. cit.*, pp. 66–67.

[22] Cf. Feuillet, *art. cit.*, col. 708.

[23] Cf. Charlier, *art. cit.*, p. 89; also Feuillet, *art. cit.*, col. 710.

[24] Cf. Charlier, *art. cit.*, 88.

[25] Cf. the remarks of E. G. Selwyn, *The First Epistle of St. Peter* (London, 1949) p. 93.

[26] The importance of Christian Antioch cannot be exaggerated. Here the disciples are called Christians (Acts 11:26). Here the celebration of the Eucharist is called "liturgy" (cf. Acts 13:2). Here, too, the missionary program of the Church in a proper sense got under way (Acts 13:3).

[27] In the Jerusalem community the "breaking of the Bread" tended to be overshadowed by the splendor of the Temple liturgy; it was performed in the privacy of the home. But in Antioch the Eucharistic rite became the center of public worship.

[28] Cf. P. Benoit's introduction to his commentary on Matthew: *L'Evangile selon saint Matthieu* (Paris, 1950) pp. 13–21; also L. Vaganay, *Le problème synoptique* (Paris, 1954) pp. 223–24.

[29] V. Taylor, *The Gospel according to St. Mark* (London, 1952) p. 3.

[30] Cf. W. Manson, *Jesus the Messiah* (Philadelphia, 1946) p. 155.

[31] Cf. O. Cullmann, "Jésus serviteur de Dieu," *Dieu vivant* 16, 28.

[32] This is the reading of the Western text, which is also found in Justin, Clement of Alexandria, Origen, Methodius, Hilary, and Augustine.

[33] This reading of Jn 1:34 is attested by Sinaiticus, several mss. of the Vetus Latina, and the old Syriac version; it is to be preferred to the *lectio facilior* ("Son of God"): cf. D. Mollat, *L'Evangile selon saint Jean* (Paris, 1953) p. 73.

[34] Cf. Feuillet, *art. cit.*, col. 710. Note the observation of van der Ploeg, *op. cit.*, p. 159.

[34a] Cf. Mk 9:12 for the same idea.

[35] Cf. Cullmann, *art. cit.*, p. 27.

[36] Cf. A. Loisy, *Les évangiles synoptiques* 2 (Ceffonds, 1908) p. 241.

[37] In the first part of the verse, the Evangelist uses the term *diakonein*, which is not found in the LXX: cf. H. Wolfgang Beyer, "*diakoneō*," *Theologisches Wörterbuch zum Neuen Testament* 2, 82. However, in v. 44, *diakonos* is paralleled by *pantōn doulos*, thus bringing noun and verb (*diakonos, diakonein*) within the ambit of Servant terminology.

[38] The *āsām* in Lv 5:14–26 and 7:2–7 is a sacrifice for guilt. In Deutero-Isaiah it is probably more broadly used for an *atoning* sacrifice (cf. the wide use of *minhah* in Mal 1:11). In Is 53:3 the Servant is regarded as one of "those before whom men veil their face," i.e., a leper. The *āsām* prescribed for a leper upon his cure is two lambs and a sheep (Lv 10:10 ff.). In Is 53 the Servant is at once the leper and the lamb; he carries the sin of the world and at the same time takes it away. Thus in the context the offering of the Servant is evidently regarded as a *lytron*.

[39] Manson, *op. cit.*, pp. 155–56, says: "In the Gospel of Matthew the correlation of the two conceptions is open and explicit. . . . But this is the language of the evangelist and of the Church." It is indeed; and the doctrinal development of the Servant theology in our Gospels testifies to the existence of tradition. Cf. Walter J. Burghardt, "The Catholic Concept of Tradition in the Light of Modern Theological Thought," *Proceedings of the Sixth Annual Convention* [1951] *of the Catholic Theological Society of America* (New York, 1952) pp. 42–76.

[40] Cf. n. 5 above.

[41] Cf. n. 15 above.

[42] Cf. Manson, *op. cit.*, p. 54.

[43] While Lk 6:29 translates this logion into terms a Hellenistic audience will grasp, Mt 5:40 almost certainly retains the original form of this saying of Jesus.

[44] Cf. A. Feuillet, "La synthèse eschatologique de saint Matthieu (XXIV–XXV)," *Revue biblique* 56 (1949) 361.

[45] Cf. Is 25:19; 29:18–19; 35:5–6; 61:1–2.

[46] Matthew does this by placing the miracles in chaps. 8–9 as a prelude to the Baptist's disciples' question (11:3) under the rubric of the Servant theme (cf. Mt 8:17), and also by citing Jesus' reply to John's disciples, which is a second reference to the book of Isaiah.

[47] Cf. Schmitt, *op. cit.*, p. 185, n. 2.

[48] Cf. J. Coppens, "Le problème du sens plénier," *Problèmes et méthode d'exégèse théologique* (Gembloux, 1950) p. 19.

[49] During New Testament times the title "Servant of Yahweh" was applied to Christ and considered of paramount importance.

[50] Cf. Lk 3:4 ff.; 4:17 ff. Among the implicit citations of the Servant Songs in this Gospel, van der Ploeg (*op. cit.*, p. 159) mentions Lk 2:21 (Is 49:1) and the Nunc Dimittis, Lk 2:30–32 (Is 49:6).

[51] Cf. E. Osty, *Les évangiles synoptiques* (Paris, 1947) p. li.

[52] So that, as Knox (*op. cit.*, p. 56) asserts, this journey gives its literary form to the second half of Luke's Gospel.

[53] Cf. F.-M. Braun, *La mère des fidèles* (2nd ed.; Tournai–Paris, 1954) p. 79.

[54] Cf. M.-J. Lagrange, *Evangile selon saint Jean* (7th ed.; Paris, 1948) pp. 39–41; also F. Prat, *Jésus-Christ* 1 (16th ed.; Paris, 1947) p. 174.

[55] Cf. P. Joüon, "L'Agneau de Dieu," *Nouvelle revue théologique* 67 (1940) 318–21.

[56] Cf. G. Kittel, "*amnos*," *Theologisches Wörterbuch zum Neuen Testament* 1, 343. However, it is not necessary to go as far as Kittel does here in order to find a connection between the Servant and the lamb, since Is 53:7 already reveals the comparison.

[57] Cf. n. 38 above.

[58] Cf. Mollat, *op. cit.*, p. 190.

[59] Cf. A. M. Ramsey, *The Resurrection of Christ* (2nd ed.; London, 1946) pp. 18–19.

[60] Cf. M.-E. Boismard, *Le prologue de saint Jean* (Paris, 1953) p. 71.

[61] This is the ultimate reason why the Passion is viewed as part of the "glory" of Jesus in the fourth Gospel.

[62] Cf. Is 6:1–3. In the LXX, both Lord and Yahweh in this passage are translated by *Kyrios*. This passage in the fourth Gospel is an important attestation of the conscious manner in which the divine Name was applied to Jesus Christ in the primitive Church.

[63] This is clear from the citation of the opening lines of Is 53 in v. 38 (John appears to intend to recall the whole chapter to his reader's mind).

[64] 1 Peter represents a later development of the Petrine viewpoint expressed in the primitive kerygma (e.g., in Acts), while Hebrews in some respects is a development of Johannine theology.

[65] Cf. Mollat, *op. cit.*, p. 62.

[66] Recent studies of the relationship between the third and the fourth Gospels include: E. Osty, "Les points de contact entre le récit de la passion dans saint Luc et saint Jean," *Recherches de science religieuse* 39

(1951) 146–54; M.-E. Boismard, "Le chapitre XXI de saint Jean: Essai de critique littéraire," *Revue biblique* 54 (1947) 473–501; F. C. Grant, "Was the Author of John Dependent upon the Gospel of Luke?" *Journal of Biblical Literature* (1937) 285–307.

[67] Cf. C. Spicq, *L'Epître aux Hébreux* 1 (Paris, 1952) 92–138.

[68] Cf. Selwyn, *op. cit.*, pp. 56–63.

[69] Cf. Spicq, *op. cit.*, pp. 256–61.

[70] Regarding 1 Peter, cf. Selwyn, *op. cit.*, pp. 7–38; regarding Hebrews, cf. Spicq, *op. cit.*, p. 167.

[71] *Paradidonai* (cf. the LXX of Is 53:6, 12) is a technical term in the New Testament for the handing over of Jesus to death: cf. Mt 17:22; Mk 9:31; Jn 18:30, 35; Mt 20:18; Mk 10:33; Lk 18:32; Mt 26:2; Mk 14:41; Lk 24:7; Acts 3:13; Rom 4:25; 8:32; 1 Cor 11:23; Gal 2:20; Eph 5:2, etc.

[72] Cf. Selwyn, *op. cit.*, p. 30.

[73] Cf. Spicq, *op. cit.*, pp. 92–108.

[74] Cf. Heb 5:7–10 for an *implicit* reference to the Servant.

[75] Cf. J. Bonsirven, *Epître aux Hébreux* (Paris, 1944) p. 73.

[76] Cf. Jackson-Lake, *op. cit.* 1, 384; W. D. Davies, *Paul and Rabbinic Judaism* (London, 1948) p. 275.

[77] Cf. J. Jeremias, "Zum Problem der Deutung von Jes. 53 in palästinischen Spätjudentum," in *Aux sources de la tradition chrétienne* (Neuchâtel–Paris, 1950) pp. 113–19.

[78] The idea of substitution is present in the Deutero-Isaian expression of the work of the Servant: cf. the nuanced discussion by C. Charlier, "Le serviteur glorifié," *Bible et vie chrétienne* 1 (1953) 67–69.

[79] For Paul, the atoning death of Jesus did not release man from the obligation of death for his sins; rather it entailed it. Thus the baptismal death (Rom 6:3 ff.) of the Christian is somehow more than a symbolic one.

[80] Cf. n. 71 above.

[81] Paul was the first to exploit the positive role of Jesus' death and resurrection. For the interesting history of the interpretation of this text, cf. D. M. Stanley, "Ad historiam exegeseos Rom 4, 25," *Verbum domini* 29 (1951) 257–74.

[82] Here, as elsewhere in Paul, the resurrection of Christ is considered as benefiting the redeemed (1 Cor 15:20; 2 Cor 5:15; Col 1:18; Rom 5:10; Acts 13:16 ff.).

[83] The obedience of the second Adam was probably taken over from the

Servant theme. Pauline theology is thus shown to be a development of that of earlier preachers and writers.

[84] The résumés of Paul's sermons in Acts contain no references to the Servant theme.

[85] Paul appears to have been the speaker on this occasion, as he was the preceding Sabbath (Acts 13:16–41); cf. also Acts 13:13.

[86] Paul refers to Christ in the role of the Servant in 1 Cor 15 and Phil 2:6–11, thus proving he was aware of the place it held in the primitive apostolic preaching.

[87] Cf. the LXX of Is 49:4 (*kenōs ekopiasa*) and Phil 2:16 (*eis kenon ekopiasa*); cf. also Gal 4:11 and Acts 20:35.

[88] Cf. Cerfaux, *art. cit.*, pp. 362–63.

[89] *Ibid.*, pp. 359–60.

[90] Cf. Rom 1:1; Phil 1:1; Tit 1:1; Gal 1:10; 2 Cor 4:5.

[91] Is 49:3, 5 in the LXX.

[92] Col 1:24.

[93] 1 Cor 15:45; Rom 5:12 ff.; Col 1:18 ff.

[94] Cf. S. Lyonnet, "S. Cyrille d'Alexandrie et 2 Cor 3, 17," *Biblica* 32 (1951) 25–31.

[95] Cf. P. Benoit, *Les épîtres de saint Paul aux Philippiens* . . . (Paris, 1949) pp. 17 f.

[96] Cf. J. Huby, *Les épîtres de la captivité* (14th ed.; Paris, 1947) p. 271.

[97] *Morphē* is found elsewhere in the New Testament only in Mk 16:12; *harpagmos* is a *hapax* in the New Testament; *to einai isa Theō* is only paralleled in Jn 5:18b; *tapeinoun* is normally used by Paul only of himself (Phil 4:12; 2 Cor 11:7; 12:21); *hyperypsoun* is a New Testament *hapax* (*hypsoun*, which John habitually applies to Jesus' glorification, is never so used by Paul); *charizomai* is never used by Paul with reference to Christ; *katachthonios* is a New Testament *hapax*.

[98] Cf. J. Weiss, "Beiträge zur paulinischen Rhetorik," in *Theologische Studien* (Göttingen, 1897) p. 190.

[99] Cf. H. Lietzmann, *Messe und Herrenmahl* (Bonn, 1926) p. 178.

[100] Cf. M. Dibelius, *An die Thessalonicher I, II. An die Philipper* (3rd ed.; Tübingen, 1937) p. 72.

[101] Cf. E. Lohmeyer, *Kyrios Jesus* (*Sitzungsberichte der Heidelberger Akademie der Wissenschaften*, 1927–28) p. 7.

[102] Cf. L. Cerfaux, "L'Hymne au Christ-serviteur de Dieu, Phil. II, 6–

11 = Is. LII, 13—LIII, 12," in *Miscellanea historica in honorem Alberti de Meyer* 1 (Louvain, 1946) pp. 129 f.

[103] Cf. Benoit, *op. cit.*, 18–19.

[104] Cf. pp. 105–106 above.

[105] Cf. Bonsirven, *op. cit.*, p. 67; also Huby, *op. cit.*, p. 324.

[106] Cf. L. Cerfaux, *Le Christ dans la théologie de saint Paul*, pp. 288–90, for an interesting explanation of the passage.

[107] *Ibid.*, p. 293.

[108] Calvin was opposed to the notion that Jesus' exaltation was a reward, and so he translated *di' ho* by *quo facto*. The fourth-century Arians used the verse to buttress their subordinationist theory.

[109] Cf. P. Henry, "Kénôse," *Dictionnaire de la Bible: Supplément* 5, 35.

[110] Cf. P. Boylan, *St. Paul's Epistle to the Romans* (Dublin, 1934) p. 3: he takes "the spirit of holiness" to mean the Holy Spirit. Cf. S. Lyonnet, *Les épitres de saint Paul aux Galates et aux Romains* (Paris, 1953) p. 67: he takes a different meaning from the phrase; A. Feuillet considers it to refer to the divinity of Christ: "Le plan salvifique de Dieu d'après l'épître aux Romains," *Revue biblique* 57 (1950) 338.

[111] Cf. Schmitt, *op. cit.*, p. 98.

[112] Cf. Bonsirven, *op. cit.*, p. 64.

[113] Cf. Schmitt, *op. cit.*, pp. 94–95.

[114] Cerfaux, *art. cit.*, p. 129, takes seriously the possibility that this hymn was used in the celebration of the Eucharist. The aptness of the ode as part of a baptismal liturgy can be seen in the prominence given to the Servant theme, which, as we saw, played a significant part in the presentations of Jesus' baptism. In addition, Acts 8:26–40 would seem to suggest that there was a special adaptation of the Servant kerygma in some circles to the prebaptismal catechesis.

NOTES TO CHAPTER 12

[1] J. B. Orchard, "Thessalonians and the Synoptic Gospels," *Biblica* 19 (1938) 19–42.

[2] That Paul's *preaching* resembled the traditional apostolic kerygma which later developed or was incorporated into the Synoptic Gospels is the opinion of F. Prat, *La théologie de saint Paul* 1 (8th ed.; Paris, 1920) 36 ff.; cf. also Jules Lebreton, *Les origines du dogme de la Trinité* (3rd ed.; Paris, 1910) pp. 289 ff.

[3] I shall discuss the Pauline conception of "imitation" as a means of handing on apostolic tradition in the study which follows immediately in this book.

[4] Mark, like Paul, envisages the possibility of a woman divorcing her husband—an action which in the Semitic culture of Palestine would be unthinkable.

[5] This last part of the text may contain an allusion to the logion found in Mt 5:14–15.

[6] Cf. J. Guillet, *Thèmes bibliques* (Paris, 1951) pp. 11–16.

[7] Cf. Lucien Cerfaux, *L'Eglise suivant saint Paul* (2nd ed.; Paris, 1948) pp. 69–88.

[8] In Rom 8:16 Paul refers to another *martyrion* (cf. Mt 10:18) by the Spirit of a more personal character, experienced by the Christian in prayer: "The Spirit Himself witnesses together with (*symmartyrei*) our spirit that we are God's children."

[9] M.-E. Jacquemin, "La portée de la troisième demande du Pater," *Ephemerides theologicae Lovanienses* 25 (1949) 61–76.

[10] Another logion Paul may be alluding to is that found in Lk 23:34a (cf. also Acts 7:60).

[11] F. W. Beare, "Jesus and Paul," *Canadian Journal of Theology* 5 (1959) 84.

[12] Whether, in employing the term *lytron* and its derivates, Paul thought

of the money deposited in a pagan temple by the slave who bought his own freedom from his master, is doubtful: cf. Stanislas Lyonnet, "La sotériologie paulinienne," in *Introduction à la Bible* 2 (Tournai, 1959) 863.

[13] Cf. J. Schmitt, *Jésus ressuscité dans la prédication apostolique* (Paris, 1949) pp. 194–99.

[14] Incidentally, this is the earliest New Testament passage in which the Church is depicted as the new Eve.

[15] In 1 Cor 7:29–31a, there is possibly an allusion to the Lucan version of the Wedding Feast (Lk 14:16–24): "I mean this, brothers: the time is short. It remains for those who have wives to live as those who do not have them, and for those who weep [to act] as those who do not weep, and for those who rejoice [to act] as those who do not rejoice, and for those who buy [to act] as those who will not retain possession, and for those who make use of the world [to act] as those who do not use it as their own. . . ." Several details in the parable seem to explain this rather puzzling paragraph in Paul. "The time is short," since the Messianic age has begun, i.e., it is "the hour of the supper." The poor and the underprivileged who receive the invitation become like "those who do not weep," while those who refuse to come join the category of those "who do not rejoice." The excuses of the first two guests who refuse explain Paul's strange reference here to commerce—in a context where he is discussing marriage ("I have bought a farm . . . I have bought a pair of oxen . . .")! These guests, like the man who has just "married a wife," are excluded from the Messianic banquet because they "are making use of the world . . . as their own."

"Become Imitators of Me": Apostolic Tradition in Paul

NOTES TO CHAPTER 13

[1] Apart from 3 Jn 11 (*mē mimou to kakon alla to agathon*), the only other instances occur in Hebrews, a letter largely Pauline in its inspiration. The first example is Heb 6:12, "une des plus parfaites définitions de la vie chrétienne dans le Nouveau Testament" (C. Spicq, *L'Épître aux Hébreux* 2 [Paris, 1953] 159). It reads as follows: *hina mē nōthroi genēsthe, mimētai de tōn dia pisteōs kai makrothymias klēronomountōn tas epangelias.* Heb 13:7b provides the second example, where the author urges the second-generation Christians, his addressees, to imitate the "faith"—"vertu fondamentale, inspiratrice de toute la vie morale" (*ibid.*, p. 421)—of their hierarchical leaders in the community: *mimeisthe tēn pistin.*

[2] Cf. Wilhelm Michaelis, "*mimeomai, mimētēs, symmimētēs,*" *Theologisches Wörterbuch zum Neuen Testament* 4, 665.

[3] *Ibid.*, pp. 661–64.

[4] *Memorabilia* 1, 6, 3.

[5] Moreover, Paul deprecates this very idea and inveighs against it at some length: cf. 1 Cor 1:12 ff.

[6] Apart from the Gospels, the word is found only in Ap 14:4.

[7] This attitude is displayed by the author of Hebrews towards the apostolic eyewitnesses: cf. Heb 2:3; 13:7.

[8] Cf. 1 Th 2:13; Eph 5:1.

[9] This is true as regards 1 Th 2:13, as we hope to show presently.

[10] O. Cullmann, *Christ et le temps* (Neuchâtel–Paris, 1947) p. 164.

[11] S. Lyonnet, "La 'morale' de saint Paul," *Catéchistes* 4 (1953) 149–59; "Liberté chrétienne et loi de l'Esprit selon saint Paul," *Christus* 4 (1954) 6–27.

[12] Cf. Michaelis, *art. cit.*, pp. 674–75.

[13] *Ibid.*, p. 676: "*Die Forderung einer imitatio Christi hat in den paulinischen Aussagen keine Stütze. . . .* Paulus keine eigentliche Nachah-

mung Christus (und Gott) gegenüber kennt, sondern nur ein gehorsames Nachfolgen als Ausdruck der Lebens- und Willensgemeinschaft . . ." (emphasis is that of the author).

[14] Cf. H. Schlier, *Der Brief an die Epheser* (Düsseldorf, 1957) p. 231, n. 1: "Dass Michaelis . . . die *mimēsis* auf den 'Gehorsam' im Sinn der Annahme des Wortes reduziert, entspricht weniger den Texten als einer eigentümlichen protestantischen Abneigung gegen das 'Vorbild.' Diese beruht aber doch wohl auf einem Missverständnis dessen, was *typos* ist."

[15] Cf. Charles Masson, *Les deux épîtres de saint Paul aux Thessaloniciens* (Neuchâtel–Paris, 1957) p. 21, n. 2: ". . . W. Michaelis, par réaction contre l'*imitatio Christi* de la tradition catholique, a mis trop fortement l'accent sur l'obéissance due à l'apôtre et au Christ qu'on imite, au détriment de l'idée d'exemple à suivre du caractère normatif du comportement du Christ et de l'apôtre. . . ."

[16] Cf. J. Hering, *La première épître de saint Paul aux Corinthiens* (Neuchâtel–Paris, 1949) p. 89: "Toutefois, il est remarkable combien il (Paul) attache de l'importance à la vie terrestre de Jésus, et combien par conséquent il serait erroné d'interpréter le fameux texte 2 Cor 5:16 comme exprimant un désinteressement à l'*imitatio Christi.*"

[17] These neologisms, no less than eleven in number, vividly portray Paul's firm belief in the reality and supernatural character of the Christian's assimilation to Christ. We list them here in alphabetical order: *synkathizein* (Eph 2:6), *synkakopathein* (2 Tim 2:3), *syzēn* (2 Cor 7:3; Rom 6:8; 2 Tim 2:11), *syzōopoiein* (Col 2:13; Eph 2:5), *symbasileuein* (2 Tim 2:12), *sympaschein* (Rom 8:17), *synapothnēskein* (2 Cor 7:3; 2 Tim 2:11), *syndoxazesthai* (Rom 8:17), *synegeirein* (Col 2:12; Eph 2:6), *synthaptesthai* (Rom 6:4; Col 2:12), *systaurousthai* (Rom 6:6; Gal 2:19). It is interesting to observe that in contrast with the vocabulary expressing "imitation" of Paul himself (which all belongs to Paul's earlier correspondence: 1 and 2 Th, Phil, 1 Cor), these terms —insofar as they express the existential union of Christ and the Christian —belong to Paul's mature style and thought (2 Cor, Gal, Rom, Col, Eph, 2 Tim), and they express a conception of paramount importance in Pauline theology: (1) they express or imply the redemptive activity of God the Father; (2) they restrict the assimilation of the Christian to Christ by associating it only with those events of the New Testament *Heilsgeschichte* which for Paul constitute the essential work of redemption, viz., Jesus' death and passion, burial, resurrection, and glorification.

[18] B. Rigaux, *Saint Paul: Les épîtres aux Thessaloniciens* (Paris–Gembloux, 1956) p. 363.

[19] *Ibid.*, p. 366.

[20] *Ibid.*, p. 436: "Cette parole apostolique qui n'est pas parole humaine mais parole divine, communication des secrets de Dieu et opératrice du salut, apparaît ici déjà chargée de résonnances chrétiennes. . . . Elle n'indique pas une prononciation de discours mais l'objet du discours lui-même." As our study will, I believe, demonstrate, however, the Pauline notion of the gospel is rather that it is a divine-human Word, containing not only God's self-revelation but also an element personal to the preacher, viz., his testimony of personal faith to the truth of what he proclaims.

[21] Paul's own conversion had undoubtedly impressed this truth upon his mind. Despite the unique privilege he had of beholding Christ in His exalted state, Paul had still to be admitted to the Christian community—and this was effected not by the Lord who met him on the Damascus road, but by Ananias (cf. Acts 9:6, 17–19; 22:16). We have another illustration of this same truth in the case of Cornelius and his household, who, though enjoying the pentecostal experience of the primitive community, were baptized at Peter's command (Acts 10:44–48).

[22] Hence Paul made it a rule never to evangelize in those places where others had preceded him (2 Cor 10:15–16; Rom 15:20).

[23] This relationship is present to Paul's mind even when he has to rebuke the Corinthians for their partisan spirit (1 Cor 1:11–4:16).

[24] As I have pointed out in an earlier essay in this book in discussing the character of scriptural inspiration (cf. p. 75), God's self-revelation in the Bible *is at the same time* the self-revelation of the human writer. The divine message necessarily reaches man clothed in the inspired author's reaction of faith to that message.

[25] Cf. Masson, *op. cit.*, p. 21, n. 4.

[26] It is still more obvious that there can be no grounds of comparison between the Thessalonians' acceptance of the Word and Christ Himself.

[27] Rigaux, *op. cit.*, p. 383.

[28] This doctrine is taught indirectly by the explanation of the seed which fell upon rocky ground: cf. Mt 13:20–21, where the terms *meta charas* and also *thlipsis* occur.

[29] Cf. L. Cerfaux, "Saint Paul et le serviteur de Dieu d'Isaïe," *Studia Anselmiana* 27–28 (1951) 351–65, and my own views on this point ex-

pressed in the study of Paul and the Servant of Yahweh, pp. 312–51 above.

[30] The order of the Greek sentence seems to suggest this. Michaelis (*art. cit.*, p. 672) calls it "eine Art Selbstkorrektur."

[31] For Paul, the title "the Church (or Congregation) of God" belongs primarily to the Jerusalem community of the early days (1 Cor 15:9; Gal 1:13; cf. Phil 3:6). Then by extension, as here, the name is applied validly to all the Palestinian communities. The churches which Paul founded in Europe come to participate in the title—a sign of their communion with the "Mother Church" of Jerusalem: cf. 1 Cor 1:2.

[32] Cf. Michaelis, *art. cit.*, pp. 668–69.

[33] Cf. E. Trocmé, *Le "Livre des Actes" et l'histoire* (Paris, 1957) pp. 49–50.

[34] M. R. Vincent, *Epistles to the Philippians and to Philemon* (Edinburgh, 1897) p. 115; P. Bonnard, *L'Epître de saint Paul aux Philippiens* (Neuchâtel–Paris, 1950) p. 70. For another meaning given to the prefix, cf. P. Joüon, "Notes philologiques sur quelques versets de l'épître aux Philippiens," *Recherches de sciences religieuses* 23 (1938) 307–8.

[35] This appears to be the best way of understanding this much-disputed phrase in v. 16.

[36] Cf. L. Cerfaux, "L'Hymne au Christ-serviteur de Dieu," in *Miscellanea historica in honorem Alberti de Meyer* 1 (Louvain, 1946) 129–30.

[37] The *paidagōgos* was the slave whose duty it was to accompany his master's children to school. Paul uses the same figure in Gal 3:24.

[38] It is significant that nowhere in the letters to the Churches of Rome and of Colossae is there any suggestion that Paul be imitated. In Eph 5:1 the "imitation" is of quite a different order.

[39] The use of *typos* (10:6) and *typikōs* (10:11) in this passage illustrates, I believe, the sense in which *typos* is used in the "imitation" passages (1 Th 1:7; 2 Th 3:9; Phil 3:17). It denotes an example drawn from sacred history which has a doctrinal significance. In Scripture it is a person or an event which, considered in the reality it possesses *as written*, provides a vehicle "for our instruction" (10:11). Applied to himself by Paul, the term describes his personal kerygma as preached and lived by him, thus emphasizing its supernatural and didactic character. In short, Paul as *typos* is the representative of apostolic and evangelical tradition.

[40] Rom 15:7, which proposes Christ's redemptive work as an example to be followed, presents "God's glory" as the aim of His career also.

[41] For the meaning of *areskein* in monumental inscriptions (= "to render service"), cf. A. Robertson and A. Plummer, *First Epistle of St. Paul to the Corinthians* (Edinburgh, 1914) pp. 224–25.

[42] In Rom 15:1–3 a similar exhortation to put the service of one's neighbor first is based upon Christ's own example: *ho Christos ouch heautō ēresken.*

[43] Cf. Michaelis, *art. cit.*, p. 675, n. 29.

[44] P. Bonnard, *L'Épître de saint Paul aux Galates* (Neuchâtel–Paris, 1953) p. 91.

[45] H. Schlier, *Der Brief an die Galater* (Göttingen, 1949) p. 147: "V. 12 leitet die Ausführungen mit einer Mahnung zur Nachfolge ein. . . . Auch sonst stellt sich der Apostel als nachahmenswertes Vorbild der Gemeinde hin (1 Cor 4:16; 11:1; Phil 3:17; 2 Th 3:7). Er ist nicht nur ihr Lehrer und ihr Hirte, sondern auch ihr Heiliger."

[46] P. Benoit, *Les épîtres de saint Paul aux Philippiens, à Philémon, aux Colossiens, aux Éphésiens* (Paris, 1949) p. 73.

Index of Subjects

Abraham, and Christian faith, 156–59; and Gentile Christians, 158; promise to, 158

Acts, kingdom of God in, 27; literary forms of, 289–92; plan, 7; references to Deuteronomy in, 405 (n.40); summaries, 120–21; theme, 288–89

After life, O.T. conception, 42

Aggiornamento, xii

Antioch, celebration of Eucharist, 23–24; Christian community, 22–23; Christian liturgy, 23–24; mission to pagans, 24

Apostle, evolution in concept of, 289

Apostolic college, the Twelve and, 396–97

Apostolic preaching, 50; sayings of Jesus, 62

Apostolic teaching, and Eucharist, 122; Holy Spirit, 209–10; and O.T., 206–07; Paul, 210–21

Apostolic testimony, 7, 14, 289; nature of, 58, 257; object, 59

Apostolic tradition, Paul, 353

Auctor, 73

Author, Holy Scripture, 75; Old Testament view of, 72–73

Baptism, anointing, 162–63; Calvary, 180–81; Cana, 174; catechesis, 427; Christian initiation, 187; circumcision, 158–59; covenant-sprinkling, 161; creation, 150–54; Deluge, 155–56; the desert, 160–61; eschatological character, 169; infants, 127; "in Jesus' Name," 189–92; of Jesus, 172–73; Johannite, 21; John the Baptist, 166–67, 188–89; Jordan, 162–64, 427; light, 153; "living water," 176; marriage symbolism, 161; natural symbolism, 422; Nicodemus, 175; O. T. symbolism, 150–51; paradise, 154; Paul's view of, 182, 185–86; Pentecost, 183–87; Pliny, 99; primitive preaching, 65; profession of faith, 191–92; Red Sea, 160; seal, 159; signification, 20–21; Trent, 172; Trinitarian formula, 191–92

Baptismal formulae, 125–26

Barnabas, 22

Bible, authors' purpose, 77; incarnational view, 72; inerrancy, 79–80; nature, 74–75; nineteenth century criticism, 68–69; purpose, 87; rationalist view, 69–70; religious or psychological view, 70–71

Breaking of bread, 13

Canon, formation, 84, 86

Credal formulae, in O. T., 92–93
Christian wisdom, Paul, 406 (n.53)
Christology, Apocalypse, 107; and history, 272–73; John, 267; Luke, 266–67; Mark, 262, 406 (n.58); Matthew, 263–66; primitive, 39
Church, contemporary concept, ix; Holy Spirit, 51–52; institution of, 36–37; N. T. conception, 4; kingdom of God, 5, 36
Cornelius, admission to community, 20
Covenant, marriage-theme, 162; divinity of Christ, 117
Creation, O. T. view, 151–52
Cultus, 91–92

Dabar, 260–61
Day of Yahweh, 43, 44, 49
Deluge, in O. T., 155–56
Development of doctrine in New Testament, 39
Diathēkē, 435
Didachē, Gospel form, 212–13
Divino afflante Spiritu, 244–45
dokimazein, 372

Elijah, O. T., tradition, 170–71
Enthronement theme, 102, 109–11
Ephphatha, 174
Eschatology, Jesus' teaching, 46–47; Matthew, 230–32
Euangelion, 195, 313–14
Eucharist, apostolic teaching, 65; joy, 95–96; Bread of Life, 146–47; as Christian Passover meal, 133–34; liturgical formulae, 126; Lucan Last Supper, 132; Pliny, 99; risen Christ, 13
Exile, and salvation, 41
Exodus, and salvation, 41–42; I Peter, 332

Fundamentalism, 241–42

Glory, fourth Gospel, 329–30
God, author of Scripture, 73
Gospel, aim and scope, 2, 215; as teaching, 203–04; hermeneutics, 244–45; and history, 254–55; John's purpose, 258–59; literary form, 270–71; Luke's purpose, 258; Mark, 205–06, 218–20, 258, 262; Matthew, 26, 29–36, 225–26, 268–69; Pauline concept, 275

Hellenists, 16, 17
Historical method, 253–54
Historicism, 242–43
History, concepts of, 251–52
Holy Spirit, 51–52
Humani generis, 245
Hymn, Phil 2:5–11, 105–06, 346–49, 406

Imitation, 371–74, 389
Inspiration, analogous concept, 79; Benoit, 78–79; Brinkmann, 85–86; Charlier, 71; Coppens, 80–81; and founding of the Church, 82; patristic view, 73–74; Rahner, 81–85; recognition by Church, 84; and revelation, 78–79; two analogies, 88–89

Ipsissima verba Jesu, 75–76, 196, 211–12, 215, 274

Jesus Christ, creator, 114; divinity recognized, 55–57, 61, 100–01, 403 (n.22); last Adam, 280–81, 344–45; preaching, 201; pre-existence, 105; redeemer, 114–15; redemptive death, 64–65; seed of Abraham, 157–58; Servant of God, 314–15; teaching, 205–05
Jewish proselyte initiation, 166–67
Johannine baptism, 168
John the Baptist, baptism, 8–9; Elijah, 167–68, 200–01; mission, 167–73; preaching, 45–46, 200; "restoration of all things," 170–72
Joy, N. T. concept, 95
Judgment, Johannine concept, 177

kerygma, 59–60, 195, 202–03, 378
Kingdom of God, and exalted Christ, 63–64; and "the Name," 57–58; in Acts, 27; and Church, 36–37; Jesus' preaching of, 46; in Matthew, 29–30; O. T. concept, 44
Koinōnia, 13, 16; relation to Eucharist, 121–22
Kyrios, meaning in N. T., 106; in credal formulae, 190–91

Literal sense, 245–46
Literary forms, 80, 269–70, 273–74, 249; genealogy, 272; midrash, 274; popular story, 273; Pius XII's teaching, 245
Liturgical hymns, 96–97, 124–25
Liturgical recital, O. T., 92
Liturgical texts, 275
Liturgy, Acts, 130–32; and Gospels, 119, 127–28; instruction, 98; Passion narratives, 123–24; Pliny, 98–99; in primitive Church, 123–24; and Christian salvation, 138–39; and vocation of Israel, 91
Liturgy of Israel, and Gospels, 134–37
Luke—Acts, 6, 7
lytron, 223

Martyrion, 195
Messiah, 101
Messianic times, 9, 10, 14, 15, 51; significance for Church, 403–04 (n.27)
Messianism in O.T., 42–43; Abraham, 54; Moses, 54; royal, 42–43; Servant of God, 42–43; Son of Man, 42–43
Metanoia, 62–63, 168, 200
Mission to the pagans, 65
Moses, 159–60

New Adam, 152–53
New creation, 152–53
New Israel, 51, 53–54
New Testament, creation of, ix

"Obstacle" in Paul, 399
Old Testament, Christian interpretation, 140–41, 143–44

Parables, Luke, 400 (n.31); Matthew, 33–35; and salvation, 46–47; in Paul, 363–69

Parousia, 15, 24–25, 49, 392
Paul, at Antioch, 22–23; and apostolic kerygma, 38; "Church of God," 461; Christian wisdom, 383–84; conversion, 292–96; *dokimazein*, 372; gospel, 280; imitation, 371–74; and law, 372–73; love and neighbor, 361–63; Jesus' parables, 363 ff.; Parousia, 360–61; prayer, 358–60; prophet, 305–07; Servant of God, 307–09; 339–44; O. T. typology, 160
Pentecost, 9, 11, 50–51, 143–44, 184–85
Peter, and Cornelius, 19–20; primacy in primitive community, 14
Pliny, 99
Prayer, ecstatic, 397; in Paul, 358–60
Preaching, 200
Presence, N. T. notion, 48
Primitive Jerusalem community, 8, 11, 396 (n. 8); idyllic existence, 12; last function, 26–27; principles, 24–25; "the Way," 14
"Private interpretation," 250–51
Prologue, fourth Gospel, 115–17
Prophets, in N. T., 10

Qumrân, legalism, 142; Messianism, 45; lustrations, 166–67; two baptisms, 168–69

Remnant, 15–16, 44, 53; and the Deluge, 155
Resurrection of body, in O. T., 42
Revelation, N. T. historical process, xi

Sacramental symbolism and sacred history, 145–46
Sacramental theology, Luke 128–29; John, 128–29
Sacraments, juridical view, 149; symbolism from sacred history, 145–46; efficacy, 147–48
Sacred history, 75, 144–45, 276–77, 254–55; relation to sacraments, 146
Salvation, concept of, 54, 55, 141; and the Exodus, 159; Jesus' preaching of, 45; in John, 180–81; limitations of primitive Christian idea, 64–65; and liturgy, 138–39; Luke's concept, 233–34; in Mark, 220–25; in Matthew, 226, 229–30; of pagans, 15, 279; in Paul, 181–82, 280; conception in primitive community, 63; O. T. concept, 40; Synoptic contribution, 236–37; in Synoptic Gospels, 216–17; telelogy, 65–66; in wisdom literature, 41–42
Sayings of Jesus, in Paul, 354–56
Second Adam, 112 ff.
Sermon on the Mount, 31
Servant theology, 102–03
Signs (Symbols) in O.T., 147–48
Son of Man, 103–04; and Jesus, 46
Spiritual sense of Scripture, 71, 72; in St. Thomas, 144–45
Stephen, 17, 18, 280, 316–18; contribution to primitive Christianity, 18–19; interpretation of O. T.,

143–44; parallels with Jesus, 18; view of sacred history, 18
Summaries in Acts, 12–14
Symbol, light (baptism), 153
Symbols in O. T., baptismal, 150 ff.
Synthēkē, 435

Teaching of Apostles, 12, 13
Temple, and primitive Jerusalem community, 26; ruin of (Matthew), 34
Testimony, concept of, 58–59; of the Church, 1–2
Theology of history, 48–49; in Paul, 25
Theology of miracles, 202; in Matthew, 228
Theology of "the Name," 57–58
The Twelve, and apostolic college, 396–97
Titles of Christ, in John, 104
Truth, Semitic conception of, 76–77
Typology, Stephen's view of, 60

Urkirche, 82

Worship, "in spirit and truth," 176

Index of Names

Ahern, B. M., 395
d'Alès, A., 423, 426
Allo, E. B., 424
Alonso Schökel, L., 241, 438
Auvray, P., 412

de Bachiocchi, J., 404
von Balthasar, H., 44
Bardy, G., 414
Barrett, C. K., 177, 426
Barucq, A., 410
Bea, A., 73, 123, 410, 413, 419
Beare, F. W., 456
Behm, J., 416, 423
Bellamy, J., 423
Benoit, P., 67, 78, 79, 80, 126, 127, 183, 242, 347, 396, 398, 402, 403, 408, 410, 411, 412, 413, 416, 417, 419, 420, 425, 427, 431, 432, 435, 437, 446, 454, 455, 462
Beyer, H., 451
Beyschlag, W., 409
Boismard, M. E., 112, 329, 415, 417, 452, 453
Bonnard, P., 461, 462
Bonsirven, J., 401, 417, 427, 441, 453, 455
Bouyer, L., 402, 422, 424, 426
Boylan, P., 455
Braun, F. M., 402, 425, 434, 452
Brinkmann, B., 67, 85, 86, 88, 408, 413
Brodrick, J., 447
Brown, R. E., 420
Brown, W. A., 401
Bultmann, R., 141, 421, 426
Burghardt, W. J., xiv, 451
Burrows, M., 421, 425

Cambier, J., 241, 261, 416, 439
Causse, A., 398, 407
Cazelles, H., 410
Cerfaux, L., 105, 114, 347, 395, 400, 416, 417, 430, 443, 445, 448, 450, 454, 455, 456, 460, 461
Charlier, C., 68, 71, 248, 318, 403, 409, 411, 432, 437, 450, 453
Coppens, J., 67, 80, 81, 408, 409, 412, 437, 451
Courtade, G., 408
Cremer, H., 398
Cullmann, O., 127, 128, 261, 321, 372, 403, 416, 420, 426, 428, 439, 440, 450, 458

Daniélou, J., 135, 420, 424
Davies, W. D., 441, 453
Dejaifve, G., 411
Démann, P., 157, 424
Descamps, A., 425
Dewailly, L. M., 413
Dibelius, M., 347, 454
Dinkler, E., 251, 439
Dix, G., 248, 401, 409, 438

Dodd, C. H., 199, 240, 252, 254, 400, 402, 429, 439, 445
Dubarle, A. M., 402
Dupont, J., 429, 432, 441

Farrer, A., 150, 409, 423
Féret, H. M., 417
Feuillet, A., 232, 400, 424, 430, 436, 439, 448, 450, 451, 455
Fischer, B., 415
Fitzmyer, J. A., 438
Foakes-Jackson, F. J., 448, 453
de Fraine, J., 411
Franzelin, J. B., 67, 74, 79, 408, 412, 413
Friedrich, G., 313, 429, 430, 432, 448, 449

Gaechter, P., 427
Gaertner, B., 402, 406
Giblet, J., 435
Goguel, M., 407, 441
Grail, A., 424
Grant, F. C., 453
Grosheide, F. W., 432
Grossouw, W., 414, 431
Guillet, J., 160, 422, 424, 456
Gunkel, H., 69

Haag, H., 402, 431
Hauret, C., 437
Henry, P., 416, 455
Héring, J., 373, 459
Holtzmann, H. J., 409
Hoskyns, E. C., 163, 420, 424, 426
Houbaut, H., 425
Huby, J., 346, 454
Humbert, A., 423

van Imschoot, P., 402, 426

Jacquemet, G., 427
Jacquemin, M. E., 456
Jeremias, J., 453
John XXIII, xii
Jouon, P., 327, 452, 461

Käsemann, E., 417
Kittel, G., 327, 446, 452
Knox, W. L., 289, 307, 399, 407, 443, 447, 448, 452
Koehler, L., 427
Kümmel, W. G., 395
Kurfess, A., 415

Lagrange, M. J., 67, 221–22, 231, 235, 327, 403, 408, 413, 423, 426, 431, 436, 452
Lake, K., 442, 448, 453
Lake, S., 442
Lambert, G., 438
Lattey, C., 421
Laurentin, R., 136, 274, 420
Lebreton, J., 456
Lebreton-Zeiller, 442
Leclercq, H., 415
Leenhardt, F. J., 423
Lemonnyer, A., 400
Leo XIII, 409
Léon-Dufour, X., 439
Lercher, L., 427
Lestringant, P., 407, 442
Levie, J., 411, 437, 439
Lietzmann, H., 347, 454
Lilly, J. S., 441
Lindeskog, G., 423

Lohmeyer, E., 223, 347, 454
Loisy, A., 6, 69, 322, 395, 446, 451
Lyonnet, S., 13, 121, 249, 372, 396–98, 419, 424, 428, 433, 438–39, 454–55, 457–58

MacKenzie, R. A. F., 67, 72, 242, 406, 408–10, 414, 423, 427, 437
Malevez, L., 141, 421
Manson, W., 450–51
Masson, C., 159, 424, 459–60
McKenzie, J. L., 239, 243–44, 273, 410, 437–39
Meinertz, M., 412
Menoud, H., 404
Michaelis, W., 373, 379, 386, 389, 458, 461–2
Michaux, W., 431, 434, 439
Mollat, D., 137, 204, 328, 420, 425–26, 431, 452
de Montcheuil, Y., 398, 407
Moore, G. F., 425
Moriarty, F. F., 437
Moulton-Milligan, 431
Munck, J., 400

Neunheuser, B., 424
Newman, J. H., 412
North, C. R., 423, 448

Orchard, J. B., 352, 456
Osty, E., 430, 432, 452

Paul VI, i, ix, x
Pautrel, R., 401
Pedersen, J., 40, 401
Pesch, C., 413
Pirot, L., 444
Pius XII, xi, xii, 70, 198, 239, 244–45, 247–50, 275, 411
van der Ploeg, J. S., 309, 423, 447–50, 452
Plummer, A., 462
Prat, F., 327, 452, 456

von Rad, G., 423, 448
Rahner, K., 3, 67, 73, 81–85, 88, 138, 408, 410–14, 420, 437
Ramsey, A. M., 7, 329, 395, 443, 452
Rétif, A., 429–30, 432
Rigaux, B., 437, 460
Robert, A., 439
Robert-Tricot, 408
Robertson, A., 462
Robinson, J. M., 436
Romeo, A., 438
Rowley, H. H., 448
Ruotolo, D., 243

Sahlin, H., 424
Schildenberger, J., 437
Schlier, H., 96, 373, 415, 459, 462
Schmaus - Geiselmann - Grillmeier, 425
Schmitt, J., 53, 169, 325, 398–99, 402, 404–07, 416, 421, 425–26, 449, 451, 455, 457
Schweitzer, A., 441
Selwyn, E. G., 331–32, 399, 424, 450, 453
Smith, G. D., 438
Soubigou, L., 435
Spicq, C., 333, 402, 404, 407, 410, 417, 421, 424, 426, 453, 458

Stanley, D. M., 395, 400, 402–3, 420, 422, 425, 435, 439–40, 449, 453
Stendahl, K., 395, 436
Swete, H. B., 425, 447
Synave, P., 408, 411, 437

Taylor, V., 222–24, 416, 419, 424, 434–35, 450
Toynbee, A., 251
Trocmé, E., 461
Tromp, S., 413

Vaccari, A., 439
Vaganay, L., 433
de Vaux, R., 424
Vawter, B., 129, 420, 437
Vincent, M. R., 461

Weiss, J., 346, 409, 454
Wellhausen, J., 69
Wikenhauser, A., 396–97, 441–42
Worden, T., 240

Zerwick, M., 438

A NOTE ON THE TYPE

IN WHICH THIS BOOK WAS SET

This book has been set in Weiss, an interesting face created by E. R. Weiss of Germany, who prefers to be called a painter. While he has studied almost every known letter in the world and copied inscriptions from Roman monuments, Renaissance capitals and fantastic baroque letter-forms from gravestones, he still remains a painter. The Weiss types, while traditional letters, are the product of our own time. Lines of text take on a gracious air—an easy, limpid flow when set in this modern type design. Weiss types have good color and create dignity whenever one sees them, either in a book or advertisement. This book was composed and printed by the York Composition Company, Inc. of York and bound by Moore and Company of Baltimore. The design and typography are by Howard N. King.